Psychoanalytic Explorations in Art

Psychoanalytic Explorations in Art

ERNST KRIS

Yale University School of Medicine
Child Study Center

International Universities Press, Inc.
Madison   Connecticut

First Paperback Printing, 2000
ISBN 0-8236-8220-X (paperback)

MANUFACTURED IN THE UNITED STATES OF AMERICA

CONTENTS

ACKNOWLEDGMENTS 8
PREFACE 9

Part One—INTRODUCTION

1. APPROACHES TO ART 13
   I. The contribution of Psychoanalysis and Its Limitations .. 13
   II. Daydream and Fiction 31
   III. The Aesthetic Illusion 39
   IV. Magic, Communication and Identification 47
   V. Creation and Re-Creation 56

2. THE IMAGE OF THE ARTIST
   A Psychological Study of the Role of Tradition in Ancient
   Biographies 64

Part Two—THE ART OF THE INSANE

3. COMMENTS ON SPONTANEOUS ARTISTIC CREATIONS BY PSYCHOTICS   87
   Appendix: A Psychotic Artist of the Middle Ages 118
4. A PSYCHOTIC SCULPTOR OF THE EIGHTEENTH CENTURY 128
5. THE FUNCTION OF DRAWINGS AND THE MEANING OF THE "CREA-
   TIVE SPELL" IN A SCHIZOPHRENIC ARTIST (with *Else Pappenheim*)   151

Part Three—THE COMIC

6. THE PSYCHOLOGY OF CARICATURE 173
7. THE PRINCIPLES OF CARICATURE (with *E. H. Gombrich*) 189
8. EGO DEVELOPMENT AND THE COMIC 204
9. LAUGHTER AS AN EXPRESSIVE PROCESS:
   Contributions to the Psychoanalysis of Expressive Behavior   217

Part Four—PROBLEMS OF LITERARY CRITICISM

10. AESTHETIC AMBIGUITY (with *Abraham Kaplan*) 243

5

11. Freudianism and the Literary Mind 265
12. Prince Hal's Conflict 273

Part Five—PSYCHOLOGY OF CREATIVE PROCESSES

13. On Inspiration 291
14. On Preconscious Mental Processes 303

Bibliography 321
Bibliographical Note 341
Index 344
Illustrations

List of Illustrations

Fig. 1 Psychotic Artist. (Fairy Tale)
Fig. 2 Psychotic Artist. (Portrait)
Fig. 3 Ernst Josephson. (Pan)
Fig. 4 Ernst Josephson. (David and Goliath)
Fig. 5 Hysterical Patient. (Drawings)
Fig. 6 Psychotic Patient. (Anti-Christ)
Fig. 7 Psychotic Patient. (The Shepherd)
Fig. 8 Psychotic Patient. (Six Heads)
Fig. 9 Psychotic Patient. (Profile)
Fig. 10 Cameo. (Combination of Heads)
Fig. 11 German 19th Century. (Caricature of Napoleon)
Fig. 12 Psychotic Patient. (Hindenburg)
Fig. 13 Psychotic Patient. (Emperors)
Fig. 14 Ernst Josephson. (Adam)
Fig. 15 Ernst Josephson. (Drawing)
Fig. 16 Ernst Josephson. (Drawing)
Fig. 17 Ernst Josephson. (Portrait)
Fig. 18 Psychotic Patient. (Drawing)
Fig. 19 (a and b) Psychotic Patient. (A Photograph and Its Copy)
Fig. 20 Opicinus de Canistris. (Autobiography)
Fig. 21 Opicinus de Canistris. (Christ and the Universe)
Fig. 22 F. X. Messerschmidt. (Quiet Peaceful Sleep)
Fig. 23 F. X. Messerschmidt. (The Artist How He Imagined Himself Laughing)
Fig. 24 F. X. Messerschmidt. (The Courageous General)
Fig. 25 F. X. Messerschmidt. (The Melancholic One)
Fig. 26 F. X. Messerschmidt. (A Surly Old Soldier)
Fig. 27 F. X. Messerschmidt. (The Reliable One)
Fig. 28 F. X. Messerschmidt. (The Ill-Humored One)

6

Fig. 29 F. X. Messerschmidt. *(The Satirizing One)*
Fig. 30 F. X. Messerschmidt. *(The Yawning One)*
Fig. 31 F. X. Messerschmidt. *(The Obstinate One)*
Fig. 32 F. X. Messerschmidt. *(A Haggard Old Man With Aching Eyes)*
Fig. 33 F. X. Messerschmidt. *(Just Rescued From Drowning)*
Fig. 34 F. X. Messerschmidt. *(A Hanged One)*
Fig. 35 F. X. Messerschmidt. *(The Vexed One)*
Fig. 36 F. X. Messerschmidt. *(Strong Odor)*
Fig. 37 F. X. Messerschmidt. *(A Simpleton)*
Fig. 38 F. X. Messerschmidt. *(An Old Cheerful Smiler)*
Fig. 39 F. X. Messerschmidt. *(A Hypocrite and Slanderer)*
Fig. 40 F. X. Messerschmidt. *(First Beak Head)*
Fig. 41 F. X. Messerschmidt. *(Second Beak Head)*
Fig. 42 F. X. Messerschmidt. *(The Sinister Man)*
Fig. 43 F. X. Messerschmidt. *(The Incapable Bassoonist)*
Fig. 44 F. X. Messerschmidt. *(Afflicted with Constipation)*
Fig. 45 F. X. Messerschmidt. *(Grief Locked Up Inside)*
Fig. 46 F. X. Messerschmidt. *(Childish Weeping)*
Fig. 47 F. X. Messerschmidt. *(The Enraged and Vengeful Gypsy)*
Fig. 48 F. X. Messerschmidt. *(The Troubled One)*
Fig. 49 F. X. Messerschmidt. *(Jan van Swieten)*
Fig. 50 F. X. Messerschmidt. *(The Capuchin Monk Fessler)*
Fig. 51 Psychotic Architect. *(Victory)*
Fig. 52 Psychotic Architect. *(Sphera)*
Fig. 53 Psychotic Architect. *(Eternal Hell)*
Fig. 54 Psychotic Architect. *(The Dies Are Cast)*
Fig. 55 Psychotic Architect. *(Sphera and Damnation)*
Fig. 56 Psychotic Architect. *(Sphera and the Stars of David)*
Fig. 57 Psychotic Architect. *(The Universe)*
Fig. 58 Psychotic Architect. *(God Father Himself)*
Fig. 59 Psychotic Architect. *(Ostensory)*
Fig. 60 Psychotic Architect. *(God, the Sculptor)*
Fig. 61 Psychotic Architect. *(The Process of Sculpturing)*
Fig. 62 Italian 17th Century. *(Caricature)*
Fig. 63 Italian 17th Century. *(Caricature)*
Fig. 64 Italian 17th Century. *(Dwarfs)*
Fig. 65 Honoré Daumier. *(Napoleon III)*
Fig. 66 Greek Art. *(Dwarf)*
Fig. 67 Lorenzo Bernini. *(Captain of the Fire Brigade)*
Fig. 68 Lorenzo Bernini. *(Cardinal Scipione Borghese)*
Fig. 69 David Low. *(Tabs of Identity)*
Fig. 70 Early Christian Period, Wall Engraving. *(Mock Crucifix)*
Fig. 71 German 15th Century. *(Man on the Gallows)*
Fig. 72 Dutch 17th Century. *(The Preacher and the Devil)*
Fig. 73 Italian 17th Century. *(Sketches and Caricatures)*
Fig. 74 Giovanni Battista Porta. *(The Man and the Ram)*
Fig. 75 Phillipon. *(Louis Philippe)*
Fig. 76 Corneliss Floris. *(Ornament)*
Fig. 77 "Rabelais." *(Grotesque Figure)*
Fig. 78 "Rabelais." *(Grotesque Figure)*
Fig. 79 Hieronimus Bosch. *(Grotesque Figure)*

7

ACKNOWLEDGMENT

The present volume could not have been published without the generous permission of the editors of the following Journals: *The British Journal of Medical Psychology, The International Journal of Psycho-Analysis, The Psychoanalytic Quarterly, Philosophy and Phenomenological Research, Imago,* and *Internationale Zeitschrift für Psychoanalyse und Imago.* For a detailed list of papers formerly published in these journals see p. 342. I also wish to thank Dr. S. Lorand, the editor of *Psychoanalysis Today,* and the International Universities Press, Inc. for the permission to use sections of an essay.

PREFACE

The essays collected in this volume, prepared and published during a period of well over twenty years, were originally planned with a double purpose in mind. Psychoanalytic ego psychology, which was at the time rapidly taking shape, drew attention to new potentialities not only for psychoanalytic technique and theory but also for the attempts to apply psychoanalytic insight to the problems traditionally treated by the humanities in which I had originally been trained. But the complexity of the new psychoanalytic approach and the vistas which it opened made it no longer seem possible to rely on data traditionally offered, and collected without a psychoanalytic perspective in mind. A new type of interdisciplinary contact was required, and its potentialities were yet to be demonstrated.

As the years progressed this first purpose lost some of its urgency, since the new types of interdisciplinary coöperation, particularly between psychoanalysis and the social sciences were rapidly developing. Thus the second purpose gained in importance: The study of art and of creative processes in the broadest meaning of the word seemed to facilitate contributions to psychoanalytic psychology itself and to crystallize certain impressions gained in clinical work. The shift of focus is reflected in some of the contributions presented here.

The very fact that after so many years the original intention of publishing a series of independent though interconnected essays should have been retained instead of there being a more systematic presentation, indicates that in this volume no psychoanalytic psychology of art is offered. I do not feel that the time for a systematic presentation of this type has come.

Except for one instance the original essays were left essentially unchanged. Only the introductory essay (pp. 13-63), which combines material from two previous publications, was largely rewritten and expanded in the light of recent advances in psychoanalytic knowledge, both in theory and clinical experience. In other instances I have limited myself mainly to adding references to the recent literature and have tried to indicate where more recent findings or views support the formulations which I had reached, where they suggest alternatives and modifications. I have not attempted to eliminate all repetitions, nor to reformulate all passages in the terms I used in the introductory essay. I have also—again with one exception—resisted the temptation to add new material. In the one instance where I have yielded—The Appendix, pp. 116-127—the extraordinary character of the case reported justifies, I believe, the exception.

In both areas, in the collection and interpretation of data and in inquiries into the theory of psychoanalysis, I was privileged to enjoy the advantages of team work. Three of my collaborators have graciously consented to have jointly published papers included in this volume: E. H. Gombrich, Slade Professor of Fine Arts in the University of Oxford, who also revised the text of our original contribution and read through the first draft of the introductory essay; A. Kaplan, Professor of Philosophy at the University of California in Los Angeles whose suggestions in dealing with the problems of aesthetic ambiguity have proved useful beyond the incidence of coöperative effort; and Else Pappenheim, M.D., of Yale University, with whom I studied a case which confirmed older and suggested new hypotheses.

The development of psychoanalytic ego psychology owes much to the thought of H. Hartmann. The close association with him has, over the decades, stimulated much that is said in this volume but particularly the formulations in the introductory and concluding essays. Some of what is said there and elsewhere in this volume refers also directly or by implication to discussions with both him and R. M. Loewenstein.

The list of others to whom I might wish to express my gratitude has grown too long over the years. Only a few can be mentioned. The instigation to the long-delayed work on the present volume came first, before the War from Herbert Read, when I presented some of the material discussed here in a series of lectures in the Courtauld Institute of London University. My interest was recently revived by the fact that the Arthur Davison Ficke Foundation of Hillsdale, New York, made a grant to the School of Medicine of Yale University in order to stimulate research in creative activity in the Child Study Center and the Department of Psychiatry. I felt that the experiences gained during the inquiries about which I here report might be able to stimulate others to more detailed, more systematic and better integrated work.

Dr. Eleanore Nicholes was good enough to revise the translations of those papers which had not previously been published in English and to make suggestions on many points. Miss Lottie Maury who has assisted me in translating some and editing other parts of the manuscript has supplied numerous productive suggestions. I found both her help and her criticism invaluable.

ERNST KRIS

Part One

Introduction

Chapter 1

APPROACHES TO ART

I. The Contribution of Psychoanalysis and Its Limitations

What are those things like which, by contemporaries or (under changed conditions) by posterity, tend to be endowed with the specific aura which the word ART conveys? What must the men have been like who made these things, and what did their work mean to themselves and to their public?

These are some of the questions which the study of art suggests and which no one discipline of knowledge can hope to answer; moreover, no answer can hope to be satisfactory unless these questions are interrelated. In this essay we are concerned with the actual and potential contribution of psychoanalysis to this wide field of inquiry, which, however ill defined, cannot fail to exercise a singular fascination.

In speaking of psychoanalysis we refer to a complex set of constructs and general assumptions on which specific hypotheses are based, to a broad framework for the study of human behavior which allows for the study of a large number of interdependent factors. Psychoanalytic propositions fulfill the general requirements of theory in science. They unify special assumptions under more general ones, indicate what tests for validation and refutation of specific hypotheses are meaningful, and facilitate the formulation of new hypotheses which in turn can be tested (Kris, 1947). Hence constructs and basic assumptions must be revised from time to time in order to retain their usefulness.

In many instances, particularly when psychoanalysis is being "applied" outside of clinical work, its contribution tends to be characterized by one or several quotations from Freud's writings. Not that their value should be minimized; but isolated quotations, however poignant, tend to convey a static impression and suggest that Freud mainly attempted to demonstrate the validity of a given set of hypotheses, adding, as it were, insight from various sources. Nothing could be more misleading. Freud's work consists of continuous attempts to unify detailed observations by an explanatory framework and to revise the theory thus obtained

13

in the light of new empirical data or impressions. This revision led repeatedly to radical reformulations of constructs, basic assumptions, and specific hypotheses—a development which tends to be obscured by the reliance on "representative quotations."[1]

From the early days of psychoanalysis many authors, utilizing primarily clinical observations, participated in the process of revision of theory, sometimes stimulating Freud's own revisions and reformulations and at other times contradicting his views.

This process has gained momentum with the increase in numbers of trained analysts. When alternative propositions reach a certain point, "schools" of analytic thought arise and are propagated. Next to rather obvious psychological factors, the nature of the subject matter itself is responsible for such consequences of controversy: The difficulty of deciding between alternative propositions favors the tendency to substitute dissent for discussion. We do not mean to imply either that decision between alternatives cannot be reached or that opposing views are destined to coexist: The testing of hypotheses would in many instances (particularly the more important ones) require a considerable amount of time as well as complex testing procedures, and crucial experiments can only rarely be specified. In most instances clarification depends on the gradual progress of insight derived from many sources of evidence, mainly the progress of clinical observation and of therapeutic technique. Of their subsidiaries, psychoanalytically oriented studies in child development illustrate best the productive aspects of "validation" (Benjamin, 1950). By bringing new problems to the observer's attention, validation becomes part of the regular progress in science (Kris, 1950).

Dissent in psychoanalysis must be mentioned in this context not only to characterize the writer's position, but also for reasons pertaining to the subject at hand. In discussions on psychoanalysis and art the tendency to simplify or to abbreviate psychoanalytic thinking is particularly noticeable. This seems to imply that the psychological understanding of art requires simpler assumptions than the psychological understanding of the activities more regularly or exclusively investigated by psychiatrists—a view that need not be refuted once one has pointed to its clan-

---

[1] In order to illustrate the difficulties which arise, particularly in interdisciplinary communication, we mention as an instance only Sterba's (1940a) summary of Freud's views on art which eliminates many misunderstandings due to what might be called the "quotation method." Sterba stresses the gradual unfolding of Freud's ideas and— perhaps not quite sharply enough nor in enough detail—the reformulations which occurred. When used by nonanalysts—e.g., in the otherwise excellent book by Weitz (1951) —this intention of Sterba's summary is largely neglected; psychoanalysis continues to be treated as a "static" system.

destine existence. It might, however, be useful to illustrate in what way simplification tends to be misleading. While in their clinical work psychiatrists are accustomed to assess carefully the requirements of a specific environmental situation, the "reality" in which the artist creates is often neglected. "Reality" is used here not so much in the restricted sense of immediate needs and material environment as in another and extended sense: The structure of the problem which exists while the artist is creating, the historical circumstances in the development of art itself which limit some of his work, determine in one way or another his modes of expression and thus constitute the stuff with which he struggles in creation.[2]

The widespread neglect of such circumstances, supreme in C. G. Jung's contributions to the vast area of psychoanalysis and art, is facilitated by the use of an abridged, and hence frequently vulgarized, conceptual framework. The nature of this abridgment, as far as Jung is concerned, has been discussed in considerable detail by Edward Glover (1950). To no other system of alternative propositions has a similar discussion been devoted. However, it seems that the schools of psychoanalytic thought—whatever their scope—which have developed during the last decades resemble in one respect the earlier ones, exemplified by Jung's approach: They have to organize isolated alternatives into a systematic presentation. They tend to reduce the complexity of psychoanalytic thinking and to offer abridgments by creating artificial dichotomies. Some abandon the "biological" roots for the emphasis on "social" aspects —an antithesis which in itself is spurious (Hartmann, Kris, and Loewenstein, 1951)—or reverse the relationship by ignoring environmental conditions. They may limit the scope of the instinctual drives for the sake of the inhibitory and controlling organizations, or take the opposite attitude. Many of them eliminate constructs—preferably, concepts of energy[3]—which seem highly serviceable and do not replace what they omit except by recourse to concepts unrelated to psychoanalysis itself; and thus the usefulness of psychoanalysis as a theory is impaired. The later work of Otto Rank, particularly his voluminous book on *Art and the Artist* (1932), offers the most regrettable example of a similar procedure. While it excels by its array of information, there is no thought to unify this material, but rather an endeavor to disprove what Freud, and Rank himself, wrote earlier. The vast amount of quotation from

[2] See also M. Deri's (1931) formulations on these points which, though published by a distinguished art critic in a psychoanalytic journal, tend to be overlooked in psychoanalytic writings. For further discussions see pp. 94f., 133 and 147f.

[3] On their position within psychoanalysis see particularly Glover (1947).

sources of various degrees of reliability screens the fact that the conceptual framework of psychoanalysis has been simplified to a point where it can contribute hardly more than common-sense psychology of the pre-Freud era.

The present attempt, opposed to abridgments and simplifications, rests on the assumption that the complete system of psychoanalysis offers at present the best chances for understanding and predicting human behavior. It is an "open system," achieved by synchronizing hypotheses which have been formulated during the total course of the development of psychoanalysis—a system not only exposed to constant amplification and emendation, but based on the clarification of some semantic contingencies.[4]

The potential contribution of psychoanalysis to the study of art can, I believe, be assessed only if one takes advantage of the differentiated tools psychoanalytic theory offers. But this is not the only precondition; at least one other must be mentioned. Art—the humanities in general—tend to be viewed as a province outside the confines of science (H. B. Lee, 1947), and if science penetrates into their field it is in the disguise of history. Historians are skilled in establishing the nature of events of the past (and no one is less inclined than the writer to underestimate the rigor of their methods). The events themselves, however, concern human behavior and are part of that broad, ill-defined field which reaches from anthropology to the confines of medicine—the cultural and social sciences. Seen in this context, the study of art is part of the study of communication. There is a sender, there are receivers, and there is a message.[5] These all are, it is true, of a very special and enigmatic kind, and yet only if viewed within a similar framework can the study of art become part of the gradual integration of our knowledge of man.

During the last twenty years there has been repeated discussion of the question of the distance from psychoanalytic thinking at which the social sciences in general find it useful to formulate their assumptions. While the sociologist or economist studies predominantly aspects of human life different from those with which psychoanalysis deals—man's central psychological conflicts—the student of art shares presumably common ground with the psychiatrist: It has been said that he deals with similar stuff. As in other areas of research, the attempt to use psychoanalytic thinking may well lead art criticism to propositions derived from psycho-

---

[4] For a more detailed orientation on aspects of psychoanalytic theory relevant in this context see Hartmann (1939, 1948-1951); Hartmann and Kris (1945); Hartmann, Kris, and Loewenstein (1946, 1949, 1951); Rapaport (1950); and here Chapter 14.

[5] In a similar sense, Fairbairn (1938, a, b).

analysis but designed to meet the special requirements of its own field; a significant step wherever interdisciplinary contact is established.[6]

While the potential contribution of psychoanalysis to the study of art is thus bound to lead into uncharted land, an evaluation of its actual, past, contributions can best be obtained if we briefly turn to the history of psychoanalysis itself. In its heroic age the validity of the earliest hypotheses had to be established. Clinical data were scarce and could in many instances not be communicated in support of the hypotheses. Moreover, when clinical data could be used, there remained the objection that Freud's general psychological findings were valid only within pathology. The study of documents of culture, foremost among them works of art, seemed a field where supplementary evidence could be gained. The intensive research activity which followed on the opening of this non-clinical field was mainly concerned with three problems: first, the "ubiquity" in mythological and literary tradition of certain themes known from or related to the fantasy life of the individual; second, the close relationship between the artist's life history in the psychoanalytic sense and his work; and, third, the relationship between the working of creative imagination, the productive capacity of man, and thought processes observed in clinical study.

The very fact that certain themes of human experience and conflict are recurrent wherever men live or where, at least, certain cultural conditions prevail (best known from the tradition of Mediterranean civilizations) —the fact that from Sophocles to Proust the struggle against incestuous impulses, dependency, guilt, and aggression, has remained a topic of Western literature—seems after almost half a century, as well established as any thesis in the social sciences. It has proved immensely stimulating, opening vistas that had remained inaccessible as long as the comparative study of mythological and literary themes had been based exclusively on general cosmological or specific historical considerations. Progress beyond these initial findings—richly documented in the early encyclopedic writings of Otto Rank (1907, 1909, 1912, 1919)—has on the whole turned in one major direction: psychoanalytic interpretation was expanded. The complexity of these themes became more firmly established. The existence of a larger number of contributing determinants seemed better to account for the intensity of appeal which these themes retained.

This expansion of interpretation of mythological and literary themes reflects some trends in the development of psychoanalysis. When the

[6] Such propositions tend to be of "medium generality." See Gomperz (1929); Mannheim (1940); Hartmann (1944).

emphasis on the uniqueness of the mother-child relationship during the preoedipal phase had gained importance in Freud's thinking, the destiny of Oedipus, for example, came to be viewed not only as a fate determined by the rivalry between son and father, but also by the son's unsatisfied longing for, and retaliatory impulses against, a mother who had betrayed her infant. Hamlet's conflict was no longer viewed only in relation to his repressed parricidal impulses (Freud, 1900; Jones, 1911), but as codetermined by his hidden and dangerously submissive attachment to an idealized father (Jones, 1950). Some authors went further and stressed the part which matricidal impulses play in Hamlet's musings (Wertham, 1941; Maloney and Rockelein, 1949). Similar additions and reinterpretations of widely spread themes have become rather frequent. They use a fair sample of the hypotheses which during the last decades have developed, some intending to supplement, others to supplant, older psychoanalytic interpretations. Wherever controversy arises—it is rarely made explicit—decision must be expected to come from the area in which these hypotheses were formulated, that is, from clinical and experimental studies.

However significant some of these additions to previously assembled knowledge are, they have not basically enlarged our views. It is striking that extensions of research have neglected one aspect. The wide distribution of certain themes was particularly revealing as long as Freud's hypotheses on the generality of certain instinctual strivings was being tested, that is, as long as the study of the id dominated psychoanalytic interest. Since psychoanalytic ego psychology has sharpened our eyes for the specific within the general, one might have expected that the variations of general themes previously studied would have attracted attention and that the question would have been asked: Under specific cultural and socioeconomic conditions, during any given period of history or in the work of any one of the great creators within each period, how have the traditional themes been varied? What aspects of the themes are more and which less frequent, and how are they modified? It seems that a wide field of research waits for those interested in interdisciplinary integration.[7]

For different reasons, progress in the second area of original psychoanalytic interest has been limited. It no longer seems doubtful that what

[7] A significant attempt in this direction by Wolfenstein and Leites (1947, 1950) is connected with the study of recent American and European films. For other fruitful suggestions see Friedman and Gassel (1950), and particularly Kanzer (1948, 1950), who stresses that any "cultural" interpretation presupposes a correct and inclusive psychological interpretation. The anthropological literature supplies more instances of an approach similar to the one postulated above. See also Chapter 12.

a man has experienced during infancy or childhood (particularly if experience is not restricted to external events but includes patterns of conflicts and their solution) may influence as a recurrent theme (or as a defense against it) his thought processes, his dreams, and his artistic creations. The extent to which psychoanalytic insight has advanced in this respect need hardly be stressed. In particular, the constructs of ego psychology, interacting with the constant refinement of techniques for handling developmental problems, have sharpened our eye for the relevance of early experiences. And yet it is significant that we have remained incapable of penetrating to the central problem which evaded Freud's (1910 a) ingenuity. When studying Leonardo da Vinci he had been able to enter deeply into the secrets of a man of genius. Determinants of Leonardo's scientific interest, his obsessional and frequently self-defeating working habits, could be plausibly traced to infantile imprints. The child raised by two mothers—the peasant mother and the wife of his father, in whose house he grew up—was stimulated to unite almost for the first time in Italian painting the Virgin and St. Anna with the infant Christ. Unity between the three was established not only by gestures; they seem to merge into each other since they are inscribed into a pyramidal configuration. By similar devices Leonardo created in several of his paintings compositions which exercised considerable influence on the development of the art of his time. The phenomenon investigated has thus been approached from two sides, the life history of the artist and the solution of the artistic problem:[8] One can demonstrate the interaction of an incentive in the individual life history with the stringencies of an artistic problem, determined in Leonardo's case by the development of Italian painting.

Significant as it is, this very possibility illustrates the limitations of our understanding. Two such limitations deserve our particular attention. The first concerns mainly the individual; the second, his relation to his medium and its potentialities under given historical conditions.

We have no answer to the question why an individual with the infantile experience and the particular pattern of defenses Freud was able to reconstruct in Leonardo's life history was fated to become the great creator. It is not the lack or imprecision of the data used by Freud and accessible to him in this case which can be made responsible for this limitation. Even when we are in a position to rely on the innumerable and detailed observations which clinical study of creative individuals in psychoanalytic observation and therapy brings to the fore, this question

[8] See for a similar point of view M. Deri (1931) and now Christensen (1944) ; see also Clark (1939).

remains unanswered. All progress we have made has led into one direction, which for the sake of simplicity I shall call here vocational choice.[9] Psychoanalytic material enables us to point to the interaction of factors which made one individual turn to painting, the other to dancing, writing, or music. At times even broad generalizations are suggested; we may feel able to say why one prefers action, another contemplation or speculation, why—with apparently similar predispositions—one devotes his life to science and the other to art (Sharpe, 1930, 1935).[10] We have gained a good deal of experience in accounting for obvious failures in performance, and psychoanalytic therapy achieves some of its most gratifying results in helping individuals overcome both general impairment of their working capacity and inhibitions in specific types of endeavor. However, after all this has been properly taken into account, there remains the question not only of why one is successful and the other is not, but, particularly where science or art is concerned, why one is great while the other barely reaches medium height.

We do not at present have tools which would permit us to investigate the roots of gift or talent, not to speak of genius.[11] However, recent advances in ego psychology enable us better to focus on this gap in our knowledge and suggest inquiries which promise to improve our understanding. We have come to view psychological conflict not only as an unavoidable accessory to personality development, but also—within cer-

[9] Findings of psychoanalysis in this area can apparently not be duplicated if the data are obtained by other methods than psychoanalytic observation and therapy, even if in the interpretation of data a psychoanalytic viewpoint is adopted. See in this connection Ginzberg, Ginsburg, Axelrad, and Herma (1951).

[10] Investigations of problems that are related to this area have been undertaken by Roe, largely based on projective tests. Roe started out to study and was led to tentative generalizations in the area of vocational choice, generalizations which are of considerable interest, e.g., a comparison of feminine traits in artists, scientists, and a large group of professions comprising teachers, ministers, and physicians. For a survey see Roe (1947), where further references are given.

[11] See for a beautiful formulation Freud (1930 b). For an apparently different approach see Bergler (1950, p. 257), who writes, "Personally I believe that we are able to define the biological and psychological x producing the phenomenon 'of the writer.' Biologically it consists of a quantitative increase of oral tendencies, including the derivations of orality-voyeurism." At this point Bergler's formulation seems strictly opposed to the view developed later in this essay. However, Bergler continues, "These two biological facts do not *per se* make a writer. In addition there is a specific psychological elaboration, the defensive *"unification"* tendency [Bergler's italics] denying infantile fancied disappointments experienced at the hands of the preoedipal mother, by autarchically setting up the 'mother child shop'". . . . At this point a specific defense mechanism *"encountered exclusively in the artistically creative person"* (Bergler's italics) is postulated. It seems conceivable that such a specificity of defense mechanism might be positively correlated with a certain autonomy in ego function, both primary and secondary; see Hartmann (1950).

tain limits—as an essential ingredient and incentive. We are about to study ego development not only in relation to typical conflicts, but also as far as the ego's capacities and functions emerge from conflict involvement and acquire autonomy. In this connection the endowment of the personality, its innate equipment, plays a significant role. We had been used to view it in terms of potentialities of the individual which might be favored or smothered by life experience, stimulated or suppressed by some of the numerous factors on which maturation and development depend. We are about to appreciate complementary aspects, that is, the influence which endowment may exercise on life experience, and particularly the role endowment may play in facilitating the detachment of certain ego functions from conflict, in establishing autonomy in certain activities (Hartmann, 1939, 1950, 1951).[12] These views prove not only useful in organizing clinical impressions, but particularly stimulating in observing child development. However significant the results of these studies may prove to be one day, their impact on the problem at hand, the psychology of the artist, will, for a considerable time, remain indirect.

The question of endowment of individuals for specific activities may gradually, and only in years to come, play an increasing role in psychoanalytically oriented research. The second problem to which we were led by our discussion of Freud's contribution to our understanding of Leonardo's work suggests even more arduous detours.

Historical and social forces, we said, shape the function of art in general and more specifically that of any given medium in any given historical setting, determining the frame of reference in which creation is enacted. We have long come to realize that art is not produced in an empty space, that no artist is independent of predecessors and models, that he no less than the scientist and the philosopher is part of a specific tradition and works in a structured area of problems. The degree of mastery within this framework and, at least in certain periods, the freedom to modify these stringencies are presumably part of the complex scale by which achievement is being measured. However, there is little which psychoanalysis has as yet contributed to an understanding of the meaning of this framework itself; the psychology of artistic style is unwritten.[13] We may expect that the method of approach will be an

[12] In this simplified rendering of an important part of psychoanalytic theory we have implied certain distinctions suggested by Hartmann (1950), particularly his distinction between primary and secondary ego autonomy.

[13] For psychoanalytic approaches to this problem see Sachs (1942). It is significant that no other psychological approach has led to tangible or meaningful results. Thus the attempt to use Gestalt psychology by Sedlmayr (1930) has not led to insight into the psychology of style, nor have recent contributions by Arnheim (1949) and

extremely complex one; what psychoanalysis may have to offer will probably depend on our ability to view the phenomena of style in art at least
in part in terms of the processes of discharge which they stimulate in
artist and public.[14]

Investigative procedures which have this goal in mind will have to
vary according to the medium of artistic expression examined. Psychoanalytic experience can suggest mainly one principle: Instead of accepting the division of form and content, maintained in many areas of the
history and the criticism of art, psychoanalytic orientation suggests the
value of establishing their interrelation.[15] To illustrate the difficulties of
such attempts, we return once more to Leonardo's painting. Our understanding of his achievement would gain if, in addition to being able to
demonstrate that the desire to unite the Christ with two mothers is
rooted in his childhood experiences, we were able to find a similar root
for the specific type of merging—for instance, for the construction of a
pyramidal unit into which the figures are made to fit.[16]

The third of the main avenues on which psychoanalysis approached
the wide area of art led to the study of the artist's imagination. In the
initial stages of his work, Freud felt that only the attempt at vigorous
scientific thinking established a difference between his approach and
that of the intuitive psychologists among the poets whose writings he had
always admired.[17] Even when there was no longer any doubt about the

---

others, who still seem to be engaged in searching for a "good" Gestalt, valid under all
historical circumstances. Ehrenzweig (1948-1949) has recently successfully broken away
from this tradition and attempted to combine Gestalt psychology and psychoanalytic
thinking. However, his interest is largely centered on a phylogenetic explanation.
There are few references to concrete phenomena familiar to the psychoanalyst or other
investigators of empirical data. Without referring explicitly to Gestalt psychology,
Weiss (1947) has pointed to what I think may prove to be a bridge between what
Gestalt psychologists would refer to as *praegnanz* and psychoanalytic thinking when he
suggests that "formal aesthetic pleasure is economy of expenditure of psychic energy
in perception."

14 For some attempts in this direction see pp. 142ff., 159, and 262f.

15 Freud's translation of the formal characteristics of the dream into latent dream
thoughts offers the model for similar investigations; see also pp. 105ff., 147f., and 161.
The psychoanalytic approach to the problem of formal elaboration has been
studied also in relation to music, a field which I do not feel competent to discuss.

16 One is tempted to establish a connection between the insertion of the figures
into a superimposed body and Leonardo's interest in procreation and pregnancy. However, I do not feel that the evidence at our disposal is specific enough to establish
a relationship between "form and content" on a level which would essentially improve
our understanding. Pfister's (1913 b) attempt to recognize in the painting the vulture
of Leonardo's screen memory, analyzed by Freud (1910 a), has not convinced me.

17 See p. 266.

independent character of the contribution psychoanalysis was able to make, late in his life, he spoke of philosophers, writers, poets as "the few to whom it is vouchsafed . . . with hardly any effort to salvage from the whirlpool of their emotions the deepest truth to which we others have to force our way, ceaselessly groping among torturing uncertainties" (1930 b, p. 122).

Throughout the history of analysis statements of men of introspective genius who had anticipated some aspect of psychoanalytic insight have been quoted. No attempt has as yet been made to survey this material. While Plato, Sophocles, Shakespeare, Pascal, Hobbes, Lichtenberg, Coleridge, Goethe, Melville, Hawthorne, Nietzsche, Henry James, and Proust, to mention only a few, have contributed views which in many ways coincide with what psychoanalysis has ascertained by another method, the fact that with each of these men another aspect of psychological dynamics becomes important has to my knowledge never been fully discussed; the history of intuitive insight waits to be written, if for no other purpose than to demonstrate how the great are less than others subject to the limitations which cultural and historical conditions impose.

This at least is the impression one gains in another area, in which the creations of the masters of intuitive psychology were made subjects of analysis. Behavior and motivation of characters in literature are viewed as the analyst views his patients;[18] the scope of these studies has gradually developed, and they have added a new dimension to our understanding of literature.[19] Recurrent themes in the works of certain writers, treatments of certain conflicts and avoidance of others, have brought us closer to an understanding of the process of creation in literature than any other approach; and yet it cannot and should not be claimed that this approach exhausts all aspects relevant to what can be called here, loosely, an adequate understanding of literature as art.[20]

The reaction of the writer himself to psychoanalytic interpretations of his work has proved revealing in the few instances in which it has been recorded. When Freud published his most detailed analysis of a work of narrative art, the essay on dreams and delusion in the novel *Gradiva* (1907), the aged author, Wilhelm Jensen, a distinguished

[18] For the first steps in this direction, stimulated by Breuer's and Freud's *Studies in Hysteria* (1895) see Chapter 11; for Freud's own initial attempts see his remarks on novels of C. F. Meyer in his letters to W. Fliess (Freud, 1950).

[19] For a recent and particularly significant example see Wangh (1950), who pointed to the part Iago's homosexuality plays in the structure of *Othello*.

[20] See Trilling (1947, 1950), and Chapter 12.

but not outstanding German writer, reacted to the publication in several letters. He was impressed by Freud's interpretation, found that it had fully come to grips with the intention of the novel, but was unaware of the multiple determinants in the hero's dreams and delusion to which Freud's analysis had pointed. "It might be best," he wrote, "to attribute the description of the psychological process . . . to poetic intuition, though my original training as a physician may have played a part"[21] (Jensen, 1907). When, during analytic treatment, previously produced works of art are investigated, similar responses seem to be typical. Jensen's approval was limited to the recognition of the link between conscious and preconscious thoughts which Freud had established, but his introspection could not encompass what was repressed.[22] During psychoanalytic treatment it seems comparatively easy to establish connections between preconscious elements in the artist's work and those of which he had always been aware. The contributions derived from the storehouse of memories and the sometimes very numerous clues borrowed from one or the other source in the environment and condensed into a single trait appear in analytic material sometimes without particular effort.[23] But only extended analysis leads to repressed psychic material, to motivation from the id—and only this allows full demonstration of the interaction and interconnection of elements derived from various stages of awareness.[24]

The study of this interaction entered the orbit of psychoanalytic investigations early in its history, since its understanding could be based on a comparison of the dream work with what one might call the "art work"; a comparison particularly significant because of the differences which it emphasizes.[25] Freud himself first approached the topic in his

[21] Judging from similar instances, that part can only have been a minor one.

[22] See a similar reaction of Stefan Zweig's reported by Freud (1928 b).

[23] The psychological approach to literary criticism has achieved its most impressive results where the attempt was made to trace similar material by a study of the artist's life history and the sources available to him. It suffices here to refer to Lowes' (1927) work on Coleridge, Murray's (1949) on Melville, or Paden's (1942) on Tennyson. For the specific psychoanalytic evaluation of material thus assembled see, e.g., Beres' (1951) recent study on Coleridge.

[24] It is regrettable that clinical material of this kind has only rarely been available and in most instances cannot be made available. It should, however, be said that it tends to remain highly incomplete, because its exploration is part and parcel of the analytic process and subject to the limitations imposed by the therapeutic purpose. Similar considerations concern artistic productions during the course of analytic treatment; this situation is, however, even more complex, since artistic productions tend to be influenced by the existence of the analytic contact and serve, additionally or essentially, the purpose of communication in analysis.

study on *Wit and Its Relation to the Unconscious* (1905 a), and since several of the essays which follow elaborate his thoughts, we limit ourselves here to one remark only, anticipating what will later be discussed in greater detail.[26] The relationship of the ego to the id encompasses not only the question of the extent to which id strivings are being satisfied or warded off or the compromises which are achieved. It also encompasses the relationship of primary to secondary processes; but the relationship familiar in dream work is reversed: We are justified in speaking of the ego's control of the primary process as a particular extension of its functions. What in the dream appears as compromise and is explained in terms of overdetermination appears in the work of art as multiplicity of meaning, which stimulates differentiated types of response in the audience. The fruitfulness of these points of view in the progress of modern criticism and the theory of art has been considerable; it seems to have stimulated years ago the work of William Empson, who lately has extended his approach to the study of linguistics (1951).[27] At the same time it offers an access to that complex field which we mean when we speak of "the psychology of *the* artist."

The capacity of gaining easy access to id material without being overwhelmed by it, of retaining control over the primary process, and, perhaps specifically, the capability of making rapid or at least appropriately rapid shifts in levels of psychic function, suggest psychological characteristics of a definite but complex kind. The most general, one might say the only general, hypothesis advanced in this respect came from Freud (1917), who speaks of a certain "flexibility of repression" in the artist.[28] This flexibility, or whatever other and more satisfactory characteristics we might establish, is clearly not limited to the artist: These characteristics are related to those conditions in which id impulses intrude upon the ego and this leads to the question of the extent to

[25] See Rickman (1940) paragraph 5, and recently also Schneider (1950); see for a fuller treatment here pp. 177, 253f.

[26] See Chapters 3, 6 and 7.

[27] For Empson see Chapter 10; on his relation to Freud see particularly Hyman (1948).

[28] Related to this flexibility is another of Freud's hypotheses, his emphasis on the artist's bisexuality (1928 b), which plays frequently a role in the passive experience during creation. (See here Chapters 13 and 14, esp. pp. 317f.).

Various authors have contributed hypotheses which could be viewed as pointing to ontogenetic factors related to both of Freud's suggestions. I mention particularly Lowenfeld (1941) who assumes that early traumatic experiences form one of the preconditions to artistic creativity in stimulating a lasting need to repeat actively what was once experienced passively. There is a possible connection between this suggestion and those of Bergler's (1950) (see p. 20), who in a large number of analyzed cases

which pathological dispositions may be part of what constitutes the artist. It is this problem to which Freud referred when he said (1905 b) that "a considerable increase in psychic capacity results from a predisposition dangerous in itself." The protection against these dangers lies, according to Freud, in the function of the ego, in its capacity for sublimation.[29]

In order to equip ourselves for the subsequent steps in our discussion, it is necessary at this point to widen the scope of our presentation and to touch upon matters seemingly distant from our topic. The usage of the word "sublimation" in Freud's own writings is far from consistent and was subject to a number of vicissitudes (S. Bernfeld, 1922, 1931; Sterba, 1930); as a consequence a number of shades of meaning persist in general psychoanalytic usage. However, the variations of meaning tend to be less frequently discussed than the conditions under which, according to clinical observation, sublimation is favored, a topic of central importance in all therapeutic contingencies.[30]

Sublimation, listed also as one of the defense mechanisms of the ego, designates two processes so clearly related to each other that one might be tempted to speak of one and the same process: it refers to the displacement of energy discharge from a socially inacceptable goal to an acceptable one and to a transformation of the energy discharged; for this second process we here adopt the word "neutralization."[31] The usefulness of the distinction between the two meanings becomes apparent when we

---

of "writers" found among other factors the prevalence of the defense against oral-masochistic tendencies. A survey of these and other views on the psychoanalytic psychology of "the artist" is not intended here. Such a survey would have to distinguish between two approaches: There are those who connect the psychology of the artist mainly with typical patterns of conflict and those who focus mainly on structural problems in the artist's personality. At the present time the second approach seems to be the more fruitful one.

[29] For a survey of problems concerning ego functions in creativity see now Hart (1950). For similar views presented in a somewhat misleading terminology see Born (1945); see also Schneider (1950).

[30] The most comprehensive discussion of the term in psychoanalytic writings and its bearing on metapsychological problems, is still to be found in Glover's paper of 1931. For later formulations see, e.g., F. Deri (1939), Flugel (1942), Róheim (1943), Bergler (1945), Brierley (1950). For sublimation and its relation to art see critical comments by Levey (1939, 1940), which neglect the problem of energy transformation in its relation to psychic structure. For the specific relationship to destructive impulses see Sharpe (1930, 1935) and particularly Menninger (1938, 1942).

[31] We do so since "sublimation" when used to designate energy transformation tends to designate that of libido only; since we assume throughout that the transformation concerns both libido and aggression, the term "neutralization" offers better opportunities to avoid misunderstandings. See Hartmann, Kris, and Loewenstein (1949). The term "sublimation" could thus be reserved for the relation to the goal.

realize that goal substitution and energy transformation need not be synchronous; the more acceptable, i.e., "higher," activity can be executed with energy that has retained or regained its original instinctual quality. We speak then of sexualization or aggressivization. Clinical experience points to this danger which may be responsible for malfunctions of various kinds from symptom formation to inappropriate performance.

There is one further theoretical problem, particularly complex yet probably of considerable significance, that has still to be mentioned: Freud's distinction between primary and secondary processes was based on the idea that in the former energy was fluid, ready for immediate discharge, in the latter, bound, at the disposal of the ego. One might be inclined to assume that in speaking of neutralized energy we have in fact only substituted another word for bound energy, that the two conditions are identical. However, there are reasons (discussed in part in Chapter 14) which make it advisable to refer to both conditions as frequently but not always synchronous; they are to some extent independent variables. Hence the degree of neutralization may be low, yet we may be dealing with secondary processes; while fully under the control of the ego, fully bound, the energy may still have retained the hallmark of libido or aggression.

The tools which psychoanalytic theory puts here at our disposal have not yet been fully utilized. It seems possible not only to organize the structural characteristics of various types of activity according to the opportunities they offer for more or less direct discharge of instinctual energy, but also to organize them according to the degrees of neutralization of libidinal and aggressive energies which they "require."[32]

The topic is a wide one and fundamental to many general problems in adaptation and personality development. It includes the problem of secondary autonomy in ego functions (Hartmann, 1950) since one is led to the assumption that secondary autonomy depends on the irreversibility of energy transformation, i.e., on the permanent or relatively permanent investment of the ego with neutralized aggressive or libidinous energies. However, in addition to these partial and relatively permanent changes in energy distribution which seem to be of signal importance for personality development, one would have to account also for the energy flux, i.e., the transitory changes in energy distribution and redistribution such as the temporary and shifting reinforcement of sexual, aggressive or neutral energy as it may occur in the course of any type of activity. Sublimation in creative activity might conceivably prove to be

[32] For a discussion of the usefulness of a similar approach to social phenomena see Axelrad and Maury (1951).

distinguished by two characteristics: the fusion in the discharge of instinctual energy and the shift in psychic levels.

The idea of the fusion of libidinal and aggressive energy plays a considerable part in Freud's formulation on psychoanalytic theory. In the study of creative activity, however, one special aspect of this broader problem may prove relevant, namely, the special assumption that a certain degree of energy neutralization provides favorable conditions for fusion (Hartmann, Kris, and Loewenstein, 1949) and hence for the mastery of even particularly intense instinctual demands.[33]

In speaking of shifts of psychic levels we refer to the organizational functions of the ego, to its capacity of self-regulation of regression and particularly to its capacity of control over the primary process;[34] problems which in some of the subsequent essays are treated in relation to special areas of investigation.

We cannot in the present context and at the present stage of our understanding attempt to elaborate on these suggestive possibilities and have to abandon the idea of a systematic presentation lest we impose too great a strain on our as yet limited ability to handle highly complex problems of psychoanalytic theory in extreme abbreviation. We may only point to what may be the goal of such a systematic presentation. As far as artistic activities in the broadest sense are concerned we might be led into areas of problems with which traditionally the theory or philosophy of art deals or has dealt, problems concerning the hierarchy of various media and various works of art. However, there is no doubt that we are familiar with similar problems, though on a different level. In clinical practice, by rule of thumb, views concerning both specific problems of energy discharge and of ego functions in relation to specific types of creative behavior are taken for granted.

Our expectations are significantly limited when we hear that a certain patient is an actor, a dancer, a cartoonist, or a dress designer. They are less limited but still significant when we hear that he is a writer, painter, architect, or poet. In all these cases—in the first instances more definitely—we expect that certain typical conflict constellations will more likely occur than others: The problem of rapidly changing identification may be crucial in the actor, that of coping with exhibition in the dancer, the wish to distort others in the cartoonist, and to adorn them in

[33] For a clinical instance of such a fusion of libidinal and aggressive discharge processes on a comparatively "high" level of sublimation, see p. 52.

[34] See for some further discussion pp. 305f. See now also Rapaport (1951), who in his annotations to Hartmann's paper on adaptation (1939 a), and to my own on preconscious mental processes (see here Chapter 14) has repeatedly discussed related problems.

the dress designer; but each of these dominant wishes—which we here have mentioned only in order to characterize one direction of our expectations—is clearly merged with innumerable other tendencies in the individual, and each of them is rooted in his history. According to clinical experience, success or failure in these professions depends, among other factors, on one to which we referred before: on the extent to which the activity itself has for any particular individual become autonomous, i.e., detached from the original conflict which may have turned interest and proclivity into the specific direction. It is at this point that the much-discussed question of the function of psychoanalytic therapy in relation to creative capacities can be considered. Therapy may facilitate or even bring about this detachment of creative ability and of the urge to create from immediate conflict involvement.[35] At this point the relation to the "special gifts and predispositions which are not commonly found in sufficient degree" gains importance; endowment facilitates the detachment from conflict of those "higher and finer" types of activities "in art and science which at all times are the privilege of a selected few."

Gifts and predispositions have to be studied not only in their relation to the conflict in which they may have been rooted, and from which they emerge, but also in relation to the structure of the activity in which they are put to use. Here again a variety of conditions has to be taken into account, foremost among them the properties of the media and their function under those special historical conditions which determine the modes of expression and the "problems" to be solved. It will not be found that the same equipment, the same psychological proclivities, will in all periods of history make for success—in any given medium or in artistic creation in general. Thus the artist whose endowment is determined at least in part by the "flexibility of repression" to which Freud referred—the one who borders on pathology and conquers it by his work —is likely to appear as a leader in art at certain periods and not in others. In this sense the "selection" of artistic leaders may well proceed according to the same general principles which seem to determine the selection of leadership in other areas. In the same sense that the structure of a political situation may attract certain personality types as main actors (Hartmann, 1944; Kris, 1949), the structure of a situation in the

[35] The alleged sterilizing effect of analytic experiences on the creator seems in this context as another example of a spurious topic; we would be faced with instances in which creation was solely determined by conflict (e.g., solely serving the purpose of defense) and did not have a place in the autonomous sphere of the ego. This seems broadly to coincide with the clinical experience of psychoanalysts: The gifted artist "spoiled by analysis" seems to be a rare occurrence. See in this connection Trilling (1945, 1950).

development of art in general, or of a specific medium, may elicit participation from those whose predispositions are likely to fulfill the requirements at the given moment. These requirements may in turn be modified by the participants; thus new and different types of personalities may become important.

Put in these general terms, the problems seem simple. To apply the principle to any concrete field is another, infinitely more difficult, matter —one that once more reminds us of the wide open spaces, the areas where integrated research alone can become fruitful. From what is known at present we may deduce that the artist whose creative capacities are close to potential pathology will find his place more easily in "romantic" than in "classical" periods of art; and since these very terms are not too well defined, except when applied to the historical movements of the eighteenth and nineteenth centuries, the psychological aspect may help to clarify some of the problems traditionally linked to what we call "the style." However, the very contrast we mention is a narrow one; we may come close to relevant dichotomies when we think of cultural conditions in which skill alone predominates and is seen as value in art and others where skill without inspiration is held in low esteem—and others again where inspiration with even less skill becomes acceptable and admired.

In the history of almost all the arts since the eighteenth century the trend to an increased insistence on inspiration seems to be detectable —dominant in certain phases, more submerged in others, and yet clearly continuous as a movement that gained increasing strength, to the point where dream and fantasy could be painted and put into words, where relation to stringencies became less important, and where finally the work of art became a document of the process of creation. In the field of literature this trend has repeatedly been characterized, particularly by Praz (1933) and Fretet (1946); in the representational arts it is outlined by the genealogy which leads from Goya to van Gogh and to surrealism.[36]

From another angle we now approach the relation of psychoanalysis to art: During the last decades psychoanalytic insights into the processes of artistic creation have themselves become part of art.[37] Creative artists of our day are wont to use free association as a training ground for creative thinking or as an independent mode of expression, and some among the surrealists have assigned to their work the function of documenting the process of creation itself, thus making explicit what previously had

[36] Fretet (1946), a literary critic and physician, stresses that "since Rousseau, melancholic and delirious states play a prominent role in the history of art. They have a literary tradition . . ."

[37] See Chapter 11.

been implicit.[38] In the present context this is only mentioned since it indicates a reversal of functions; psychoanalysis and its discoveries act as a social force upon art and artist.

If in the light of these limitations we review once more the contributions of psychoanalysis to the study of art, the question arises of the extent to which these contributions are specific, applicable to art as distinct from other human endeavors. Obviously, this specificity is true only in a limited sense: Newspaper reports are frequently concerned with events no less similar to general themes in mythology and individual fantasy than are great works of literature. The impact of childhood on all human activities is permanent. Psychological intuition is a prerogative of many leaders in society, and while it is particularly important in many types of art, problems of sublimation and neutralization concern a much wider field.[39]

The quest for what is specific to the psychological processes connected with art, its creation and its re-creation, constitutes a problem that we can hardly hope to solve. All we can hope is to approach it from afar, but we are entitled to value every step we are able to take in the desired direction. We propose to take structural, dynamic, and economic changes which seem to be characteristic of what one might call the aesthetic experience into account. Our starting point will be the function of art as a specific kind of communication from the one to the many.

II. Daydream and Fiction

In order initially to avoid the complexity of clinical material, we start with a model:[40]

A huge Alsatian dog comes yelping at a little boy playing outdoors. The child is frightened by the creature's size and bark, and turns away, screaming for help. He may later elaborate this scene in many ways. In his play with his toys, roles will be reversed; the boy will conquer the threatening enemy and tame the animal, which may become his special friend and protector. The scene may occupy the boy's thoughts at night in bed before he goes to sleep. The dog may grow in size and shape. Dangers that he had experienced before and other thoughts, common to all little boys, may merge with the latest encounter. When these

38 On the specific sociological significance of this transition see pp. 262f. See also Read (1936 a) .

39 For a similar point of view. leading however to different conclusions, see now H. B. Lee (1949 c, particularly p. 356) .

40 It is a variation of a similar model used by Burt (1933) .

thoughts recur during the day, the boy relives the pleasurable experience of the conquest of danger in his daydreams. The delight of the triumph explains why play and daydreams can be repeated time and again.[41]

The influence of the traumatic experience described in this model may be more or less lasting; play or daydreams may continue for a long time. They may change their content and still bear the imprint of flight from, or conquest of, danger, and when the boy comes of age he may translate fantasy into action, remaining one of those who expose themselves to vicissitudes of many kinds and who relish the continual conquest of circumstances. Or else, the specific matter of play and daydream may persist and cause him to become a fancier of pets or a scientific student of animal nature. These and similar solutions may occur in response to significant experiences, and it is rarely possible to predict which one will be adopted. Clinical observation indicates, however, that the chosen solution serves many purposes at the same time and is, as it were, the resultant of many forces.

Traumatic experiences do not presuppose an objective danger situation: There need not be a yelping Alsatian dog in order to arouse fear of big animals. In urbanized civilization fear of big animals is frequent with little boys as a convenient displacement of the ambivalent attitude to the father during the oedipal phase. The trauma of the scene of our model is therefore itself the result of experiences rooted in the successive phases of earliest childhood, when the demand for love and protection, the response of the environment to these demands, and the striving for independence in the child, first mold the human personality.

We have mentioned but a few of the possible reactions to the traumatic experiences of our model situation, omitting both the pathological and the most normal. Little need be said here of the dog—or animal—phobia which might ensue as a transitory symptom or firmly establish itself, not to yield without treatment. The most normal solution concerns the child's contact with his environment. When the boy screams for help and the mother rushes to help him, he feels her love as a guarantee of future safety.

In safety a new desire may arise: In search of admiration, the boy may speak of his encounter in order to insure attention. At this point fantasy elaboration acquires its social function. Play or fantasy may be shared with a faithful companion or with a group of boys who may be led by the little hero. Fantasy play then turns into the game of the group, and the pursuit of adventure may only in insignificant details re-

---

[41] I here refer to "functional" pleasure, a pleasure arising from a sense of mastery. See pp. 210f., and 315.

veal its origin in the traumatic experience of the group leader. He has found followers because the emotions reverberating in his plan for the game were akin to their emotions. The solutions he invented met with their latent demands.

Leadership on this level has no relation to art. But should the boy turn not to action but to contemplation, and develop his daydream in the form of an ordered account, he may find an audience willing to share with him the adventures of his tale without turning to action. If the activity of the storyteller is analyzed at this point, it will be found to serve a multiplicity of functions: It is an attempt to gain control over the traumatic experience which, long repressed, still exercises influences; and at the same time it brings enjoyment in reproducing, with variations, the pleasurable experience of conquest. This reproduction is turned into a means of gaining contact with others by letting them share in the experiences under the storyteller's guidance.

We now are prepared to turn to a clinical parallel, which leads to deeper and more relevant psychological problems. There are individuals —normal in all essential respects—who never part from the habit of weaving their hopes and fears into "continued stories," to which they return whenever life inflicts frustration. However varied the stories may be, they not only contain a nucleus of recurrent themes, but they also share a common fate. The most refined elaborations which lead the hero to grandeur sooner or later become unusable. Once the plot is elaborated, the urge to reach the climax grows. The quest for immediate gratification destroys the product of inventiveness. Gradually the climax swallows up the story.

Psychoanalytic literature reports a number of such daydreams,[42] but as far as I know, there is only one instance in which the transformation of the daydream into a story, its socialization, has been recorded in detail. Anna Freud, in one of her first publications (1923), described this development in a female patient. The daydream itself was rooted in a masturbation fantasy of a well-known type, repeated with monotony: A baby was being beaten by an adult. The figures were sometimes multiplied but remained anonymous.

In analysis the patient did not remember all the details, but she did remember that the fantasy was accompanied by sexual excitement and some masturbatory action. The fantasy in itself was, of course, of highly complex origin, springing from the wish to be loved by the father. With progressive psychic evolution, attempts were made to retain the fantasy

42 See particularly Sachs (1924) and the abbreviated translation (1942) . For further literature see Chapter 14.

but to detach it from the elements leading to autoerotic gratifications. Continued stories, sets of daydreams, each with a different plot and describing different figures, were composed. In her fourteenth or fifteenth year the patient inserted in those stories one which she had made with the help of some book she had just then read, but her own ideas had been intermingled with its contents to such an extent that it proved to be impossible to separate the two sources.

At that time the story read as follows: "A medieval knight has for years been feuding with a number of nobles who have leagued together against him. In the course of a battle a noble youth of fifteen [the age of the daydreamer] is captured by the knight's henchmen. He is taken to the knight's castle and there kept prisoner for a time, until, at last, he gains his freedom again." In this comparatively simple daydream there are only two really important figures, the noble young prisoner and the harsh and brutal knight. Their relation furnished the basis of an apparently irreconcilable antagonism between the strong and powerful character and the weak one who was at his mercy. The patient had described the meeting and the relation of both these characters in many varied situations. The climax of each was the moment when the anger and rage of the mighty one, represented as a torturer, were transformed into kindness and pity. Then the excitement was resolved into a feeling of pleasure. But such an episode only proved satisfactory in the daydream for some days. Then the tone of gentleness which at the beginning had marked the climax spread further and further over the story and finally absorbed all the interest formerly taken up by the introduction and the development of the plot.

Some years after the first appearance of this story, the young girl made an attempt to write it down. She produced a short story describing the youth's life during his imprisonment. The story was well arranged, all the events being transposed into the past and described through the medium of a conversation between the prisoner's father—a figure unknown to the daydream—and the knight. There were no climaxes in this story; it showed a steady growth of the friendship between the knight and the prisoner, and its development took up the whole length of the story. The end, the final harmony between those who were the late embodiment of the infantile beating fantasy, the father, the knight, and the daughter transvested as the noble youth, was thus anticipated but not described. Thus the precipitation of the climax was replaced by a careful build-up of the plot: The daydream had become socialized and adapted to an audience (Freud, 1908).

Up to this point we have dealt in our model and our clinical example with productions which, though in some respects of the nature of art, are still at a great distance from where art begins, however wide we intend to draw the confines. To establish the connection between daydream and narrative art requires a large set of data, such as only psychoanalytic material offers; but though much of what is said in the context of this essay is derived from, or was crystallized by, clinical experiences, they do not lend themselves to publication, particularly not at this point in our discussion, at which it seems appropriate to include some reactions of the public.

The history of literature is replete with instances in which in a writer's account the biographical element predominates, and it is common knowledge among critics that there is one type of writer in whom this element determines success: The writer whose first book is different from others, since it was this first which contained the one story—his own—which he had to tell. Famous achievements in the history of literature could be included in an investigation of such autobiographical novels. One might inquire into the distance from immediate life experience at which any given writer, or writers of any given period, tends to create—questions which in the future may well attract students in psychologically oriented expansions of criticism. We suspect that the greatest among them may be no less concerned with their own experience, no less self-centered, than the minor ones; but their achievement might well be due in part to their ability to detach themselves more completely from the immediate reality of their actual experiences, and to make a wider range of subjects their own.[43] In the present context, however, not the self-centeredness of the artist's choice of subject is at stake but rather a special version of self-centeredness, i.e., the relation of his work to a daydream in which he has lived. It seems, therefore, permissible to introduce here a personal experience with a work of narrative art that corresponds to the requirements we have in mind.

During the early years of this century the writings of Frederick William Rolfe (1860-1913) attracted attention. Rolfe lived and wrote for part of his life as Baron Corvo, an Italian title allegedly acquired by adoption. He has remained known as one of the original contributors to *The Yellow Book,* a literary magazine published in London during the

---

[43] See for a more detailed discussion Chapter 12. It should be noted that other criteria which might be applied seem less specific. One might ask what difference it makes, e.g., to what degree narrative art expresses the striving of wish fulfillment or the defense against instinctual demands. According to my experience this difference exists already in the structure of daydreams and the question therefore applies already to fantasy itself. For the role of defense in narrative art see also Bergler (1950).

last years of the nineteenth century,[44] and as author of a series of short stories in Italian setting, a vivid and extraordinarily selective history of the house of Borgia, a short novel devoted to the description of one day in the life of an Italian nobleman of the Renaissance, and, particularly, as the author of a book published in 1904 under the title *Hadrian VIIth, a Romance*. This tells the story of an unfrocked British monk who in the early years of the twentieth century is raised to the Holy See; it has retained its place in the interest of the reading public, in both England and this country.[45] It owes this distinction to several characteristics praised by critics and admirers, of whom D. H. Lawrence seems to have been the most representative. They extol the extraordinary virtuosity of language, which though rich and almost exotic—"embroidered with words glittering like jewels" (Haigh, 1935)—is yet of a rigor hardly impeded by artificiality, the remarkable wealth of descriptive material set out in great detail, and the plausible and impressive character of the hero, G. A. Rose, the future Pope. Apparently all contemporary readers sensed the affinity between hero and author.

When by an accident I became familiar with this book during the late nineteen twenties, I knew nothing about its renown and, as all other readers, nothing about the author. I reacted to it with a mixture of fascination and disgust. In order to check on the nature of my reaction, I encouraged a number of friends from various walks of life to read the novel. While I did not in detail record their reactions, I kept notes to check on my hypothesis. I expected that my own reaction would prove to be a fairly typical one and would be shared to some degree by other readers. A strong but ambivalent reaction seemed appropriate since I was convinced from the first that the writer, a man of great ability and imagination and some learning, had presented his readers with what was in all essential aspects a daydream in the full and clinical sense of the word, not merely a novel in which "the author identified himself with the hero." This view was suggested by the passionate character of the account, by the rapture in which climax was heaped upon climax, and by the fact that in all episodes the hero emerged triumphant and uncontested.

The reaction of my subjects was to a considerable degree confirmatory: Appreciation was expressed in various degrees of intensity, disgust

[44] For the cultural atmosphere see Gaunt (1945) who does not, however, refer to Rolfe.

[45] It was republished by the original publishers, Chatto and Windus, in 1929 as part of their Phoenix Library, reprinted in 1935 and, I believe, several times since. Its American publisher, A. Knopf, selected it for the "Borzoi" series.

in some instances mitigated by more or less admiration. Only two of my subjects did not react in this ambivalent sense: One, a man of considerable sophistication, who in abandoned enchantment declared that this was one of the great literary achievements of all times, was the son of a bishop. The other had earlier in his life considered an ecclesiastic career for himself; in him negative reactions predominated. Both these reactions seemed plausible if my hypothesis was correct: They could be explained by the fact that the subject matter of the novel stimulated in the two men responses of a highly personal nature; in one memories concerning his father, and in the other memories concerning a phase in his own development, which he resented.

At the time when I conducted this inquiry no information on the author's personality was available. A few years later, in 1934, a biographical account was published by A. J. A. Symons, who had himself started out as a devotee of "Hadrian." It combines under the title *The Quest for Corvo* the biography of the hero with an enthralling account of the search for data and has in turn stimulated interest in Corvo's writings.[46] It tells the story of an unfrocked British seminary student, whose misadventures coincide in many details with those of Rose; the story of a paranoid homosexual psychopath with great gifts, who started out with interests in painting and music, who turned to writing around forty, during a respite on his way from charlatanry to criminal offense, and who died as a man of very ill repute indeed in Venice. His self-willed and lifelong battle against misery and destitution fits into a clinical picture in which the masochistic self-debasement appears as an expression of the same proclivity which transforms sponsors into enemies. The misdeeds of the first part of this painful life appear as defamatory reproaches in the novel. One might say that only a paranoid personality could have engaged in presenting a daydream as a novel.

The three illustrations in turn throw light on some aspects of the function of art as communication: The most significant ones are supplied by the case history. It illustrates the transition from the striving for immediate discharge in a masturbation fantasy (where fantasy is a phase of or an aid to action) to the solitary daydream (which retains elements of the striving for action and gratification) to the attempt at interposing organizing factors into the account. We are accustomed to recognize the control over time, the ability to delay, as one of the earliest functions of the ego; or, more accurately, the fact that such delay has become possible

[46] A review of this book by Haigh (1935) in *The Psychoanalytic Quarterly* is, I believe, the only reference to Corvo's work and personality in psychiatric writings.

supplies one of the indicators for early stages in ego development.[47] The delay in discharge of tension is evidence of first and nuclear processes of energy neutralization. A continuous line leads from one stage, on which masturbatory action is in part substituted and in part supplemented by the continuous daydream, to another, on which the narrative account develops; both steps, but particularly the latter, presuppose the development of certain skills in imagination and formulation and the translation of the visual into the verbal. Daydreams tend to retain as a similarity with dreams, with which they share some important functions, the use of certain visual elements; the extent to which this occurs is for unknown reasons extremely variable. The purposeful translation of the daydream into narrative form is dependent on a total translation of visual into verbal expression (Sachs, 1942), the shortcut of visual imagination must be replaced by words which can evoke the vision in others. We are not told whether Anna Freud's patient aimed consciously at an audience, and whether she tried to submit her narrative to this test. But if we use experience from similar instances we might infer that such a test was at least preconsciously intended and probably linked to the idea of gaining self-esteem through the reaction of her readers. Self-esteem in this connection may gain a variety of meanings, one of which, according to clinical experience at least, is very general: The approval of an audience encourages self-approval. If others can share, the fear of the superego is abated; unconscious self-criticism can be kept in abeyance. The illicit has become licit.[48]

Corvo's romance illustrates another aspect of a similar psychological problem: In presenting the daydream as novel and reducing disguise to a minimum, the audience is challenged, and a battle ensues: there will be admirers and opponents. In the relation of author to his public the neutralization of energy has been in part undone; instinctual drives break through, and in the context of Corvo's life history the self-defeating tendencies remain supreme. The tendency to uninhibited self-exposure, the preference to minimal disguise of the plot, draws our attention to the fact that the delay of discharge of which we spoke is not achieved to the same degree in all parts of the creative process: While in the treatment of his medium, in his language, Corvo has created a style of his own,[49]

[47] See Hartmann, Kris, and Loewenstein (1949); Kris (1951 b).

[48] See Freud (1908), and Sachs (1924, 1942).

[49] There is no doubt that in this instance some of the characteristics of style might be accessible to further analytic investigation: The access would be through the imagery used.

the striving for direct gratification left a more noticeable imprint on the plot.

Both examples tend to illustrate the problem of the distance between the narrative account and instinctual conflicts in the narrator. A general survey of similar problems was offered in the model of the boy frightened by the Alsatian. From reactions in play, solitary or with companions, we led the way to the emergence of the narration. The direction we followed was that of the increasing distance from direct reaction to the traumatic experience, distance from immediacy of discharge. We considered the possibility that at a similar distance from immediate discharge processes, various avenues of sublimation may have proved accessible; the one we fancied establishes a particularly close relationship with the audience.

Let us assume that our subject was one of the endowed individuals, a poet, by whatever interaction of factors this may come about; then in his account the age-old theme of child against beast may be transposed into a world where Mowgli lives, abandoned by man, protected by wolves, pursued by Shir Khan—the pet of the jungle and later its master.[50]

At this stage the artist assumes a position of leadership. His message, the work of art, is not a call to common action—which is the nature of propaganda—nor a call to a common spiritual experience, linking communicator and audience to an ideal to which both submit—which is the function of the priest; nor does the artist teach his public in order to widen its insight.[51] All this he may do. At any given time all or some of the arts may be more or less closely linked to the call to action or be part of religious or secular teaching. While some such links exist of necessity at all times, the specific meaning in which the word "art" is used in our civilization refers to another function: The message is an invitation to common experience in the mind, to an experience of a specific nature.

III. The Aesthetic Illusion

From a topic well known from traditional aesthetic literature we may borrow our first and introductory example:

From a remote country place, where he has passed his life, a farmer comes to town and visits a theater. The implications of dramatic art are unknown to him. The play is an inspiring one: A great hero is seen

50 For the relation of animal phobias to the protection by animals, see Anna Freud (1936).

51 In all these instances we assume that the distance from immediate gratification has been achieved, though in slightly different degrees, that psychic energy has been neutralized; but subsidiary pathways of discharge play different roles.

at the height of his glory; a group of his alleged friends are threatening
to destroy his life and career. They claim that he is usurping the government and planning to violate the constitutional right of the people—
although he has no such intention. The farmer is on the hero's side; the
man's greatness and frankness attract him. At the moment when the con-
spirators are preparing to murder the hero, the farmer, who cannot bear
to see the victory of traitors over the genius, decides to interfere. He gets
up from his seat and shouts through the hall: "Look out, they are
armed!" And thus the great scene of Casca's first stroke against Caesar is
suddenly interrupted.

This anecdote illustrates a typical misunderstanding of art: The
farmer ignores "the aesthetic illusion";[52] his participation has not led
to experiences in the mind but to action. His response, different from
the one expected from a theatrical audience, is primitive in various
meanings of the word. The historical development of dramatic art during
a comparatively late, the so-called classical, phase of Greek civilization
was, according to well-documented assumptions, preceded by various
stages in which no rigorous separation between audience and stage
existed. All were potential actors, participating in festival or ritual,
celebrating or reliving what myth had taught them as the essence of
tradition. What later developed into various, more or less independent,
branches of art was part of one performance: music, dance, and verbal
expression were fused. No other response but active coöperation—or better, coaction—was possible. Distinctions between the participants rested
mainly on their *charisma*. The difference in ability which enables some
to play major parts was probably viewed by the community and quite
possibly experienced by the endowed individuals not only as a matter of
skill and hence of social status, but as reflection of a special relationship
to the divine.

The development from magic ritual to dramatic art in Greek civilization has many analogies in other culture areas.[53] The common element
of these developments is the tendency to the reduction of action and its
more or less complete replacement by other experiences. The degree of
this substitution varies even within Western civilization confronted by
the same performance; there are the young, the "less educated," certain
culture groups, and certain individuals whose response is so vivid that

[52] See now Sperling's (1951) discussion of "illusions naïve and controlled" in which,
however, no reference is made to the "aesthetic illusion" and the vicissitudes of control here discussed.

[53] For a survey of the literature and recent theories see Adolf (1951).

they tend to act in their seats.[54] Moreover, on the fringe of art there are social arrangements of many kinds which encourage various degrees of participation of the audience. Group dance, revival meeting, and political assembly—the latter particularly under totalitarian management—tend to limit freedom of individual reaction and to drive individuals to regression, transforming the group of participants into an intensely reacting crowd.[55] On these occasions "actual" participation is expected, and no aesthetic illusion is ignored by those who respond by action.

The lack of distinction between stage and reality is a primitive mode of behavior also in an ontogenetic sense: A child of five is taken to a play in order to see his grandfather, a famous actor, in the part of the tyrant who is killed on the stage. Though the child is familiar with theatrical affairs, at this instance his experience offers no satisfactory guidance. At the fatal moment the child breaks out in a cry: "Grandpa is dead!" Under the impact of rising fear and aggression, the function of reality testing breaks down; stage and reality are being confused. It is a well-documented finding that more recently acquired ego functions are more exposed to regression than older and better established ones (Anna Freud, 1951). The border between stage and reality proves to be not too resistant—an impression which is confirmed by many experiences in the observation of the child (and even the adolescent). Psychoanalysis assumes that during the earliest phases of infant development the intensity of the child's needs has the power to "evoke" the need-gratifying object; it presumably appears as perception, whatever senses are involved. As the distinction between self and environment is gradually more sharply defined—and this presupposes processes of physiological maturation—the line can be drawn which divides need and perception: The child learns to test reality. The older proclivity, however, lives on: Imagination enters; and soon, instead of doing what one wishes, one can play at doing it or can pretend to do it. The step is vital in the experience of the child; it seems that the method used in this step has in many, and quite possibly in all, instances to do with one decisive mechanism in the child's early development: What to outside observers frequently appears as an imitation of adults proves to be only one instance of a more general tendency, that is, to repeat actively what has been passively experienced.[56]

54 For a special instance of such intense participation, which confirms various of the assumptions made in this essay, see Sterba (1939).

55 We do not at this occasion discuss the structural and psychological differences existing within the range of such social arrangements. For some such distinctions see Kris (1943); see also Lasswell (1948).

56 Freud was at first inclined to consider this mechanism as the nucleus of the

This mechanism not only supplies a pathway for the child's identification with the adult, but is simultaneously linked to the function of
reality testing, which establishes the confines of the actual and its distinction from the possible. The world of make-believe is at first thinly separated from the real world, but the distinction becomes ever more
durable. The mechanism of denial can operate; a firm belief in the
"reality of play" can coexist with a certainty that it is play only. Here
lie the roots of aesthetic illusion.[57]

In play and fantasy the child's wishes live on, adapted to but still
unhampered by reality, and in this very world a further step is made
which carries the child in the direction in which it may later find pleasure in art. Instead of his own fantasies the child is ready to accept, and
at certain points of his development prefers to accept, fantasies of others,
the stories and fairy tales offered to him. Adults who look from their
point of view at famous children's books or fairy tales find it difficult to
understand that children can enjoy them. Their crude and often openly
sadistic content seems repugnant, their symbolism too obvious. All this,
however, appropriately fulfills an important need in the child's life. The
bad stepmother, the merciless king, the dumb princess—these are all
creations of his own mind. His fears and feelings of guilt, his hopes and
desires, find their expression in this world. From clinical experience we
know that in those dreams of adults which are the unveiling of the fantasies of early childhood, fairy tales tend to express what for the child's
own life once had vital importance (Freud, 1913). The fairy-tale theme
was in most of these cases chosen by the child as less dangerous and less
forbidden; it was not a product of his own imagination, but a pattern for
his emotional reaction offered to him with the consent of the adults.[58]

It is obvious that a similar attitude survives in the adult, that it is at
the root of the demand for cheap fiction, in whatever medium it may be
presented, and that it expresses itself frequently as insistence on a happy
ending or at least an ending so ambiguous that the happy one is not
excluded. This attitude is by no means limited to the public at large,
whose reaction allegedly forces upon media of mass communication,
mainly radio and movies, lowered standards; we meet it in people in-

---

child's play (1920) but pointed later to its more general importance in child
development; see Freud (1931 b), Brunswik (1940), and an unpublished note of
Freud's quoted by Kris (1951 b).

[57] For some similar formulations see now an obviously preliminary draft of Freud's
(1904 b) which was posthumously published (1942).

[58] See for more detailed comments and some experimental data Friedlander (1942)
and Wolfenstein (1947).

timately connected with the world of art, the actors. Garrick's protest against the part of Macbeth is well known, but there are many similar incidents reported. When Ibsen's *Doll's House* was first to be performed at the Burgtheater in Vienna—then the most famous theater in the German-speaking countries—the actress who was to play Nora refused to act the part in which she leaves her husband without hope of return— and the author's consent had to be obtained for a slight change in the last words of the play.[59]

This instance could lead us to the very center of the psychology of the actor, a subject which has found expression in the plays of Piran- dello—best in his *Six Characters in Search of an Author.* Only one part of its meaning has a bearing on our problem. The actor who performs a part may sometimes lead its very life; if he wants to give another ending to the play, he wants to correct something "in life."

This is the particular predicament and the singular privilege of the actor, in whose work the incentive to trespass upon the confines of the aesthetic illusion is great—and yet it is an undoubted ingredient in what makes for artistic distinction.[60] However, proclivities of a similar kind exist in the audience, when the identification with any one character of the play may detract attention from the play as a whole.

A young woman of distinctly upper-class origin led at the beginning of her analysis a promiscuous sex life, the expression of unconscious prostitution fantasies which combined the gratification of aggressive im- pulses against her partners with self-debasement. After part of this con- flict had been brought to consciousness and some of its origin had been clarified, she reported what she described as a startling experience at a performance of Bizet's *Carmen*: In former years the part of Carmen had been her own. She was the victorious seducer and the final victim. This time she not only felt like the faithful Michaela, but, as she put it, as if she *were* Michaela, an experience which preceded by some time an actual change in behavior.[61]

Reactions of so personal a kind are not limited to dramatic art; they occur wherever a stimulus of "the nature of art" is offered. A young man who dabbles in various arts successfully relates the extreme uneasiness he experiences at certain events in fiction or plays. This uneasiness over-

[59] Schlenther, Vol. VI (no date).

[60] The very large number of variables which enter into and seem to determine some of the psychological types of the actor cannot be discussed here. See, however, Fenichel (1946).

[61] For similar observations and a somewhat similar discussion see, for instance, Langfeld (1920), and for a clinical instance now Maloney and Rockelein (1948).

comes the patient when a hero he admires proves himself unable to fulfill his expectations. The young man is faced with the same difficulties when reading history. Napoleon was the beloved hero of his childhood, and he had contrived to preserve his admiration in spite of manifold experiences which had taught him to look with little sympathy at dictators. The life history of Napoleon was known to him in detail, but only up to the climax in the emperor's life, up to the Russian war. At the very moment when Bonaparte's actions seemed to lose their adjustment to reality, when, driven by hatred and pride, he began to destroy his own former success, the patient's interest stopped; more than that, he experienced an uneasiness which could hardly conceal deep fears. Analysis reveals that he is unable to detach himself from the hero, that he himself is victorious with Bonaparte, that he rises with him step by step, and that what he is afraid of in his own life, i.e., self-destructive impulses, is intolerable when perceived in the biography of his substitute in history or fiction. In short, history and fiction have for this man a primitive meaning; they are reduced to the level of a daydream.

Before we try to comment on these illustrations and on the light they permit us to throw on the problem of aesthetic illusion, we have to comment on other aspects of its function, relevant for some of the examples cited but better to be demonstrated in those that here follow. While we have dealt with instances in which the intensity of participation seems to infringe upon the aesthetic illusion, there are others where the participation becomes possible only under the protection of the aesthetic illusion. It has been noted by analysts (Bellak, 1945; Buxbaum, 1941) that this is the case with readers of thrillers, individuals who in real life tend to be opposed to the very experience they seek in their reading addiction, the thrill of danger.[62] Under protection of the detective, the new hero who himself is frequently part of an idyllic rather than a romantic setting (Auden, 1948) and whose weaknesses in other human performances are cherished no less than his feats of detection, they can indulge in what they otherwise fear. While they are thus protected against threats from outside they are not guaranteed safety from self-reproaches. They tend to turn to the thriller in moments of dissatisfaction and disappointment, and the self-excitation which the play with danger provides tends to be so remindful of the infantile experience from which it derives its power, that with some readers boredom sets in; with others there is the

---

[62] See also Bergler (1945, 1950) who stresses in the "triad producing the mystery fan" (i.e., unconscious enjoyment of passivity, of uncanniness, and of voyeurism) particularly "the feminine hysteric passivity of the mystery fan" (1950, pp. 164, 167).

feeling of having indulged once more in an escape which could not afford lasting relief.

The protective function of the "aesthetic illusion" is even better illustrated by a reliable account which reached me during the Second World War.[63] A captain of a Marine detachment on one of the Pacific islands heard from one of the outposts a dim noise of voices. Though the enemy was at safe distance, a gathering of several men required the captain's attention. He approached the spot and found one of his men with a radio set tuned in to an American short-wave station. The captain reported that he hardly had time to ask himself whether or not such listening, while on outpost, was permissible; he found himself within a short time engrossed in the story: It dealt with outposts of Marine detachments waiting on a Pacific island for a Japanese attack. No clearer example of "vicarious participation" is known to me; safety in the aesthetic illusion protects from the danger in reality, even if both dangers should be identical.

From the account of this singular and dramatic incident a way seems to lead to one of the baffling and most complex questions of traditional aesthetics—the pleasure in the unpleasant in art—and hence to the question of how tragedy is possible. Art, it is said, releases unconscious tensions and "purges" the soul. This view is frequently attributed to Aristotle and considered the common denominator between his theory and that of Freud who adopted, for the first step in psychoanalytic therapy, the Aristotelian term: *kathartic*.[64]

The progress of psychoanalytic knowledge has opened the way for a better understanding of the cathartic effect; we are no longer satisfied with the notion that repressed emotions lose their hold over our mental life when an outlet for them has been found. We believe rather that what Aristotle describes as the purging enables the ego to reëstablish the control which is threatened by dammed-up instinctual demands. The search for outlets acts as an aid to assuring or reëstablishing this control, and the pleasure is a double one, in both discharge and control. The maintenance of the aesthetic illusion promises the safety to which we were

---

[63] I am indebted to Mr. Joseph Goldsen for this example.

[64] See Freud (1920, p. 16): "The dramatic and imitative art of adults which differs from the behavior of children in being directed to the spectator does, however, not spare the latter the most painful impressions, e.g. in tragedy, and yet can be felt by him as highly enjoyable. This convinces us that even under the domination of the pleasure principle there are ways and means enough of making what is in itself disagreeable the object of memory and of psychic preoccupation. A theory of aesthetics with an economic point of view should deal with these cases ending in final pleasure gain."

aspiring and guarantees freedom from guilt, since it is. not our own fantasy we follow. It stimulates the rise of feelings which we might otherwise be hesitant to permit ourselves, since they lead to our own personal conflicts. It allows in addition for intensities of reaction which, without this protection, many individuals are unwilling to admit to themselves; with many, we know, this is due to educational pressures, which under certain cultural conditions have generally devalued high intensity of emotional display except in regulated and institutionalized channels: Art offers such socially approved occasions. The vicarious participation in the hero's destiny is the mechanism by which this effect comes about. True, this intensity should not grow too much, but should be kept moderate. We are warned to remain at a safe distance. Too great an intensity of reaction may threaten the aesthetic illusion; the two patients whose reactions we described were both limited in their response: the daydreamer, because he was reluctant to see the hero in calamity; the young woman who shifted her allegiance from Carmen to Michaela, because instead of living one borrowed life she merely borrowed another.

We touch here upon a problem which in the philosophy of art has played a considerable role, at least since Kant and Schiller, i.e., that the dispassionate spectator alone can appreciate beauty. Formulations of this fundamental attitude in a brilliant essay by E. Bullough (1912) [65] permit us to establish a connection with the conceptual tools with which we have equipped ourselves. When Bullough speaks of "underdistance" in the attitude of the public to the work of art, of "too strong" participation, we are inclined to use the concept of energy discharge in its relation to control of the ego. We may assume that not enough energy was neutralized or, alternatively, that neutralization was not complete enough; too much of libidinal and aggressive energy was at work: The function of the ego was too closely in the service of the id. There is an opposite case which deserves our attention: Bullough refers to it as "overdistance." We are too detached, and we are unable to establish contact or to maintain it if nothing in our own proclivities is stimulated. It is a condition which tends to arise if the work of art is totally foreign; if, for instance, no cultural tie connects us with it. Though the range in which we still understand art of the past or of foreign lands has grown immensely—for reasons which will be discussed in Chapter 12—the impediment of "overdistance" exists even today between the spectator and certain artistic productions. With some productions, the impediment exists for every individual. The problem of individual limitations and

[65] For Bullough's position see Radar (1935), and Listowell (1933). For Bullough's later views see his articles published in 1919 and 1921.

individual taste seems accessible from here. We might attempt to explain provisionally the phenomenon of "overdistance" by assuming that we are, as spectators, unable to find a point of identification, or that there was no, or not sufficient, incentive for an energy discharge. We may even tentatively raise the question as to what extent any discharge of neutralized energy presupposes some id incentive, some admixture of libido and aggression, and we may be impressed with the possibility that the initial motor power must stem from there. Its lack would produce the lack of interest, the "overdistance," of which we spoke. At this point, however, we have in a different language approximately repeated what in other words has been said many a time. We are with Coleridge, who speaks of the "willing suspension of disbelief." Safely balanced between two extremes we gain pleasure from art.

The argument developed up to this point, however essential to our exposition, is so obviously incomplete, the result is so disappointing, that we are impatient to interrupt it. Our attempt at discussing the aesthetic illusion apparently does not enable us to differentiate between the reaction to Hamlet and to the thriller—and worse cannot be said of a psychological approach to the study of art. All we have achieved is the description of an element entering into the aesthetic reaction, the reaction appropriate to art. Before we proceed, a detour is necessary to enlarge our vista. We turn to some reflections on another medium of artistic expression in the hope of gaining clarity in some general problems.

IV. Magic, Communication, and Identification

The special social position granted by most societies to those who exercise certain arts rests upon two grounds: upon admiration of the artist's *skill* and upon awe of his *inspiration*. The artist appears either as a master of his craft or as genius. Which of the two views predominates, and how they are combined, depends on an interplay of cultural and psychological factors. The literary tradition of arts and artists in Mediterranean and Western civilizations sharply differentiates between the arts: To the Greeks of the classical era Phidias is the greatest of artisans and Aeschylus an inspired creator.[66] Painters, sculptors, and builders, reach the status of "genius" later than poets and musicians, and only since the sixteenth century has this differentiation gradually disappeared. When in the Renaissance recognition was given to the creative genius of painters and sculptors, they were generally mentioned in association with technicians, inventors, mathematicians, and scientists, as members of

[66] For the following see Chapters 2, 7 and 13.

a group that investigates and controls the external world. The poet throughout the ages remained associated with the scholar, the philosopher, and the sage, with those who know about man's history and his inner experience. This classification still dimly reflects mythological traditions. Painters and sculptors are descendants of cultural heroes. Experts in many skills, masters of many secrets of nature, these heroes competed with the gods: Prometheus, who created man, Hephaestus or Daedalus, who created moving automatons of man, and their counterparts in Nordic or Central Asiatic mythology, were punished for their transgression of divine prerogative—codified in biblical tradition—of the sculptor God, which condemns emulation. The interdict against art in Hebrew and Mohammedan, and the temporary and partial interdict in Christian, civilization is based upon the belief of the magic potency of imagery: According to a widely spread notion, images give power over what they depict. In the folklore of art, the creator of the image is close to the sorcerer and magician. Even when and where the belief in the magic of images has been partly overcome, it may be reflected in the social status of the artist: With the Greeks and Romans his degradation is rationalized as social prejudice, and the plastic arts are considered as slave labor; to the Greeks he is an artisan; Roman and medieval tradition do not record his name.

The ramification of the belief in image magic need not be traced here.[67] It is sufficient to mention that the survival of the belief in the magic power of the work of sculptors and painters has often been reflected in their social position on the fringe of society in a "bohemian" reservation. Thus isolated, they could enjoy special recognition; they were the ones who had power over memory and could eternalize human appearance. The elimination of this monopoly by the technological progress of the nineteenth century initiated a revolutionary period in the fine arts which extends into the present.

The magic element in representational art invites further comment and tempts to some speculation: We may ask ourselves where the border lies between its magic and its communicative function. Many of the works of painting or sculpture which we admire most were not created for a public, or at least not for a public only. Statues of basalt were entombed with mummies; they were intended to eternalize the departed, not merely to represent him. Were the colossal lions and the winged bulls which flank the doorway of Assyrian palaces real watchdogs for the Royal houses, or were they meant to symbolize protective forces in animal form? Where is the delimitation between the two interpretations, the one which

---

[67] See pp. 201-203.

takes the image as real and the other which recognizes it as a representation of the real? In many instances a distinction seems difficult to make. There is, however, no doubt that both beliefs coexisted over long times and wide spaces, and the question might well be asked whether the effect of representational art is not, however small the degree, dependent on this coexistence. The dichotomy between magic and representation might then constitute an ambiguity comparable to that which we discussed as the aesthetic illusion, differing from it by the structure of the artistic media.

To illustrate the complexity of the problem, we start from one well-known observation. In almost all periods and cultures one meets with some works of representational art which are characterized by a higher degree of "primitiveness" than other contemporary art products. We refer to idols. The shape may only distantly recall the form of the object the idol represents, either man or animal. While idols exist in many stages of cultural development, in some periods art as a whole approaches the stage of the idol; there is hardly anything but idols. Wherever they occur, idols are proof of sorcery or magic of some kind. The devotional images offered in temples to the remote godhead are idols, and the effigy of the deity itself may be idolistic. Even in epochs with developed artistic tradition, images in front of which the believer kneels may be dressed like puppets. It may be an old and well-established image, powerful in protection, and one might attribute its primitiveness to its age, which seems to guarantee its power. But there is more to it; in the period when Greek art was at the highest stage of its evolution, the citizens of one of the leading cultural centers in Asia Minor requested more primitive statues for their temples than those last and refined achievements of Greek art. Idols are effigies, the belief in whose magic is unshaken; they are centers of action, acting themselves or acted upon. This may account for their primitiveness. To the extent to which the belief in the identity of image and model predominates, the shape of the image is unimportant. Man projects his hallucinatory vision onto the object. The idol exists by virtue of the omnipotence of thought. In front of the idol all have the same belief. But when this identity of social conception is shaken, omnipotence of thought no longer endows it, and the image gains another function. The public must be "informed" what it represents, and it must "resemble" the object represented.[68]

[68] Lest this assertion might be misinterpreted in an evolutionist sense it seems appropriate to state that we refer to a specific functional context in which the effigy is used and not to a magic stage of art or civilization which stands at "the beginning of things." The relation between function and formal characteristics of art has been elaborated by Gombrich (1951). See also pp. 142f., and 168.

In the function of communication, the image takes its place beside gesture and word. However, the picture is distinguished by one particular trait: It does not presuppose the presence of the person addressed. Gestures must be seen when they are made; words must be heard when they are spoken. Pictures can be read in aftertime. They persist, control time, and overcome its passage. In this very fact there is magic. This potentiality of representation has led to various developments. That which is exclusively devoted to communication soon becomes independent from art. What was once a picture later on became a sign, a mere letter. While the invention of alphabetic writing was formerly viewed merely as a degeneration of representational symbols into letters, there now is reason to assume that the use of a sign for a letter was due to agreement—as in the establishment of the Morse alphabet (K. Bühler, 1934) : Wherever the step toward alphabetic writing of some kind occurs, it is due to an interaction of various ego functions. The development of concept formation and the structure of the intended communication must be taken into account.[69]

The communicative tendency lives on amalgamated with and implied in other functions which representational techniques fulfill in society. We cannot attempt even to enumerate them; they all have fertilized the soil out of which has grown what one loosely calls figurative or representational art. Enumeration would require discussion of that important and most fascinating function of representation connected with decoration. We would have to account for that evolution of ornamental form which leads back to the decoration of the human body, or to human attire, with its power to attract, to protect, or to intimidate (Loewy, 1930) . At some stage of development all these functions have been connected with that one great achievement—the preservation of that which vanishes.

Pictures do not convey a thought or meaning only, they catch reality for the man who is to see them. Seeing contains both elements: that of recognizing what is known, the element of thought, and that of actually holding reality. Modern investigators tend to agree that the art of the cave dwellers was meant as magic. But what could the function of the

---

[69] Needless to say that the relation of representational and verbal communication to each other remains complex, and not only the more "archaic" character of visual versus verbal thinking (see Chapter 14) plays its part. Children, even of early school age, retain the need to *see* the text illustrated; with adults illustrations fulfill a specific function, they heighten the effect, epitomize it, stimulate additional discharges or—as graphs or aids in scientific work—they clarify issues. This example tends to illustrate that media of communication acquire differentiated functions. In psychotic production this differentiation is abandoned. The magic purpose reduces differentiation. See Chapter 5.

pictures have been in these magic rites? Some speak of them as centers of ritualistic scenes, or dances around the image of the bull. They visualize the way the darts were thrown at the effigy in the practice of sympathetic magic. This may have happened in some instances. But some of the frescoes in the depth of the earth show us the darts sticking in the body of the animal. The animal is depicted after the hunt. The picture thus renders a historical scene. Moreover, we know that in certain rituals the medicine man and sometimes the tribe are dressed like the hunted animal. On some of the frescoes in the Spanish caves we see a man dressed as an antelope represented on the same wall above the hunted animal, as if he ruled over the world of prey. Whether hunt or, as I rather think, ritualistic action, what we here have is a "historical" painting, which depicts past hunting or ritual and anticipates future ones. Instead of action—hunt or ritual to come—the painting stands as a substitute. Substitution here has most likely a double meaning. The painting in itself, the transposing of what one could call the passing reality into the eternity of pictorial representation, may have been meant to produce some magic effect on the object. The tribe was there to see what the medicine man had painted. For them, for their eyes, it was made to commemorate and anticipate the fight with the prey, to show them what they had in mind as a memory of the past or as a vision of the future.

If these inferences are correct, they would illustrate one rudimentary form in which the magic meaning of the image and its use in communication would have merged under archaic cultural conditions. Let us visualize the situation afresh. Anthropological evidence indicates that wherever human beings form groups there are specialists, men skilled in various activities—in our instance, some who have the power of tracing pictures; they could catch what was passing and thus dominate the objects. Most likely this was only a part of other magical activities and it has been assumed that the painter and the medicine man were one and the same. However that may be, there was one to create, there were others to look, and thus there was art as an institution.

The mythological and literary tradition concerning painters and sculptors is closely related to the psychological process active in man as painter and sculptor, if this process is studied in relation to unconscious tendencies contributing to it. In spite of considerable individual and cultural variations, some common elements in this process can tentatively be summarized. The artist does not "render" nature, nor does he "imitate" it, but he creates it anew. He controls the world through his work. In looking at the object that he wishes to "make," he takes it in with his eyes until he feels himself in full possession of it. Drawing, painting, and carving what has been incorporated and is made to reëmerge from vision, is a two-pronged activity. Every line or every stroke of the chisel is a simplification, a reduction of reality. The unconscious meaning of this process is control at the price of destruction.[70] But destruction of the real is fused with construction of its image: When lines merge into shapes, when the new configuration arises, no "simile" of nature is given. Independent of the level of resemblance, nature has been re-created.

In analytic observation of individuals who turn to art as a profession or preferred occupation, dynamics akin to those summarized here can occasionally be traced far into childhood. The earliest memory of a patient who later became a painter of some ability but who was particularly successful as art teacher of children took her back into a period of childhood when she was in danger of losing the interest of her mother. The man to whom her mother's attention turned at a time when the little girl pleaded for her sole devotion became the first object of her artistic attempts. The scribbled lines of the skeleton man which the three-year-old produced gained increasing importance for her. Here was a way to independence. She could hold those she was afraid to lose, call those who were away, and, by crossing them out, eliminate those whom she resented. She gradually learned to express her feelings in drawings and to establish contact with others by this medium. When later in life somebody understood her paintings, there was no need for words. When there was a tragic situation, art could give her unique support. A young man of a different social class had fallen in love with her and although she saw no prospects of a common future, she could not resist the attraction he held for her. In this conflict she decided to paint his portrait. One could observe in analysis over a period of time how, through different attempts to catch the likeness, the emotional attachment to the object was loosened and the withdrawal of emotion achieved. Thus, by incorporating it into the work of art she mastered what was formerly a danger. Dreams occurring during this period revealed the wider significance of painting to the unconscious: A part of this significance was still connected with the creating of the object, but the object was also overcome and overpowered. Construction and destruction met in one process.[71] It was destruction when in looking at her model her mind was concentrated on the problem as to which part of the reality offered should be "left out." It was construction, creation, when out of the lines she drew, the object arose.

A patient of Nunberg's (1932) expressed similar experiences: "When I draw I have a feeling of tactile communication as if every line and

[70] See also pp. 116ff., and 164ff.
[71] See above p. 28.

stroke palpitated under my hand and through this process only I learn to understand the essence of the model, in taking it into myself. . . . Then it is mine. If I want to redraw it, I am independent of the object since I can reproduce as frequently as I want, it comes out of myself."

Utterances of this kind, familiar to analysts, are apt to illustrate the complexity which a metapsychological study of painting and sculpture as types of sublimation would have to take into account. Here only a few aspects can be suggested. The intimate relation of painting and sculpture to infantile experiences and needs, regularly stressed in psychoanalytic writings, does not only concern isolated impulses, i.e.—the drive to smear—but also concomitant or independent, but always interconnected, anal and phallic fantasies of "producing," with active and passive connotations. They are part of a phase of ego development in which reality testing only gradually reduces the trust in omnipotence.[72] Furthermore, manipulatory performances in painting and sculpture are likely to stimulate aggressive and libidinal strivings, which are both part and parcel of the archaic "making" of things. The perceptual process which precedes and accompanies the actual production, the process in which the model becomes the artist's own, revives even earlier instinctual impulses; power over the model may have the unconscious meaning of its incorporation. For the functions we mentioned, instinctual energy may find a more or less direct or neutralized discharge;. the function may have become more or less autonomous.[73] As far as the relation to the model is concerned, verbalizations vary greatly from artist to artist and approximate more or less the examples quoted above.[74]

Some of the statements illustrate the artist's experience when the function of perception has become autonomous. It seems that in these cases the actual function of perceiving is less invested than the inner vision, so that perception only supplies a stimulus. Leonardo's advice to his pupils to arouse their imagination by looking at a crumbling stone wall is representative of this attitude.[75] The familiar figure of the painter in search of a model, a scene, a tree with specifically shaped branches,

[72] This stage is best observable in child development, when this belief is no longer vested in the self, leading to hallucinatory gratification, but when power is attributed to adults in the child's environment as a first stage in their idealization.

[73] To the extent to which neutralization has remained incomplete, defenses may be required to establish the balance. There is the painter who prefers gray since freedom in the use of colors might suggest to him too sanguine or too dirty shades.

[74] See, for example, a contemporary sculptress who describes how in her portraits she "empties" the models (Orloff, 1937), or Picasso's famous saying: "Le dessin est une espèce d'hypnotisme: on regarde tellement le modèle, qu'il vient s'asseoir sur le papier."

[75] See Chapter 7 where the historical significance of this statement is discussed. The "inner vision" itself is naturally codetermined by the conventions dominant in a given medium at a given historical moment. See Gombrich (1951).

can well be compared to that of writers engaged in a similar quest; they scan the world around them for observations or themes which would stimulate their imagination. One of the famous novelists of our age describes this process when he confesses to the need to stroll around, to live with people of various lands and classes as one of them until, at a given but apparently not predictable moment, the feeling of satiation arises. Then he returns to the magnificent solitude of a home which through a lifetime has remained the place in which to write. The lives of the people he has seen, the minor and major experiences of his wandering, suddenly come to life in the context of a voluminous account of a family's destiny to which he has devoted the best part of his creative years. The collected experiences have acted as triggers: They help to form and to continue an account, the outline of which was ready in his mind. The stimulus from perception is needed to facilitate creation, to set the writer to work and to produce the mood in which work can proceed. It is this mood, no less than the way in which it comes about, which is common to those who create in different media, common to the process of creation.[76] The structures of the various media account for various degrees of differentiation between this common experience. The study of these differentiations cannot be attempted here, and even as far as representational art is concerned only one aspect will be mentioned here: The manipulation of the painter or the sculptor allows for various types of motor discharges: direct ones, i.e., when the painter's mood leads his brush, and indirect ones, when the innumerable details in which organization of parts or the whole of a composition express feelings rooted in postural experience.

For a better understanding of the importance of this element we turn from the artist to the response of his public in the hope of securing further insight. If we try to summarize impressions gained over long periods of time and from various sources, we are led to distinguish various components in this response: There is first the simplest and most unambiguous stage, which may be called recognition. The subject matter is found to be familiar and is brought in relation to a memory trace:[77] There is secondly a stage in which some experience of the perceived and recognized subject becomes part of the spectator. The sensory pathways by which this experience is communicated are not well known and too little explored, though systematic and experimental study seems to hold promise. The case which can at present be best discussed is the simplest

[76] For further discussion of inspiration see Chapters 13 and 14.

[77] In front of abstract art this phase gains special importance: the tendency to recognize has to be "repressed"; the path leads directly to "later" stages of reaction.

one: the reaction to a human figure in paintings or sculptures of Western civilization.

Looking long enough, one tends to become aware of a kinesthetic reaction, however slight;[78] it may be that one tries, at first imperceptibly and later consciously, to react with one's own body, or it may be that the reaction remains unconscious. We know that our ensuing emotional experience will still be colored by the reflection of the perceived posture, that our ego has in the process of perception utilized a complex apparatus, the body scheme, or (with Schilder, 1950) the image of the body.[79]

The "bodily" experience with which we react in front of the representation of the human figure suggests a formula of wide application. On the second stage of reaction we identify ourselves with the artist's model. The two phases which we here distinguish, recognition of the subject and identification with the model, are frequently interwoven, one supporting the other. The second is not limited to the perception of the human figure; all perceptual reactions are, according to Schilder (1935), to some extent influenced by the image of the body. The two reactions mentioned

[78] We here encroach on the traditional theory of empathy. On its purest formulation in the work of Vernon Lee (Violet Paget) (1913), especially on her early work, not yet influenced by Lipps, see Listowell (1933); Radar (1935). For a more recent statement see Langfeld (1937), who remains fully aware of the possible objections against the attempt to base his view on the motor-theory of consciousness. See also Langfeld (1920). For a philosopher's evaluation see E. M. Bartlett (1937). Psychoanalytic comments on the relevance of kinesthetic experience are to be found in Freud's earlier writings (see, e.g., 1905 a); for more detailed psychoanalytic hypotheses see Sterba (1928); Winterstein (1929). The limitations of the theory of empathy have recently been discussed by Arnheim (1951), who feels that "there is no evidence that the feeling of visual dynamics is due always or mainly to kinaesthetic empathy" and assumes that there may be individuals "for whom external stimulation essentially fulfills the function of pulling the trigger which sets inner activities into motion." If this difference can be meaningfully correlated to personality characteristics, the data on the development and function of the image of the body will have to be taken into account. See for instance the investigations on children's drawing by Bender (1937); Schilder and Levine (1942); and the crucial findings of Spielrein (1931); for their relation to other observational and experimental findings see Graewe (1936); see also p. 114.

[79] Its role in the process of identification is not yet fully appreciated. From the study of child development we derive the impression that the tactile contact of mother and child lays a foundation for many other types of communication between men. Touch communicates at a time when vision is still less useful as a perceptual tool. As visual perception develops and expressive movements become understandable, as the child becomes able to distinguish in the mother's face the mood which it expresses, such understanding is in an unknown way related to the body image, probably by stimulating certain impulses to movement, which though not executed or only partly executed still evoke moods in the child similar to those it infers in the adult.

The reaction "with our body" remains part of human equipment (see Chapter 9). It is an archaic method of identification, which under certain conditions becomes manifest, but which, we assume, contributes always to some extent to all interpersonal relations. In analytic material it is usually not directly accessible since its

lead to a third, which, less general, may or may not occur according to a large variety of factors. In the first two we have recognized what was depicted and "identified" with it, in the third we supplement these processes by experiencing how the effect to which we reacted has come about. From looking at a whirl of lines, from following them, we change imperceptibly from identification with the model into the stage in which we "imitate" the strokes and lines with which it was produced.[80] To some extent we have changed roles. We started out as part of the world which the artist created; we end as co-creators: We identify ourselves with the artist.

We soon recognize that what is here described as reaction to representative art is part of the adequate response to all art. The case we chose, i.e., of the reaction to the representation of the human body—by whatever theory this reaction be explained—proves to be only the case in which our thesis can best be demonstrated. The sequence of reactions described, however, seems to be valid for a wide range of experiences. This sequence will not develop if we miss the aesthetic illusion; it will be impeded by both "overdistance" and "underdistance." It is, we believe, dependent on and—in circular fashion—frequently responsible for the appropriate distance, and seems a most significant component of the specificity of the aesthetic response.

V. Creation and Re-creation

At first it seems necessary to eliminate misunderstandings which the expression "identification with the artist" may suggest. We have neither

---

contribution is overshadowed by orality. The telescopic nature of our memory presumably produces this fusion of early imprints. In rare cases, however, particularly in cases of earliest temporary physical impairment, the traces of the bodily experience themselves seem to be detectable, not in verbalized material but rather in bodily sensations themselves.

The influence of the image of the body on artistic productions is most dramatically illustrated by the highly impressive sculptural creations of the blind child (Münz and Loewenfeld, 1934). Some normal individuals, in whom the sensitivity of the muscular apparatus is highly developed, become conscious of this reaction. A young man who from an acrobatic child grew into an expert dancer seemed to distribute his preferences among works of representational art clearly according to the bodily sensations they provided. Unfortunately, the limitations of the analytic situation have made a further exploration of this connection impossible.

80 Art critics seem to have repeatedly hinted at the existence of a similar mechanism. Roger Fry (1920) stressed that while in daily life we glance at the objects only just long enough to recognize them, in the process of seeing what the artists did, seeing itself has a different meaning. Cyril Burt (1933) has epitomized this difference when he says that in life we see what we know to be there, not what is there to be seen. What we here add is the emphasis on the active side of this latter attitude.

connoisseurship in mind nor identification with the artist as a concrete individual. Most works of art are consciously or unconsciously addressed to an expert audience. Under certain social conditions a whole community may be the expert: In certain preliterate tribes everybody may know how to dance, many may know much about carving, and yet there is a leader of the dance and a supreme master of carving; they are, actually or potentially, viewed as artists. Collective expertness seems to exist only where the function of art is not limited to the aesthetic sphere, where art in general or in any specific medium serves, mainly or partly, purposes of social control—i.e., of ritual, religion, or politics. On this level the identification with the artist can be subsumed under the wider phenomenon, the identification with the leader, be it the personalized leader himself or one who only represents supreme power. In the extreme case, the public tends to accept him as the embodiment of their superego or at least to delegate superego functions to him.[81] We meet with the opposite extreme in urbanized civilizations, where art lovers tend to form elite circles, sometimes distinct in social status, mores, and even language. We know only in barest outline about many intermediary conditions, but we are justified in assuming that art does not have, as a rule, a homogeneous public; audiences tend to be stratified in various ways and certainly in degrees of understanding. There will be those who remain on the fringe—and unavoidably, those who pretend.

And there are works of art of various degrees of depth. In the instances of "great art," the superficial gratification which a first approach affords to the public may only be a bait; the artist, as it were, draws his public closer into his net. One stands on the fringe and gradually moves to the center. On a third reading, the plot is but of little interest, and the fascination turns to active response. The formal qualities then become important and the question arises of how the artist has done it.[82] If this question is consciously posed, we are faced with the response of the connoisseur or critic, the silent or vocal competitor or prophet of artists. Most statements on reaction to art stem from him, and their study remains incomplete if his peculiar position is not taken into account. He will at times be concerned with the actual personality of the artist, will arouse interest in the artist's biography, which is then presented to the educated, first as a general model of greatness and then in order to

---

[81] This is an abbreviated and fragmentary reference to a topic of considerable significance for investigations in social psychology. For a somewhat more extended treatment see Kris (1943) and Lasswell (1948).

[82] The identification stimulated is largely an identification with the artist's ego.

deepen the understanding for the artist's work.[83] Benedetto Croce's distinction between the empirical and the aesthetic person of the artist proves in this connection to be relevant. Even those who consciously identify themselves with the artist, and whom—we here comprehend with an extension of the traditional meaning—as connoisseurs, are as a rule concerned with the aesthetic person, with the artist as creator of art, not with the artist as common man. It speaks for the usefulness of this distinction that the impact of the greatest poet of Western civilization was not impeded by his relative anonymity, and little has as yet been gained by attempts to link his work to his life history.[84]

While we designate here as connoisseurs those whose identification with the artist reaches consciousness, we assume that, however slight, some degree of identification with the artist, unconscious or preconscious, is part of any aesthetic reaction. The behavioral manifestations may be varied. We started with reactions to representational art in instances when the spectator would begin in his mind to draw the lines of the painting. The person who hums verse or melody, who repeats to himself passages and can thus reëxperience the original experience, is in a similar position.[85] Do we then refer to a reproductive rather than to a productive activity? Are we entitled to speak of identification with the artist when his work has become part of the inventory of our memory or when we can "recall" or "perform" it? The behavior to which we refer is in itself highly complex and subject to almost infinite variations of intensity and kind, but all these varieties of behavior seem to have in

[83] We take it for granted that the relation of the creator's personal life to what he creates can find expression in many different ways. A vast, and as a rule not too thoroughly appreciated, complexity exists, which constitutes a challenge for further inquiries. Hence we are willing to accept the warning of T. S. Eliot (1942) on this subject (see p. 255). Psychoanalytic writers have been for some time aware of limitations of biographical insight (see Chapter 12). For a general methodological discussion see Birnbaum (1933) and Allport (1942); for a bibliography of pathographies, Lange-Eichbaum (1928); for the history of the "pathographical" approach, Pollnow (1937); for the psychoanalytic point of view see Hitschmann (1930). For the psychology of biographical interest see Bonaparte (1939).

[84] Freud started out with such an attempt in *The Interpretation of Dreams*, when he tried to connect the impulse to the writing of Hamlet with the death of Shakespeare's father and of his son, Hamnet. [For an elaboration of this theme see Jones (1911, 1949).] When he later, 1930 and 1935, accepted Edward de Vere, the Earl of Oxford, as author of the Shakespeare plays he had similar arguments in mind. For my own view in this respect, see Chapter 12. I, therefore, feel that the validity of recent attempts of Ella Sharpe's (1946, 1950), in what one might call biographical exegesis of Shakespeare has to be evaluated with caution. Apart from this restriction Sharpe's contributions seem to me to be among the most poignant and valuable.

[85] For a clinical illustration that might be interpreted in this sense, see Gutheil (1935).

common that the audience passes from passivity to activity and that the work of art is re-created.[86] Somewhere between the misunderstanding of art by those who do not keep the right distance, who miss the aesthetic illusion or utilize art mainly for the discharge of libidinous or aggressive strivings, and between the connoisseur, the artist's rival, lies the reaction to which we refer when we speak of aesthetic response or response in the aesthetic sphere.

But more need be said: In speaking of re-creation, we mean that the process in the spectators has some semblance to that which the artist experienced.[87] "A poem," writes T. S. Eliot (1942), "may appear to mean very different things to different readers and all of these may be different from what the author thought." We cannot, at this point, attempt to discuss this process in its infinite complexities; we can only try to emphasize a few aspects which seem particularly significant.[88]

Schematically speaking we may view the process of artistic creation as composed of two phases which may be sharply demarcated from each other, may merge into each other, may follow each other in rapid or slow succession, or may be interwoven with each other in various ways. In designating them as inspiration and elaboration, we refer to extreme conditions: One type is characterized by the feeling of being driven, the experience of rapture, and the conviction that an outside agent acts through the creator; in the other type, the experience of purposeful organization, and the intent to solve a problem predominate. The first has many features in common with regressive processes: Impulses and drives, otherwise hidden, emerge. The subjective experience is that of a flow of thought and images driving toward expression. The second has many features in common with what characterizes "work"—dedication and concentration. These extremes and many intermediary modes have repeatedly been described in observation and self-observation.[89] We are aware of the fact that not all artistic creation derives from inspiration—neither all kinds nor one kind wholly. But wherever art reaches a certain level, inspiration is at work.[90]

[86] See also Chapter 10. For various types of re-creation see now H. B. Lee (1949 a).

[87] For a different view or emphasis see Schneider (1950) who believes that the artist forces his view upon the audience by identification. "The audience should be drawn in and overcome" (p. 51).

[88] We summarize what in various of the essays collected here is discussed in greater detail; see particularly Chapters 13 and 14.

[89] A collection of stimulating material has been compiled by Harding (1940, 1948); see also Rees (1942).

[90] This may, to some, seem to constitute a transgression from science to evaluation, from psychology to normative aesthetics. I doubt whether it is a transgression, but if

Inspiration—the "divine release from the ordinary ways of man," a state of "creative madness" (Plato), in which the ego controls the primary process and puts it into its service—need be contrasted with the opposite, the psychotic condition, in which the ego is overwhelmed by the primary process. The difference is clearest where the relation to the public is concerned.

Psychoanalytic investigation of artistic creation has abundantly demonstrated the importance of the public for the process of creation: Wherever artistic creation takes place, the idea of a public exists, though the artist may attribute this role only to one real or imaginary person. The artist may express indifference, may eliminate the consideration for an audience from his consciousness altogether, or he may minimize its importance. But wherever the unconscious aspect of artistic creation is studied, a public of some kind emerges. This does not mean that striving for success, admiration, and recognition, need be the major goal of all artistic creation. On the contrary, artists are more likely than others to renounce public recognition for the sake of their work. Their quest need not be for approval of the many but for response by some. The acknowledgment by response, however, is essential to confirm their own belief in their work and to restore the very balance which the creative process may have disturbed. Response of others alleviates the artist's guilt.[91]

The relationship of the artist to his work is complex and subject to many variations. In the typical case the work becomes part of and even more important than the self. Narcissistic cathexis has been shifted from the person of the artist to his work (Sachs, 1942). If this shift outlasts the process of creation, the work gains a permanent place in the artist's life; in extreme cases he may find it difficult to part from what he created. If the shift of interest lasts only while the work is being produced, the artist may look upon his earlier work with moderate curiosity and detachment; or the work may become dissatisfying, unbearable evidence of failure. Psychoanalytic observation suggests that such unfavorable judg-

---

so, it is one I intended, not one that slipped through my fingers. I believe that the most sensible and most frequently applied evaluations of art by contemporaries or posterities refer intentionally, or unintentionally less often to skill, i.e., perfection of elaboration, than to depth of meaning and expressive quality, of which inspiration is an essential ingredient.

91 See Chapters 6 and 13. For an opposed view (or different clinical findings) see H. B. Lee (1947 a, p. 284), who states that "the artist gives least or none of his thought to the effect his work will have upon others." I have, in the light of this passage, reviewed clinical impressions and find no reason to modify my views stated above.

ments tend to be experienced as directed against the art work as part or substitute of the self.[92]

To the artist the public is not necessarily, and not only, a distant and powerful judge, on whom he projects his own superego. He also puts himself into the place of the public and identifies in ego (and superego) with his audience. Once more it is a process of infinite complexity. While the artist creates, in the state of inspiration, he and his work are one; when he looks upon the product of his creative urge, he sees it from the outside, and as his own first audience he participates in "what the voice has done." Art, we said, always, consciously or unconsciously, serves the purpose of communication. We now distinguish two stages: one in which the artist's id communicates to the ego, and one in which the same intra-psychic processes are submitted to others.

We may now supplement the distinction of inspiration and elaboration as extreme phases of creative activity in stressing that they are characterized by shifts in psychic levels, in the degree of ego control and by shifts in the cathexis of the self and the representation of the audience.[93]

In the creations of the insane it is this cathexis which tends to be minimized; while in initial phases of some psychotic states productive power increases and works of art produced at this stage are frequently most significant to the public, what is produced at more advanced stages of the psychosis tends to lose its meaning for the public. The endless stereotypical variations of one theme, in words or shape, gain for the insane a new meaning, unintelligible to others. Case histories suggest that these productions are no longer meant to influence the mind of an audience, but that they are intended to transform the external world. By his word the insane artist commands the demons, and by his image he exercises magic control. Art has deteriorated from communication to sorcery.[94]

If we turn from the artist to his public, we find that, through the unconscious identification with the artist, a psychological process comes into being akin to that experienced by him in creation. As in the artist,

[92] This brief summary does not take into account several not infrequent variations. Indifference or abhorrence of the artist before his work are by no means rare. We have reason to believe that such attitudes are related to the unconscious determinants of production.

[93] For a rich collection of material on the phase here designated as elaboration see P. Bartlett (1951).

[94] The substitution of aesthetic by magic functions in the process of regression has a counterpart in a process of substitution of magic by aesthetic functions in progression; see Chapters 4, 5, 7, and p. 184.

shifts in psychic levels occur, but the process is reversed in order. With the public it proceeds from consciousness, the perception of the art work, to preconscious elaboration and to the reverberations of the id. From what little detailed study of similar processes has been made, it appears that the core of the process lies in the shift of cathexis between the psychic systems and in the function of the ego during these shifts. In a first phase the ego relaxes control; i.e., it opens the way to an interplay with the id. This phase is predominantly passive: The art work dominates the public. In a later phase, the ego asserts its position in recreation. In doing so, it not only wards off fear of the demands of the id and of the pressure of the superego, but it controls the flow of mental energy. The degree of activity in the response to the work varies not only with individuals, but also with the structure of the work of art itself and with the media of art. There are styles of art in which the response is more rigorously prescribed, less elasticity in response is required or possible, than in others.[95] As our discernment grows, we may learn to evaluate works of art according to the responses they elicit from wide or limited, contemporary and noncontemporary, audiences, i.e., according to their survival value as art.[96] It is a plausible but not verified impression that survival value does not depend on the closeness with which the reaction of the audience tends to repeat the experience of the creator[97] but, among other factors, on the dynamic effectiveness of the experience in the audience and thus also on the degree of activity it stimulates. The cathartic effect, then, of Greek tragedy is not only related to the universality of the theme with which it deals but to the "purging of the soul" in experiencing the power of destiny. The process of "purging" is infinitely more intricate. "Tragedy," says Aristotle, "is the representation in dramatic form of a serious action, of a certain magnitude, complete in itself, expressed in agreeable language, with pleasurable accessories, with incidents arousing pity and fear, wherewith to accomplish its catharsis of such emotions." The process of catharsis Aristotle has in mind is determined by the complexity of the tragedy as work of art and hence by the variety of reactions it stimulates in the audience. They all can be described as shifts in psychic levels, as transitions from activity to passivity, and as varying degrees of distance in participation. To insist only on one point: The understanding of the formal qualities of the verse[98]—while

95 For other aspects of this problem see Chapter 10.

96 For a somewhat similar point of view, see Frois-Wittman (1929, 1937).

97 In this sense one may speak of reconstruction rather than of re-creation, the former being one of the prerogatives or pretenses of connoisseurship; see pp. 259f.

98 The "pleasurable accessories" of Aristotle's text (the more literal translation of

certainly effective to a different, and on the whole quite possibly lesser, extent with a modern than with a Greek audience—is still such that it imposes upon the audience the task of detaching itself from the immediacy of passions evoked.[99] It imposes, one might say, the necessity for more, or more complete, neutralization of psychic energy. But is "impose" the word we need? Is it not rather that the way to such detachment is opened, and an incentive to transformation of energy is supplied?

At this point we feel finally in a position to formulate a thesis: The shifts in cathexis of mental energy which the work of art elicits or facilitates are, we believe, pleasurable in themselves. From the release of passion under the protection of the aesthetic illusion to the highly complex process of re-creation under the artist's guidance, a series of processes of psychic discharge take place, which could be differentiated from each other by the varieties and degrees of neutralization of the energy discharged. All these processes, however, are controlled by the ego, and the degree of completeness of neutralization indicates the degree of ego autonomy.

In assuming that the control of the ego over the discharge of energy is pleasurable in itself, we adopted one of the earliest, and frequently neglected, thoughts of Freud (1905 a) in this area: the suggestion that under certain conditions man may attempt to gain pleasure from the very activity of the psychic apparatus.[100] It is obviously at this point that a closer and more detailed discussion of the aesthetic attitude might be initiated: One might, for instance, try to answer the question of the differences in energy changes in reaction to different types of aesthetic experiences, e.g., the comic and the sublime,[101] or one might approach an even more complex and ambitious problem and ask to what extent the aesthetic attitude is limited to the reaction to art. To attempt more than speculation would mean to enter into areas of research which are particularly difficult to approach. Our expectation, however, is that psychoanalysis supplies useful equipment for these investigations and that the progress of psychoanalytic work in practice and theory might continue to improve the value of the tools which we have to offer.

Butcher speaks of "several kind of embellishments") are in the next paragraph explained to be verse and song.

[99] I am aware of the fact that this view implies some revision of the traditional interpretation of the passage. For the traditional interpretation see Butcher's edition of Aristotle's "Poetics" and John Gassner's introduction to it (1951).

[100] See Chapter 14.

[101] See Chapter 6 (pp. 187f.).

Chapter 2

THE IMAGE OF THE ARTIST

A PSYCHOLOGICAL STUDY OF THE ROLE OF TRADITION IN
ANCIENT BIOGRAPHIES

I

A psychological understanding of the meaning and function of biographies might be arrived at by various routes. The student could well begin with an investigation of the psychology of the biographer. According to Freud (1910, 1930 a), the biographer is frequently attached to his subject in a strange manner and in idealizing him strives to enroll the biographical subject among his infantile models. Or the biographer might be ambivalent: Heroizing and debunking in biography might thus be contrasted, and the fusion of the two demonstrated in various ways.

Another approach—the one we shall adopt here—is concerned not with the attitude of individual biographers but with biography as a literary category and with its social function; hence, one might also say, with biography as an institution. For material we draw on the findings of a science which can look back upon a long and significant history: the critical—philological and historical—evaluation of source material, a method more than accidentally related to that of psychoanalysis itself.[1] One of the findings from this method is that in ancient biographies stereotypical formulae tend to occur.

Two different lines of investigation are suggested: Since the same incident, or the same personality trait, is frequently reported in biographies of outstanding personalities, we might expect to gain some knowledge of the characteristics they have in common and proceed, on a statistical basis, to outline the characterology of "genius." This line of investigation presupposes the validity of the typical reports and their reliability in all

[1] Freud referred to this relationship when he compared psychoanalysis to archeology; see also Hartmann (1927), S. Bernfeld (1932), Gero (1933), and now S. C. Bernfeld (1951).

64

cases. A more skeptical line of reasoning would question these assumptions and emphasize that the uniformity of reports indicates instead a uniform attitude of biographers to their heroes. These explanations may actually supplement each other.

We are all familiar with descriptions of Archimedes' behavior upon the conquest of Syracuse; namely, that he received the soldiers storming into his room with: "Noli turbare circulos meos." If we frequently find the same report in ancient as well as modern biographies, the repetition of the same incident and the same behavior tends to arouse our suspicion and lead us to assume that biographers have utilized this well-known incident of Archimedes' life in order to characterize the scientist's or artist's preoccupation with and concentration on his purpose. Critical studies of source material have indeed established beyond doubt that such typical reports—which I shall simply call biographical formulae—were regularly inserted where the biographer did not have access to factual data on his hero's life history and actually could not have had access to them. These considerations suggest the basic line of investigation which we propose to follow: We intend to examine biographical formulae without regard for their correspondence to actual occurrences, although even in this respect the formulae are highly instructive. They strive toward an approximation of real life situations and generally create the impression of being true. One could speak of their "plausibility." However, we start from the fact that we are dealing with a typical biographical device. Once the existence of biographical formulae has been recognized, the question arises of the factors which can account for the widespread acceptance and popularity of the formulae.

Our investigation requires a limitation of our topic. Ancient biographies tend to be organized according to the hero's professional and social position. If we select for the purposes of our investigation a specific professional group, a content analysis of the typical formulae may give us some understanding of how members of this group were regarded by their environment, what specific aspects characterized their position, and what specific qualities the public attributed to them. The biographic formulae, we here study, are concerned with the image of the artist.[2]

2 The concept of the "image" has since the publication of this essay (1934) been used repeatedly in a similar sense; see e.g. Erikson (1942); Kris, Speier et al. (1944); and Heller (1951). There is a close relationship between the "image of the artist" and what Linton (1943, pp. 129-130) has since described as "status personality." He writes: ". . . in every society there are additional configurations of responses which are linked with certain socially delimited groups within the society. Thus, in practically all cases, different response configurations are characteristic for men and for women, for adolescents and for adults, and so on. In a stratified society similar differences may be

The establishment of these data will furnish a bridge leading from the psychology of biography to the psychology of its heroes. We may assume convergences between characteristics of the hero and the formulae; that is, certain of the formulae will more nearly fit the biographical realities.

The biographical accounts and the formulae I shall use refer to painters, sculptors, and architects. It was while studying this material that I was some ten years ago (1924) first struck by the recurrence of formulae in biographic writings. The collection of the material became a meaningful task only through psychological insight—which illustrates the view that the vistas opened up by psychoanalysis may lead to new problems in the humanities. The collection of the material has been published in a monograph entitled "The Legend of the Artist," where all references are given (Kris and Kurz, 1934).[3] From this material I have selected examples which are meant to illustrate, first, one of the fundamentals on which biographies in general rest; and, second, the special position of the artist. Because the artist-biography has special features within the larger category, some discussion of biographies of artists must precede the illustrations.

II

Only in societies in which the artist is held in high esteem and in which his name is linked to the work he produces, can the biography of the artist as a literary category develop. Such conditions are comparatively rare; there are societies with whose history we are intimately familiar, there are periods of the past about which we possess detailed information and in which outstanding works of architecture, sculpture or painting were produced, without an artist's name having been recorded.

A schematic survey reveals that the artist enters upon the stage of history when artistic creation becomes differentiated from other social

---

observed between the responses characteristic of individuals from different social levels, as nobles, commoners, and slaves. These status-linked response configurations may be termed status personalities."—Is not the artist a status personality of a special kind and does not the question of the comparative stability of his image pose a problem that deserves further attention by sociologists?

[3] The conditions of joint publication made it seem undesirable to compel the co-author (O. Kurz, now Librarian of the Warburg Institute of London University) to share responsibility for the psychoanalytic views which had suggested the problem to me, and I reserved the right to treat the material of our joint venture once more in order to discuss psychological problems in some detail. This division of labor allows for a briefer presentation of those problems on which psychoanalytic considerations have a more immediate bearing.

functions and attains its own value; that is, when art no longer serves purposes of ritual exclusively but has become an independent and legitimate pursuit. The process of separation is a gradual one, stimulating the creation of artists' biographies in two cultural areas only—the Far East and the Mediterranean. Biographical formulae used in both areas tend to resemble each other strikingly. We shall be concerned only with the European tradition, which has a "two-phasic" origin. One phase of development started in ancient Greece and can be traced back to about 300 B.C.; the other began in Italy during the Renaissance. There is a gap of "anonymous art" during the Middle Ages, between those two periods. Even the greatest masterpieces of this era are anonymous.

Sketchy as this outline is, it will suffice for our purposes as long as we add that all formulae contained in Greek and Roman literature were revived in the Renaissance, during which period, however, some new formulae emerged, deriving from the differences which had come about in the position of the modern artist. The Greek and Roman sculptor was of lower rank, a *banausos* who "smacked of the workshop," and the high esteem granted to other creators—to poets, bards, dramatists, and philosophers—was denied him. The gods had not graced him; he was not endowed with "enthusiasm," with that inspiration which enabled the others to create. During the Renaissance he gained in status; in fact he enjoyed a favored position.

III

The general problem we shall examine pertains to the position which biographers have assigned to the hero's youth. Two viewpoints must be distinguished. The first one regards the hero's youth as the prehistory of his life. This conception of youth, which is our own, developed gradually. From the eighteenth century on it can be found in ever broadening circles, and under the influence of psychoanalysis it has gained momentum. The second viewpoint regards the experiences and achievements of the young hero—the child altogether—not as part of his history, but as premonition of his future character. This conception is older and more widespread; it is rooted in the mythical thinking of mankind and extends, almost unbroken, into the present. It has at the present stage of our knowledge only a limited part in scientific thinking, but it strongly affects our pre- and extra-scientific attitudes.

Ancient biographies rarely record data concerning the hero's youth; whenever mentioned, however, they serve the purpose of demonstrating the special nature of his personality. The new significance and the enhanced prestige the artist attained during the Renaissance can best be characterized by the fact that biographers began to take cognizance of his youth. This interest is mirrored in an extraordinarily widespread biographical formula. It was first reported of Giotto, the outstanding Italian painter of the fourteenth century; it spread widely when Italian Renaissance biographies placed him almost at the beginning of the great national revival of art. Almost at the beginning, for to a still earlier generation belongs another painter, Cimabue, of whose life very little indeed is known. The names of the painters appear side by side not only in artists' biographies of the fifteenth and sixteenth centuries; they were connected already in Giotto's lifetime. Both names are mentioned in Dante's "Divine Comedy," where we learn that the once outstanding fame of the older Cimabue was overshadowed by that of Giotto. The context in which this reference occurs accounts for its meaning: Dante gives an example of the transience of worldly glory, an *exemplum morale*. The reference in the "Divine Comedy," one date in Cimabue's life, a few dates in Giotto's, whose great artistic achievements have remained familiar and admired whereas Cimabue's style seems to fade into darkness—these are the only certain biographical facts handed down to us.

The short reference in Dante was elaborated by Dante's commentators. The interpretation of the "Divine Comedy" had soon become a required subject of higher studies in Florence, and the "department" was at one time headed by Boccaccio. The commentators derived from Dante's verses a historical account and made Giotto into Cimabue's pupil. Although this "interpretation" cannot be supported either by documentary proof or by any resemblances in the style of the two artists —on the contrary, art critics are aware of counterarguments only—there soon arose a legend which spread from mouth to mouth. First recorded in the Dante commentaries, it took finally the following form:

> Giotto, a farmer's son, watched the flock of his father and drew pictures of the animals in the sand. It so happened that one day Cimabue accidentally came by, recognized the boy's miraculous talent, and took the boy with him. Under his guidance, Giotto grew up to be the great genius of the new Italian art.

The legend soon became "common property" of biographers; it was ascribed to all sorts of artists, even to those whose well-recorded life histories excluded the occurrence of a similar incident. But it was chiefly employed when the biographer lacked definite data, when he was, as it were, forced to fabricate a part of the biography. The extent to which this legend met the requirements of biographers can be seen from the fact that it is still used in artists' biographies of the twentieth century. A well-known biography of Segantini's wove this legend into the story of his youth—under the protest of Segantini's relatives; and we find it again in the life history of a contemporary artist, the Yugoslav sculptor, Mestrovic. In this latter instance, however, the artist is said to have related it himself to one of his earliest casual biographers. The legend has become so typical of the early years of the artist's life in general that it has also been adopted by poets: Andersen used it in one of his tales, and Octave Feuillet transferred it to the youth of a musical genius to whom he dedicated one of his plays.

Short as this legend is, it is nevertheless composed of various themes, some of which are traceable to antiquity. The general intention of post-humously bringing famous men in contact with each other is familiar as a ferment of Greco-Roman historiography; and so is the attempt in this way to link several generations to each other in order to establish a "genealogical" connection between them. Of independent origin—rooted in the attitude of peripatetic philosophers—is the element of chance and that of social ascension which, in our case, makes of the farmer's son a celebrated artist. Despite the numerous variations which the legend of the discovery of talent underwent—one of them soon elaborated also on Cimabue's life history—social ascension and the child-artist's miraculous gifts remained its nuclear themes.

To what characteristics did this formula owe its popularity and wide-spread acceptance? The legend of the discovery of talent shows striking resemblances to sagas and myths, particularly to those which have come to be known as "Myths of the Birth of the Hero" (Rank, 1909). The parallels in human fantasy life to which the disposition to the formation of these myths is due are well known. They derive from the conflicts inherent in the family situation which give rise to the family romance (Freud, 1909 b). We have here an ontogenetic model which psycho-analysis can offer the humanities. It is, however, necessary to compare and examine more closely the interrelationship of the nuclear themes of the child-artist and his social ascension. The common elements lie essentially in the area of the environment and the developing situation; i.e., the hero's starting life as a shepherd and the subsequent change of milieu. There is an even closer connection with other sagas of heroes which only partly coincide with the group discussed by Rank, with accounts in which the hero is recognized as such by virtue of his accomplishments. Such miraculous accomplishments are not infrequently recounted in myths. The most famous is that of the young Heracles who throttled snakes. Of the many other mythological parallels which could be enumerated, one legendary account has an immediate bearing on our subject. It pertains to the childhood of Christ and is recorded in one of the apocryphal Gospels, in which the New Testament's version of the coming of the Lord has been amplified and distorted by writers of the syncretistic period.[4]

We hear that as a child Christ made out of clay birds into which he breathed life. This ability characterizes the divine child as the world's creator and connects his early achievements with the tradition of God the sculptor of man, which opens the Old Testament account of Genesis. In the apocryphal Gospel, however, this ability is viewed not only as divine prerogative but also as evil sorcery: Into the characterization of the God-Child elements have entered which, rooted in pagan tradition, view the omnipotence of the gods as indication of their potential arbitrariness.

The tale of Christ as a young sculptor of animals was undoubtedly familiar to those Florentines who "invented" the legend of the discovery of talent. We may consider it as another root of the legend which supplied the idea of the early and miraculous achievement of the artistically endowed boy. We are thus faced with the question of where in the fantasies of individuals this particular aspect of the legend may have its counterpart. It seems at this point appropriate to insert two clinical illustrations; though they do not cover the entire question, they come close to its essence in establishing a bridge between the ideas of the infant prodigy and the family romance.

A twenty-five-year-old man related in his analysis that in his fifth or sixth year he developed the following fantasy. He was the son of the deceased Crown Prince Rudolf of Austria. Apart from the typical and gradual separation of this fantasy from the domain of the oedipus complex—that is, the evolution from legitimate to the illegitimate son of his parents, finally becoming their foster child, who is in reality the son of the unfortunate prince—another element gained ascendance in the fantasy; namely, the patient's desire to be discovered in a miraculous fashion, in order to protect his country from wars of succession to the throne—a feat of which he alone was capable. It was this part of the fantasy which was destined for importance and only analysis could disclose the role which the expectation of future discovery played first in the patient's fantasies and finally also in the actual course of his life. In the analysis of another patient I found a similar fantasy with a felicitous rationalization. A young sculptor, in whose life the idea of be-

---

[4] The tale has stimulated the Swedish writer Selma Lagerloef to one of her most imaginative stories; see her "Christ Legends."

ing "discovered" could play a considerable role, associated the fantasy of the sudden unfolding of his talent with the idea, disclosed in his dreams, of being given a real, i.e., a fully grown, penis by the father image of the discoverer. The matrix from which this fantasy evolved was the old competition with the patient's real father who had been successful in the same branch of art.

I am inclined to surmise that similar elaborations frequently accompany the typical family romance. The fantasy of the hero's discovery would constitute the link.[5]

We must now consider another explanation, less remote than the hypothesis that the legend of the discovery of talent contains elements which can be related to the family romance. If we consider even part of the hypothesis as justified, we would find that it would hold true only for the typical garb in which the legend is clothed. One might reason that underlying the legend was an empirical finding—the early talent of the future artist—and that it was only this empirical finding which gave rise to the embellishments of the semilegendary accounts. There is no need to argue against this consideration. In our introductory remarks we have already pointed out that biographical formulae may aim at comprehending the hero's character, being tailored to the peculiarities of his nature. The artist's precocity could be accepted as an actual finding. On the other hand, we cannot summon conclusive evidence to prove the correctness of this assumption. The inclination to representational art is not necessarily found among those tendencies which developed at a very early age,[6] nor do we know to what extent this early awakening of voca-

---

5 Since this was written I have had repeatedly the opportunity to study similar fantasies in analysis, sometimes as elements of conscious daydreams, sometimes as repressed fantasies which occurred at the height of the oedipal conflict or in early latency. They regularly seem to contain a compromise between the competition with and the submission to the father figure. In all instances the longing for closeness was nearer to consciousness than the aggressive content, and the conscious emphasis on feminine traits covered the hostile oedipal impulses. Moreover, in at least one case the fantasy of discovery was linked to the theme of the well-known rescue fantasies (see Sterba, 1940 b) with which they share the "double root." In two instances I met the fantasy in female patients; needless to say, the "discoverer" was in both cases a woman. In all cases the fantasy was recalled, or gained its meaning, in relation to transference problems, and had invariably colored conscious daydreams of the adolescent period; in at least one case the adolescent fantasy seems to have been in all essential traits identical with the earlier one.

6 We certainly do not want to discard the opinion which holds that the decisive anlage manifests itself already at an early age. On the contrary, the more insight we gain into the impact of life experiences on personality, the more we are impressed with the significance of earliest individual differences. See pp. 20f.

To determine the specific nature of these differences from the infant's or small child's behavior seems to be an important field of study which could perhaps in the not

tional determination in artists varies with historical conditions. The fact that the very accounts which we have recognized as formulae tend to be cited as evidence for the early manifestations of talent suggests the danger of a circular argument.

This consideration, however, draws our attention to our general readiness to overvalue children's accomplishments and to regard them as extraordinary and singular, an attitude obviously connected with the search for augury in the child's early behavioral manifestations. It is not difficult to deduce some determinants of this attitude. We can often catch ourselves in the desire to discover in our own children those abilities and attributes which were denied to us or of which we are especially proud. We are under the spell of narcissism. We might also remind ourselves of the eternal wish for one's own childhood—a wish which is likely to result in the overestimation of the child's achievements. It is as if we wanted to emphasize the richness and happiness of our own development before this or that fateful event altered its course. Another reflection has even wider implications. The abilities and achievements which in our admiration we ascribe to the child (we do not intend to deny that the child possesses abilities which the adult loses) may be an expression of our own desire for superiority, when we were children, a desire which would have enabled us to gratify instinctual demands or escape instinctual conflicts. "So past, present and future are threaded, as it were, on the string of the wish that runs through them all" (Freud, 1908, p. 178).

The role which our own childhood plays in shaping our attitude to the child prodigy facilitates our understanding of one detail of the legend "of the discovery of talent." The legend attains its full meaning if we remember that a child is discovered in a "childish activity," receiving instead of the anticipated punishment, the father's encouragement and support.[7] This approval constitutes one of the fundamental pre-

---

too distant future greatly enhance our knowledge in respect to such questions as the strength of the instinctual drives and the individual's selective reactions to external stimuli. But this side of our (scientific) interest in the child's early functions represents only an additional motive of our endeavor to search for forebodings in the child's behavior. Even "the search for the child prodigy" does not completely describe our attitude. Direct observation, clinical experiences in psychoanalysis, and material known from folklore, concur in suggesting a further reason for the interest in nature and personality of the very small child: the fact which legal tradition designates by *pater incertus*.

For a survey of problems concerning hereditary factors in the development of gift for drawing and painting see Haecker and Ziehen (1931).

[7] The syncretistic account of Christ's childhood supports this, for it is birds that the young magician forms.

conditions to which our unconscious tends to link the future great-ness of the child—one of the preconditions which in our own life would have led to happiness or greatness.

After this sketchy delineation of some of the themes which con-certedly appear to explain our readiness to search for the child prodigy, we listen to a poet:

> . . . and here he sat, a gray old man, looking in while this hop-o'-my-thumb performed miracles. Yes, yes, it is a gift of God, we must re-member that God grants His gifts or He withholds them, and there is no shame in being an ordinary man. Like with the Christ Child.—Before a child one may kneel without feeling ashamed. Strange that thoughts like these should be so satisfying . . .

These words of Thomas Mann (1948, p. 177) invite a host of con-siderations. Data from ethnology, folklore, and the history of religion, could be cited in the pursuit of the answer to the problem to which he points. We, however, are directed back to our point of departure. There is a clear dividing line in our reflections upon the parallels of the legend of the discovery of talent and the myth of the birth of the hero. In the latter, the abandoned hero-child is of high parentage and is, so to speak, rediscovered. In our legend, however, the child is of low origin while the discoverer is the new and simultaneously elevated father figure.

The child prodigy's early striving for artistic expression is a theme which was introduced for the first time into the biographies of artists in the Renaissance. Earlier eras had reserved this distinction for a dif-ferent type of hero; in antiquity it was essentially confined to the hero as a man of action, in the Middle Ages to the legends of the saints. From these sources is derived the theme which now finds its way into biographies of sculptors and painters.

In the sharp light of Western civilization no full-fledged mythology of the artist could originate, but the attitude to which we point constitutes an important ingredient of modern ideologies which surround him, an ideology reflected also in the widespread literature on the theory of art. The ideology of which we speak embraces many creative and intellectual leaders of society; the theory of art is being supplemented by the theory of genius—which the eminent historian of this theory, Edgar Zilsel (1918, 1926), could on good grounds designate as "the religion of genius." The divine ascent of genius is part of the doctrine typical of this theory. In the biographies of artists this view is clearly expressed. Giorgio Vasari's work on the Italian artists (first published in 1550), the impressive standard-work of Renaissance historiography, was conceived as a pyramid at whose peak stood the towering figure of Michelangelo Buonarotti. The life history of this greatest of Italian artists commences in the manner and tone of myth:

> Since God saw that it was just in Toscana that sculptors, painters, and architects had with the greatest devotion dedicated themselves to the fine arts, He desired that this mind sent by Him should have his home in Florence . . . This son of whom I am talking was born on a Sunday, in the evening of the sixth of March at eight o'clock. He was given the name of Michelangelo without any further reflection, as if under the influence of higher forces one wished to indicate that he surpassed every human measure and possessed heavenly and Godlike gifts.

It is consistent with the general structure of myths and the succession of their themes that we learn next that the boy was brought to Settignano, where he was nursed by the wife of a stonemason, so that "already with the milk of his wet nurse he sucked in the proclivity to hammer and chisel."

If we regard the image of the artist which developed in the Renaissance after the fourteenth century as a uniform and gradually unfolding one—and all arguments support this view—we are in a position to narrow the gap between the legend of the discovery of talent and the myth of the birth of the hero. The princely origin of the abandoned infant is replaced by the divine origin of genius. The discoverer whose model we encountered in Cimabue happens to pass by and discovers the child whom God has chosen.

This instance was selected to illustrate the thesis that biography originates in myth and could not, in earlier times, entirely free itself from the influences of this heritage. Even biographers of modern days seem from time to time to be carried away by the very tendencies which led the oral tradition in Florence to revert to legendary themes.

IV

The special characterization of the artist by his biographers shall first be illustrated by two particularly widespread formulae. One of them relates that the Greek painter Zeuxis, when he painted Helena's portrait for the city of Croton, assimilated in his work the most perfect features of five different beautiful models. The legend is rooted in Plato's theory of art, according to which the artist's task is to surpass reality. Whatever beauty nature offers in various individuals, the artist is to unite in an ideal of beauty.

The second legend shows the artist's achievements from an opposite side. Its oldest version tells us of a contest between two Greek painters, Zeuxis and Parrhasios. Zeuxis painted grapes, and sparrows came flying to pick the grapes. Parrhasios, however, outshone Zeuxis, because he invited Zeuxis to his studio and asked him to draw back the curtain which covered Parrhasios' picture. But the curtain was the picture. Zeuxis could deceive birds, but Parrhasios deceived men.

Both legends lived on after the decline of Greek culture, and one might well say that they are still with us. The second is more widespread and popular, appearing in innumerable variations. It is the most famous and the most typical legend of the artist—the legend of the artist *par excellence*. Before we examine its meaning more closely, however, we must emphasize that the content of the legend, if taken literally, appears to be a senseless exaggeration. Neither the works of art of the Greeks nor any of the subsequent works to which this legend has been linked have been able to copy and represent nature as the legend wishes us to believe.[8] The gist of the legend does not merely underline a certain high level of artistic achievement; the emphasis is rather on the deceiving effect of the artistic product. The meaning of this statement becomes apparent if we turn to two groups of variation of the legend. Achievements like those of Zeuxis and Parrhasios are also attributed to artists of Greek prehistory, the era of Greek myth; e.g., to the ancestor of Greek art, Daedalus. There is sufficient evidence to warrant the assumption that the account of the deceiving effect of Daedalus' works represents a weakening of older traditions which tell us that Daedalus created moving statues of women. Similar stories are related of other mythical artists, e.g., of the Finnish Smith-God Illmarinen or of Hephaestus of whom it is said:

> . . . And in support of their master moved his attendants.
> These are golden, and in appearance like living young women.
> There is intelligence in their heart, and there is speech in them
> and strength, and from the immortal gods they have learned how to
>   do things.[9]

As the legend of the competition of the artists for the greater deceptive power of their works traveled from mouth to mouth, ever new variations arose. In one of them part of the original contents which we assume

[8] For an elaboration of this problem and others discussed here see Gombrich (1951).

[9] *The Iliad of Homer,* translated by Richmond Lattimore, Chicago: University of Chicago Press, 1951 (Book 18, lines 417-420). An essential element of these accounts seems to be that the statue be that of a woman—a fact which suggests a parallel to the account of Genesis.

to have been repressed emerge again in an undisguised form: According to a Central Asiatic version of the legend, a painter and a maker of automatons competed with each other; in this instance also, the work of the automaton-maker was a female figure.

The legend of the deceptive power of his works belongs to the oldest stratum of biographical reports on the artist. It originated in a collection of biographies, usually attributed to Duris of Samos (fourth century B.C.) of which only fragments have been preserved. The legend seems to imply that the artist who had just entered upon the stage of historical tradition had inherited the position of the great artists of myths. In order to complement this finding, in itself hardly astonishing, we resort to a second group of variations of the legend. They throw light upon a different aspect of the deceptive power of the work of art: their development too can be traced throughout the course of Western history. I have in mind reports which state that a work of art, an image of a human, has reached such a high level of perfection that it has been taken to be alive and has excited some to violent sensual love. We are told that an Eros or a Venus of Praxiteles evoked such reactions in their beholders. The most famous legend—most famous, probably, because of the interaction of several factors—is that of the sculptor king Pygmalion who fell in love with the statue of a woman he himself had created. Substitutions of this kind do not take place only on the basis of love; they can also occur under the primacy of aggression. Not only affectionate acts are carried out on the image; the image may also be the object of punishment and destruction. Those who destroy the image of a faithless lover or revolutionaries who overthrow a ruler in effigy, act basically like the "lover of statues" among the Greeks: For both of them the boundary between artefact and reality, between the image and the depicted, is blurred. The evanescence of this boundary, the identity of picture and depicted, belong to the domain of image magic. It is necessary to interpolate at this point that we rarely find the belief in the identity of picture and depicted in a pure form.[10] It is harbored more readily in preliterate societies than in literate ones,[11] and is more likely to occur with children than with adults. States in which the affects—particularly anxiety—gain primacy will give rise to the belief more readily than states of composure. In summarizing, we can say that this belief appears when the ego

[10] As far as we know this occurs only in psychoses; see Laforgue (1928). However, the example given there is invented. For further discussion see also Chapter 7.

[11] How controversial and open an issue the attitude of primitives to representations of the human figure is can be seen from the obviously one-sided discussion by Olivier Le Roy (1927).

has not yet gained full command or has loosened the reigns of its control. In each of these cases the nature of the picture is—for very different reasons—of little significance.

The determinants of this attitude can further be characterized in terms of our "ontogenetic model." In a certain phase of children's games —role-playing or illusory games—the nature of the object with which the play is enacted is of little relevance. A broom turns into a horse, a bobbin becomes a weapon. There is no indication that the child necessarily believes in the "reality" of the play situation,[12] but the intensity of his imaginative powers cannot be evaluated unless we realize that the "intensity" of illusion matches that of fantasy productivity; i.e., of the narcissistic cathexis. Children's role-playing, the content of which emerges at a later phase in daydreams, has from the economic point of view a parallel in that behavior of adults in which the ego has suffered a loss in its regulating and controlling functions. When the distinction between picture and depicted diminishes for the adult, he has "regressed" to a form of behavior which we call "magical." He is then dominated by the belief in the omnipotence of thought.

The connection to our topic can be established on the basis of the following brief consideration: The more firmly the belief in the "magical identity of the picture" prevails, the less attention we need to pay to its external attributes.[13] Likeness is the tie which links picture and depicted when the belief in their identity has vanished. In the prehistoric Greek art, likeness in this sense played but a minor role; it became significant as a result of a development lasting for more than two centuries—at the very time when Greek artists first became the object of a biographer's endeavor. The meaning of the first formula we know from these biographies: The artist, by virtue of his perfection, reëstablishes the link between picture and depicted object which on an earlier level of development existed by virtue of the magic meaning of imagery.[14]

The possible usefulness of this hypothesis seems to be confirmed if we submit historical data to an opposite test. Those works of classical antiquity which represent the most obvious peak of the new naturalistic spirit, its sculptures, appear as anxiety-evoking objects in the Middle

[12] For a detailed discussion of this problem see Bühler (1927).

[13] See Gomperz (1906) and here p. 168.

[14] This hypothesis cannot contribute a solution of the problems pertaining to the changes of style. It is conceived merely as one step toward a better understanding of the artist's biographical portrait. The relationship between narcissistic involvement and antinaturalistic art has repeatedly been pointed out in various disguises and terminologies during the last decades.

Ages, a time of renewed antinaturalistic tendencies.[15] This was a time when the artist once more vanished from the limelight of history. The names of artists of Greek antiquity which literary tradition had preserved now became the names of dangerous sorcerers. This notion, which had influenced also the image of the artist in ancient times, persisted as an undercurrent throughout and far beyond the Middle Ages, finding reflection in numerous fables; among the most famous is that of the pacts with Satan—a legend not confined to artists. This notion has continued, and even today influences the position of the artist in society.

The belief in the artist's magical power, and at the same time also the belief in the forbidden nature of his activity, is deeply rooted in the mind of man. For, it was precisely those demigods of myth who had been rebellious and punished—the imprisoned Daedalus, the lame Wieland, the crippled Hephaestus, and their great ancestor, the enchained Prometheus—whose heritage early biographers awarded to the artists.

At first one might be tempted to assume that the prohibition upon which they trespassed concerned image making: Magic can be practiced on an image and should the image be that of the deity, the authority of the gods might be jeopardized.[16] This explanation, however, is of necessity unsatisfactory. The taboo attached to the artist's activity is not confined to instances in which he depicts reality. Architecture as well is held to be an offense to the gods. The legend of the Tower of Babel reflects the universal custom according to which the completion of buildings must be expiated by human sacrifices.

But shaping images and erecting buildings are not the only activities which myths assigned to the artist. Artistic ability is part of the power of the demiurge. He is part of a world in which magic practices comprised art; it is the time of the sacred archaic craft which contains in undivided unity mantic, magic, and various specialized skills (Eisler, 1910). Daedalus and his nordic brother, Wieland, are credited with having fulfilled one of man's oldest dreams. The myth associated with their names has connected the control of the skies with artistic endeavors. The stealing of the fire attributed to the Fire God Prometheus—whose heir is the fire demon Hephaestus—was only in subsequent and contradictory fusions linked with his sculptures and thus his creation of man.[17]

[15] Here too a psychoanalytic interpretation could advance somewhat further: we are at the border of the uncanny.

[16] Since classical antiquity we find it frequently said that the work of art—mostly studies of facial expressions—is fashioned after a model the artist has killed. This fórmula lives on in many contemporary short stories and has been applied even to the photographer's work.

[17] See in this connection for older psychoanalytic views Abraham (1909), Jung (1911, 1912), Baudouin (1928), and leading into a different direction Freud (1932 b).

If we relate these ideas to our topic, we can advance the assumption that creative production—the making of images and the erection of buildings —is universally held to be the prerogative of the divine, since the creation both of the universe and of man are considered visible signs of divine omnipotence. This prerogative determines the manner in which the artist is heroized. Renaissance artists asserted their sovereignty in depicting themselves as "God and Creator" (*dio e creatore*) of the work of art (Leonardo) ; and their environment, in turn, unhesitatingly bestowed on them the attribute "divine" (*divino*) which soon became frozen in a figure of speech. The figure still survives in the epithet of the actress, the *diva,* but originally it carried the full literal meaning of the term. The theory of art justified this exaltation of the artist.[18] The anecdotes about Zeus and the maidens of Croton set the task for the artist not to imitate the real but to create an ideal.

The image of the divine artist, the *divino artista,* has an exact counterpart. The sculptor God of biblical tradition is frequently viewed as artistic mastermind, as *deus artifex,* and hence as prototype of the divine artist.

V

Since the sixteenth century new formulae tend to appear in the biographies of artists, who now have become members of the great brotherhood of the endowed and creative and share with them the temptting and dangerous traits of genius. The genius can dispense with divine favors. Inspiration, originally conceived as animation by the breath of God, has become secularized and is acknowledged as the artist's inner voice.[19] Like the mythical heroes whose domination they have put aside and whose status they have partly inherited, the creative personalities are to some extent beyond the pale of society, beyond the dictates which normally rule it and hold it together. They enjoy special prerogatives[20] —e.g., the prerogative of greater sexual freedom—but the radius of their

18 From the theory of art this doctrine seems to have entered aesthetics in general; see, e.g., recently the discussion on the "beauty of nature and art" as topic of philosophy by H. B. Lee (1948) who very suggestively points out how the function of the artist is made to resemble that of "the minister of religion as a specially gifted mediator between God and man" (p. 509).

19 See Chapter 13.

20 These prerogatives also extend to their works. The "license" of the poet is the freedom with which the "aesthetic value" endows his achievement. Provided it is art, he may do what otherwise would be forbidden. See Sachs (1924), Muschg (1933); also p. 294.

lives extends only from Parnassus to bohème; they are the objects of our admiration and the targets of our ambivalence.

This is the matrix in which the more recent biographical formulae originate. They are less specific and on the whole closer to life. One gains sometimes the impression that the actual behavior of one or another of the famous artists of the time has been used as a prototype, frozen into a formula which is being handed down as such to succeeding generations. In most instances the formula has striven to comprehend the artist's personality, to fathom and humanize the riddle of his life and his creativity.

In order to characterize this new spirit we refer to at least one group of formulae: The special position which the artist's work holds in his life becomes a focal point for the inquiry into the mystery surrounding him. An ancient comparison describes the particular attachment of the artist to the work he creates in terms of his parenthood; the work of art is seen as the artist's child. Jokes utilize this comparison, and in establishing a parallel between sexual and artistic creation they seem to anticipate part of the meaning of sublimation. Other formulae describe how the artist is unable to part from his work; they dwell upon his conflict with his customer, which arises because he cannot part from what he has created. In order that he might retain exclusive ownership, the idea takes shape in the artist's mind that his work should not outlive him. The opposite thought is also expressed: The artist's life remains tied to his work, whose destruction is followed by his suicide. Most obvious, and in a statistical sense most frequent, are the accounts reporting that the artist has killed himself upon the discovery of an error in the already completed work. (One of the most frequently cited errors is the omission of horseshoes on the equestrian statue.) In such instances, the special form of artistic narcissism determines the formation of the formulae.

In discussing these more recent formulae, we have wandered from the psychology of biography more and more into the psychology of the artist. We are now reminded that we expected a similar connection between biographical formulae and the psychology of the artist as far as the older legendary accounts are concerned. Something in his nature, we argued, must have suggested, evoked or justified, the traits which were given by his biographers to his image. We have seen that the legends characterizing the artist as sorcerer, magician, and rebel reach back far into the mythological matrix. Should we assume that this heritage also finds a representation in the artist's behavior or experience?

I should like to illustrate the complexity of this problem by referring to the life history of an artist whose work is discussed in one of the subsequent essays.[21] We will be able to use but little of what the traditional biographers record on Franz Xaver Messerschmidt (1736-1784). They saw the course of his life from a specific angle and considered him as a misunderstood genius. In doing so, they unwittingly accepted the version which Messerschmidt himself, under the pressure of a persecutory delusion, had proclaimed to every one with whom he had had contact. Moreover, the basis of all, or at least most, biographical data about Messerschmidt is a popular tract in which the entire inventory of biographical formulae pertaining to the artist has been assembled. We hear of Messerschmidt as the shepherd boy who carved wooden images of the animals of his flock. We are told that as a boy he became oblivious to food and drink when studying his anatomy book, that he killed his model in order to capture the features of the dying. This list, from which the pact with Satan is not excluded, could be very considerably enlarged. But the examples suffice to illustrate the thesis that popular opinion readily accepts the stock of stereotypical formulae as part of the artist's characterization. This formulation, however, misses the more serious question of whether or not a sharp line of demarcation can be drawn between the biographic formulae and the actual life experiences of the artist himself. Reliable reporters who met Messerschmidt recorded that he again and again voiced his intention to destroy his works before his death; it also seems to be an established fact that he asked ridiculous sums of money for his sculptures. The scope and depth of the problem become accessible to our understanding when we realize that not only were some external aspects of his behavior governed by the themes to which the legends of the artist point; the very structure of his delusion can be viewed as typical of the creative artist. For in the center of his delusion we find the thought that the gods, envious of his perfection as an artist and particularly of his knowledge of the "divine proportion," persecute him—a delusional thought which can easily be recognized as a projection of that other notion according to which the artist competes with God.[22]

The pale reflection of literary parlance, of the contest between the *divino artista* and the *artifex deus* gains suddenly a new vividness: In the thought processes of the schizophrenic, a tradition is renewed which leads back far into the past of the race.

This connection between literary tradition and the experience of the creator can be further illustrated if we turn to formulae which do not concern painters or sculptors but architects: they describe the architect's

[21] See Chapter 4.
[22] For a further discussion and other clinical examples see pp. 118ff., 131ff.

suicide upon the completion of his work. The accounts appear in many variations. The suicide is motivated by competition with a superior pupil, by the discovery of an error in construction after the building's completion, or by the escape from the pact with Satan. But these motivations establish only a façade.

A detailed study of the incidents accounted in more recent biographies suggests their division into two groups. There are cases in which the suicide was actually committed, and there are others where the formula is inserted into the biography but where the suicide never occurred. There clearly is no psychological contradiction between the two kinds of reports: They illustrate two aspects of the same phenomenon. What the biographers describe as the architect's typical fate meets with an unconscious expectation of the public for which the artist works; at the same time it determines the unconscious experience of the artist himself. And again there is a way leading back to mythological tradition. The widespread custom of offering human sacrifice upon the completion of the edifice seems strangely connected with the experience of Ibsen's "Master Builder."

At this point Jungian psychology with its concept of the collective unconscious seems to offer a ready-made solution. But it is one which we have every reason to reject. We have discussed in Chapter 1 the unconscious experiences which tend to be connected with creation in the figurative arts;[23] we were able to establish how these experiences shape the delusion of the schizophrenic, how the experience of creation, the experience of omnipotence produces conditions into which literary and mythological tradition fit—a vacuum as it were which they fill. There is no need to enlarge upon the idea that the *erection* of the edifice, the creation of the building, evokes similar unconscious fantasies, that here, too, the sexual and aggressive symbolism of the activity itself creates a disposition to accept what the tradition offers: Every building may in this sense be viewed as a Tower of Babel. Myth and tradition, the expectation of the public, the experience of the artist, the delusion of the psychotic creator, originate in the same unconscious complex of ideas.

But the problem of this study is not exhausted by pointing to the fact that common unconscious attitudes account for the survival of biographical formulae or for the renewal, out of new experience, of their impact. There exists a less "deep," a more pragmatic, relationship. The biography sets up models. We are reminded of a simple incident to which we referred above, of the artist who told his first biographer "the legend of

23 See p. 52 and Chapter 3.

the discovery of talent" as an account of his own youth.[24] Whatever else we may think of this incident, in such distortion we can still recognize a widespread process which is frequently of considerable significance. I propose to call it the enacted biography.[25]

Thomas Mann has recently given clear presentation of extreme cases of such enactment. In his book *Joseph and His Brethren* he repeatedly expresses the thought that the succession of generations may become indistinct, that proximity and remoteness of time tends to diminish by virtue of identification; this is particularly illustrated in the figure of Eliezer, a freedman of Jacob, "not to be confused (as occasionally happened to Joseph and as the old man himself liked to have happen to him) with Eliezer," Abraham's oldest servant.[26] In a world whose semi-darkness is again and again submerged in myths, the boundary between the individual and tradition grows hazy and identification with the ancestor decides the nature and direction of the individual's existence.[27] Under normal conditions, in our society, this bond plays on the whole a subordinated role. And yet many of us live even today the life of a biographical type, the "destiny" of a particular class, rank, or profession.

Such identifications can again and again be traced back to typical models, which in turn have been set up by biographies. Under normal conditions, these identifications supply late contributions to the formation of the superego. The most obvious cases are those in which they significantly fashion its conscious components. These identifications frequently find expression in professional ethics. The extraordinary achievements which they can prescribe or release should warn us not to think lightly of their power.

We cannot in the present context attempt to explore further the various influences biographical models tend to have on human life and conflict. They form, it seems, an important chapter in the psychology of

[24] See p. 69.

[25] It is difficult to decide on the extent to which, in any individual case, "models" exert influence. Again using the case of Messerschmidt as our example, we do not know the extent to which the "typical" utterances and acts of which we are told came about as emulations of "models" or were "new creations" stemming from an analogous attitude.

[26] Thomas Mann has used a discussion of the present paper and some of its hypotheses for a starting point of his address on the occasion of Freud's eightieth birthday. See Mann (1936).

[27] An illustration of this was supplied by an example I heard Gregory Bateson quote in a discussion. A young Iatmul, aged seventeen, was asked to describe the course of his life. He started with birth, went through childhood, adolescence, manhood, and his advanced years, without becoming aware of his actual age. What he described was the prescribed course of his life, the life of a man in a specific culture.

adolescence but retain influence even during the later stages of personality development. Problems of this kind will, I believe, gradually become part of ego psychology, and our best access might well be the study of identifications which have miscarried.

It also seems that the freedom of the individual, particularly his freedom in an era of rapid social change, is to some extent related to the problem of enacted biography. It is particularly acute among the stratum of social leaders. There are the pathetic and ridiculous figures who live only for diary or obituary, whose sole purpose in life seems to be one day to become themselves biographical models; and there are those who need not emphasize the bond of heritage. They have renounced the conscious aspirations which haunt the others, and by virtue of their achievements they realize the old ideals of biographers in a new form.

Part Two

The Art of the Insane

Chapter 3

COMMENTS ON SPONTANEOUS ARTISTIC CREATIONS BY PSYCHOTICS

I. INTRODUCTION

Since the middle of the nineteenth century the study of drawing, painting, and sculpture produced by psychotic patients has attracted the attention of psychiatrists. The trends in the selection of problems and in the interpretation of the data reflect so clearly the changing approaches of investigators from many lands that one might well be tempted to consider a survey of these studies as a fitting introduction to the history of psychiatry in this century.[1]

Psychoanalysts and psychiatrists with psychoanalytic orientation have contributed to these studies: Publications by Baudouin (1929), Bertschinger (1911), Lewis (1925), Mohr (1906), Pfister (1913 a and b), and Rorschach (1928) have demonstrated the role of "symbols" in psychotic art; individual creations by psychotics have been studied in relation to the patient's delusional system, and data related to the ever-growing interest in problems of psychodiagnostics have been assembled.[2]

We do not in this paper propose to follow their example. Our purpose is limited to a consideration of what psychoanalytic ego psychology can contribute. By ego psychology we refer to that part of psychoanalytic theory which, since the publication of Freud's *Inhibition, Symptom and Anxiety* (1926),[3] has brought many valuable additions to the older

[1] Since the publication of this paper (1936) a number of informative survey articles and bibliographies by Anastasi and Foley (1940-1942) have appeared, and a survey article by Born (1946).

[2] Since 1936 the literature has vastly grown, producing many valuable insights. A survey of psychodiagnostic investigations using the art of the insane is given by Anastasi and Foley (1941, IV). Interpretations of individual creations based on psychoanalysis have been published in considerable number; papers by Bychowski (1947), Grotjahn (1947, 1948), and Mosse (1940) may be mentioned here, particularly two detailed monographs by Naumburg (1949, 1950). Representative of the Jungian approach is the publication by Baynes (1940). For pertinent psychiatric descriptions see also Ferdière (1947, 1951).

[3] The American translation is entitled *The Problem of Anxiety*.

approaches within psychoanalysis. This vantage point determines the problems on which we focus. While clinical data gained from individual case histories will form the basis of our discussion, our interest will be centered on a few specific problems. We shall attempt to clarify the meaning which artistic creation may acquire during a psychotic process, and we shall try to comment on some of the formal characteristics of psychotic productions—topics which have been treated in Prinzhorn's volume on "The Art of the Insane" (1922 a) . We are indebted to Prinzhorn for much stimulation and for rich material, on which we shall draw liberally, but our approach is radically opposed to his. Prinzhorn's views are based upon the psychology of Ludwig Klages. He is, in his own words, not interested in psychological explanation but in intellectual intuition (*Wesensschau*) . This attitude not only permeates his presentation but determines also his choice of material.[4] It was meant to support an aesthetic thesis and to plead the cause of German expressionistic art. We differ from Prinzhorn not only in our theoretical orientation and the method of inquiry which we intend to adopt, but also by the avoidance of some far-reaching speculations. The study of psychotic art does not, in our view, encourage a general answer to questions concerning the origin of the urge to create in man, nor does it account for the nature of primitive configurations, suggested by the comparison between psychotic art, the art of children, and that of certain preliterate societies. However, some of our findings may permit us to formulate problems in this second area.

Our inquiry has to start from a survey of some widely accepted clinical observations.

II. Creative Activities of Psychotics and Untrained Normals

At one point in the course of their illness some psychotic patients begin to devote themselves to creative activities. In some cases, on which we concentrate here, creative activities are undertaken not only occasionally but fill a major part of the patient's life. A distinct urge to create, to utilize the most varied materials and tools, becomes manifest. Any scrap of paper, the walls or floors, may be used to draw upon; any pencil or stick may serve as tool; bread is kneaded into figures; each piece of wood is turned into a carving, with broken pieces of glass serving as knives.

The occurrence of such an urge or spell to create is—statistically

---

4 This statement is based on checks which I was enabled to make in 1931 in the Collection of the Psychiatric Clinic in Heidelberg.

speaking—rare. According to possibly optimistic estimates, somewhat less than 2 per cent of hospital inmates can be considered as artistically active. They are said to have few characteristics in common.[5]

There is no fixed point in the disease process at which the drive to create appears. It seems to have a somewhat higher incidence in the initial phases.[6] The new preoccupation frequently indicates a change in the course of the disease and may also initiate one of its later acute phases. No specific relationship between the occurrence of the urge to create and other personality characteristics is reported in the literature. The urge to create may occur in patients in whom language and writing is intact or in cases of far-gone language deterioration. In most instances artistic creation becomes a means of expression which is equal to, or slightly preferred to, speech and writing. Frequently these forms of expression are used in conjunction.[7]

One further observation, which is of particular importance in the context of this paper, has to be reported: No definite relationship to skills and talents of the prepsychotic personality can be established. The factor of "training"—whether or not the patient has drawn, painted, or carved before the onset of the psychotic process—seems not to influence the sudden outburst of artistic activity. It should be noted, however, that previous training does not necessarily supply clues to the patient's natural gifts. While we have no scientific means to assess presence or extent of this factor, and can therefore not operate with it, its existence should not be denied. In summarizing, we may state that in the "ideal" case the psychotic "creator" is untrained.

A clinical example, which has been chosen for its clarity, may serve as illustration: Villamil (1933) reports that a peasant suffering from acute alcoholic intoxication was brought to the hospital in Conja, Spain. This acute state was superimposed on the symptom complex of a "mania" which unfolded progressively after the patient's commitment. In the

[5] For discussion of the diagnoses see p. 153. The increase in productive activity during the development of a neurotic process differs clearly from the spell to create here described. For a clinical example see Eisenstein (1948, Case I).

[6] A rough statistical survey of the case material published up to 1936 suggested this result; for a more cautious formulation see p. 153.

[7] See Hassman and Zingerle (1913). Anastasi and Foley (1944) studied a population of 680 subjects, equally divided between normal and abnormal men and women. Each subject was asked to make four drawings, one of his own choice, one representing danger, a picture of a man, and a copy of a floral design. In some instances abnormal subjects tended to mix writing and drawing whereas normals did not. They showed a slight preference for the fantastic and for disjuncted additions; there was more "scribbling or scrawl" on abnormal drawings. These differences, however, concern but a small part of the sample.

course of the psychotic process the patient turned to carving. His creations were bizarre and resembled those of many other psychotics. In our
context, one feature is important. The patient's progressive improvement
was reflected in the following change: First he replaced symbolic creations by the construction of practically useful objects, for instance, of a
jug or a pipehead; when he was subsequently introduced to occupational
therapy where the physician wanted him to work in the carpenter's
workshop, the patient explained that he was a farmer and wanted to
work as such. Hence, the artistic activities appear to have been elements
foreign to the healthy part of the personality.

Inasmuch as the emergence of the spell to create is independent of
previous training and, in the "ideal" case the psychotic creator is untrained, we are forced to detour in our investigation. Before we can
characterize the productions of psychotic patients, we must determine
which features of their production can be related directly to lack of
training. Doodlings by untrained adult normals and by psychotics tend
to "look alike"; that is, they resemble each other to such an extent that
a distinction is only rarely possible.[8]

The difference seems to lie mainly in the function which doodling
has in the lives of untrained normal and abnormal individuals. While
doodles may occupy a significant part in the life of the mentally ill, they
are incidental products of the normal. Occasional observations of untrained normal individuals, as well as self-observations, suggest that
doodling tends to occur while one is either "unoccupied" or in a state
of distracted attention, i.e., when the ego is fully occupied with something else. At first one is frequently aware of a certain purposive idea,
an "intention to draw," which may refer to any geometrical or decorative design. In some instances, one may "intend" to reproduce some
object in the environment; in others, there is no such intention. In the
course of doodling this intention gets lost. The drawing hand "creates"
autonomously; lines or steps "suggest" subsequent ones.[9] Clinical observa-

---

[8] What one might call a "graphological" difference is sometimes apparent. Prinzhorn mentions as special characteristics of psychotic doodles the "disturbed" sense of
rhythm "which in extreme cases can be lost entirely." Other characteristics can be
detected in a quantitative exaggeration of elements present also in doodles of normals.
These impressions (reported in 1936) have been confirmed by the investigation of an
unselected sample of doodles by Maclay, Guttmann, and Meyer-Gross (1939); see also
Arundel (1937). For another clinical approach to doodling see Auerbach (1950).

[9] For a detailed discussion see Maclay, Guttmann, and Meyer-Gross (1938). In this
respect, the process of doodling seems to be similar to the conditions attending production by the skilled. One of Pfeifer's (1923) subjects, for instance, reports: "The idea
is mine, but once I start drawing, it is the skilled hand that functions and thinks for
me." This description reminds us of some self-observations by artists during creation.

tions suggest that doodling has a frequent if not regular dynamic function for the normal: Fantasies and thoughts hidden in doodles are those of which the doodler wants to liberate himself, lest they disturb the process of concentration.[10] While there are cases in which the function of doodling is similar for psychotics, in many, and probably in most, instances its function is quite different. The doodle tends to be taken "seriously"; it may become a highly invested product.

The far-reaching visual resemblances between the doodles of untrained normals and those of psychotics suggest comparison of other products of their representational rendering. But at this point we meet with deficiencies in the available data. Comparisons to which the literature refers tend to be based on heterogeneous material[11] or on reasoning by analogy. The products of untrained adults tend to be compared with those of children or with primitive and folk art. Conclusions based on such comparisons must be viewed with reservations.[12] Our own approach starts from the consideration that in Western culture representational skills are limited (and were limited during all periods investigated by historians) to a segment of the population.[13] We are accustomed to distinguish between talented and untalented individuals, a distinction which will become meaningful in a psychological sense only when the various ontogenetic factors which contribute to the development of talent or its inhibition will have been investigated in greater detail. By and large, individuals in our culture tend not to be particularly concerned

---

A discussion of the differences between the psychic processes of the doodler and those of the artist would have to focus on the ego's involvement in the working through of emerging images and ideas. If we compare various observations—among them also analytic experiences—doodling comes extraordinarily close to "preconscious fantasy thinking" (Varendonck, 1921) from which it differs, however, in so far as only visual images are involved. The "archaic pictorial thought processes" have asserted themselves and the content of thoughts is transformed into visual material as in Silberer's description of hypnagogic phenomena (see Rapaport, 1951).

10 See Pfister (1913 a and b) and the example discussed here p. 307. For clinical illustrations see also Erickson and Kubie (1938), particularly the first two drawings of their patient.

11 Prinzhorn's book on the art product of prisoners (1924) has supplied material which for obvious reasons cannot be used as basis of further deductions. Anastasi and Foley (1944), in a paper from which we quoted above, do not deal with spontaneous products. Impressions derived from their findings would suggest that the difference in the formal expression of untrained normal and psychotic subjects should not be overrated.

12 Michailov (1935) distinguishes between lay and folk art (in contradistinction to folk art, "the independent product of a lay person . . . is in a certain sense always an unconditional new creation") without contributing anything toward a more circumscript clarification of concepts.

13 For an example concerning the Renaissance see p. 198.

about the absence of the ability to "express themselves" in representational art. The untrained adult does not as a rule become "artistically productive," and when he desires to do so—when he suddenly feels the wish or even urge to draw, to paint, or to whittle—he does not remain untrained. He learns and practices, his skill increases, his "form niveau" changes and expands. While it is thus erroneous to say that the mobilizing by the psychotic of atrophied or undeveloped functions for purposes of creation is in itself pathological, the pathology reveals itself by the fact that though the productions of the psychotic tend to be prolific, the level of his skill remains essentially unchanged.

Prinzhorn attempted in several instances to trace a developmental sequence in the creations of his "schizophrenic masters." His arguments, however, are not convincing. I can see variations of style but not a "development," by which I understand a change (continuous or diffluent) in the actual accomplishment, which can be regarded as a meaningful sequence of attempts at problem solutions. I believe that "development of style" presupposes intactness of ego functions—or, more precisely, a certain degree of intactness. This, then, is the reason why comparisons between single products by untrained normals and untrained psychotics, however instructive, usually leave us dissatisfied. It is not the single work but the meaning of production which seems to supply the important clues. As a consequence, psychodiagnostic impressions based on isolated products of representational art remain in many instances unreliable.[14]

14 One may raise the question how far this is true also of written communication and tend to argue that, if a psychotic blacksmith or carpenter fills hundreds of pages with poems, essays, and theological treatises, he behaves in no way different from the psychotic painter or sculptor. But even one example of his literary productions will frequently justify a diagnosis. We here touch upon the simple and yet highly important structural difference between media of communication. The level of command of language of any individual can be assessed approximately; his prepsychotic "drawing level" cannot in most instances be ascertained. Everybody talks, but not everybody draws. Our attitude toward language and toward pictorial representation reflects this difference. We are infinitely more aware of "correct" speech than of "correct" drawing, and the question as to the standards of correctness in drawing is meaningful only in rare and specific cases (for instance, in technical illustrations). Any kind of pictorial representation tends to gain an "aesthetic" significance for us. Though this phenomenon is subject to considerable cultural variations, it nevertheless is widespread. While the structure of human language has been the subject of many and searching investigations, summarized and expanded of late by K. Bühler (1934), a comparable investigation of the structure of representational art has not been undertaken for more than a century. See here Chapter 7 and Cameron (1938 a, b). A word need also be said about a recent remark of Read's on this subject (1951 b). He writes: "I do not know whether it has ever been put forward by scientists, but it seems to me very likely that the human race, like the child of historical times could draw before it could speak." This suggestion can only make sense if in the child of historical times, speaking is equated with the capacity to vocalize and drawing with rudimentary scribbling—and

We may now approach the question of the dynamic significance of the creative urge or spell in the schizophrenic, which leads to the mobilization of previously untrained or neglected modes of expression.

Psychoanalytic experience suggests that we view this spell as part and symptom of the attempt at restitution. This limits the validity of our explanation: It refers mainly, if not exclusively, to the psychodynamics of schizophrenia.[15]

The disturbance of psychic economy, pathognomonic of the schizophrenic process, concerns the relationship of the ego to the environment, to reality. In Freud's view, this relationship is loosened or impoverished, cathexis of the world around is diminished, and in extreme conditions disregard of and indifference to reality become supreme. During the phases preceding this final stage, the loosening of the relation to the world around is counteracted and covered by vehement attempts to recathect objects outside. We are inclined to view the increase of productivity as an attempt of this kind. The manifestation of attempts at restitution in schizophrenic creativeness are manifold; they may lead to the predominance of geometrical scribblings in which, as it were, only the essence but not the life of the object world can be reached or— particularly during initial stages of the process—to moving and grandiose expressions in which the feeling of the loosening contact inspires powerful images previously not attained by the creator; such is, for instance, the case in the late poems of Hoelderlin, whose greatest achievements we owe to defense against the threat of schizophrenic detachment.[16] Parallel phenomena with normals are well known. Anna Freud (1936)

---

even then one will be inclined to wonder as to the exact chronological relationship of both capacities. The idea that in philogeny the "language of words" should have been preceded by the "language of images" would indeed require a very specific redefinition of terms and reorganization of our ideas of developmental processes.

[15] The term restitution was introduced by Freud (1911 b, p. 463) in his analysis of Schreber's autobiography; the English translation, however, uses the term "attempt at recovery" and speaks of "an endeavour to bring libido back again onto its objects." For the development of the idea of restitution see Fenichel (1946). For a closer analysis of some phenomena see Katan (1940). Recently the concept of restitution has frequently been considered as identical with "reparation." The schizophrenic, it is assumed, has destroyed the world around him and his delusional system is intended to reconstruct it; see pp. 116f., 167ff.

[16] See Jaspers (1926) who proposes a line of investigation which seems to, but actually does not, lead into the direction we shall subsequently pursue. ("It is a fruitless approach to apply rough psychiatric categories to Hoelderlin's poetry. Certain characteristics of his poetry, however, might elucidate the nature of schizophrenia, though only of a special type within the extensive area of this disease, and permit a descriptive delineation of the concept of schizophrenia.") A similar interpretation can be applied to the work of the English poet John Clare; see Nicholes (1950).

has discussed in what sense the behavior of adolescents can be compared to that of schizophrenics during the process of restitution. We may add here that the adolescent, too, tends to use heightened productivity—in many instances artistic productivity—as a defense against threatening upheaval.[17]

III. THE CHANGE OF STYLE IN THE WORK OF PSYCHOTIC ARTISTS

The suggestion of viewing the creative spell of psychotics as part of an attempt at restitution determines our next question. According to general experience, detailed investigation reveals that activities undertaken for the sake of restitution have recognizable characteristics. We detect them by their difference from previous behavior. We may expect to be able to observe a change of style. However, since in the instances to which we have referred up to this point the productive activity was initiated with the onset of, or during, the psychotic process, we have to turn to another area: to cases where trained creators use their skill in the service of restitution.

In attempting to discuss changes which psychotic processes produce in creative artists, we are faced with a difficult task. In schematic outline four possible types of outcome may be distinguished:[18] First: the artistic ability remains unimpaired and no relevant changes occur; the creative activity is then not part of the psychotic process.[19] Second: The artistic activity is interrupted and—without noticeable change—resumed after the patient's improvement.[20] In both the remaining types, changes in the artist's work occur which are connected with the psychotic process. The difference between them lies in the nature of the change. In the third type, the disorder manifests itself in a change of style, but even though the style has changed, the connections with the artistic tendencies of the individual and his environment are preserved. Viewing the total work of the artist, we may still speak of its intactness. According to general

17 For different motivations and further discussion of the creative spell in psychotics see Chapters 4 and 5.

18 For a different enumeration see Weygandt (1925) who, for instance, looks at Van Gogh as a case of "deterioration of technical abilities."

19 Prinzhorn has pointed out that certain types of representations may remain outside the orbit of the psychotic process; for instance, certain psychotic artists continue to draw still life, animal pictures, or landscapes, in the traditional manner, while their free compositions show psychotic configurations.

20 M. Eitingon has informed me in some detail about one remarkable case of this kind. A patient of his resumed, after a severe schizophrenic episode, work on a sculpture which he had started before the onset of illness, on the very place where he had relinquished it.

opinion, van Gogh would be a case in point;[21] another similar case, that of the sculptor Messerschmidt, is discussed in one of the following essays.[22] Only one group of his sculptures is connected with his delusional system. The change of style, however, which manifests itself in these productions is consistent with the contemporary artistic trends. In the fourth type of outcome the change of style can be explained only on the basis of the psychotic process.

To suit our purposes, diagnosis as well as change of style must be clearly established. I shall, therefore, limit myself to a discussion of two cases which meet these requirements.[23]

The first patient, a decorator and painter, was described by Pfeifer (1923) and Weygandt (1925). Immediately before the onset of the disease, she illustrated fairy tales. One of these illustrations is reproduced here (Fig. 1) as characteristic of the patient's prepsychotic style. One detail deserves our attention. A snake can be seen in the basket beside the girl. This snake had escaped the attention of all observers and was noticed only when the patient herself, confronted with this drawing, pointed it out.[24] In the patient's delusions, the snake was an anxiety-inspiring animal which, as it were, had sneaked into the drawing without disturbing its meaning. The ego had been victorious in front of an isolated delusional element. The drawings made during the course of illness are very different indeed. One might be inclined to view Figure 2 as a page out of a sketchbook. But this is certainly not the case; nothing is being sketched, prepared, or practiced. Every element has a special and definite significance: the star at the corner of the mouth, the plant on top of the hat, the heads in the upper corner. But we are ignorant of what the significance is. It is a picture riddle, the key to which remains unknown to us.[25]

21 See Westerman-Holstijn (1924), Jaspers (1926), Minkowska (1937), and more recently Kraus (1941). For a different psychiatric diagnosis see Evenson (1926).

22 See Chapter 4.

23 Among artists whose work invites further inquiry I mention Frederic Hill, a Swedish contemporary of Josephson (see Hodin, 1949), the English painter, Richard Dudd (1817-1886) who was for many years committed to institutional care (see Binyon, 1937), the enigmatic French engraver Charles Meryon (1821-1866) or William Blake (for some comments see Born, 1946). In each of these cases, however, the available data would have to be enlarged in order to make comments profitable.

24 Weygandt, though, informs us that this was not the case: "We are rather dealing with an embellishment or decoration, as the patient herself assured us." I believe the distinct outlines of a snake can be seen; it seems that the patient interpreted the same form in two different ways.

25 How to interpret such "riddles" has been repeatedly demonstrated in cases in which schizophrenics in therapy were encouraged to draw and then to comment on

The second case is that of the Swedish painter Ernst Josephson (1851-1906), a complex and fascinating artist. At the age of thirty-seven, in 1888, he developed a psychosis, during the course of which he continued to draw and—at certain times—to paint. In his youth he had been the organizer and leader of the younger generation of Swedish artists, the leader in the attack on the Academy of Stockholm. In the early eighties he received general recognition also in Paris. Shortly thereafter, under the impact of repeated disappointments, a delusional state developed.

It is difficult to convey an impression of his manifold interests and abilities. He was active as a poet and interested in spiritualism. Both poetic creations and the concern with the supernatural are interwoven with his delusions. In letters published in the comprehensive biography by Wahlin (1911) one notices the gradual approach of the schizophrenic breakdown: The world is full of darkness. "One has to struggle to catch a glimpse of light" (1887). Before the full development of the psychotic condition there seems to have been a period in which by increased realism of style he was attempting to resist the onslaught of regression. When the delusion developed, he abandoned oil painting, at least for a period. During the height of his illness, most of his work was contour drawings. Some represent themes familiar from his past; others, however, are part of his delusional system, which brought him in touch with the world of spirits. After he rejected spiritualism, he believed that his room was St. Peter's abode and that everybody admitted to heaven had to use him as an intermediary. He interviewed the applicant souls, drew their pictures, had the power to forgive their sins, and admitted them into the presence of God. These delusional drawings were always executed in seven outlining strokes, such magic ceremonials being linked to Swedenborg, the great Swedish medium and mystic (1688-1772) whose name appears on the corner of the drawings.[26] Conversations with applicants were recorded, and the discussion of their sins played a considerable part. Those received in heaven occasionally returned to express their gratitude. In heaven Josephson was praised as the highest spirit after God, as the elementary force of the universe; there were no limits to his power.

The style of his drawings from the acute phase of the delusion is of utter simplicity: There is no expression; there are only a few lines.

---

their productions. Naumburg (1951) in her richly illustrated and fully documented report made the most consistent attempt of this kind.

[26] On Swedenborg see Hitschmann (1913).

During the long course of his illness—he died in 1906—and presumably during periods of partial remission, he occasionally resumed oil painting and drew some of the subjects in which he had excelled before. It seems that the simplification of graphic expression did not disappear. We cannot attempt to render a fuller account of this development here, nor can we relate individual features of his drawings to the dynamics directing his delusions. It is, however, significant that studies of the nude which he drew later in his life not only show a simplification of presentation but also a definite androgyne character. It must be left to those who will—we hope it is soon—present a psychoanalytically well-founded investigation of Josephson's development to inquire into the details of this truly fascinating case.[27]

In the present context we have to limit ourselves to a confrontation which, though it unduly simplifies an intricate life history, may prove illuminating.

A picture which he painted in numerous variations may be considered as representative of Josephson's prepsychotic style (Fig. 3). It has a definite place in the history of art, following certain artistic conceptions prevalent in the eighteen eighties. We contrast it with a drawing made during the initial phases of the illness (Fig. 4), confining ourselves to enumerating some of the striking features of the line drawing. Much skill has been lost, the structure is rigid and disconnected, and much remains obscure. Who knows the meaning of the "skein-like" slings which David holds in his hands and which are connected with his mouth by threads? We do not point to other "unintelligible" elements but turn our attention to one detail only, to Goliath's countenance. It shows three eyes: The middle one may be regarded as the forehead eye of giants (recalling, in the figure of Polyphemus, how widespread this notion is). But the other two eyes also show peculiarities; one of them is closed. We might conjecture that various thoughts have been combined here. According to the Bible, David's stone penetrated Goliath's forehead; since this account has always carried the connotation that the stone entered through the eye, the ideas of blinding and of killing the giant may have been fused. Hence, one eye might be closed because three would be "too many." At the same time, a future event, David's victory, might thereby be indicated. Similar guesses obviously are not only vague,

27 There is an ever-growing literature on Josephson with which I am only to a very small extent familiar. I have to thank Dr. T. Vangaard for help in translating passages which seem particularly important. For a psychiatric appreciation, see B. Gadelius (1922, III, p. 153); for that of the art critics see now a set of papers by Jacobsson (1946). For a short biography without reference to source material see Millner (1948).

but they cannot even aim at understanding what was "intended." We recognize once more how little we are capable of entering the world of the insane on the basis of his artistic product.

In both cases the change of style confronts us with a regression, or, more precisely, with an alteration which, biologically speaking, may be called a loss of functions. This is illustrated by two characteristics. First, the configurations have become "unintelligible." Instead of a representation which is accessible to us, we find a fusion and combination of various divergent elements which are of a distinctly symbolic nature, but the logic of their fusion escapes our comprehension. The star at the corner of the mouth of Figure 2 or Goliath's three eyes (Fig. 4) may be cited as examples. The second striking characteristic is that everything pertaining to the representation of the human figure is particularly rigid and stiff, impressing us as unnatural and artificial.

We are aware of the fact that these remarks do not exhaust the problems suggested by the material. All we have intended was to point to some aspects of the change of style in psychotic artists, aspects which establish a similarity between their work and that of untrained psychotic creators.[28]

IV. The Primary Process in Psychotic Art

A patient of Bertschinger's (1911) made the following comment on two of her drawings: The ram (Fig. 5 a) represents man's mentality of which it is a part; the two men are young lovers. We understand that in this case the ram serves as a symbol of masculinity; it has the same phallic connotation as the snake which one of the men holds up. We learn from the patient's case history that the sight of a ram's erected genital made a deep impression on her in her youth; significant events of a sadistic nature which she experienced later in her life were related to a man whose features and beard she again connected with the ram. The patient commented on the second drawing (Fig. 5 b) by saying that it was a man who wanted to subdue "the pig in himself" but actually was a beast.

These drawings may be looked upon as illustrations of hysterical fantasies; the patient's comments enable us to understand their meaning. This understanding corresponds to our understanding of a dream if it is accompanied by associations. The drawings give evidence of the working of the primary process; i.e., the processes operating in the id. We are familiar with the primary process mainly from the part it plays

[28] For the purpose of further documentation see a third case, pp. 118-127.

in dreams, in which the residue of infantile, preverbal thought processes survives. But the work of the primary process is not confined to dreams; it can be found in numerous pathological conditions and in many phenomena on the border of normalcy. Their common characteristic seems to be that the ego suffers a temporary or permanent loss of some of its functions. Attempting to describe the ego's position relating to the primary process, we may say that the ego is constantly "occupied" with warding it off; a special expenditure of energy is required to prevent a sliding back to the mechanisms of the primary process (Foulkes, 1936). The various mechanisms of the primary process do not contribute in an equal measure to the phenomena to be described in what follows. We shall find relatively little use of displacement, the effects of which become comprehensible only when content interpretations are directed at finding the affect and its utilization. On the other hand, we shall frequently encounter condensation and the use of symbols in manifold variations.

The drawings of Figure 5 illustrate clearly how the mechanisms of the primary process—namely, condensation and symbolization—operate. But these drawings are distinctly different from typical schizophrenic creations. A few examples from Prinzhorn's material will characterize their peculiar qualities, at least from one viewpoint. Figure 6[29] shows a composition which the patient, a mechanic, called "Anti-Christ." He further remarked that it represented how "St. Thomas, God's spirit in the figure of the false prophet, standing upon a cloud, proclaimed to the Redeemer the last judgment condemning sinful mankind." In spite of these explanations many features remain unintelligible. We do not know, for example, why the cloud, on which the figure stands, has the shape of a head. Some other parts of the drawing become clearer, however, in the light of the patient's additional remarks: "I have called this spirit Thomas, The Spirit of Disbelief, because his figure resembles a 'T' which is made up of three commas; the head is made up of a 42 cm shell[30] which turns into a Papal tiara and finally into a magnificent pile of straw." We thus learn that certain forms have a double significance: The head is a tiara and a shell. It is more difficult to say "where" the pile of straw is; perhaps the lower part of the body might be seen as a bundle of sheaves.

This phenomenon calls for a psychological explanation which we can best find by turning again to the language of the dream. In dreams words

[29] Prinzhorn, Fig. 121; the patient who drew this picture had had a high-school education.

[30] The biggest German shell used during the First World War.

and objects are frequently interchangeable; clang associations replace object associations; that is, the double meaning of words is used in the dream like the double meaning of shapes in drawings. Analogous phenomena are not too rare: They occur whenever the primary process breaks through. This phenomenon is best known in the speech of schizophrenics, i.e., in verbal attempts at restitution. Freud gave an extensive description of how the schizophrenic, attempting to reëstablish the impoverished relationship to the external world, to regain the "lost" object, does not reach the objects and their characteristics but fails on his way to them. He apprehends only the word but treats it like an object; the "word representation" replaces, according to Freud, the "object representation"[31] and is itself subjected to the elaborations of the primary process.

This explanation of puns and of the use of words in schizophrenic verbigerations can be applied to many features of the schizophrenic processes in representational creations. A further example illustrates this point: Figure 7[32] was drawn by the patient who drew Figure 6. He gave such a plastic description of how the drawing originated that the fusion of forms, their successive joining, seems almost to unroll in front of our eyes: "At first the cobra stood in the air, iridescent, motley and blue. And then came the leg. [It is seen parallel to the snake.] And then the other leg was added. [At the extreme right one can still see the toes. The description leads back to the left corner.] The second leg was formed out of a root. [He associates with this: *Rübezahl*,[33] repentance pays. The description continues in the right corner.] On this second leg the face of my father-in-law appeared. [I abbreviate the next part of the description which pertains to the horizontal part of the snake's body.] Then it came out as a tree. The back of the tree was broken off in front so that the hole formed the mouth of the face. [What follows pertains to those parts of the head which resemble Indian feather decorations.] The hair formed the branches of the tree. . . . Between the leg and foot there then appeared a female genital which broke off the man's foot; that is, sin comes from the woman and brings about man's ruin.—One of the feet plants itself firmly against heaven: this means the fall into hell."

Further remarks pertain to other parts of the drawing; e.g., to the central figure of the shepherd; they do not contain any new elements. It is not our intention to explain in detail the secret meaning of the

---

31 I no longer feel that this part of Freud's theory is fruitfully formulated.

32 Prinzhorn, Fig. 123.

33 *Rübezahl*, a giant of German folklore and fairy tales. (*Rübe*=beet, root, *Zahl*=pay.)

content or of the symbolism, the extensive use of which can hardly be overlooked even in these abbreviated excerpts. We are concerned with the significance of the multiple meaning of shapes. The patient's own account permits us to follow their playful fusing. Objects change their meaning; a certain external similarity forms the bridge on which images are joined together.[34]

We may conclude that the play on words and the play on shapes are analogous phenomena, special manifestations within the verbal and graphic expression of schizophrenics. The analogy is more extensive and complex than can be shown here. In both phenomena we find similar attitudes to the existing conventions. As unintelligible as the language of schizophrenics may be, it nevertheless often preserves, and frequently to a very high degree, syntactical correctness. Similar conditions prevail in the drawings of schizophrenics: Certain formal conventions are adhered to. The drawings we have discussed seem to have preserved such general conventions—at least as far as certain structural and formal elements are concerned.

In what follows we shall not continue to elaborate on these considerations but rather pursue our main reflections. In what way can psychoanalytic insight improve our understanding of the psychological significance of the phenomena here described? It will be advisable to begin by comparing the creations of psychotics with those achievements of normals which despite external similarities illustrate fundamental differences.

One of Prinzhorn's patients offers us two typical illustrations. One drawing (Fig. 8) [35] represents a combination of six heads, a special kind of contamination. Some lines have a definite "double significance"; they simultaneously belong to different heads; viz., the heads of the lower left corner have the neckline in common.[36]

[34] The patient's commentary suggests special problems. One gains the impression that he does not feel fully responsible for the drawing, views it as if it had come into being by itself. He says, "Then it came out as a tree," "then appeared" or "there stood." Two tentative explanations can be offered which are not mutually exclusive but, under certain conditions, complementary. The patient chooses the intransitive expression because hallucinatory experiences are involved. According to the other, his description coincides with what we may call the preconscious mental processes during productive activity. This phenomenon is by no means confined to pathology; it has been mentioned as one of the conditions under which the scribblings of those who are otherwise preoccupied arise. Analogous phenomena occur during artistic creation. See Chapters 13 and 14.

[35] Prinzhorn, Fig. 103. The patient, a traveling wine salesman, had completed high school. Play on shapes, as shown in Figures 8 and 9, is characteristic of his graphic productions.

[36] In an analysis of more than 1200 drawings by some 180 patients in American

A head drawn by the same patient (Fig. 9) [37] shows a stern profile on the right while the area inside is covered with heads placed in rows next to each other, of finger joints linked with each other in chainlike formations, ending on one side in a sort of worm mouth.

In contrast to these drawings, the cameo (Fig. 10) shows a fusion of four heads: a satyr mask on the left, a female profile on the right, a bearded God on top, and a ram at the bottom. This eighteenth-century cameo, a typical example of its kind, is a faithful copy of a Roman gem. Such cameos and gems were known as *gryllus* in Roman art. Nothing is known about any special significance of their theme or content; they are regarded as pure play on shapes, as comic productions. (A connotation became attached to their name: In the Renaissance certain particularly odd and comical inventions were called "gryllic.") Historically the roots of the *grylli* reach far back. They have recently been thought to lie in old-Persian and Iranian art. However, it is permissible to assume that when the heads of a God and a ram were combined in ancient days, this graphic fusion depicted a genuine identity; namely, the thought that animal and God were one being.[38] It cannot be said, however, that the cameo reproduced here is based on such an idea of magical identity. Here the pleasure in playing dominates. This play on shapes has with few changes survived for centuries; it has been widely practiced since the seventeenth century, generally occurring in a definite context, i.e., in satirical portraits. In this case, the play on shapes serves the function of unmasking. A famous example among many similar ones is a portrait of Napoleon which was popular in Germany at the end of the war of liberation (Fig. 11). It shows the Prussian eagle as the Emperor's hat; on his shoulder, as an epaulet, the hand of God tears the spider's web which is, in the play on shapes, substituted for the

---

mental institutions, Anastasi and Foley (1943) found a small number of individual peculiarities among which they note "the overlapping function of lines, the same line serving a multiple function as a part of more than one object, sometimes producing 'chain drawings'; overlapping figures, the same space being used indiscriminately for several objects." The psychotic medieval cleric whose case is discussed on p. 118 used a similar device, which according to the judgment of the historians did not conform to contemporary usage. We might therefore be tempted to assume that we have here a definite formal characteristic of psychotic art, an easily recognizable hallmark. However, once more caution must be exercised. In the material of doodles sent in by the public to a newspaper competition, Maclay, Guttmann, and Meyer-Gross (1938) found a relevant percentage of doodles using what they call "mixture," i.e., "one line may belong to two groups and have a different meaning in each." As far as I can see, the principle is never carried as far as in the psychotic products here discussed.

[37] Prinzhorn, Fig. 110.

[38] See Roos (1935).

grand cross of the legion of honor. Although these elements certainly constitute a satirical counterpart to traditional allegorical pictures, the intent to unmask becomes nevertheless fully evident if we look at Napoleon's features: they are formed of human bodies writhing in despair. Hence the message is: "This is what the great Emperor actually is, a butcher of men."

How are we to interpret this use of condensation, which we know as a mechanism of the primary process? It is obvious that, in view of the very clear and conscious intention, we cannot say that the ego has been overwhelmed by the primary process. On the contrary, the primary process has been put into the service of the ego; the ego has utilized it.

Analogous conditions prevail as far as wit is concerned. According to Freud, wit arises when the person who invents, or thinks of, a joke permits a preconscious idea momentarily to be elaborated by the unconscious. In other words, the ego momentarily abandons its prerogatives: It can be considered a sign of the ego's strength if, occasionally and for a specific purpose, it is capable of tolerating the mechanisms of the id. But in the case of schizophrenic verbigerations and schizophrenic drawings, we meet with different conditions: The ego slips away from the processes of secondary elaboration and reality testing and indulges in plays on words and shapes.[39] It is a well-known and frequently discussed fact that the communications of schizophrenics are occasionally witty. The same may be said of their representational art. That both phenomena do not occur frequently does not detract from their significance.[40]

As illustrations I select two wood carvings of a schizophrenic (Figs. 12 and 13) [41] whose works were treated with careful deliberation in Prinzhorn's book. The patient called the first one Hindenburg. The figure can be viewed as a caricature: We see a corpulent bugbear, his hands folded idly over his stomach, the military element suggested merely by a coat of mail covering the lower parts of the body; there are enormous ears and a flattened nose. But it is better merely to indicate these elements and thus to supply "a guide" for looking at the figure. Those who follow the guide will easily perceive the element of "caricature."[42] If we

[39] See also Chapter 7.

[40] These analogies may be further extended. Like wit and caricature, puzzle and picture puzzle can be related to each other. For picture puzzles see Bradley and Meyerson (1937).

[41] Prinzhorn, Figs. 97 and 98.

[42] I have often tried to present a photograph of this wood carving as a caricature. Some subjects will immediately—one is tempted to say, with heightened rapidity—

change our attitude and look at the wood carving in a different way, we see it as what it was intended to be: an idol. Made during the First World War, it represents the power and glory of the marshal. The fantastic head decoration is meant to be a crown "which he wears in case Wilhelm should abdicate one of these days"; the neck ruff and the folded hands represent Hindenburg as a spiritual father; thus he prays— as a clergyman—with his soldiers. The enormous size of the ears also has a special reason: It signifies that Hindenburg learns of everything. Hence, the wood carving is, in the opinion of its maker, permeated with magic meanings, and rooted in magic thinking.

Whereas the possibility of looking at the wood carving of Hindenburg in two different ways is not accessible to everyone—that is, the element of caricature as potential effect is not always evident—the second wood carving by the same patient (Fig. 13) meets our requirements far better. According to the patient, this figure represents Wilhelm I and Wilhelm II at the same time, combining the beards of both Prussian rulers. It is also known as "Herr Lehmann from Berlin"—a designation which probably has been given to the figure by the people in the institution, who thereby seem to have grasped what surely is our own first impression: the persiflage of a certain, militaristic Prussian type, e.g., the small man, whose mentality culminates in adopting the Kaiser's mustache, and whose bared teeth permit a glimpse of that brutality which breaks through in full force when the civilian appears in the garb of a drill sergeant.

These examples suggest a generalization: Configurations which bear the imprint of the primary process tend to be ambiguous, allowing for more than one interpretation. The play on words in the language of the schizophrenic may have a comic effect; similarly, his pictorial representation may impress as cartoon or caricature.[43]

The mechanisms of the primary process endow productions of the individual—different from each other according to their position in

perceive it as such. Others more or less fail to do so. Individual differences in the understanding of plays on shapes are apparently as great as in the ability to respond to plays on words.

43 For a distinction of cartoon and caricature see pp. 173ff., and Chapter 7.

Other productions of our sculptor could not be viewed in such different ways. The conditions under which the double interpretation is still, and those under which it is no longer, suggested, can be described in terms of the formula which Freud (and Reik, 1929) gave for the joke: The distortion of the preconscious content through the elaboration by the id must not go beyond the point at which the content ceases to be intelligible. The person who listens to the joke must be able "still" to understand it, i.e., to retranslate it.

psychic economy—with a common element; it unifies their façade. We are faced with a principle common to many creative processes, a principle which becomes particularly important in "primitive" modes of expression. It seems that we may find here one of the rare accesses leading from psychoanalysis to the discussion of form as contrasted to content: It is a contrast which we tend to minimize; even the formal characteristics tend to lead the psychoanalyst into content.[44] In the present context, however, the coincident traits are not in the focus of our discussion. We propose to stress differences. We are not concerned with demonstrating the effects of the primary process per se but with showing that the primary process can be effective within different psychic structures. The gross antithesis of the primary process in the service of the ego (in the case of the joke and caricature) and the primary process which incapacitates the ego (the reaction of the weakened ego in dreams and psychoses) serves to demonstrate the similarities and differences in the play on shapes of normals and abnormals. Following the tradition of similar deliberations, one might be tempted now to enter into a discussion of the art products of children and primitives. The far-reaching similarities can hardly be overlooked. But in certain phases of the development of a science the concern with differences is more meaningful than with similarities. It may then be our duty to determine the extent of both difference and similarity in order to comprehend the specificity of the phenomenon under investigation.

These considerations touch upon a crucial and recently much-discussed problem of developmental psychology,[45] a problem which hinges upon the concept of regression. It has been rightly said that the sick adult is neither a primitive nor a child, despite all "point-by-point" similarities. I see no contradiction between this view and psychoanalysis. Freud succeeded in demonstrating common elements in the psychic life of children, neurotics, psychotics, and primitives. His findings and the subsequent inquiries of a generation of psychoanalysts were mainly concerned with one issue: They attempted to discover the secrets of the unconscious, to fathom the id in its onto- and phylogenetic nexus. Hence, the search for the common elements predominated. Today, however, a different vantage point suggests new interests. Whereas the com-

44 Bühler (1927) has characterized psychoanalysis as content-bound. (For a recent reiteration, see Read, 1951 a.) Without contradicting this statement we may say that ego psychology tends to suggest a number of points where problems of formal elaboration become accessible. See also pp. 142f., 168, and 238. For the translation of form into content see lately particularly Lewin (1949).

45 See for instance Meyer-Gross and Lipps (1929/1930), Lips (1937) and Werner (1933).

mon elements relate to the id, we might say that the differences are determined by the ego.

This then is the reason why the systematic investigation of structural problems has gained decisive importance in psychoanalysis. We are bound to inquire into the position which any given phenomenon holds within the individual's psychic structure, for example, into the role of the primary process in the creations of children and primitives.[46]

One has hardly to search for a theoretical model for such structural inquiries; it is offered by Freud's theory of anxiety as developed in *Inhibition, Symptom and Anxiety*. Freud's procedure is exemplary, and every psychoanalyst is familiar with some of its applications: Psychoanalytic technique itself rests on this foundation.

V. The Rendering of the Human Countenance in Psychotic Art

We have up to this point only occasionally pointed to formal characteristics of the art of the psychotic.

That such characteristics exist can hardly be doubted,[47] however difficult it may be to draw a clear line of demarcation between "abnormal and normal" features in any given case. The decision is facilitated when the phenomenon as such is viewed in general terms. We considered the psychotic's urge to create as part of the disease process, or more precisely, as an attempt at restitution within this process, and further endeavored to point out certain characteristics which seemed to be determined by this factor. No doubt, this attempt has not substantially

---

[46] We need not stress again that even such an investigation would no more lead to an "explanation" of "the art" of "the child or the primitive" than we can in the present essay "explain the art of the insane." In all similar instances we can only aim at clarifying certain issues.

A word may be said on the evolutionist approach to the problem of "thinking in images" in its relation to representational skills. The most consequent theory in this area has been developed by Kretschmer (1930) who bases his considerations on Wundt's theory of agglutination—a theory which has for some time been discarded in the area of language—and who describes the laws of image agglutination. Although his description' is in full accord with the psychoanalytic concept of the primary process, his theory, stimulating and challenging in certain details, seems not particularly fruitful. One can scarcely escape the impression that the infinite variety of phenomena cannot appropriately be elucidated in terms of a smooth and orderly sequence of evolution, without indication of what is considered "primitive" in a given context. This theory, then, can as little do justice to the phenomenon of paleolithic cave drawings, as the theory can be brought into a connection with the fascinating comparisons which Snijder (1934) made (on the basis of Bouman's investigations), between the artistic creations of an eidetic, mentally deficient child and works of Mycenaean art.

[47] For a discussion see Prinzhorn (1922), Anastasi and Foley (1944); see also above, pp. 89ff.

advanced our knowledge; a more complete investigation should succeed in defining individual peculiarities of psychotic creations which are characteristic only of them and hence may be regarded as pathognomonic. These characteristics are, after all, an aspect of a larger, and more general, clinical problem, i.e., the disturbance of expression in schizophrenia. The stereotypies, for instance, which occur so frequently in drawings by psychotics, cannot be understood unless the role of stereotypy in the behavior of schizophrenics is evaluated; the *horror vacui,* which likewise is characteristic of many drawings of schizophrenics, is so typical of their entire graphological expression that its manifestations must be examined in all areas.

In the following we turn to one group of formal characteristics suggested by the material here discussed. If one thumbs through a collection of psychotic art productions—regardless of whether it is a rather recent collection, such as Prinzhorn's or Pfeiffer's, or an older one, such as Mohr's—one is struck by the rigidity and stiffness with which the human figure is rendered. One might be inclined to attribute these qualities to the patient's lack of skill and practice and, hence, to disregard this characteristic. But this view can hardly be maintained if we recall the changes of style that occurred during psychosis in some of the "skilled" psychotics. Comparing two drawings of a designer (Figs. 1 and 2), we can determine the extent of the change that has occurred in the representation of the human figure. A similar change was apparent in Josephson's portraits (Figs. 3 and 4). In order to achieve useful results, it is necessary to adapt our question to the material at our disposal. In what follows, we shall therefore confine ourselves to discussing the disturbances in the representation of the human countenance.

Before formulating a more general observation, we compare three further drawings by Josephson. The first (Fig. 14) represents Adam's creation. The enormous head of God appears to be man's vision. There is no doubt that, however apparent to the psychiatrically trained the characteristics of a schizophrenic expression are in this drawing—clearest perhaps in the symbolic substitution of the flower for the genitalia—an artist speaks to us. We can here refer to what was said above: The intact part of the personality reaches us in spite of the pathological process, and, possibly because we react to the ambiguities of the disjuncted expression,[48] he reaches us even more forcefully. In examining the drawing more closely, our attention is attracted by certain details. The effect is largely due to the eyes of God; one may be inclined to see in the way they

[48] This thought is further developed in Chapter 10.

are drawn some reflection of the symbolism of radiant suns.[49] But we also detect that mouth and facial muscles are strangely distorted, as if the whirl of emotions, conveyed by the lines which form the face, had actually disrupted the facial expression; however, the theme of the drawing, the vision it depicts, may be said to justify such representational means.

The second drawing evokes a different response (Fig. 15). The beauty of lines is striking; it prepares for stylistic tendencies which several decades later are being resumed, particularly in France. Josephson seems to have anticipated these developments in the flow of his lines; this at least is the view of art critics and art historians.[50] Such anticipation can hardly be explained unless we assume once more that with the intact part of the personality he was able to find solutions which allowed for an expression which not only met his actual needs while he created but at the same time offered a solution of representational problems meaningful in the historical setting.[51]

The interaction of the two factors is such that under certain conditions even those traits in artistic creation which are linked to what we can clinically describe as pathological processes may actually enhance the effect. This may happen especially when for certain historical reasons the very emphasis on conflict, or some obvious contrast which we may clinically attribute to the upsurge of id impulses and the defense against them, gains high social approval. Such an evaluation was characteristic particularly of the peak of the expressionist movement in Germany, when Josephson was rediscovered. Admiration was devoted exclusively to works created during his illness.[52]

While the beauty of line of Figure 15 is striking, the emptiness of the facial expression, the artificiality of the smile, becomes the more apparent the longer we contemplate the drawing. This feeling gains power over us if we inspect the many similar drawings of Josephson which presumably originated during the same period.[53] Out of several similar

49 For this symbolism see Freud's interpretation of the Schreber case (1911 b). It should, however, be stated that if this symbolism plays a part, it is still conveyed within the tradition of representational art; eyes tend frequently to be drawn that way.

50 See Hartlaub (1920) who gives bibliographical references, and recently Hodin (1949) who discusses Josephson's influence on later painters and seems to assume that familiarity with Josephson influenced "Modigliani's Raphaelism." See also Millner (1948).

51 For a more detailed discussion of this problem see Chapter 4.

52 For comments related to this problem see pp. 260, 263.

53 We are aware of the fact that our lack of information on the course of Josephson's illness limits the value of this discussion in many ways.

drawings we choose one with the heads of two young girls (Fig. 16). At first we may be inclined to think that these are studies of models, sketches near to the normal. But on closer inspection the emptiness of expression in the faces becomes apparent. We are confirmed in this reaction if we turn to one of the portraits dating back to his prepsychotic period (Fig. 17). No doubt, Josephson at that time was a master in rendering human physiognomy. His portraits could convey the impression of a definite personality.[54] We might conclude that during the period of his psychotic disturbance, human faces in Josephson's work were rendered either in extreme excitement or in utter emptiness. A reconciliation of these two extremes seems missing; the human face in moderate or complex expression, in varying degrees of mood or conflict seems at that time not accessible to him.[55]

In this, Josephson resembles the untrained schizophrenic creators to whose spontaneous production our general remarks refer. Let us first observe an untrained psychotic creator during his work. Figure 19[56] shows a drawing which copies a photograph. The photograph was removed too late; the patient had already distorted it by drawing lines into the heads. We are inclined to assume that here as in other cases, distortion substitutes for destruction. The individuals represented on the photograph were not familiar to the patient; the photograph had apparently been offered to him accidentally as a model to be copied. Since we have no way of entering into the dynamics of his experience, we must limit ourselves to commenting upon the result: Quite obviously he has by his additions increased the effect of the faces; he made them stare at us. We do not look at the typical picture of a couple at their wedding or wedding anniversary but are caught by piercing eyes; their look seems uncanny. The copy of the photograph seems to assure us of the correctness of this impression. The unity of facial expression, of which the photograph still retained elements, is here fully lost; there is nothing but utter strangeness.

The process of creation, then, seems to pass through two phases: a distortion of reality in a sense leading to some heightened excitation,

[54] But even in front of this portrait one may feel inclined to speak of some stiffness, a foreboding of that tendency which is manifest in his later works.

[55] One may here object that such is not necessarily the artist's business. However, it is the context of the life history which makes us decide that those who were or are inclined to admire the very polarity between vision and schema in Josephson or are moved by the stiffness, since they sense in it a clandestine and hence warded-off emotionality, react to an ambiguous stimulus largely by projection; see p. 260.

[56] Prinzhorn, Figs. 138 a and b. The diagnosis is indicated by Prinzhorn as either schizophrenia or a manic condition.

and finally the turning to emptiness. We may ask ourselves to what extent these two phases can be compared to the polarity of expression which we discussed in Josephson's drawings.[57] While one side of the polarity, the heightening of expression, only rarely becomes fully manifest, the second is more than obvious: Every collection of productions by psychotics contains innumerable drawings which more or less show the same feature as Figure 18;[58] an example we have selected because it lends itself to a comparison with Josephson's sketches. It obviously shares their emptiness and distance. Moreover, we hear that the patient, like Josephson, produced not here and there a human head; she was producing series of them. According to many observers, this again is not infrequent among psychotic creators and seems to occur sometimes independently of the state of deterioration during psychosis. A young schizophrenic woman of highest intelligence and achievements, who committed suicide, devoted herself clandestinely during a period of several months to drawing a similar series of human physiognomies which were discovered after her death. She had maintained her position in life, and the severity of her condition had been recognized only by a psychiatrist who saw her many months before, during a state of acute depression.[59]

It becomes necessary to formulate what we can learn from these observations: We believe that in representational creations of schizophrenics we rarely find human faces rendered in such a way that we can "understand" them; they do not supply a clue to the moods or the personality or its characteristics and thus do not invite identification.[60] This lack of facial expression cannot be accounted for solely by lack of training. The untrained psychotic creator tends to be more successful in the rendering of other subjects, and the trained one is likely to reveal his disturbance at this point more than at any other. The validity of observations of this kind is difficult to test. As far as trained artists are concerned, the complexity of any test is great, and all that I can do is to state that I have not met with cases which would have shaken my conviction. As far as untrained artists are concerned, the evaluation of what may impress us

[57] It should be added that the distorting of the photograph by additions can be observed over and over again in the contact with psychotics. Prinzhorn has at least one more case in which a photograph was also copied (1922, p. 166) similar to the one here discussed.

[58] Pfeifer, Fig. 19.

[59] Permission to publish these drawings and further material concerning this case was refused to this colleague.

[60] In this context we shall not discuss what is meant by "understanding" a facial expression and shall avoid comments on degrees and varieties of such understanding. For some remarks on this topic see Chapter 9.

as "rigidity" or "emptiness" is difficult. However, since the first publication of this paper, various authors have gained impressions similar to my own, and even some data of an experimental nature have been published. However tentative they are, they deserve to be quoted: Reitman (1939) showed to schizophrenic patients schematically drawn human faces with ten different facial expressions. The patients were able to recognize these expressions correctly; when asked to copy them they failed to render the expressive elements. In this they differed from both hysterical and manic-depressive patients.

The attempt to account for the occurrence of this trait in representational creations of the psychotic must remain tentative. We cannot hope to point to etiological factors of equal importance in every case; we rather expect that in the future the detailed study of cases will permit the establishment of what part, if any, various factors play in each individual instance. Only case studies will answer the question of the extent to which the heads repeatedly depicted by some schizophrenics represent either love objects or persecutors. Either of these assumptions can be proven only in exceptional cases; where such information reaches us, chiefly in drawings produced during therapy, the drawing usually serves a different function. It is, as a rule, made for the therapist and meant to convey something to him. But even under these conditions, when we are not dealing with spontaneous productions—to the study of which this essay is limited—the facial expression is rendered either in an exaggerated, masklike excitement or in utter emptiness. The difference between these two apparently opposite cases, however, should not be overrated; they ultimately are witness to the same disturbance: the search for an expression. We owe this insight in turn to a case study, that of the psychotic sculptor Messerschmidt (1736-1784). The discussion of this case[61] will make it plausible that, next to a variety of culturally determined functions, the long series of "heads" he produced were frantic efforts at presenting a normal face; in this he failed. When he rendered emotions, some superimposed, a rationalizing trait or "emptiness" came to the fore. This emptiness, however, was not what he observed in others. When he acted as a portraitist, he remained a master, hardly influenced by his delusions. It was an emptiness which he felt in himself, when attempting to establish contact with others. The busts were composed in front of the mirror and all prove to have been self-portraits.

In the literature dealing with physiognomics, there are a few similar examples of which at least one may be mentioned here. In the publica-

[61] See Chapter 4.

tion of a psychotic, published around 1910 under the titles *I Will* and *The Ladder to Heaven* (Hermann Ludwig), ninety illustrations show photographic self-portraits in excited facial distortions. While any single photograph seems suggestive, in looking over the series we gain increasingly the impression of distance and strangeness. We do not refer here to the magic functions of these representational studies but to their stereotypy. While in Messerschmidt's busts we shall see that this stereotypy is determined by his repeating fundamentally one and the same facial constellation, the stereotypy in Ludwig's photographs consists in the repetition of frantic attempts at finding an expression at all: Instead of reaching the normal, he can fasten only on the exaggerated one.[62] We must now make explicit what has been implied in the foregoing. We are attempting to view the emptiness in the facial expression of schizophrenic creations, and the frequency with which the human face is rendered in their spontaneous productions,[63] as part of the general contact disturbance of the schizophrenic.

Human mimic expression is addressed to the other person; it aims at contact. It is this contact which, during the schizophrenic process, is loosened and in catatonic conditions, broken. The disturbance embraces the total expressive behavior and supplies a criterion frequently used for the purpose of diagnosis. We consider the control of motility as one of the earliest functions of the ego; the control of expressive movements is part of it, that part which serves communication. The mannerism in schizophrenic expressive movements—in posture and gait and particularly in facial expression, the wish to appear meaningful, to convey "something," combined with rigidity or emptiness, rapid changes of facial expression without reason or correspondence to changes in mood— all these may be viewed as attempts at restitution in the sense of Freud, restitution in the area of autoplasticity. But this assumption leads only half the way. Are we not confusing two things, the mimic of the schizophrenic himself and his ability to render mimic when he draws? Where is the bridge between the autoplastic and the alloplastic, the disturbance

[62] For the discussion of the magic, defensive meaning of such exaggerated facial distortions see Chapter 4.

[63] Anastasi and Foley (1944) found as difference between untrained normals and abnormals that the latter tend to render human faces in profile considerably less frequently than the former. It is well known that the untrained finds it easier to draw the profile than the frontal view of the human face. The authors assume that the psychotic subjects, among whom schizophrenics predominate, tend to overrate their ability or to be less aware of its limitation. While this may be so, the present context suggests also that the frontal view is preferred, since the profile is the position in which the facial expression becomes least visible.

of the creator and that of his product? At the present stage of our knowledge, a definite answer cannot be given; all we have to offer is a suggestion. A large field of research would have to be covered before a test would become meaningful; all I can attempt at present is to point to some facts which seem to support the hypothesis.

Whoever has had intensive contact with painters or sculptors will have had an opportunity to hear from them, in one version or another, observations concerning the artist's relation to his model, observations which as far as I know were formulated first and most profoundly by Leonardo.[64] The artist, he feels, is inclined to lend to the figures he renders his own bodily experience and hence to make them similar to his own appearance "if he is not protected against this by long study."[65]

It might be possible to interpret Leonardo's view as suggesting once more an emphasis on the importance of projection in artistic creation. But I believe that if we weigh his words carefully, we come to a somewhat more precise understanding. There is a tendency which the artist must resist, the tendency to substitute his own bodily experience for that of the model he wants to depict. What Leonardo describes here has recently become accessible in at least three different fields of investigation. Spielrein (1931) has interpreted comparisons between children's drawings done with open and closed eyes. Engerth (1933) has shown, in studying a case of finger agnosia, that as long as the disturbance persisted, the patient, trained in drawing, remained unable to render his own hand or the hand of somebody else in his drawings, and when the disturbance had disappeared the difficulty in drawing persisted when he attempted to draw with closed eyes. Finally, it seems to me that only the participa-

---

[64] See Herzfeld (1925).

[65] The most striking and most revealing parallel to this was pointed out in a paper by Wulff (1936) devoted to supplementing and criticizing the German version of the present essay. The Russian writer, art critic and theatrical producer, Jevreinoff, published a book on portraiture. He was much sought after as a model by the great masters of Russian art such as Rjepin and Ssorin, of the period previous to the First World War. Wulff proceeds: "If I am not mistaken, about ten different portraits of Jevreinoff were produced, which did not resemble each other at all or only to a small extent. It was this experience which suggested to Jevreinoff the idea of writing a very interesting and convincing study on portraiture, in which he proves that the different artists who made his portrait used this only as an occasion in order to express the peculiarity, the characteristic, in the ultimate sense the real spiritual significance [geistigen Inhalt] of their own personality. To put it even more bluntly: in truth it was not Jevreinoff's personality which was depicted but the personalities of different artists, with all the typical, peculiar and characteristic traits which constitute their personalities. Everyone who skims through Jevreinoff's book and looks at the portraits reproduced there will at once be irresistibly convinced by this book's thesis, if he is at all familiar with the personality of the portraitists."

tion of our own bodily experience (in representational creation) can facilitate our understanding of the large and impressive collection of sculptures of the blind, which Münz and Loewenfeld (1934) have gathered.

I interrupt this presentation at this point: We are at the borderline of neurological investigations, which will, no doubt, carry on from here, and will have the possibility of further elaborating and checking our hypotheses. I believe that Schilder's concept of the image of the body will lead to investigations disproving or confirming this thesis, which, to summarize it once more, contends that the disturbance in rendering facial expression in representational products of schizophrenics is related to the disturbance of their own expressive movements and that interest in and attempts at rendering facial expressions in their products can be understood as a second level of an attempt at restitution.[66]

VI. CONCLUSION

In addition to the Hindenburg "caricature" (Fig. 12) and the two German emperors combined in one bust (Fig. 13), Prinzhorn's patient also produced many fantastic and bizarre wood carvings. This patient made a remark which strikingly demonstrates the intricacy of the problem upon which we have touched. He described the process by which he created in the following words: "When I have a piece of wood in front of me, it contains a hypnosis; if I obey it, it turns into something, but if I don't, there is trouble."

This description can be compared with Michelangelo's idea that the

---

[66] Investigations on the image of the body have, I believe, borne out at least in part the hypothesis formulated here shortly before the publication of Schilder's *The Image and Appearance of the Human Body* (1935). In Schilder's own work and in the widespread literature since that time, evidence suggesting many detailed assumptions are contained, which I propose to summarize in a different context. For Schilder's own reaction to my hypothesis, see *Goals and Desires of Man* (1942). Wulff's pertinent comments (1936) on this paper have been mentioned before; his objections "to introducing neurological investgations" seems to me largely invalidated by recent findings. The "image of the body" is, in terms of psychoanalytic theory, an apparatus of the ego largely connected with its autonomous functions, i.e., with the area free from conflict. That in certain psychopathological conditions these functions should become involved or—if we take a broad ontogenetic view—reinvolved in conflict may well suggest one of the avenues on which further research will proceed. In this connection the findings of Bender (1947) on childhood schizophrenia and its relation to motor disturbances may gain decisive importance, and certain, however vague, psychoanalytic impressions on the cathexis of the body image and early object relation may prove valuable. (See pp. 55f., and Kris (1951 b). The recent findings of Machover (1949) seem finally to have established beyond any reasonable doubt that the way in which individuals render the human figure constitutes an important diagnostic tool.

unhewed block of marble already contains every form the artist will choose to give it. Michelangelo's conception is rooted in the neoplatonic theory of art, which demands that the artist does not imitate nature but that he surpass it, that he serves a certain ideal of beauty, derived from his own inner life. This conception of art, traceable through the history of Western thought (Panofsky, 1924), can be directly connected with the utterance of the psychotic. Both describe the same psychic process, the placing of an inner experience, an "inner" image, into the outside world, i.e., the mechanism of projection.

If we attempt to delineate the difference, we may contrast the compulsion of the psychotic with the freedom of the artist. Nevertheless, a common element remains. For if we say that the psychotic sees hallucinated figures in his piece of wood, we must also recognize that with hallucination we designate but one point in a series extended between imagination and perception (Flournoy, 1933), and that in this case normal and pathological mechanisms may merge.[67] The "hallucinatory" image, as experienced by the normal adult may be regarded as a prototype (Jaspers, 1923, 1948). We may add that in the more narrow province of representational creations, a certain technique of producing pictorial images evoked through chance formations plays a considerable part. Leonardo, who advised the artist to train his imagination by observing crumbling walls, merely repeated, in much the same words, an old Chinese instruction to artists, which originated in the eleventh century. There is abundant material to prove that this idea was always alive,[68] that it extends into our own time, where in the Rorschach test it has been utilized in the service of psychodiagnostics. Hence, in the psychotic artist as well as in the artistically active normal, the mechanism of projection must be regarded as operative in creative activity.

But we must add that in each instance this mechanism operates in an entirely different context. This difference does not become evident either in studying creation as a process or in investigating the psychic processes of the creator; it is, however, apparent in the created work. In extreme cases the works of psychotics are "unintelligible"—as is their speech. Depending upon the extent of the disturbance, their commentary may facilitate, or may fail to further, our understanding. On the basis of psychoanalytic insights, we may offer the following formulation: Some ego functions of the psychotic are disturbed; the ego, however, is not only

[67] Recent experimental findings suggest that the above should have been qualified: see Roman and Landis (1945).

[68] See Kris and Kurz (1934).

the apparatus of perception but also the one entrusted with that formal elaboration which shapes the contact with the environment.[69]

This formulation does not introduce a new element but constitutes merely a deduction from the facts with which we started this investigation. The representational creations of psychotics, being attempts at restitution, follow the laws of the primary process, the "language" of the id. This we know from the dream, which remains unintelligible unless definite techniques of "translation" are applied. In the dream, as in spontaneous productions of psychotics, the ego participates only to a small degree. If we endeavor to compare the creations of the artist with those of the psychotic, we find an aid in some of the already developed thoughts. In the work of art, as in the dream, unconscious contents are alive; here too, evidences of the primary process are conspicuous, but the ego maintains its control over them, elaborates them in its own right, and sees to it that the distortion does not go too far.

"One would like to know more about how, precisely, the ego achieves this" (Freud) but this question lies already beyond the scope of our topic, in the province of the psychology of art. Although we are reluctant to enter this field, we will make the attempt once more to resume the connection with our more narrowly circumscribed topic. The differences between the works of psychotics and the works of artists have been described as being sharply delineated and fundamental. But this description does not do justice to the fluid transitions which also exist—transitions which become impressive if we reëxamine the process of creation rather than the finished product. Apart from those qualities which we have already enumerated, we should focus our attention on one quality that we have so far neglected. The extent to which it is generally valid is questionable; we assume it only in the sphere of representational creations. Even the normal artist's process of artistic creation frequently evinces features which remind us of restitutive phenomena. Analytic experiences—particularly suggestions by Sharpe (1931, 1935) and Fenichel (1935), which my own experiences largely confirm—imply that the mechanism of projection in artistic creation also serves the reparation of introjected, and hence lost, objects. This idea constitutes the basis of Sharpe's view on the psychology of the

---

[69] In my opinion we are justified in deducing from this statement that the frequently used expression "unconscious communication" is ill-applied or in need of a more precise specification. While communication from "id to id" is hardly conceivable, something similar may occur under certain conditions of diminished ego control, particularly when ego and id are in harmony with each other.

artist.[70] While we cannot further pursue it here, one point should be stressed: In this process the object emerges anew, with full—at times even enhanced—reality for the artist and the community whom he addresses.

[70] Several authors have since insisted on this point; see e.g. Rickman (1940) and Tarachow (1949). It has found a consistent elaboration in several papers by H. B. Lee. The points of agreement need hardly be stressed. I feel, however, that some of Lee's generalizations remain doubtful. When he writes, "Creativeness, like pity is a dynamic and antithetical reaction against unconscious impulses to destroy" (1949 a, p. 245), this seems to me not to do justice to the nexus of determinants which may lead to creativeness; see, for instance, pp. 52 and 167f. For other comments on H. B. Lee's position see Brierley (1950).

Appendix

A PSYCHOTIC ARTIST OF THE MIDDLE AGES

The case to be presented here in comparative detail offers several unique features, not all of which enter into the range of problems discussed in the preceding paper. It is hoped that this case will attract the interest of other investigators, who might try to view the productivity of the insane in the framework of comparative psychiatry, i.e., linked to the study of culture and personality.

Opicinus de Canistris, an Italian cleric (1296 to about 1350), is known as the author of two tracts and a volume with extraordinarily large drawings and an abundance of written commentary. His sole claim to distinction lies in the peculiarities which this volume reveals. He was eminent neither as a theologian, a writer, a painter, nor did he play any relevant part in political affairs or in the intellectual and artistic life of his time. His very identity was established only because of a combination of fortuitous circumstances and the acumen of recent historians. Only because of his illness can we offer something more than the skeleton of data recorded in the archives. On one of a series of enormous sheets of drawings, most of which are filled with only partly meaningful annotations, he recorded in some detail his life history, of which we first present a summary.[1]

Opicinus was born into a world sharply torn by political and spiritual strife. The secular power of the Church, divided in itself, was waning, and for the first time in history the Popes had been driven into exile from Rome. His great contemporaries, Dante, Giotto, and later Petrarch, had opened new horizons for mankind. In Opicinus' life we find only external and minor reflections of this grandiose social change. He was born in Pavia, and by the age of ten was destined for a career in the Church. From the age of fourteen on, he found pleasure in drawing. For economic reasons he had to interrupt his studies and worked for a while

[1] We rely in what follows on Salomon's admirable edition (1936). In many points the psychiatric approach suggests a different evaluation of details; however, it seemed advisable not to venture too far in this direction, lest the crucial question be obscured of what is "culture" and what "deviation."

as a toll collector on a bridge. He had returned to school, aged sixteen or seventeen, for a short time when he had the opportunity of attending some classes in medicine. Forced by the deterioration of family finances to earn his livelihood, he became for a while a tutor in a wealthy family. When Opicinus was nineteen years of age, Pavia came under the suzerainty of a new family, and he and his people emigrated to Genoa, where he once more worked as school teacher. In order to increase his earnings, he learned to illustrate manuscripts—a skill particularly important before the invention of print. The content of the theological treatise he adorned attracted his attention, and when, in 1318, he could return to Pavia with his mother and siblings—his father had died shortly before—he continued at first his work as an artisan but soon obtained, without having been ordained, the position of chaplain at the cathedral. Supported by one of the curates, he could continue his theological studies and reach ordination. The ceremony had to take place outside of Pavia, because the town had been excommunicated for some time—one of the reasons which restricted the scope of his sacerdotal functions and which seem to have rendered his clerical career arduous. He embarked first on literary work, none of which is preserved. He was soon subject to attacks by opponents in local politics and hard-pressed by creditors, in spite of the fact that, aged twenty-seven, he had been able to obtain a small parsonage in town. He left Pavia but continued to write, living in various places in Northern Italy. In 1329, aged thirty-three, he appeared at the Papal Court in Avignon, where at the time clerics without attachment tended to assemble. His first job was the illustration of a manuscript, after which he lived on alimonies. He soon wrote a political tract on the relationship of the Holy See to the Empire, in the hope of attracting the Pope's attention, and then obtained a clerk's position in one of the divisions of the Papal Chancery, which he retained till his death. But before he could assume this position, and during his early time of tenure, he was investigated and had to stand trial for reasons unknown. The trial exhausted him physically and depleted his meager resources.

During this period of trial or shortly after its conclusion, in the spring of 1334, aged thirty-eight, Opicinus fell ill. He described the onset of illness as sudden and mentioned that he had been unconscious for ten days. During this illness a dream occurred:

> I was in Venice, a town I had known only from descriptions. When I opened my eyes I felt as if I had awoken from eternal sleep and was born anew. I had forgotten everything and could not recall how the world outside looked.

He recorded that he had had a vision in June: "In the presence of a servant who could testify to it," he saw a vase in the clouds. In his weird annotations, the vase plays a considerable role since by a play on the double meanings of the word *canistra* it is linked to his own name. "I was," he writes later, "at the time mute, paralyzed in my right hand and had lost in a miraculous way a large part of my memory for affairs of learnings."[2]

We note that the loss of "memory" is described as *"miraculous"*; similarly the (alleged) impairment of the right hand was later seen as an asset: it *miraculously* enabled him to draw and write what he considered his great and inspired work. We are not informed how long the speech disturbance persisted.

Up to this point one is inclined to consider the illness as a cerebral process and might think of an inflammatory or vascular basis. However, it seems that the symptoms described might have been either part of a psychotic process, or that subsequently a mental condition developed, which, though rich in hysterical features, bears unmistakably the imprint of a psychosis. We arrive at this conclusion for a variety of reasons. Before we discuss them in detail, we have to point to some of the psychological dynamics which we can infer in Opicinus' experience. There is in his autobiographical notes evidence of a deep attachment to his mother; when she died shortly after the onset of his illness, his reaction was strong. We also learn that in order to stay close to her he decided not to join one of the religious orders. The death of his father and, shortly before it, that of one of his brothers is simply mentioned. His sisters seem to have played a more relevant part in his life; he is, for instance, concerned with finding a place for one of them in a suitable convent. Moreover, the earliest of his self-accusations concerns sexual play with a sister at the age of eight. The very fact that such an event should be recorded in the life history of a medieval cleric is symptomatic; the very existence of a biographical record of the kind is considered to be without contemporary parallel. While it is a record without ideological implications, it is not a simple statement of facts. The account of events and experiences is interwoven with self-accusations and self-exposure, which, according to the views of experts, is only marginally related to contemporary literary patterns. Thus, one might be inclined to consider it as "acceptable" when Opicinus mentions that before the age of twenty he submitted to carnal temptations, but the scarcely veiled references to masturbatory activity are without analogy in contemporary documents;

[2] The Latin original says *memoria literalis*. We shall subsequently comment on the probable meaning of this expression.

references of this kind are without any doubt to be viewed as an expression of the dynamics of an individual conflict.

We are familiar with the fact that the stringency of cultural patterns seems to weaken, the closer we come in a personal document to the individual's central psychological conflicts, a fact noted and discussed by Kluckhohn (1945) in relation to anthropological data. Opicinus de Canistris' personal notes seem to be, if not the only, at any rate the most outstanding example of a similar deviation from medieval tradition. In many instances he remains vague: thus, when he refers to personal difficulties during his early theological studies, and in his self-accusatory fury quotes instances of his lack of understanding of this or that of the current theological concepts. But he goes further; he gives reasons for what was, at least initially, a disturbance of concentration during his theological studies, mentions persisting blasphemous thoughts during religious service, and the irresistible impulse to outbreaks of laughter while celebrating mass. These were not symptoms of his youth. Immediately before the outbreak of his illness, the obsessional-compulsive soul-searching seems to have reached a peak. During the early years in Avignon his scrupulosity is such that in spite of absolution he refrains from exercising sacerdotal functions and seems to have requested absolution ever anew.[3]

Scrupulosity, one might be tempted to assume, is typical of a medieval cleric, a part of his training, and to refer to it might be part of literary tradition; the experts, however, assure us that nowhere in this tradition is there to be found a model for such behavior as that displayed by Opicinus: As Salomon puts it, he feels that sin is with him, is reality, that there is no redemption, and he does not expose his sinfulness as moral example. He does so because of reasons for which the familiar cultural patterns offer no rationalization, perhaps with the intention of barring future vices by loud acclaim.

We should at this point remind ourselves that the record in which these autobiographical statements are contained and this obsessional symptomatology is deployed was written during what we consider his psychotic period, of which the acute illness was part or during which it was initiated. We left Opicinus in June of 1334, two months after the onset of illness, paralyzed in the right hand, with impairment of speech

---

[3] Opicinus quotes in detail the limitations to which his functions as a priest had been subjected. While Salomon tends to attribute these limitations to the fact that, while a priest in Pavia, the town was under interdict, I tend to disagree and am inclined to connect the passage with the thought: "I was at all times cautious to exercise as little sacerdotal power as possible, sinner I was and am."

("mute") and of *memoria literalis*. According to his record the following
dream occurred somewhat later: He saw

> . . . the Virgin with the Child on her lap, sadly seated on earth. She
> gave me back instead of the literary learning, which since my youth
> had been wasted, the spirit in reduplicated strength.

Salomon points out that similar formulations in which comparatively
"external" intellectual capacities are contrasted to spiritual force occur
frequently in writings of contemporary mystics, which otherwise show
no resemblance to Opicinus' mentality.

The extent and nature of the change produced by his illness can only
be appreciated if we turn to subsequent events. Early in 1335 he retired
temporarily from his job because of the weakness of his right hand.
But this very hand proved, in his own words, miraculously strong when
he was not required to draft documents for the Chancery of the
Holy See, but was engaged in the work which at the time occupied
his imagination. This work is preserved as a collection of twenty-seven
enormous drawings on parchment, varying in height between 70 and 97
cm. and averaging in width 50 cm. The vast majority of them—and only
with these are we concerned—were produced between February 1335 and
June 1336 with that right hand "which produced these images without
human assistance." They follow no definite or even detectable plan, and
no clear ideological tendency which would connect them has been established. According to Heimann, the art historian collaborating with
Salomon, almost all of the drawings have been started with some circle
into which human figures were later inserted or on which they were
superimposed. All have the character of some monumental scheme, lay-
out, or architectural design. Two of these drawings are here reproduced
to convey a general impression (see Figs. 20 and 21) .[4]

It is clearly impossible to attempt an enumeration of the content
of the whole or even of a part of one of the drawings. We mention only a
few details of Figure 20: In the center there is the Virgin surrounded
by smaller figures. Around this central panel we find forty concentric
circles, each corresponding to one year of the author's age and each carrying 366 letters for the days of the year, ingeniously subdivided by
diameters into groups of seven, with Easter being specially indicated for
each year. This is the "system" into which the author has inscribed the
record of his life; what did not find its proper place here was distributed
in the corners or elsewhere. In the axes of the ring system, we find the
four evangelists and what are intended as four self-portraits.

[4] Salomon, Plates XIV and XXII.

A wealth of details is not visible on our reproduction: Thus the background of the innermost circle is formed by a map of the Mediterranean, the African coast, and the Peloponnesian peninsula, with other parts of the coastline visible. The Virgin's head is by inscription designated as the priest; other designations are distributed over other parts of her body. The inscription in large letters on the Virgin's mantle, however, refers to Italy: On the map the outline of Italy would be visible at this point if the Virgin were removed. Similarly, the fact that her feet are designated as "husband" and "wife" respectively seems to refer to the nearby statement concerning the author's legitimate birth, on the innermost of the forty surrounding circles.

At first one might be tempted to see in this configuration evidence of medievalism; one feels vaguely reminded of glass paintings in cathedrals, with which Opicinus naturally was familiar. But medieval art has nothing similar to offer.

When Salomon, the learned editor of the codex, first approached his task he was, as he puts it, for some time tempted to put the volume aside as a "merely pathological product" not deserving the historian's attention. But under the impact of the consideration that even in pathological productions "there might be some material that advances historical insight," he did not drop his investigation. Salomon and his collaborators have devoted infinite labors to tracing whatever connections the historian can establish between Opicinus' work and contemporary knowledge or models. They have drawn attention to a vast array of influences to which he was exposed, to many sources from which he drew the vast store of information which is contained in his written comment. And we shall try to show that some of Opicinus' search for information seems to be connected with the inferred content of his delusions. The delusional character of his productions reveals itself by a large number of traits. As far as the written material is concerned, there is no doctrine or view expounded, and relations to contemporary knowledge are limited to details. There are, however, a number of "themes" to be detected, such as the predominance of damnation. It threatens Opicinus, the sinner in past and future, and also threatens the world around him. Side by side with despair stand thoughts of advancement, of high ecclesiastic honors. However, such ambitions are in turn portent of evil; the small parsonage in Pavia would still offer the most adequate protection; it could replace the world and the whole church to him. At times, while he writes, ambition grows into thoughts of grandeur, and at least in one instance he designates what he has written as "the most recent and eternal evangelium," which should be approved by the Pope and recited in all churches.

Thoughts and expression of this kind are not met with in Opicinus' previous writings, neither in the tract we have mentioned nor in a minute and very accurate description of his home town, both of which fall into common literary categories of the time in Italy. In his annotations, the writings after the "illness," Salomon finds a man who wanders on dark paths, of a kind onto which he might have never ventured before. Not only has the sinister gained the upper hand and the factual receded, but it is noted by Salomon, who admired here and there the vigor of an isolated figure of speech, that the thought is of a disjuncted character; the writer, he says, is constantly forced to ward off the onslaught of associations—a good many clang associations among them—and while he heaps arguments upon each other, he ever again loses the thread. The rapid, and at times incoherent, change of images lends to Opicinus' writings an affinity with the discourse of the prophets, and while he obviously was familiar with their style, the prophetic attitude reoriginates, as it were, afresh out of the tenor of his messages; their content, however, frequently cannot be established. Salomon often finds himself unable to translate the author's simple Latin, in which there seems to be little rhetorical refinement. We are, quite obviously, at the border of verbigeration and at times beyond it. It fits into this pattern that hidden meanings abound which can be unraveled only rarely.

Similarly, when Opicinus comments directly on the "meanings" of his drawings, he refers to many overdeterminations, heaping associations upon associations.

The analysis of the drawings themselves led the art historian Heimann to analogous conclusions: Opicinus uses patterns familiar from contemporary art, and all the technical aspects of his drawings, for instance the way in which he renders the human figure, can be related to current contemporary practices. In the details he uses there is little originality and certainly no increase of expression and no innovation; however, there is no evidence of deterioration. But the entire setup, the total composition, is deviant. Heimann uses examples to illustrate this: On some drawings we find a towering figure holding a circle or arena, like a shield in front of the body, so that only feet and fingertips are visible. While this may still be an acceptable pattern of medieval representational art, in many instances the figures, and not the geometrical schemata they carry, include other smaller figures. Even this has its analogies, but not in the same manner: Some justification is generally found in the posture of the including figure. Opicinus seems to use the "inside" in the way one uses a diagram; contemporaries, on the other hand, used a mantle to make the inclusion of small figures into bigger ones plausible: Under her mantle the Virgin protects her flock. No similar justifying device occurs with Opicinus: the inclusion of small in big figures serves to express a view of dependent interrelation, ultimately linked, I believe, to fantasies concerning the inside of the body. We have no way of establishing their content in detail. The direction, however, is suggested if we mention two sources of contemporary imagery with which Opicinus proves to be familiar and which he copies in his drawings. There is first the medieval map which he draws repeatedly—and we have every reason to assume that the link between "the earth" as a whole and the Virgin whose figure it surrounds is one familiar from widespread symbolism: The interest in maps would be linked to delusional inquiries into the human and particularly into the female body. The second source to which we refer supports this view. Opicinus was familiar with medical manuscripts, and some of the details rendered in his drawings copy fetal positions illustrated in these treatises. In a particularly obscure passage in his text he refers to the caesarean operation.[5]

There is one tendency in his drawings which deserves our particular attention: the frequency with which one line serves several functions, with which one shape transgresses upon another. The elaboration of the coastlines of the maps into human shapes can serve as a case in point; it is a transmutation to which, we presume, certain thought contents were attached. While these thoughts remain unknown, we may tentatively assume that there might be some relation to creation and decomposition of the body. At the same time, the play with shapes and the play with words are characteristics of the break-through of the primary process and part of the typical symptomatology of schizophrenic production.

In summarizing, we may now attempt to review the course of Opicinus' illness: We cannot believe that the paralysis of the right hand can have been of organic nature when we realize the sheer enormity of the task which he performed. The very physical effort of the minute and detailed drawings, of the small and yet highly legible writing, eliminates the idea of a physical impairment. We rather assume the literal truth of what he says: The hand could function only to execute what a miraculous force told him to do.

[5] For a somewhat similar significance of fantasies concerning the inside of the female body see Chapter 5. See also some of the schizophrenic drawings recently described by Chatterji (1951, particularly p. 39) who interprets drawings by Indian patients as expressing the fantasy "of going to the mother's womb and the desire of coming out of it."

In a similar sense, the loss of *memoria literalis* can be understood. To draft documents had become impossible; to write tracts or treatises was no longer his task. But a wealth of words was at his disposal when he wanted to convey a message, reveal his own life, view his relation to the Virgin who controlled it, or comment on the plans of the world, the Church, and the hierarchies he drew.

The assumption that they are plans is, it seems, well warranted by their appearance, by the strange mixture of geometry and life, by the symbolism and depiction which they contain—by their emptiness and neatness.

Their resemblance to the products of schizophrenics of our own period hardly needs to be emphasized. The similarity with the magic drawings of the architect-patient, which are discussed in Chapter 5, is apparent. We find here and there a comparable interaction between intactness of comment and privatization of expression; in both the function of communication has miscarried.

The similarity with products of other schizophrenics is not less evident. The idea of creating or organizing a world and the fear of its destruction seem to connect Opicinus' effort with that of many schizophrenics of our own day. Even the formal appearance and the occasional break-through of a *horror vacui* are similar. The difference rests in the intact part of the personality. However great this difference may be, we are struck by the similarity that exists when the particular mechanisms of schizophrenic production are at work, in spite of the fact that the medieval environment seemed to offer pathways of discharge not equally available later and least of all in our own culture.[6]

We therefore tentatively conclude that Opicinus' life after the illness, if an independent illness existed, was determined by a schizophrenic process; the obsessional-compulsive symptomatology of his earlier years had apparently acted as a defensive barrier.[7] With the outbreak of the schizophrenic process a creative spell was initiated, in which no other activity but that devoted to the great project could be executed. There are, naturally, many uncertainties in the way of a similar set of assumptions, but since we have gained insight into many similarities between Opicinus' work and that of schizophrenics of our own time, it seems permissible to assume that his urge to create, like that of others, was a protection

---

6 See Freud (1904 a) ; Hartmann, Kris, and Loewenstein (1951).

7 There is the possibility that in the years between 1325-1328, about which he is strangely silent in his record, a previous process had occurred.

against the fantasy of its total destruction: The theme of damnation would be an attenuation of this delusion.[8]

Opicinus shares many traits with the other trained creators we have discussed; in his work as in theirs, no understanding of the full, intended "meaning" is possible without a detailed and intimate familiarity with the content of the delusional system.

[8] The question how Opicinus' condition was viewed by his contemporaries, i.e., the question to what extent his behavior was considered as psychotic, remains unfortunately undecided. Following suggestions by Tatlock (1943) one might well assume that awareness of pathology existed; see also Zilboorg (1941).

Chapter 4

A PSYCHOTIC SCULPTOR OF THE EIGHTEENTH CENTURY

If I were at this point a reader and not the writer, I would find it difficult to control what might be fittingly described as bored apprehension. Apart from a general weariness when confronted by papers on "applied" psychoanalysis at a time when pressing problems of *clinic* and technique seem to demand our undivided attention, I would be inclined to justify my skepticism on two grounds: How can the psychoanalyst attempt to contribute to the biography of a man of the past? Since we are no longer interested in pointing to generalities—in establishing that "he, too," whoever he was, was torn by love and hate, ridden by complexes and unconsciously directed by them—are we not engaged in a hopeless struggle with data if we try to rely on what biographers ordinarily used to record? Psychoanalysis has, from its beginning, been dependent on special types of highly "private" information, and we have of late become more exacting. Since our attention has turned to the study of the ego, we require an even more elaborate record, relying on increasingly comprehensive yet specific details as we attempt to reconstruct the patient's life history. Can we then be expected to work with satisfaction from the data which traditional biographers tend to offer?

The second ground for apprehension concerns a general dissatisfaction with psychoanalytic attempts to contribute to an understanding of an artist's work by scrutinizing his life. True, many valuable connections can be established, but in the end the unsolved problems bulk large. Why did our man become an artist, instead of an ordinary run-of-the-mill neurotic or psychotic; or, at the very least, what was the function, the specific function, of his creation in the dynamics of his personal conflict?

Let me try to state why, in spite of these weighty arguments, I am presenting the case of Franz Xaver Messerschmidt (1736-1784). First, biographical data will be held to a minimum. As our presentation proceeds, you will find that there are special reasons for this restraint. What his numerous biographers report has proved to be particularly unreliable. The usually reported facts concerning his life have had for the purposes of this study to be supplemented by others, previously not reported but available in archives. In the light of these new data, the traditionally-held views on the artist have had to be reëxamined. Instead of accepting the propositions which the traditional humanities offer for this reëxamination, we can introduce the psychoanalytic viewpoint, claiming in support of its introduction that only now can the existence of a problem be demonstrated—where historians and art critics have seen none.[1]

The second, weightier, argument hits at the weakness of all psychoanalytic studies of art and artists. But even here I claim exemption. It seems to me that both the case of the normal and the case of the neurotic are to some extent different from that of the psychotic artist. They differ in at least one respect: In the course of regression, the individual chain of motivations, however important it remains, seems to lose some of its stringency. Delusional mechanisms are less subject to cultural and individual differentiation than mechanisms operative in the formation of other symptoms. Or, to put it differently: the id is more universal than the ego.

The questions of the extent and the manner in which psychotic mechanisms may influence creative activity, of how they merge with the intact part of the personality and how they are reflected by the artist's work, can be studied only under very special circumstances. Every case that promises answers to one of these questions seems to deserve our attention, since clinical material tends to be unusable for very obvious reasons. In this connection, data from the past gain their exceptional value. They familiarize us with the not infrequent "experiments of nature"— to use an expression which W. Dilthey (1887) introduced into the discussion of these problems—and permit an access to areas from which we otherwise might be longer excluded.

II

Franz Xaver Messerschmidt was born in 1736 in Wiensensteig, Germany, the son of a large family which—if we can trust the scanty reports —lived in poor circumstances. Early inclinations, but also fortunate family relations, seem to have determined the boy's future career. His mother's brothers were the sculptors Philipp Jakob Straub and Johann

[1] The result of the research here referred to was published independently (Kris, 1932). Reference to this extensive publication makes it unnecessary to quote here in detail the source material used. This publication also contains illustrations of all of Messerschmidt's works known at that time.

Baptist Straub, the latter known as an early representative of Munich baroque and as Messerschmidt's first teacher. After his Munich apprenticeship, the length of which we do not know, Messerschmidt is said to have moved to Graz to his other uncle. When he was sixteen years old, he went to the Academy in Vienna, where he apparently had to overcome great difficulties in the beginning. In 1757 he became a metal founder at the Imperial Armory upon the recommendation of his benefactor, Meytens, the well-known court painter and director of the Academy. From 1760 on, he worked for the higher aristocracy and the Imperial court. In 1765 he undertook a trip to Rome, perhaps also to Paris and London; and in 1769, by virtue of the reputation which his works had brought him, he was appointed assistant professor of sculpture at the Academy of Vienna. Soon afterward he seems to have fallen ill. In 1774 the senior professor of sculpture died, and although Messerschmidt "was directly entitled to the position and salary of the deceased," he was not proposed as successor, but three others were proposed who in the eyes of their contemporaries seemed less worthy sculptors.[2] The details of the negotiations leading to the appointment are known from a clever and discerning memorandum of Count Kaunitz, the prime minister, who conveyed to Empress Maria Theresa the views of the Academy's faculty. From this report we quote the following passage:

> The most important objection, as far as this man is concerned, is the fact that for three years he has shown signs of some confusion—perhaps owing to his poverty or to a natural disposition. Although that confusion in his head has meanwhile subsided, permitting him to work as he had done before, it occasionally is still evident in a not perfectly healthy imagination . . . in that he believes all other professors and directors to be his enemies: he still has odd and peculiar whims and therefore can never be completely composed.

Thus we learn of a psychic illness which began in 1771, when Messerschmidt was thirty-five years old, and which had meanwhile improved to the extent that he was capable of working but not of teaching. As Kaunitz further reported, he could not be entrusted with pupils. The characterization of his behavior points to paranoid traits.

From Messerschmidt's subsequent life history, it seems certain that he had actually suffered from a psychotic process which seems to have been followed by an extensive remission. After having experienced the serious disappointment of not obtaining the chair of Sculpture, Messerschmidt

___

2 The Academy's faculty had the right to propose a man for the chair. The right of appointment was an Imperial prerogative.

returned to his home town and soon established contact with the Court of Munich. But his new contacts seemed to have been doomed to failure. When his Viennese friends tried to induce him finally to accept a pension which the Empress had granted to him in 1774, upon the request of the faculty of the Academy and the recommendations of Count Kaunitz, Messerschmidt refused. In a letter he stated that he wished to be paid for his work but would not accept charity. The closing remarks of this letter reveal his state of mind:

> . . . since already for eight years—persecuted by my enemies—I have not been able to find employment commensurate with my artistic skill . . . indeed, it seems that all Germany feels obliged to persecute me.

This letter was addressed to Messerschmidt's brother, Johann, who lived in Bratislava. He, too, was a sculptor, an artisan rather than an artist. Only a few years earlier the two brothers had had serious differences, in the course of which the less gifted Johann had attacked Franz Xaver with a sword. However, these incidents must have been forgotten, because in 1777 Messerschmidt moved from Munich to Bratislava, where for three years he found a haven in the home of his brother. He then bought a house at the outskirts of the city near the Jewish cemetery, in what was generally considered an uncanny neighborhood. There he spent the last three years of his life.

The news spread that a great man was living in Bratislava. Travelers and art lovers were not deterred by the inconveniences involved in the trip from Vienna. They came to visit the great man whose works were famous and much discussed. Thus it is possible to gain some knowledge of his last years from the reports of contemporary travelers and from art criticism. He was considered a peculiar, scurrilous individual, whose tendency to isolation was well known. Visitors found it difficult to approach him, and he often refused to show them his sculptures. His life was dominated by the feeling of not being sufficiently recognized. When a buyer attempted to determine the price of one of his sculptures, Messerschmidt named a ridiculous sum. A series of anecdotes describe how he repeatedly deterred influential benefactors by irony and scorn. He is also said to have repeatedly threatened that before his death he would throw his sculptures into the river, and it seems that he in fact destroyed some of them before he died. All reports characterizing his personality stress a mixture of pride and madness; some of them also relate that he was generally regarded as endowed with power over the spirits.[3]

3 For an evaluation of these reports see pp. 149f.

We can understand the origin of this belief from a detailed report which we owe to Friedrich Nicolai (1781). This clever writer (who was later much and unfairly abused for his biting attacks on the all-powerful masters of Weimar, Goethe and Schiller) gives a detailed account of his contact with Messerschmidt in Volume VI of his "Description of a Trip Through Germany and Switzerland." The portrayal clearly reflects the author's sympathy with Messerschmidt's psychological condition, and on the whole seems to be more concerned with the illness than with the artist. This report, to which we shall refer again, also provides the basis upon which we can form an opinion of the nature of Messerschmidt's affliction.

In 1783 Messerschmidt died from pneumonia; he was forty-seven years of age.

Messerschmidt's activity as an artist is an integral part of his biography. His first works known to us—portraits and statues of saints—follow the tradition of the Austro-Bavarian baroque but surpass the traditional artistic level in many respects. On his travels he had come under the influence of Italian and French art, many features of which he incorporated with sublime freedom in his works. One can safely state that statues he made during the seventeen sixties, of the German Emperor and Empress and the bust of Joseph II, constitute high points of German art of the period. About 1770, in the years of his first illness, a change of style took place which to some extent had been foreshadowed during the course of his previous development. Pathos and elan recede, impersonal objectivity of characterization predominates. Messerschmidt was among the first German artists—apparently the first sculptor—who turned to classicism. The classical features of his works became more and more pronounced, yet even in the works of his later period his sovereign mastery of depicting likeness, his supreme skill as a portraitist, remained unimpaired.

Messerschmidt's artistic activity extended throughout his life, though we do not know whether he was at times forced to give up work for what may have been only brief periods. But it seems that his creative activity was, even during the time of his illness, not paralyzed. The decisive change of style seemed to have occurred during the Munich period. Even during the last years of his life which he spent in bizarre isolation in Bratislava, he never lost contact with the artistic trends of his time, to which he continued to make a special contribution. From the viewpoint of the history of art, his work shows a rounded and consequent development. In his statues, busts, and reliefs, the problems of sculptural representation with which European art was concerned at that time were elaborated on what is generally held to be a high level. It is important to establish this fact for the evaluation of Messerschmidt's personality since it permits us to assess his adjustment to reality.

This term is used here in a double sense, roughly corresponding to the distinction introduced by Benedetto Croce (1922), of the artist as an empirical and an aesthetic person; a distinction which, though not without undesirable implications, seems to be useful in clarifying the problem at hand. In studying Messerschmidt as an empirical person, we are interested in his adjustment to reality as far as it concerns his relation to his environment, for instance, to his family, his colleagues, to those interested in his art, and to those who bought his sculptures. In studying Messerschmidt as an aesthetic person, the individual creator, we are interested in establishing the position of his work within the structure of the art of his time. This structure is determined by what the historians of art describe as tendency or trend in the development of style of a given medium in a given cultural context, for instance, a particular local school of sculpture.[4] The misgivings which we feel in stressing the distinction between two aspects of adjustment to reality and in accepting the distinction between the empirical and the aesthetic person of the artist can be easily accounted for: Distinctions of this kind, while useful in the present context, are of less meaning when the analyst is dealing with the full set of data which are at his disposal in clinical work.

III

From the early seventeen seventies on, Messerschmidt was no longer interested in working upon commissions of clients or sponsors. His attention was primarily, and later in Bratislava almost exclusively, centered on a series of approximately life-sized male busts or heads. More than sixty were found in his studio after his death; forty-nine of them executed in various materials, mostly in marble or lead, have been preserved in museums or private art collections. It is chiefly these busts to which Messerschmidt's reputation remained attached, a reputation which has lived on since the eighteenth century and which has given him in the history of art the place of a respected and admired artist among the minor talents of the period. From the time shortly after his death until the second half of the nineteenth century, the series of busts was repeatedly exhibited or offered for sale in Vienna. They earned Messerschmidt the honorable designation of an Austrian Hogarth, since they were considered as studies of human "physiognomy," of "character," or as

4 See above pp. 15, 147, and 261.

representations of the human passions. The captions which within four years after Messerschmidt's death were attached to the individual busts bear out this latter idea, which was particularly stressed by the artist's contemporaries.

In most instances, however, these captions do not really describe the impressions which the busts convey; in many instances they actually are nonsensical (compare Figs. 35 or 48). While the eyes of "The Troubled One" (Fig. 48) might express grief and sadness, this impression is immediately counteracted by the grimacing, pursed lips, which do not, however, convey a new quality of expression. Another example better characterizes the odd relationship between the captions and the expressions of the busts. "The Hanged One" (Fig. 34) seems to owe its designation only to the rope around the neck, whereas the facial expression—the mouth and the eyes are strenuously distorted and closed—hardly corresponds to the expression one would expect from the descriptive label. We recognize that a part element has apparently determined the choice of the designation, and we shall subsequently come to understand the meaning of this process. Those instances in which the descriptive labels impress us as adequate—for example, "Quiet, Peaceful Sleep" (Fig. 22) or "The Yawning One" (Fig. 30)—give us a clue toward understanding the problem which Messerschmidt attempted to investigate by studying facial expressions.

At the time when he was working on the busts, a general interest in questions of physiognomy had arisen in Germany, almost simultaneously in France, and to a lesser extent in other European countries. The general public keenly followed and participated in a scintillating controversy which during the seventies was conducted by two eminent figures in German letters, Pastor Lavater of Zürich and Professor Lichtenberg of Göttingen. One considered physiognomy to be the science describing the correlation of character traits with anatomical structures of the skull; the other, a wise and witty man who has anticipated many insights of psychoanalysis (Winterstein, 1913), considered *pathognomy*, the science of the varying expressions of the human face, a promising approach to the understanding of man. Both views can be traced back to a pseudo-Aristotelian treatise on physiognomy, and both have continued to play an important role even in present-day anatomical studies and in the psychology of expression. Messerschmidt's busts, however, were not influenced by either approach. His attempt can be traced to a tradition which since the seventeenth century had become firmly rooted in the studios of artists and academies of art. Within this tradition, two approaches can be distinguished. One (which had been initiated by Charles

Le Brun in 1667) consisted of the attempt to find paradigmatic types for the expression of different emotions; the other endeavored to show how one human face changed in reaction to different experiences. This second problem (which, as far as we know, was first formulated in this manner by the English anatomist Parsons in the middle of the eighteenth century) seems to be related to Messerschmidt's venture. What he wanted to represent were the changing relationships of the facial muscles in the performance of different functions; for example, yawning (Fig. 30) or sleeping (Fig. 22). He was not concerned with representing the expression of affects.

However, while the two above-mentioned busts can be explained as such attempts, most of the other busts in the series cannot be said to be adequate studies even of such a narrowly defined problem in pathognomy.

Let us examine some of these busts which can easily be recognized as self-portraits (the "Quiet, Peaceful Sleep" and "The Artist As He Imagined Himself Laughing"—Figures 22 and 23—are to be included among them). The captions—for example, "The Courageous General" (Fig. 24), "The Melancholic One" (Fig. 25), "The Reliable One" (Fig. 27)—do not strike us as appropriate. If we examine the series of these busts, we are struck particularly by the rigidity and emptiness of their expression. They differ from each other mostly by the different type of hairdress; one is almost tempted to say, by their wigs. The occasional attempts at slight variations of the mimic expression cannot dispel the impression of uniformity.

In each of the various types into which Messerschmidt transformed his features, it is possible to point to some further variations. As such we can recognize, for instance, "The Ill-Humored One" (Fig. 28) or "The Satyrizing One" (Fig. 29), in whom the distortion of the facial musculature is carried out to an even higher degree. One bust shows eyes and mouth tightly pressed together; another one shows the eyes wide open, a wrinkled brow, and only the lips closed. These patterns of mimic constellation are repeatedly varied, in manifold ways. Compare, for example, the bust of "The Vexed One" (Fig. 35) and "A Haggard Old Man With Aching Eyes" (Fig. 32). In some instances the distortion has spread to the nose; a series of busts—for instance, "A Simpleton" (Fig. 37) and "Strong Odor" (Fig. 36)—show variations and exaggerations of this.

If we examine the above-mentioned examples, we can without difficulty recognize two interlocking tendencies. One of them—we feel tempted to say, the legitimate one—strives to represent some immediately intelligible personality trait, usually by means of external characterization. The other tendency obviously seeks to change the expression by pushing it in the direction of a grimace. In some instances, for example, "Just Rescued From Drowning" (Fig. 33), there apparently was a subsequent attempt to justify the grimace-like appearance: shutting the eyes and lips is an adequate reaction upon emerging from the water. The impression which "Strong Odor" (Fig. 36) makes can be explained in a similar fashion: the facial contraction which has spread to the nose appears to represent "smelling." We may describe this process as a subsequent attempt at rationalizing the original mimic constellation.

In the majority of busts, however, a comprehensible expression has not been achieved—a fact which can be demonstrated only if the entire series of busts is examined and not merely the few examples which have been selected here.

Before we continue, let us attempt to formulate what we mean by "grimace." In everyday life grimacing occurs under two conditions: as a miscarried expressive movement, that is, when a repressed tendency interferes with the sequence of the intended expression—the smiling upon expressing condolence—and as an intended communication ("making a grimace," "striking a pose"). Both instances involve the expression of aggressive drives which in the first instance triumph over the ego, and in the second are intentionally used by the ego. These two instances may be contrasted to others which we rarely encounter in everyday life and which we might hesitate to include among normal expressions. I am thinking of those cases in which the ego temporarily loses control over the facial expression; for example, when we are overwhelmed by physical pain or a sudden break-through of passion. In these cases we speak of a "distorted face." In a highly schematized manner—similar to the miscarried expression of condolence, yet dissimilar enough to be of importance—we may assume that the ego has been overwhelmed by passions and cannot exercise its functions, that is, it is unable to control the facial musculature.[5]

There is a special reason why the grimace demands our attention. In the miscarried or pathologically distorted facial expression, we can rec-

[5] See Chapter 9 for a further discussion of these problems. The Berlin psychiatrist Bernt Götz has advanced a different conception of the grimace in a friendly and extensive review of the paper referred to above (Kris, 1932). He says (Götz, 1933, #762 ff.): "The grimace is the distorted representation of a type, whereas the caricature is the tendentiously distorted pointing to another person." I cannot share this view. I should like to point out, however, that what the author calls my views on caricature—namely, that it is a portrait whose similarity to the subject is determined by ugliness—has been explicitly cited by me as the oldest definition known to me; see pp. 189f.

ognize an essential characteristic of all expressive movements, namely, their autoplastic function. The generally comprehensible, easily interpretable expression is distinguished from that which "does not speak to us"; the mimic constellation of Messerschmidt's character busts is of this latter kind. We hope to get a better understanding of them by employing that method which we ordinarily use in the attempt to understand other autoplastic formations—for instance, the hysterical symptom. We must conceive of the mimic constellations on Messerschmidt's busts as manifestations of unconscious processes and try to elucidate their meaning by psychoanalytic interpretations. Such elucidation can be based, in this instance, not only on Messerschmidt's own assertions but on Nicolai's descriptions of Messerschmidt's behavior, since Nicolai succeeded in establishing contact with Messerschmidt and winning his confidence during the Bratislava period. Even so, our insight must necessarily remain fragmentary. Nicolai's report, extensive as it is, naturally cannot provide us with a complete picture of Messerschmidt's thought and behavior. Moreover, even those episodes which we shall select for quotation are not fully accessible to systematic and detailed interpretation.

Messerschmidt relates that demons visit him "particularly at night." He "who has always lived in chastity" must suffer the demons' tortures, although by virtue of his chaste life they could be expected to be on good terms with him. The demon of proportion is envious of him, because he, Messerschmidt, almost achieved perfection in proportion. That is the reason why he has painful sensations in his lower abdomen and thighs when he is working on "his marble or bronze pictures" on a certain part of the face "which is analogous to a certain part of the lower region of the body."

Another remark refers to the "tightly pressed together lips" which attracted Nicolai's attention. "Man must completely hide the red of the lip," thought Messerschmidt, "because no animal showed it . . . Animals had vast advantages over man; they knew and sensed many things in nature which were concealed to man."

Nicolai also gives us an idea of the manner in which Messerschmidt worked. In order to gain control over the "demons of proportion," Messerschmidt pinched himself in certain parts of the body—particularly the right side under the ribs—and combined this act with a grimace "which is in the exact required relationship to the pinching of his flesh . . .; he pinched himself, made grimaces in front of the mirror, and believed thus to have achieved miraculous control over the demons. While he was working, he looked into the mirror every half minute and made, with the greatest exactitude, precisely that grimace which he just needed."

Before we proceed to utilize this report written in 1781, it would be advisable again to bring up the question of diagnosis. Messerschmidt's thought processes and behavior, as described by Nicolai, bear out the opinion which the professors of the Academy had already formed in 1774. We are indeed dealing with a psychosis with predominating paranoid trends, which fits the general picture of schizophrenia. The delusions contain many well-known features which are characteristic of artists: the old problem of proportion—the divine proportion, as it has been called since the sixteenth century—is linked to persecution by demons. The heads of animals, which since the classical period have been the basis of physiognomic studies,[6] are connected to the form of the lips, which on many of the busts are drawn inwards.

The second part of Nicolai's report furnishes a starting point for further considerations. During the course of his work, Messerschmidt made grimaces in front of a mirror—grimaces to which he tried to give permanence in his sculptures. In this connection, let me remind you again of my previous remarks about certain character busts, and the physiognomic problem that must have preoccupied Messerschmidt; for example, in "The Laughing One" (Fig. 23) or "The Yawning One" (Fig. 30). Quite obviously, it was always Messerschmidt's own face whose mimic transformation he studied. He merely framed it differently, portraying it with straight hair, giving it a wig, or leaving it bald. But now we can make an assumption about the meaning of the grimacing: We gain the impression that we are dealing with an apotropaic act; the grimaces are aimed at warding off, or intimidating, the demons, and Messerschmidt believed he had achieved, by grimacing, miraculous control over them. The assumption that a regression to magical behavior had occurred is in keeping with the clinical picture. The means used by Messerschmidt, however, seem to facilitate our understanding of another, more general, problem. The role of apotropaic or defensive magic in the rituals of many preliterate societies is well known. It has repeatedly been connected with the widespread use of masks, which tend to survive primitive civilizations and to acquire subsidiary meanings and functions when they occur in a more differentiated cultural context. Messerschmidt's practice leads us to the assumption that we may view grimaces as the autoplastic ancestors of masks.

In order to elucidate the specific meaning of Messerschmidt's grimaces, we return to Nicolai's report, particularly to two of his remarks which can easily be brought into connection with our material. One of

6 During the sixteenth century this view was represented by Giovanni Battista Porta (Fig. 74), during the seventeenth century by Le Brun. See Kris (1932).

them purports that the demons could have been expected to be on friendly terms with Messerschmidt because he had always lived in chastity. The other implies that man, like the animals, must "hide the red of his lips" in order better to understand the demons. This hiding of "the red of the lips" might, first of all, be interpreted as a denial of sexuality, in which the lips are the symbol of sexual impulses. But we also have to consider their meaning in terms of a displacement downwards, a mechanism which played an obvious part in Messerschmidt's delusions: Working on certain parts of the face was accompanied by painful sensations in the genital region. On the basis of general clinical experience we can make the further assumption that the tight closing of the lips was aimed at shutting out the influence of the demons. If we consider the usual double role of the persecutor in paranoid delusions—namely, that he simultaneously punishes and seduces[7]—it is not too far-fetched to assume that we are here dealing with an attempt at warding off the seduction to playing a female role.

In a similar sense we may interpret the alternation in the treatment of the eyes, which are either kept wide open or tightly pressed together. We can conceive of this as an attempt to brave or deny the sight of the demons. We might even endeavor to understand the particular rendering of the nose in a similar fashion, and we shall see that more can be said to bear out this suggestion. Another series of busts, so far neglected, is consistent with these interpretations. One of them, "The Troubled One" (Fig. 48), was mentioned when we examined the captions attached to the busts. There are a number of busts with similarly flaccid, folded-down lips (Fig. 31), and also one which shows the lips half open in disgust (Fig. 46). It does not seem too far-fetched to interpret this feature as representing a yielding or surrender to the demons.

More important, however, than this attempt at interpreting various separate aspects of the mimic constellation—an attempt which cannot be founded on more solid evidence although it would be possible to extend and further develop it—is an insight which pertains to the entire series of busts. In spite of the variations of the mimic constellation itself—only a small number of the "combinations" of traits used by Messerschmidt have been mentioned here—the pervasive impression of uniformity must be emphasized once more. The longer one looks at bust after bust in the series, the more familiar one is with them (and this finding was verified by an experiment), the less interest the observer tends to retain in any

---

[7] For easily accessible examples of this double role, see the autobiography of Schreber (Freud, 1911 b), cases quoted by Kraepelin (1913, III, 2, p. 937 and particularly p. 997), and Fenichel (1946).

individual bust. Endeavors "to interpret the expression" are soon abandoned; the mimic constellation is soon recognized as a grimace; the
laughing of Figure 23, for instance, is perceived as a masked grinning.
In the second stage of reaction, the observer becomes aware of the uniformity of the grimaces. At this point an impression arises which cor-
roborates and complements the diagnosis of the clinical syndrome in
question: The impression grows that the artist's activity has been severely
limited by special conditions, that spontaneity has given way to a stereotypy, which even without knowledge of the specific determining factors
tends to be experienced by the observer as pathological.

Only two busts stand out from the others (Figs. 40 and 41). They
differ also by their smaller size. Instead of describing them, we shall again
refer to Nicolai's report:

> In one corner of the room, however, there were two busts of a
> shape which is difficult to describe. Imagine that all bones and muscles
> of a human face are pressed together and pulled forward in such a
> way that the most advanced point of the flattened forehead and the
> farthest point of the protruding chin form an angle of 20°, that is, the
> face is almost pulled into the shape of a beak, without, however,
> losing its human elements.

This description, indeed, conveys the essence of the impression. One
might say that the head is merely an accessory of the beak.

> I noticed [continues Nicolai] that Messerschmidt glanced at these
> busts briefly with fixed eyes, and quickly turned his head away.
> Thereupon I asked him rather cautiously what these busts repre-
> sented. Messerschmidt seemed reluctant to come forth with an expla-
> nation . . . and his otherwise vivid eyes turned glassy when he finally
> answered in broken words: "That one" [i.e., the demon] had pinched
> him, Messerschmidt, and he in turn pinched the demon and these
> figures were the result of it. "I thought, at last I will subdue you, but
> he nearly died in this effort." From what he said I realized that these
> caricatures of human faces were actually the figures in which the de-
> luded fantasy of Messerschmidt saw the demons of proportion.

Messerschmidt also added that he felt fully capable of doing the
entire series of busts over again "with the exception of the two beak heads
which he felt unable to produce a second time."

It is indeed highly plausible that we are here confronted with
an image of the demon in his role as persecutor and seducer. In these
busts, as in the others, the lips are the center on which attention is
focused. However, they are not only pressed together as they are on the
other busts; they are pulled out and elongated into a protruding and

pointed shape as if they were made out of dough. A phallic impression, a general sense of activity and directedness, is thus evolved. This activity, we may venture to assume, is attributed through projection to the demons as persecutors. But on closer inspection, a second and more convincing interpretation is suggested by the very appearance of the busts and by the content of the delusion—at least if we try to supplement by general clinical experience the information conveyed by Nicolai: What on one level may impress us as activity is on another a break-through of the passive feminine fantasy, which the tightly closed lips of Messerschmidt's other busts seem to have warded off. We gain the conviction that what the busts represent can be conceived of as direct illustration of fellatio, to which the demons invite Messerschmidt and which they force upon him. A glance at the rectangle of the neck in the frontal view (Fig. 40) confirms the impression that the features of the human head have been distorted or stretched in order to combine or include both male and female sexual organs.

Such attempts at interpretation, though they seem to fit into the general clinical context, tend to by-pass another important problem which the beak heads suggest. Let us start from the effect on the observer: It is not merely more intense than that of the other busts but different in kind. No mimic constellation, no grimace is rendered. The theme of the "face" is retained, and, as Nicolai suggested, the human features are not "lost," but the artist deals with them in supreme freedom. Messerschmidt has risen from the rendition of a grimace to the creation of an ornamental configuration. We may speak of a transition from the autoplastic function of a mimic ritual to the alloplastic function of the work of art. Hence a different position of the beak heads as works of art, evidenced by the reaction of observers, seems to correspond to their particular psychological position, evidenced by the fact that they evoked anxiety in the artist. If we try to account for this coincidence, the following hypothesis suggests itself: The artist's "transformation" of reality, to which the beak heads owe their effect, seems to be related to the fact that we find in them the clearest expression of the sexual nucleus of Messerschmidt's delusions.[8] In accordance with our knowledge of the nature of dream work, we may assume that here the artistic "transformation of reality" had to be carried so far in order to disguise the latent fantasy.[9]

[8] For an elaboration of this thought see now Bergmann (1935) whose remarks on the psychoanalytic theory of evaluating works of literature deserve more attention than they have received.

[9] Compare Götz's (1933) suggestion in his review of the German publication of this material (Kris, 1932), where he interprets the tightly pressed together lips "as repre-

We are well familiar with the connection between stylization, to which natural forms are subjected, and the wide area of sexual symbolism which we know from numerous examples of prehistoric or "primitive" art. In Messerschmidt's busts we can find another, analogous, instance of stylization which promises to give us deeper insight into the conditions under which it comes into being. Some of the busts show the lips specially formed and elaborated, shaped, for example, into a band covering the mouth (Figs. 42, 44, 45). After what we have so far established, we may well attempt to inquire into the symbolic meaning of this rendering: This meaning becomes apparent if we conceive of the band as a girdle—as the girdle of chastity. In some instances, for example, "Grief Locked Up Inside" (Fig. 45), this stylization is not confined to a single element. It spreads to the entire lower part of the face. An almost independent ornamental configuration arises, composed like a mask and formed out of lines framing the band-lips and merging into the area of the chin. If we take into account that mouth and lips, whose red mucus had to be hidden, are those parts of the face which play a paramount part in Messerschmidt's delusion, we are led to realize that the artist tended to abandon the natural rendering of those parts of the face whose magical meaning predominated.

This assumption is in agreement with what we know about the sequence in which the busts were made. Messerschmidt started to work on them in the early seventies; by 1776 he had finished six of them; one year later twelve bronze busts were ready; and in the early eighties over sixty busts were seen in Messerschmidt's studio. When Nicolai visited Messerschmidt, he found him working on the sixty-first bust; two years later, after Messerschmidt's death, sixty-nine busts were found. If we group the busts which have been preserved on the basis of formal characteristics—a procedure usually followed in art history with material of otherwise undetermined origin—we might be inclined to place first those heads which Nicolai regarded as "the simple busts, in harmony with the laws of nature." He was obviously thinking of the "self-portraits" (Figs. 22-25, 27). Next in line we might be inclined to put those which "in order to imitate the supernatural sense of animals" are depicted "with

---

senting a vague fear of streaming into endless space, as a fear of dissolution of the self." He believes that the "beak which sticks out and points away from the center of the head" represents not merely "sexual 'un-selfing' but 'un-selfing' per se." The beak heads are "the embodiment of the essentially questionable." Götz obviously failed to see that I had tried, in my way, to interpret what he views as the "fear of unselfing" and the "despondency" of the schizophrenic "in the course of continual depersonalization." For other interpretations of Messerschmidt, see now also Birnbaum (1935).

lips tightly pinched together and strained convulsions."[10] Within this large series, a sequence can easily be suggested. The bust showing least distortion could be joined to the self-portraits, and the extreme and therefore presumably latest position could be given to those in which the nose has become part of the grimace, particularly the one labeled "Strong Odor" (Fig. 36). This would establish the transition to the concluding links in this chain of assumed development, the beak heads.

Such an assumption on the chronological origin of the busts is based on the idea that during the course of his work Messerschmidt's style had developed from one close to nature to one highly stylized—an assumption in general agreement with investigations on the "history of style." In this instance, however, such a procedure can be proved to be erroneous. However little we can ever hope to establish the exact chronological sequence in which the busts were made, we can establish that the beak heads did not originate last, and that some of the plain self-portraits—for instance, "Quiet Peaceful Sleep" (Fig. 22)—were made after the beak heads.[11] We can thus supplement, or in fact replace, assumptions based on the history of style by others based on the psychological function of style. Instead of indicating an early or late phase in Messerschmidt's development as an artist, the formal rendering of the beak heads is linked to what the busts represent, that is, to their psychological meaning in Messerschmidt's imagination.

These considerations have enhanced if not overreached the potentialities of the data available in this case. We have ventured beyond the topic of this essay and entered the central domain of the psychology of art in inquiring into the interrelationship between formal structure and context, a question clearly inaccessible from the narrow starting point which we have chosen in this instance. We therefore return to Messerschmidt's busts. Their closer inspection suggests a large number of questions of which only a few can find an answer.

Nicolai's report verified what the comparison of the different busts and the recognition of their common typical elements, their pattern of grimacing distortion, had suggested: Messerschmidt did not use different models but always copied his own image studied in the mirror. The strange attempt to disguise and vary his own appearance, to show himself as a baldhead, as an old man with flowing curls, as a youth with slicked-

10 Nicolai counted fifty-four such busts. It seems that Messerschmidt himself destroyed some of them before his death and replaced others with those that have been preserved. With the exception of eight busts, all those that have been preserved belong in this group of replacements.

11 For a more detailed discussion on these points see Kris (1932).

back hair, gains a special significance. On the basis of what we know about the psychology of schizophrenics, we can conceive of these variations as the artist's attempt to prove the existence of his own person again and again, and simultaneously as determined by the quest for new and satisfactory external trappings. In the light of these considerations Messerschmidt's work on the character busts appears in a new light, as an attempt at regaining contact, a procedure of self-healing.

This assumption is concerned with more than the manner in which Messerschmidt attempted to solve the task he had posed himself. The mere fact of his turning to physiognomic problems, that is, the choice of the topic, which by virtue of its didactic meaning might have been close to his sphere of interest, can be thought of as being determined by one of the basic disturbances frequently met with in schizophrenics. We know that Messerschmidt started his work on the busts during the "first" period of his disorder. If we further recall the series of self-portraits (Figs. 24, 25, 27) with their peculiar dullness and dearth of expression, we can hardly escape the notion that we are here dealing with a person who struggles before the mirror for a genuine facial expression in order to retain the rapidly vanishing contact with the environment. It is an attempt in which he fails. The expression of his self-portraits remains artificial.[12]

Not only Messerschmidt's turning to physiognomic studies in general, but also the specific way in which the project was pursued can be regarded as an attempt at restitution. In this attempt, the readily comprehensible facial expression is replaced by a system of rigid mimic constellations which, though unsuitable in serving a social function and in establishing contact with the environment, have become the bearers of a magic ritual. Only the connection with this ritual enables us to understand the meaning of individual mimic elements. We may also assume that Messerschmidt's psychic condition determined to some extent the special task he chose within the general area of physiognomy. He was not concerned with studying the variations of expression under the impact of different affects; he was interested only in the reaction of the facial muscles. His was an attempt to attain in a roundabout man-

---

12 For further discussion of this problem see Chapter 3, and for its relation to diagnostic criteria in psychiatry see Chapter 9. At this point I mention only that according to an information which I owe to Nunberg, Bleuler frequently made the diagnosis of schizophrenia after separately observing the upper and lower part of the patient's face, by covering either part with his hand. Messerschmidt's busts, too, frequently convey an impression of disunity of expression; certain separate mimic elements appear to be in distinct opposition to others. A sensitive observer who visited Messerschmidt in 1780 stressed the "devastated expression" of the artist's features.

ner—as it were from the outside or the surface—a socially effective, mimic expression. He accomplished this goal only in a few instances, e.g., "The Yawning One" (Fig. 30). But here he was dealing with no more than a mimic pattern which can be regarded as a reflex movement. Yawning is ontogenetically among the first "mimic" expressions of the newborn and has originally no psychological determinants. In some of the other busts, the expression appears to be merely an added element, superimposed on the grimace—an attempt to give the grimace some emotive tint, i.e., to rationalize it. Upon superficial observation, the actual expression of some busts seems to prevail over their grimace-like quality: e.g., "The Enraged and Vengeful Gypsy" (Fig. 47). Here we feel inclined to believe in the rage, the unrestricted paroxysm of passion. In characterizing such outbreaks of emotion and the uncanny feeling they evoke, we usually speak of "senseless" or "insane" rage. This cannot be accidental; we sense the proximity to psychosis. If we consider the fact that among more than fifty busts this rage is almost the only genuine, and certainly the most intense, expression of affective experience, we can assume that on other occasions all affects had to be avoided to prevent the break-through of dammed-up rage. These considerations are, however, not based on solid evidence. If one looks at the bust of "The Enraged Gypsy" (Fig. 47) somewhat longer and more often, comparing it with the other busts, one soon realizes that even here the expression of affects tends to glide into a grimace.

With greater assuredness we are able to interpret the facial expression of one other bust to which we still have to refer; it is one of those which show the lips rendered as a band. The traditional caption— "Afflicted With Constipation" (Fig. 44)—is here completely convincing. But, if one looks at this bust for a longer period of time and somewhat more carefully, one is struck by the fact that this bust, too, shows many features which are to be attributed to the stereotypy of Messerschmidt's grimace. The individual elements, however, are subordinated to the general posture of the person who struggles against constipation, and are attuned to the endeavor to aid evacuation by pressing. Nevertheless, one does remain uncertain about the extent to which all details can be derived from these conditions. Some observers are inclined to interpret the tenseness as anxiety.

Anal fantasies fit well into the general context of Messerschmidt's delusional system. Here, too, we complement by analogy the scant material we owe to Nicolai's anamnesis. We might conjecture that defecation signified for Messerschmidt the barrier which separated him from his environment; or, perhaps, that the fecal column stood for the anal penis of the demon which he tried to remove from his body. Little as such assumptions can be documented by the "case history," they nevertheless coincide with our expectations that grimacing (the psychological significance of which we are trying to elucidate) might be connected with anal fantasies. Another important pathological phenomenon of the mimic apparatus, the tic, has been explained by Abraham and other investigators as a fixation on the anal level and even as a conversion symptom on this level.[13] That anal preoccupations played a role in Messerschmidt's delusions is apparent from Nicolai's report. In a passage which follows the description of Messerschmidt's anxiety upon looking at the beak heads, Nicolai reports this:

> When filled with mortal dread he [Messerschmidt] pinched the demon, and the demon in turn pinched him, the demon fortunately jumped up suddenly, let go a hellish flatus and disappeared. If this had not happened, Messerschmidt surely would have died. The devil [Nicolai adds] has for some time been said to disappear in the midst of dreadful stench.

We may here recall the busts in which the position of the nose is of special significance. But just at this point there is a major gap in the series of busts which have been preserved: Apart from "Strong Odor" (Fig. 36) there originally existed other busts dealing with similar themes.[14] In some of the preserved busts, the grimace-like cramp has indeed spread to the nose, the head is slightly bowed forward, and thus the impression is created that the primary aim is to avoid both sight and smell.

Nothing, however, is more characteristic of Messerschmidt's work than the fact that the same position of the head, the same mimic constellation is in one bust (Fig. 44) clearly linked to *one* psychic sensation, whereas in other busts it is not merely extended but actually transformed into moods in which a comic element predominates (Figs. 38, 39). Here too, the tightly pressed together lips and the alternatively closed or open eyes predominate, while the moods of "smiling" or "hypocrisy" are a mere coloring. Since these features recur frequently, they can be taken as evidence of Messerschmidt's endeavor to dissimulate the grimace and to deny the fundamental condition which directed his working. It is hardly surprising that cheerful or comical effects should have been adopted with preference since precisely these attitudes can readily be put into the service of disguises of and defense against anxiety.

13 See also p. 232.
14 See Kris (1932).

Let us summarize: A distinguished portraitist of the late baroque period (as such we met the young Messerschmidt) turns to physiognomic studies. This shift of interest is motivated by several factors, some of which are directly linked to his mental illness and to the specific content of his delusions. They gain an influence on his rendering of the human face; human expressions are turned into grimaces serving magic functions, which could in outline be interpreted. This interpretation became possible by recognizing that on a second level of artistic activity, as it were, the artist has endeavored to conceal the magic meaning of his grimaces by external attributes, such as changing coiffures or generally coloring the facial constellation with some expressive elements. An attempt is made to justify the largest possible number of those elements, which were prescribed by the delusional thoughts and the magic function. Thus he strived to endow with a meaning understandable to his public (but secondary) what was originally meaningful only to himself and was a part of his delusional thinking.[15]

What Messerschmidt tried to surmount was what from the viewpoint of the theory of art one may be tempted to call the aesthetic barrier. It is the same boundary by which Freud tried to distinguish dream or daydream from narrative writings, or fantasy from poetry. Tempting as it may be further to elaborate and extend this thought, such a venture would be beyond the scope of this essay. All we can do is illustrate the problem to which Freud has pointed by a concrete example of a particularly striking kind.

In the early eighties, when Nicolai found Messerschmidt working on the character busts, the artist had made among other portrait-busts one of the Capuchin monk Fessler (Fig. 50), a strange and restless man who was later to conclude his stormy life as bishop of the reformed community of St. Petersburg in Russia. It is difficult to break the spell exercised by the portrait of this man. If we compare it with one of Messerschmidt's early busts—e.g., the bust of Jan Gerhardt van Swieten, commissioned by Maria Theresa in 1767 (Fig. 49)—we realize that the grandiose baroque pathos has been replaced by concise and concentrated soberness.[16] This

---

15 The occasionally rather peculiar "captions" of the busts serve obviously the same purpose. They as well as the general theme of the whole series—its function as representations of passion or character studies—retain precisely that interpretation by which Messerschmidt tried to justify his work and to "explain" it to his environment. That he succeeded in this endeavor is demonstrated by numerous opinions voiced immediately after his death. Moreover, later, during a period of more than half a century, art historians have treated the busts as documents of and even as milestones in the history of style.

16 It seems that we are not yet equipped to answer the questions of the psychological meaning of this change of style. The existing material gives us no clue as to

conciseness may be in part derived from the skill Messerschmidt had acquired while he worked on the character busts, which in many features of rendering reflect the influence of classical, particularly Roman, portraits. The relation to the character busts is evidenced also by one detail: the small tightly closed lips. In the character busts the lips are the carriers of secret magic thought—connections linked to the nucleus of the delusions. In the portrait of the monk, however, the lips are integrated with the lines and features of the face and decidedly contribute to its physiognomic characteristics.[17] Nothing reveals the delusional thoughts which, as we know, Messerschmidt tended to connect with the rendering of this part of the human face.

Among the considerable number of reflections which an observation of this kind is likely to stimulate, there is one that seems particularly worth pursuing: May we not assume that private or "secret" meanings are attached to all or many elements of the artist's work, and particularly to the formal elements for which he shows preference in one way or another? Favorable circumstances provide us in the case of Messerschmidt, a psychotic individual, with data which throw some light on this problem. We are enabled, at least in a crude and approximate fashion, to distinguish those elements in the treatment of his medium which are determined by his individual psychological predispositions (in this case by his delusion) from others which are generally intelligible without recourse to such an individual frame of reference and could therefore be generally effective. Individual and "private" meanings of this kind are obviously an integral part also of the structure of the works of normal artists. In the ideal case these meanings cannot be separated from the whole of the structure; presumably all details and traits are socially meaningful. It seems reasonable to assume that the manner in which "the private meanings" are integrated into the structure of the artistic product is of decisive importance for the nature (and perhaps the "value") of the artistic creation. The capacity of the artist for using derivatives of unconscious processes in a socially and historically adequate way may well constitute a significant factor in his endowment.

which sources determined this artistic development of Messerschmidt, which was, as we pointed out earlier, fully adjusted to the current trends in contemporary art. A highly schematic and hardly satisfactory generalization might merely point to the fact that a relationship may be assumed to exist between the restrained conciseness of the formal characteristic of Messerschmidt's late works, the characteristics of classicism, and the detached attitude of the schizophrenic to his environment.

[17] It was possible to establish beyond any doubt that this was not a characteristic of the model; moreover, we encounter the same feature in the one other portrait bust which Messerschmidt made at that time.

I fear that I have digressed too far, and I shall again return to Nicolai's report. Two fragments of his account, and hence two elements in Messerschmidt's delusion, can apparently be further elucidated. One of them is Messerschmidt's notion that the demon of proportion persecuted him because this demon knew that he had attained perfection in the mastery of proportion. The other pertains to an action which Nicolai describes; namely, that Messerschmidt repeatedly pinched himself below the ribs while working. These two parts of Nicolai's report can be connected. But before this can be done it is necessary to make another digression which will lead us back to our initial reflections.

I said in the beginning that, contrary to the established tradition of psychoanalytic pathographies, I would use only a few biographical data, because I had good reasons to distrust their validity. I now have to justify this suspicion. It is based on two distortions which we find in practically all biographical reports concerning Messerschmidt. One of these distortions can be traced back to Messerschmidt himself. Ever since the time of his pensioning he had believed himself to be persecuted and a victim of the academic "gang." We know that precisely this attitude—i.e., that he "deemed all professors and directors to be his enemies"—was among the first symptoms of his illness. He informed everybody he met that people were plotting against him. Soon after his death this idea entered the accounts on his life, found generàl acceptance, and constituted gradually a theme elaborated by later biographers, since it was familiar to the ideology of the earlier and middle part of the nineteenth century, when the role of artist as a genius opposed to the dominant trends of his time was in full ascendancy. This coincidence explains why Messerschmidt's life history was treated repeatedly by art critics and how it entered the province of the fiction writer until the paranoid delusion of the artist had been fully molded into the image of the genius misunderstood by his contemporaries. When, several years ago, I first approached the study of Messerschmidt's life and work, I found myself faced with this image. It took some labor and a careful revision of contemporary source material to reconstruct the facts and disentangle them from ideologically colored distortions. In the course of this process a considerable part of what the biographers reported lost its value.

The other distortion which we must take into account can be explained in terms of an even older literary tradition. Numerous reports pertaining to Messerschmidt are related to us in the form of anecdotes. Some of them can be tentatively related to actual occurrences, for instance, allusions to his sexual life which seem to throw light on his latent homosexuality. We hear that he was reluctant to marry, that he fell in

love with his brother's wife; there are also intimations of a strong attachment to one of his apprentices. But even these reports seem based essentially on rumors. In other instances the unreliability of the traditional
reports can definitely be ascertained, since the majority of these anecdotes
are not told only of Messerschmidt but are part and parcel of the typical
"image of the artist" in literary tradition.[18]

That Messerschmidt grew up as a shepherd and acquired his skill
while whittling the animals in his flock would be extremely important information, if we did not know that the same anecdote has been
related about more than a dozen great artists since the Renaissance. The
same is true of reports of Messerschmidt's miraculous speed of working
or of stories reporting that he took revenge on his enemies by portraying
them as animals. The "image of the artist" of which these and similar
reports are constituent parts leads back into mythological tradition, into
the world in which the artist as a creator is endowed with the powers of
the magician and is penalized by the Gods for rebellion and rivalry.
This tradition is not dead; it lives on and powerfully determines conduct, its major themes reëmerging in the unconscious of many artists.
Hence we are not astonished to find it as part of the delusion of the psychotic creator. When Messerschmidt pinches his ribs while working on
a sculpture, we are, I believe, entitled to assume at least two determining
thoughts: His castration anxiety drives him to prove that the rib is still
there, from which God has created the woman; this thought provides the
link to the delusional fear of being overpowered and raped by the
demons, a fantasy the existence of which we had previously surmised.
The other determining thought is Messerschmidt's identification with
God—the sculptor creator: While working he feels his own ribs in order
to create human figures. We may add that at this point a circle seems to
be closed: What he sculptures—his own image, his face—has for Messerschmidt a feminine connotation.

The schizophrenic artist's identification with God, the creator, also
determines Messerschmidt's delusion according to which the envious
demon of proportion persecutes him. For Messerschmidt as for many
other artists, proportion—*divina proporzione*—is the secret of God. In
wrestling to attain it he violates a divine prohibition. In this delusion
the Promethean rebellion emerges in the form of a projection—he, the
rebel, is persecuted by God.

[18] See Chapter 2.

Chapter 5

THE FUNCTION OF DRAWINGS AND THE MEANING OF THE "CREATIVE SPELL" IN A SCHIZOPHRENIC ARTIST

Written in Collaboration with ELSE PAPPENHEIM

I

Psychiatric interest in the art of the insane dates back well over eighty years. Though many of the several hundred contributions listed in recent bibliographies[1] start from clinical material, most of them are explicitly or implicitly centered around a crucial problem: the relationship of genius and insanity. The problem is an ancient one in the world of learning and speculation. It was first and with remarkable wisdom posed by Plato. His distinction between the "productive insanity" of the creative genius and the pathology of insanity itself approximates formulations suggested by contemporary psychoanalytic insight. In the psychiatry of the nineteenth century the problem was reintroduced by Lombroso. Under his aegis much time was spent in a search for insanity in the genius. Since 1920 a shift of position has occurred: under the influence of the expressionistic and surrealist movements in contemporary art there has been a search for the genius in the insane. This point of view dominates Prinzhorn's volume on the subject (1922 a), but there is reason to believe that his eloquent aesthetic partisanship during the last two decades has delayed rather than accelerated interest in the clinical problems with which the study of the productions of the insane confront us. When we speak here of the "art" of the insane, we are not considering aesthetic values, but merely recognizing the fact that the productions are "of the nature of art."

Detailed clinical case histories and clearly formulated propositions are not plentiful in the literature. In most cases authors refer to the creative activity of psychotics for the sake of illustration alone. A mere

[1] See Anastasi and Foley (1941-1944) ; also Lange-Eichbaum (1932).

few have used experimental methods for diagnostic and therapeutic purposes.[2]

Most of the clinically oriented contributions deal with the artistic productions of schizophrenic patients who represent the largest contingent of the asylum population, and who more frequently than other psychotics express themselves artistically. Absolute figures of artistically creative patients are at any rate small; even according to Prinzhorn's liberal count less than 2 per cent of the asylum population ever shows a tendency to artistic production.[3]

The spontaneous artistic expression of schizophrenics is predominantly in the medium of the written word; drawings, interspersed with script or a transition between them, are more frequent than works in plastic, either modeled or carved.

Psychiatric students of schizophrenic imagery stressed a number of characteristics: the tendency to fill space, to "crowd in," the stereotypy and the rigidity of all shapes, and the hypertrophy of symbols. These characteristics were then related to the behavior and thought process typical of the schizophrenic. Psychoanalytic comments have repeatedly drawn attention to the working of the primary process in schizophrenic imagery, with its condensation, displacement, allusion, symbolism, and play upon words and shapes.[4] Partly under the influence of psychoanalytic thought it has become traditional to compare the productions of the "insane, the savage and the child."[5] Such true and alleged similarities made it routine for Jungian psychology to rely upon graphic material to demonstrate the general characteristics of the "archaic unconscious." To others, dissatisfied with the uncertainties of this explanation, they indicate a host of unsolved problems. The problem of the affinity of all undifferentiated psychic structure, i.e., the universality of the id, is here at stake, apart from the question of whether the lack of differentiation is due mainly to biological, pathological or cultural factors. Whatever we

[2] See Anastasi and Foley (1944), Becker (1934), Reitman (1950), Sapas (1918), Schube and Cowell (1939).

[3] The Heidelberg collection upon which Prinzhorn's views are based (1919, 1922) contained drawings and paintings of psychotic patients from various European countries. The distribution of diagnoses was: schizophrenics 75 per cent; manic-depressives 8 per cent; and the rest various other mental illnesses. In view of the varying diagnostic standards in the institutions from which the material came, these figures should be looked upon with reservation. In the literature the diagnosis "manic-depressive psychosis" is made in a good many cases where the published case history suggests schizophrenia.

[4] See Bertschinger (1911), Merzbach (1930), Schilder (1918, 1923, 1942); see also pp. 101-106 and 196-203.

[5] Lips (1937), Naecke (1913), Réja (1901), Lewis (1928).

may be able to contribute to this range of problems will be a by-product.

Clinical data, to which we now turn, are most ample for the paranoid schizophrenic group of psychotics. Clinical investigations tend to suggest the necessity of distinguishing between those skilled in the arts previous to the manifestation of the psychosis, and those who start to create spontaneously during the course of their illness without previous training.

Little is known in detail about these sudden outbursts.[6] Every mental institution in Western civilization has its inmates who cover every scrap of paper, every free place on wall or window sill, with words or shapes; there are some who carve with any instrument at hand in any material to which they can gain access or who model in bread if there is no clay. Psychotic writers, painters or sculptors may persevere in their activity for weeks, years, or, as in a case fully reported by Morgenthaler (1921), for decades. All authors agree that "the spell to create" does not develop during the acute phase of the psychotic attack and that periods of creative activity are interrupted by acute exacerbations. Some start to create for the first time during the course of illness, others stop after a remission.[7]

The pathological process produces marked changes in the style of most skilled schizophrenics who have been studied.[8] These changes may lead in two directions. In some cases it is claimed that the artist's work has gained by "the change of style," a claim which seems plausible anent changes during the prodromal or initial stages of the schizophrenic process. In other cases the deterioration is obvious.[9]

The patient we are presenting falls into the group of skilled artists whose productions change during the psychotic process. This change is due neither to an increase nor a decrease of ability, but rather to a change in the function of artistic activity. The new function it acquires can only be understood in the light of the patient's delusional system. His delu-

[6] Reitman (1947) uses the term "creative spell," derived from this paper, in order to characterize the activity of two patients after leucotomy. One patient produced after the operation, upon request of the psychiatrist, several paintings, which seem to have had a cathartic effect. The second patient changed her previous creative work in consequence of the operation. We would hesitate to speak of "creative spell" in either case. In a subsequent publication (1950), Reitman left the question of the effects of brain surgery upon creative expression open, since the necessary follow-up studies had not yet been carried out.

[7] See a case of Villamil's (1933) discussed here, p. 89; see also Bürger-Prinz (1932), Guttmann and Maclay (1937), Maschmeyer (1926), Prinzhorn (1919, 1922) and Schilder (1918).

[8] See Aschaffenburg (1915), Fay (1912), Prinzhorn (1922 a and b), Weygandt (1925), Jaspers (1926), and here Chapter 3.

[9] See Audry (1942), Evenson (1936), Anastasi and Foley (1940-1944).

sion seems also to determine why he must create in abundance. We therefore focus our attention on two problems which the title of the paper indicates: the change of function of drawing and the urge to this activity.

II

We observed the forty-nine-year-old architect, F. W., from January 17th to March 13th, 1938, at the University Hospital for Mental and Nervous Diseases in Vienna. Our data concerning the development of his psychosis are limited to two scanty hospital records of the years 1932 and 1935, to the patient's own information, and to his drawings. The only outside person we interviewed was his housekeeper, a woman of fifty-two, but her statements were not very revealing. She was committed together with the patient because she claimed with equal emphasis that he was chosen for a special mission, but within two days she gained enough insight to be discharged. According to her report the patient had lived in dire need for many years, completely withdrawn from all social contact. She was the only person he saw regularly, and she evidently took care of his barest physical needs.

The reason for the patient's first admission in 1932 is unknown. He was then oriented and coöperative but had some vague ideas of reference. He was hospitalized for only five days and discharged with the diagnosis schizoid psychopath. In 1935 he was committed because he had made confused speeches in the Cathedral of Vienna. The content of his delusions was similar to but more systematized than that which we studied later in 1938. He called himself the Son of God who dutifully fulfilled God's will. He dwelt a great deal on his ability to foretell political events, such as the Viennese revolution in February 1934; yet he never claimed to be God himself or to be able actually to bring about political events. In 1938 he most emphatically made these claims. His second hospitalization (1935) lasted for two months; he was discharged in the care of his housekeeper, with the diagnosis paranoid schizophrenia. Nothing was heard of him until January 1938. His commitment at that time followed an outburst of rage in which he destroyed several busts in his studio.

The patient referred to the formal data of his life history in rather vague and mystical terms. Fortunately one of us (Kris) had had an opportunity to watch his work at some distance in about 1920 and was able to supply further data. The patient was born in 1889, the second of five siblings, in a small village near Vienna. His father was a lumberjack. The patient claimed that he was interested in drawing and technical construction as far back as he could remember. He had been trained in architectural design, drawing and painting in a professional high school and later at the Academy of Fine Arts in Vienna. His school record must have entitled him to admission to a university, for he served as an infantry officer during the First World War at the time when a commission in the Austrian Army depended on educational status. He was well read in an autodidactic way, an admirer of Nietzsche ("the only man possibly greater than myself"), familiar with the Bible and the standard works of German literature. Around 1920 he worked as draftsman for one of the largest interior decorating firms in Vienna and his career flourished. About 1924 he established himself as an independent architect and had several contracts with one of the richest men of the day. His good fortune apparently did not outlive that of his patron; the wave of depression that swept Austria at the end of the decade carried both downward. This is all we know about him before his hospitalization.

The patient was seen immediately upon admission. He was offended and agitated because he felt his commitment was unjustified, but he was oriented in all spheres and fairly coöperative. He brought a bundle of papers along, covered with peculiar drawings. When asked about them, he became friendly and seemed to lose his initial suspicion.

In spite of his psychosis the patient was an imposing figure. He was tall, rather broad, with expressive features. His movements were always measured. Though he accompanied his speech with theatrical gestures, he never lost a certain dignity. He spoke about himself with obvious satisfaction and with a certain unctuous pomposity, even at moments of anger or excitement. He often appeared suspicious and cautious, yet he rarely lost an air of condescending amiability.

In the hospital he submitted to the routine. There was no sign of deterioration in formal intelligence or appearance. He showed no mannerisms. His theatrical gestures never went beyond those which any temperamental person might display while passionately elaborating on an idea. He played chess and cards with some of the other patients, but on the whole had a meager contact with them. Toward most patients and attendants he was haughty and often quarrelsome. Sometimes he would single out one of the more intelligent patients and stride up and down with him for hours while he delivered a monologue. Similarly with us: Although he welcomed our interest and expressed gratification when his speeches were taken down in shorthand, our response did not really matter. We were ordinary mortals, unable to grasp the real significance of his life, and important only as mere tools since we would spread his gospel. He discussed his drawings willingly but confined himself to the details he thought meaningful. He rarely answered our questions, and when we insisted he sometimes became impatient and irritated—we should think for ourselves and not bore him with trifles. At times, in an almost tragic fashion, he acknowledged his actual situation, the fact that he had been committed and that he was destitute. He became especially bitter when notified that he would be evicted from his studio unless he could produce a certificate testifying to his mental health. When he was denied this certificate, he reacted at first with anger and denounced it all as persecution, but soon he tried to console himself. It was all for the best; he had to be declared insane by the authorities so that the truth could become known to the world. He elaborated on the persecution of which he was a victim and became more and more excited, threatening his enemies with revenge, first in a bragging way, soon with full conviction of his omnipotence and self-sufficiency. He could get out of the hospital if he chose, but his mission could be better fulfilled if he remained.

III

The patient's delusion was well systematized and showed no unusual features. His megalomania culminated in his identification with God the creator and ruler, the builder of the universe and the sculptor of men. He did not always strictly adhere to the idea of being God but repeatedly referred to himself as the Son of God through whom and in whom God worked; frequently he claimed that both were one and the same. He had become aware of his mission at the age of twelve when a revelation came to him while he was lying on a lawn at night, filled with longing for the stars. All his drawings, he said, were conceived at that time.

His ideas of reference and persecution were extensive. Among his persecutors were everyday people, the janitor, neighbors, or former employers and colleagues such as the association of architects. He was ambivalent toward his housekeeper: she was either in the service of his enemies or the only person attached to him. His more important persecutors were the whole Austrian government under Dollfuss and Schuschnigg, a secret organization of Jews and the Catholic Church—particularly Cardinal Innitzer of Vienna. The church was responsible for the death by poison of his mother and brother-in-law years ago. He himself had become desperately ill at that time. He had learned about the church's plot when he confronted his housekeeper with the accusation: "You miserable creature, you poisoner," and in tears she uttered the word: "Rome." To some extent the patient used the traditional language of Austrian anticlericalism and the slogans of National Socialism. He looked upon Hitler and, to a lesser degree, Mussolini, as his representatives on earth. The earth was too small to be of great interest to him, so he would dedicate it to Hitler and only partly to Mussolini to prevent a fight. But even Hitler would not be allowed to do anything without the patient's authorization. His enemies were, in fact, powerless, since the patient was God himself, and a single stroke of his pen would have destroyed all of them irrevocably. When Hitler actually invaded Austria, the patient was beside himself with joy. He was seen for the last time on March 13th, two days after the occupation, when he said triumphantly: "Now it is done; I accomplished it all with my sword."

The ideas of persecution were clearly linked to his identification with God. While on one occasion he claimed to have written the New Testament himself, he referred to Christ with violent scorn. "To worship Christ is blasphemy; all those who worship him perish. They shall wade in blood." When asked whether he was the true son of God, he answered, "What has not been true so far became true now. Christ was supposed to remove all wrong doings; my secret is that I have done so. Today I took the sin of all men unto myself . . . I have stated there is no dead God and that no dead God shall be resurrected . . . They are praying to a dead body." In several drawings he symbolized Vienna by a *Pietà* to indicate that she would be destroyed like Jerusalem, whereas Berlin, the city of light in the future world, would assume Rome's present significance. Nevertheless, pointing to the corpse of the *Pietà*, he said, "The dead body, like myself lying on the lap." His hatred of Jesus is probably an expression of sibling rivalry for his mother's love. It also seems to be an illustration of his experience of depersonalization, since he frequently spoke of himself as being dead. The destruction of Vienna seems to symbolize the death of his mother and his experience of *Weltuntergang*.

His direct competition with Christ is manifest when he refers to Christ's origin in "an unclean marriage." Therefore, he could not have been the redeemer. The patient, however, was the product of a "clean marriage"—his parents were exempt from Original Sin. "The heart of Jesus was always an offense to me. Chaste love is always marriage, the great mother always above it. Always Christ and his mother. [With irritation] They always put the old mother and her son in front of each other! They destroyed it." The patient said of his father: "He was love in its purest form. Very silent, never outspoken." His mother too was "pure." He is going to elevate her and make her the queen of heaven.

The patient's sexual delusions were less clearly crystallized or at least less clearly verbalized than his political and religious ones. We know next to nothing about his actual sex life. In 1932 he had stated: "Basically the female body never stimulated me." In 1938 a girl, Josephine, allegedly his fiancée, played a considerable part in his redeemer fantasies. She was a friend of his youth, with whom he had had sexual relations for some years but he had not seen her since she moved to Germany ten years previously. Austria could only be saved if Schuschnigg effected her return to Vienna. Innitzer, Cardinal of Vienna, was blamed for wanting to have her "womb torn out." We do not know whether she had undergone a hysterectomy but as we shall see later, this idea is closely linked with the patient's fantasies about the nature of sexuality and bisexuality. However, before we turn to this point, we have to refer to his drawings.

IV

Later, after his commitment, he asked us to bring from his studio all those drawings that he had been unable to carry to the hospital with him. Most of them were done in pen or pencil; occasionally he would use chalk or brush. The size of the drawings varied greatly. Many were drawn on odd bits of paper, on margins of newspapers, magazines or books, and in empty spaces of architectural drawings. Others were on larger sheets of clean paper, and a good many on sheets of truly gigantic size such as architects use in their work.

The hospital records of 1932 and 1935 do not refer to any drawings connected with the patient's illness. Since he treasured his "psychotic" creations, we can exclude the possibility that any part of his work was lost. His production started in June 1937. At that time he scribbled on the margin of newspapers; the first drawing on a clean sheet is dated July 1, 1937. He did about ten larger drawings before October of that year. From then until his outburst of rage and his subsequent commitment in January, he produced from three to six large sheets daily. These are indications of "a creative spell."

The drawings superficially resemble ancient architectural sketches. They are mostly well spaced in the center of the sheets and show a limited number of themes, the most typical of which we shall discuss later. However, before entering upon a closer inspection of them, a brief discussion of their meaning for the patient seems appropriate. Figure 52 shows the most frequent of his themes, which we call the *sphera*: the city of light with angels flying toward it or from it. In it there is a detail, a triangle containing the letter "F" and the date, which we find on all the drawings, usually repeated several times, often with different dates. Sometimes we find instead of the letter "F" the word God (*Gott*) in the triangle. The triangle clearly serves as a signature. But what the patient signs are not works of art that he wishes to *authenticate*, but statements that he wishes to *validate*. The drawings are not meant for admiration by a public; they were not produced with any artistic intention in mind. They have, the patient said in reply to one of our questions, "no artistic value" and are not drawings but "written drawings." However, he has not lost his ability to draw, nor did he "change his style." In the midst of one of our interviews during which he occasionally and with great rapidity sketched one or the other of his "motifs," he drew at our request a human torso with the skill of the professional draftsman. However, such performances no longer interested him. We once praised a drawing of Victory on a baroque chariot drawn by deer (Fig. 51) which he had done for a stage decoration in about 1920. It supplies a typical example of his considerable craftsmanship. Instead of reacting to our praise, he immediately related the drawing to his current delusion: it showed Josephine's glorious return to Vienna; he had used the deer because they were pure and not tainted by man as were horses. He went on to focus his attention on the lines which he had recently sketched in the empty space in the background; they represent one of his familiar themes, "the gates of Paradise," which would be opened by his fiancée's return.

This self-interpretation was typical of his attitude to the drawings: his interest was exclusively directed to their content. The content is read as one might read a prophecy: what the drawings contain will happen one day. When we first brought the drawings from his studio he grabbed them eagerly and leafed through them, pointing at a detail here and there, literally jumping from one sheet to the other and occasionally returning to one he had passed. He studied them as documents that indicate the course of events. They were verdicts of damnation and announcements of salvation. And the signature indicated the prevailing intention: the triangle with the peak turned downward is, in the patient's words, "the sign of destruction." "If I am merciful," he added, "the triangle points upward."

The drawings were part of an elaborate magical ritual. Its main tool was the holy sword, made out of cardboard and covered with gilded paper. Whosesoever name he touched with the sword was lost. He ruled the world with it. We found it in his studio on a shabby desk, leaning against the wall. The wall space behind it was covered by layers of drawings, a self-portrait uppermost. The whole arrangement clearly suggested an altar; the holy sword, lying on what represented the mensa of the altar, as its center. It was flanked by two wooden busts, one of them portraying his fiancée.

We had several occasions to observe how the patient performed sorcery with sword and symbols. An attendant with whom he had had a minor controversy happened to pass. The patient made a cross next to a skull on one of his drawings, pressed his sword against his heart in a solemn gesture and said, "Holy sword, only salvation." Then he covered the cross with it and said that by his action he had destroyed the attendant. On the day after he was denied the certificate for his landlord, he took a paper napkin out of his pocket, folded it triangularly, drew a triangle on it which he hatched black and pronounced: "Eternal darkness, eternal God, now God is acting, everything is all right, now."

In some of the drawings damnation is the only theme: in the center we find the sword (upper part of Fig. 53), dividing "eternal hell" in two parts. The crosses represent dead souls or corpses, but, adds the patient, in drawing one cross next to the other he causes the destruction of his enemy. In image magic he uses the typical schizophrenic handling of concepts with which we are familiar in the schizophrenic usage of words and which he extends to that of shapes. Hence the network (Fig. 54) means, "The dice are cast. The grating is shut, imprisoned." Thus while the individual squares are seen as dice, their summation is seen as grating. The black band in Figure 53 represents "many graves" and at the same time the street in which he used to live—"there never was a bigger grave than L street." (The lower drawing represents graves of the Catholic clergy, the many small ones those of priests, the squares those of the hierarchy.)

To return to Figure 52, the sphera, a theme that he repeated time and again with small variations: its arrangement is probably influenced by Italian frescoes of the seventeenth century. On the ceiling of many a rotund chapel one sees angels flying toward a celestial center, thus conveying the impression of a centripetal movement. The patient seems to have elaborated on such a model. In the center there is "the throne of God," an upright triangle with seven arcs. The inscription reads: "Berlin, eternal city of God for all the people on earth." From this center radiate rays of light, crossing the border of the sphera. Angels are flying toward the center on these rays, those closest to the center carrying the victor's wreath. There are several triangles with his signature and inscriptions above and beneath the drawing.

On some of the drawings (as Fig. 55) we find in the corners the symbols of hell and damnation that we have just discussed. We therefore believe that in endlessly redrawing "Berlin," with the throne of God as city of light and center of the universe, the patient professes not only a political program—National Socialist Berlin as a world center—but that the drawings are at the same time a magic means of bringing about the fulfillment of this program; hence the repetition of the signature which reasserts validity. This seems like a compulsive ritual to silence the remaining rational part of his ego which still doubts his omnipotence.

The angels with which the sphere is populated are asexual and/or bisexual beings: "Angels," he says, "represent the spiritual conception from the heart. God's creation of angels is the deepest meaning. If two human beings feel the deep urge and want to testify God and the creation of angels, a new being emerges, a creation of God and angels comes about. The desire to love each other arises also without begetting a child."

The angels are sometimes replaced by interlocked triangles; they form a star of David from which a bundle of rays like the tail of a comet emanates (Fig. 56). The patient explained this triangle as follows: "Always one, the form leading back, the streaming in and leading back. The female casting aside, not leading back and the male. The rays are united. The female torso: $\bigcirc$ and the male: $\triangle$ which streams inward." Under the tail of the rays is another triangle, pointing toward the center. Thus the upright triangle is the male principle, the triangle pointing downward the female. The combination of both results in "Unity." He describes sexual union in marriage thus: "Marriage has been destroyed by the Old Testament, by the Jews. This was the original sin of Adam and Eve which closed the gates to paradise." The patient and his fiancée are going to reopen them. He also refers to marriage as the "holy wafer." "Every conception is through the holy ghost. *God sculptured semen and egg and united them.* The male semen enters the woman and pervades the blood. It is the holy wafer. Marriage is the holy wafer permeated with rays or semen." The interlocked triangles with the tail of rays, therefore, also suggest semen. Finally, he refers to the earth as the holy wafer presented to him by his mother.

We turn to one of the patient's largest drawings (Fig. 57), an image of the universe vaguely influenced by medieval wall paintings. The upper part depicts the throne of God in greater detail. Seven figures are seated in the seven arcs. In the middle, God, to his right and left, the patient and his fiancée, and to their right and left, their respective parents. Each holds on his lap a globe on which we see a sign which resembles the letter "M" but in fact represents an angel. In commenting upon this detail the patient says: the angel represents "the sculptor whom everybody possesses in his heart." Each figure is crowned by a triangle serving as a halo. To each figure one day of the week is assigned but, says the patient, "7–5–3–1" is *the great unity.* Behind and above God is a female figure: "God containing the mother," though the female really represents God. Unity here clearly means bisexuality. Sex differences are eliminated and both sexes are combined in one being. God is split into male and female yet both are united under one arc. The patient and God are as we know one and the same, and the "female" nature of God is ever present in the patient's mind; he claims that Josephine and he are "one and the same," he speaks of "God mother" who "established peace on earth with her sword" or of "God containing the mother."

In the lower section of the drawing the bell-shaped configuration stands for the existing world. It is of phallic shape yet also suggests a uterus. It is divided into irregularly shaped sections, somewhat like a geographical map, representing the different countries of Europe: the Reich, Austria, Italy, Russia, France, etc. The arrangement signifies their successive absorption into the Reich. In the section representing the Reich we find another version of the throne of God. This time only one figure, God or the patient, is seated on a throne, the globe on his lap, holding a scepter and sword. Directly above him, forming the tip of the bell-shaped configuration which protrudes between the gates of paradise, is again the sphera. It is divided into halves by a standing figure, God or the patient carrying the globe. Above him flies an angel, Hitler, about to place the victor's wreath on his head. The gates to paradise are flanked by two angels, the patient and Josephine. The gates form the connection between the upper and lower half of the picture. They are open—the two worlds can merge because the "great unity," bisexual peace, so to speak, reigns.

The idea of a bisexual unity finds a variety of expressions in the patient's works. In an impressive drawing (Fig. 58), which he entitles "God Father Himself," three tall figures stand on columns. God is in the middle, his right hand on the patient's shoulder, his left on Josephine's, extended in a gesture of blessing. The patient carries the globe with an angel standing on it. Josephine's folded arms rest on another globe which covers her abdomen like a shield. A bell-shaped configuration enters the globe from below. The columns are entwined by garlands, the outer ones by one garland each, wound in different directions, the middle by two which cross each other. He explains: "On the outer columns everything is separate, one heart differs from the other. In the middle column we see union, completion. The downward movement and the woman leading back, because the father is all one. The stream leading downward and the woman leading back."

The themes or "motifs" which we have hitherto described occur both in isolation and in combination. One of these combinations (Fig. 59) adds somewhat to our understanding. It represents an ostensory and therefore suggest the problem of oral incorporation because from the ostensory comes the host offered by the priest to the faithful during holy communion. The patient expresses these ideas in his own words: "The world is seen as part of God, as incorporated in him and part of him." The foot of the ostensory is framed by the lower part of God's body. His head, chest and arms are barely visible in outline in the two concentric circles of the upper half. His hands are joined exactly at the place where the gates of paradise are located. The inner circle is the usual sphera, here called "Valhalla" by the patient. The outer circle represents: "The holy creation, like a gigantic girdle. The holy wafer has to be put around, it is all embedded in God's body. I had to portray the spirit somehow." The "holy wafer" seems also to refer to oral conception: "Only when the holy wafer is fulfilled on Josephine will the gates to paradise be reopened." Above the seated figure of God in the lower half is Hitler again as an angel with the victor's wreath. The picture is entitled "Pax" and the patient said he had sent it to Hitler.

The patient's identification with God the creator can best be studied when we turn to two drawings representing subjects less frequently portrayed: In Figure 60. God himself sculptures the human couple. We see a man and a woman standing with uplifted arms, carrying the triangle, and above them God, the sculptor, with a modeling tool and compasses. From his heart seem to hang two angels, almost like breasts. They are called "soul angels." The female body is filled with little dots (semen). Both are standing on hexagons which represent corpses or coffins, but "flooded waiting for resurrection." The picture portrays: "the beauty of creation. God sculptures semen and egg. He breathed his own immortal soul into every being of his creation . . . Pregnancy, everything flooded, just as in the case of Mary. There is no other pregnancy. A permeated marriage. Everything is spirit. I became the sculptor, because the sculptor is the highest. Now it became true that I am the great sculptor, here you see him. There is no conception without spiritual conception. The truth has been destroyed."

In a variation of the same subject (Fig. 61) —described by the patient as "man and woman in the process of being sculptured"—God is barely visible. Instead, there are three triangles, surrounded by flames. Two seem to replace the two angels on God's breast in the former picture. The whole drawing and the coffins are also encircled by flames. This represents "the heart being set afire." He said that he never had "brain thoughts," only "heart thoughts." He used to think with his heart and its softness prevented him from taking action. Since his heart and spirit are dead he no longer has any feelings, but the moment he begins to feel again all of humanity will be embedded in love. "The flames around the coffins show that they are flooded with life." The angels flanking the couple are "the spiritual conception from the heart." These two drawings clearly illustrate his identification with God as the sculptor. As he said, "When I draw that, it is God within me; it is God himself."

V

Neither the patient's delusions nor any of the general clinical aspects of the case are unusual enough to warrant further discussion. We therefore turn to some of the various problems raised by his psychotic productivity. They are highly complex and our data are fragmentary. All we can hope is to present some hypotheses.

Our information about the patient's prepsychotic personality is too meager to indicate any definite link between his delusion and earlier experiences. We know nothing about his behavior in the interim between the first two attacks. After his second attack in 1935 he lived in misery, withdrawn from the world. His sole companion, the housekeeper, participated in his delusions. In June 1937 he suddenly started to draw. We are led to believe that this marked the onset of the third attack which, eight months later, led to an outburst of rage.

In attempting to explain the function of the drawing activity in the patient's psychosis, we start from the assumption that he had an experience of *Weltuntergang;* he would talk of himself as dead and refer to his loss of feeling. We furthermore assume, following Freud's analysis of Schreber's delusion (1911 b), that his psychotic system is to be explained as an attempt to recapture a world that threatens to slip away.

Within this general framework the drawing spell has two functions which are so closely linked together that they are here distinguished only for purposes of exposition: first, to prevent the further defusion of instincts, and second, to reassert the truth of the delusion against the patient's own doubts.

Defusion of instincts refers here to the juxtaposition of the wish to destroy an existing world on the one hand, and to construct a fantastic world on the other. The mounting urge to magical creation indicates, according to this hypothesis, the growing conflict between the two tendencies. The attempt fails; destruction becomes paramount. After the outburst of rage comparative calm is established. He ceased to draw and when questioned why, replied, "I am through, everything is accomplished for eternity!"

The sequence of outburst and cessation of creative activity is familiar: a case of Morgenthaler (1921) showed it in various subsequent phases. A patient of Prinzhorn's (1922 a, p. 255) stopped drawing and explained, "that it was no longer necessary." In the future he would simply dust graphite on paper and force it into lines and shapes with his eyes. The growing narcissistic regression could hardly be better exemplified.

The second function of the spell to create seems to be a reassertion of the truth of the delusion. When in doubt the patient reasserts the validity of his verdicts by re-signing them with one of the magic triangles of blessing or damnation.

Only once during the period of our observation did the patient draw spontaneously, when he heard about his imminent eviction from his studio. We reported how anger and disappointment gave way to ecstasy. He went around smiling, shook hands with everybody, and proclaimed that now he was fully God. He asked for paper and drew the sphera, calling it "the kingdom of heaven with the doors of paradise." Thus when humiliation at the hands of reality threatened, and the intact part of his personality responded to reality, magical production served to reassert the delusion.

VI

We are unable to explain the fact that the patient implemented his delusion by creation only during his third attack, unless it was due to the greater intensity of this attack. The difference in intensity is best exemplified by his relation to God: during the second attack he claimed to fulfill the will of God, during the third he felt he *was* God. The progression of the psychosis is also shown in the increased systematization of his delusions.

His identification with God, the creator of man and the builder of the universe, has specific meaning for him. Occasionally he describes his relationship with God in terms of the medieval artist's guilds: first God's apprentice, then his helper, finally the master himself. One of the earliest of his psychotic drawings was done on the margin of a poem by Emanuel Geibel (1815-1884), entitled "Die Sehnsucht des Weltweisen" ("A Philosopher's Yearning"), in which God's power to give shape to man is extended from the corporal to the spiritual sphere.

All artistic creation tends to be linked to the Divine. In summarizing briefly what can be learned from myth, folklore and literary tradition, it seems appropriate to distinguish two main types of relationship with

God: one in which the artist is God's rival and the other in which he is his tool.[10]

The first relationship, the artist as God's rival, appears most frequently in the creation of imagery. Those who create animate men and thereby violate divine prerogatives are punished, like Prometheus, Daedalus or Hephaestus. Interdicts of imagery to protect the divine from magical practice prevail over centuries in many cultures. Such attitudes live on in the literary tradition and folklore dealing with the artist. Painters conclude pacts with the devil in order to compete with God, while builders, heirs to the builder of the tower of Babel, commit suicide. These thoughts are rarely absent in the unconscious of the practicing artist; he is always supreme in the world he creates. In schizophrenic delusions similar thoughts are fully expressed: a patient of Nunberg (1932), who rubbed off the skin of her breast and molded it, claimed that she formed man in Godlike fashion. The sculptor Messerschmidt believed that the Gods were jealous of his secret knowledge and therefore persecuted him.[11]

The second type of relation, that in which the artist acts as the tool of the Divine, is even more universal. Its nucleus is inspiration. The underlying psychological mechanism is familiar: an unconscious thought is externalized and when it reaches consciousness is experienced as if it came from the outside. Myth and religious beliefs name the Deity as the outside source. If the artist is thus inspired he is free to speak of what otherwise cannot be mentioned (Muschg, 1930) or to give life to creation in imagery.

Our patient approximates this type. He occasionally describes the state of creative rapture in words similar to those normally used by productive artists when they speak of their inspirational experiences; he asserts its compulsive character, the experience of being driven. But the force from the outside which inspires him does not remain outside. It is introjected (or more precisely, re-introjected) ; the patient becomes God himself.

There is reason to believe that all creators are in a passive relation to the Divine in inspiration, possession, or revelation. Many autobiographical reports indicate the complete passivity, and others the painfulness, of creation; hence the metaphor of giving birth to a work of art.

While we do not know nearly enough of the various types and modes of these conditions, it is worth mentioning that in certain civilizations

[10] See Chapters 2 and 13.
[11] See Chapter 4.

religious inspiration clearly bears the stamp of a sacrifice of virility—certain shamans actually become female when chosen. The fertilization of the creator by God uses various orifices. Auditory and anal inspiration were stressed by Jones (1914), oral insemination by Kris.[12] The drawings of the patient indicate that his modes of incorporation are manifold: God contains all, the world is in him. Man becomes woman, woman man; but both are in God and God is the patient. Thus the delusion solves the conflict of bisexual drives and in creating, the patient acts for both sexes.

VII

The patient, identified with the creator God, omnipotent and omniscient, produces no works of art. His drawings do not serve the function of communication.

Freud (1908) has discussed this very problem in one of his most essential contributions to our understanding of art. In describing the literary work of art, and differentiating dream, daydream and novel, he said that only the novel reaches the level on which thought is communicated to others, the level where art exists; the dream is autistic, the daydream of no interest to others.

In his work the artist uses "inspiration": his unconscious produces thoughts which he permits to reach consciousness provided that they are presented in aesthetic disguise.[13]

This process can also be described in terms of ego psychology. When the artist creates during inspiration he is subject to an ego regression but it is a partial and temporary ego regression, one controlled by the ego which retains the function of establishing contact with an audience. The artist identifies himself with his public in order to invite their participation, a participation postulating their subsequent identification with him.

No such intention prevails in our patient. He does not produce in order to communicate with others any more than he converses with others. Basically his speech is soliloquy. His drawings have even less bearing on people around him. They are verdicts or statements bearing on the future which he creates.

Part of this clearly stems from the patient's vocational training. Architects' plans are not primarily imagery but plans for future actions. One might therefore say that the patient has simply drawn the plans not

12 See Chapters 13 and 14.
13 See Sachs (1942) and here p. 38.

of real objects that he wishes to construct, but of a delusional world that he wishes to bring about. However, it seems that this simpler explanation does not entirely satisfy the impression we gained that drawing itself is the activity which effects the change. He not only produces images which are being used in sorcery (image magic) —although he does so in touching with his sword a name he has written down as one kills an enemy by piercing his effigy—but he also brings about magical changes in the world by the very act of drawing.

This magic function of the creative process itself is clearer in the destruction of enemies than in the construction of a new world. Perhaps we overstate the case in putting both on the same level—and yet it seems that any such distinction between the destructive and constructive function of his work would be artificial. The two authors differ to some extent on this point. One of us (Pappenheim) believes it is significant that the patient is more convinced of his destructive powers whereas he retains some critical faculties toward his constructive abilities.

The patient handles shapes as schizophrenics typically handle words. Parts are split from wholes and used independently, many meanings are condensed, etc. The primary process is paramount. Some changes are particularly significant. In Figure 57 a series of angels illustrates the transition from a resembling shape to a sign which—possibly only accidentally—forms the letter "M." This confirms the general rule that the closer an image is to magical thought, the less the semblance with the depicted image is required.[14] The patient gave us several examples of this procedure. He abbreviated and condensed his own symbols so to speak, progressively, as for instance, in transforming the angel to the outline of the letter "M" or in usually depicting the throne of God simply as a triangle with the seven arcs. (An alternative explanation as a transition from pictography to script meets with some difficulties.) The triangle on the other hand has many meanings. Its model is probably the eye of God in a triangle, which is frequently found as a religious symbol in Austrian baroque. The upright blessing triangle is linked to the male, the reversed condemning triangle to the female; since no other explanation seems obvious, one is reminded that the patient refers to the sword of Mother God, and one might well see in this combination a derivation of castration fear.

Symbolisms of this kind are not "evident," do not reverberate in others, and isolate the productions of the insane.

To return to our introduction: a comparison of the patient's creative

14 See p. 77.

process and of his work with that of normal artists seems to add clinical precision to Plato's distinction. The controlled and temporary ego regression during inspirational creation was described by Plato as productive insanity and only the more permanent narcissistic regression of the psychotic as a pathological process.

Although the work of the psychotic is part of magic itself, that of the normal artist is not devoid of magic. He too attempts to control a world, and in his creation there is embodied some of the magic belief. But the difference is clear in two areas: first, the normal artist creates not to transform the outer world but to depict it for others he wishes to influence; second, the task of production has a definite realistic meaning. The artist proceeds through trial and error; he learns and his modes of expression change, or his style changes. The psychotic artist creates in order to transform the real world; he seeks no audience and his modes of expression remain unchanged once the psychotic process has reached a certain intensity.

For reasons not discussed here, the search for genius in the insane has become fashionable. Clinical experience, however, demonstrates that art as an aesthetic—and therefore as a social—phenomenon is linked to the intactness of the ego. Although there are many transitions, the extremes are clear.

Part Three

The Comic

Chapter 6

THE PSYCHOLOGY OF CARICATURE

I

Freud's contributions to the psychology of the comic are derived from two different phases in the development of his thought. First, there are those essentially concerned with the understanding of topographical and economic relations, embodied in his *Wit and Its Relation to the Unconscious* (1905 a). They were stepping stones on the road which was to lead through the knowledge gleaned from pathological phenomena to a new, general psychological outlook. The second set of Freud's contributions was based on nearly twenty-five years of further study, and refers mainly to dynamic and structural problems. They are formulated in his paper on "Humour" (1928 a) and are part of the efforts made to arrive at a clearer view of the ego's position in the mental structure.

A number of investigators have been at pains to correlate and differentiate the two points of view (Reik, 1929, 1933; Alexander, 1933; Winterstein, 1934; Dooley, 1934). As an attempt in the same direction is to form the substance of this paper I shall frequently have to repeat what is already known.[1] As a point of departure I shall select a subdivision of the comic which does not seem to have been evaluated according to its merits either in analytic, or for that matter in extra-analytic, literature, namely, caricature.[2]

The material on which I shall rely is of three kinds: sociological data from the history of caricature, clinical material, and observations made on children. In the present context I shall, of course, be unable to give an account of the material itself; instead I will try from my point of

---

[1] For this reason, there seems to be no object in making express reference to the fact *every* time I follow Freud's conclusions. Where I have drawn upon ideas put forward by other writers I think I have always stated the fact, although naturally only when these constitute an advance on Freud's position.

[2] In this essay (originally published in 1935) the term caricature is used in an unduly wide sense, since no distinction is made between "caricature" and "cartoon." For the fruitfulness of such a distinction see Gombrich and Kris, 1940, and here Chapter 7.

departure to formulate some reflections and suggestions of general significance for the psychoanalytic theory of the comic.

II

To begin with, there are some preliminary questions which we shall have to consider, the first among them relating to the source of the pleasure gain in caricature. We know already what to expect; a part of the pleasure derives from a saving in mental energy, another from the relation to infantile life.

If we would try to find our bearings in relation to our theme, we might well choose as our point of departure the verbal designation itself. The Italian *caricare* and the French *charger* (*charge* = caricature) convey the same idea: to charge or to overcharge; we would add, with distinctive features. Thus a human countenance may have a single trait accentuated so that the representation is "overcharged" with it.[3] What then occurs in our imagination has been described repeatedly, although by none more clearly than by Bergson. In our thoughts, as it were, we cause our model's features to become twisted in a grimace.

A distinction between a simple and a complex form of caricature seems to prove useful. The former has reference to caricatures that are comic[4] in the strict and narrow sense of the term so penetratingly defined by Freud in his book on wit. These affect us like the circus clown. We learn from Freud that the occasion of our pleasure is a comparison; in caricature this relates to reality as compared with a distorted reproduction of it. It is easy to see that here again, just as with the phenomena of the comic in the (limited) sense of Freud's definition, it is really a matter of a saving in expenditure on thought, and our pleasure may be regarded as originating in the preconscious.

This point of view, however, can hardly be regarded as very satisfying; "comic" caricatures of this kind are, to say the least, extremely rare. There can be no doubt that we should be justified in regarding its tendentious character as an essential attribute of caricature; indeed an overwhelmingly large proportion of all caricatures serves a tendency. They are aimed either at an individual or at a type, whom they portray with single features exaggerated; the natural harmony of an appearance

---

3 See in this connection Juynboll (1934, p. 148) and here Chapter 7.

4 Since it is intended here to deal with the various peculiarities and characteristics shared in common by phenomena which language brackets together as "comic," I cannot avoid employing the term in two different senses: the one general, following the usage of speech; the other limited, following Freud's definition.

is destroyed, and this has the result in many cases of revealing a contrast in the personality between looks and character. But this procedure is not specially characteristic of graphic representation. The dissolution of unity in the interests of aggression is familiar to us as a technique whereby it is precisely this incongruity of form and content which is so often demonstrated; thus parody devaluates the content, travesty the form.

The aggressive nature of all caricature, which seems to condition its mechanisms, is mentioned in the earliest definitions, which have lately come to light. According to one of these, which originated in the seventeenth century within the circle of the great Giovanni Lorenzo Bernini, caricature seeks to discover a likeness in deformity; in this way, so runs the theory of the time, it comes nearer to truth than does reality. This settles the nature of its achievement; it serves the purpose of *unmasking* another person, familiar to us as a technique of degradation. To return now to our point of departure: the saving in mental energy which accompanies caricature (of a tendentious kind) is evidently to be regarded as a saving in expenditure on suppression, or as one resulting from a liberation of aggression. Some measure of the effect produced by the comic (in its limited sense) is present as an element in all caricature, and the effect is determined in part by the pleasurable saving in expenditure on thought resulting from a comparison. We shall later have to refer to the interrelations of these two sources of pleasure.

As a basis for this discussion, let us take the scheme of a caricature of which I will try to give you a short description in words. The subject of the caricature is Napoleon and the continental blockade. We see the Emperor before us, in hat and cloak; he is strikingly small in size, far more so than in reality. He is raised on stilts, and holds out with both hands a pair of seven league boots. Instead of the well-known features of Napoleon, he has the unmistakable appearance of a shopkeeper; a number of details in his attire are also an allusion to this status.

I shall have to refrain from giving a more detailed account of the relations of the single elements to their theme, the conflict between Napoleon and the unconquerable might of Great Britain. For while it is true that this period produced a great number of caricatures of a very similar type, the one which I have tried to describe is not a caricature at all. It is taken from the dream of an Austrian patient, dreamed at the height of his conflict over castration anxiety, in which the separate elements are determined with as much, indeed with more, ingenuity than those of a caricature. I will only add that the shopkeeper, a figure from the patient's youth, bore a name rich in associations, that of Kitzler.[5]

The correspondence between dreams and caricature revealed by this example is easily accounted for. It is evidently to be referred to the circumstance that the formal language of caricature, like that of dreams, owes its nature to the operation of the primary process. There is nothing really surprising in this; for even in his first contribution to the psychology of the comic, Freud proceeded from a similar analogy; I have in mind his demonstration of the parallels existing between wit and dreams, which he was able to derive from the operation of the primary process. But this similarity can be developed further. Caricature is seen to be a graphic form of wit—a banal result, which could easily be elaborated in detail on the basis of a typology of caricature. But before we can try to advance to a more profitable conception, let us obtain some light on the analogies between the two processes by contrasting the "work of wit" with "the work of caricature." In doing so, it will be best—again following Freud's presentation—to proceed from the negative of wit, from the riddle. The riddle conceals what wit reveals. In wit the matter is known and the manner is secret; in riddles, the manner is known and the matter to be discovered. The essence of the relation between wit and the riddle—the features common to both incidentally have their roots deep in mythical thought, as we see when we recall the special position of the riddle in all mythologies—may be illustrated by reference to the behavior of a patient; he was incapable of deriving pleasure from a joke, but was under a compulsion to read the first line only and then guess the point. He converted a joke into a riddle.[6]

An analogous form of reaction may be tested experimentally by anyone engaged in studying a caricature. If the connections and allusions forming its content are obscure—this applies to all earlier caricatures, since for reasons which we shall try to indicate later on, achievements in comic expression age very quickly (posterity has no crown of laurel for the comic artist) —the hieroglyphic nature of caricature becomes a reality. We are impelled to resolve connections and allusions by guesswork; the caricature has changed into a rebus.

This attribute of caricature to which our comparison leads reappears in another branch of pictorial art, which we cannot consider further here, the realm of allegory.

---

[5] *Kitzler* = tickler, also clitoris.

[6] For the relation of the riddle to the comic in a historical setting, see now Rapp (1949). See also p. 245.

III

We have now to elucidate in greater detail the relations of wit and caricature to dreams: in dreams, the ego abandons its supremacy and the primary process obtains control, whereas in wit and in caricature this process remains in the service of the ego. This formulation alone suffices to show that the problem involved is a more general one; the contrast between an ego overwhelmed by regression and a "regression in the service of the ego"—*si licet venia verbo*—covers a vast and imposing range of mental experience.

There are numerous conditions, extending from the levels of normal life deep down into the realm of the pathological, in which the ego abandons its supremacy; besides dreams, we find, not far removed from the norm, states of intoxication, in which the adult again becomes a child, and recovers "the right to ignore the limitations imposed by the demands of logic and to give free rein to his imagination" (Freud), or again, the multiplicity of well-known clinical pictures in neurosis and psychosis. The economic aspect of some of these processes suggests a formulation which we will mention here for the sake of its connection with certain considerations later to be adduced: it seems that the ego finds its supremacy curtailed whenever it is overwhelmed by affects, irrespective of whether an excess of affect or the ego's own weakness is to be held responsible for the process.

But the opposite case, where the ego enrolls the primary process in its service and makes use of it for its purposes, is also of the widest significance. It is not confined to the sphere of wit and caricature but extends to the vast domain of aesthetic expression in general, and that it applies to the whole field of art and of symbol formation, preconscious or unconscious, which, beginning with cult and ritual, permeates the whole of human life.[7]

The primary process, the operation of which, in Freud's view, conditions the uniform character of primitive modes of expression, is not merely of decisive importance for the thought processes of primitive peoples but appears also to determine the evolution of the "grammar" and "syntax" employed in those of the child. This notion, I believe, enables

[7] See also Chapters 1 and 14, where recent, wider formulations in this area (Hartmann, 1939 a) are discussed.

An investigation of the specific achievements of the ego in wit and caricature would have to take its "multiple function" (Waelder, 1936) into account. The process of mastering strong exhibitionistic tendencies seems likely to provide us with a sure foundation.

us to discover points of contact between the views held by psychoanalysts and those of Piaget, the interrelations of which have of late occupied the attention of many analysts—I may mention de Saussure (1934) and Kubie (1934). Once more it will be better not to pursue the thread further. For any attempt to base the view here indicated on a firmer foundation would necessarily take us back to the interpretation of dreams, the old *via regia* of psychoanalysis.

IV

Besides the saving in mental energy, Freud regards a close relation to infantile life as a distinguishing mark of all forms of the comic. The expression in words, which includes wit, revives modes of expression employed by the child when speech was developing; for example, the play on words restores to its ancient rights the clang association of their sounds, as opposed to that of the things they represent. We have to ask ourselves: what is the nature of the connection between the child's behavior and that branch of the comic which employs, not verbal but pictorial (principally graphic) means of expression? So far as regards caricature, the question is easily answered. Just as wit returns to particular verbal forms of expression, caricature returns to typical elements in the graphic forms of expression (drawings) of the child.[8] Anyone who tries to understand children's drawings finds himself often enough obliged to "interpret" them, just as we are accustomed to do with dreams. For the graphic art of the child is to a great extent controlled by the primary process. I shall have to refrain here from adducing more detailed evidence in support of this theorem. Instead I will try to link up these considerations with our previous ones by propounding the following statement: the primary process controls graphic expression in the child, whereas it appears in the pictorial art of the civilized adult as a freely and deliberately chosen technique.[9] It would be well to supplement these reflections of an ontogenetic order by calling to mind a third form of comic expression, the comic of gesture. Detailed analysis reveals in all comic gesture a technique of imitation, which owes its character to the reanimation of a particular phase of reaction in the child. I refer to that stage of development in which the acquisition of motor capacities,

[8] A separate problem, but one capable of a psychological explanation, relates here to the significant interval in time between the corresponding phases in the evolution of verbal and graphic expression in the child. See now Cameron (1938 a, b) and here p. 92.

[9] I am aware that this formulation is too general in its terms. For qualifications see now pp. 92ff., and Chapter 7.

particularly that of "representation" by "mimo-motor" means, receives a decisive impetus by the imitation of the motor activities of adults.

To these hypotheses directed to ontogenetic origins we would append others concerned with phylogenetically early forms. We might well begin with comic expression in gesture, since in the realm of the comic this activity evidently approximates most closely to archaic types of reaction. We are familiar with its effect. Nothing is so sure to hurt our feelings as to see our words or gestures imitated (the imitation of our speech as a "gesture" may be included here). It is easy to see that the exposure and devaluation are not alone responsible for the wound to our narcissism, but that a deeper signification underlies "caricature in gesture." When we are imitated, we feel threatened in our individuality, superseded and dismissed.[10] We realize that in this power which gesture has something primordial survives: the ancient part played by gesture in cult and magic. The part played by words in wit too leads to this domain, and Reik (1929, 1933) who considers that comic expression in words developed out of and supplanted comic expression in gesture, was able to show that at several points in its technique wit reanimates the old magical significance of words.[11] These observations find some support when we consider the corresponding problems in graphic forms of comic expression with reference to caricature. For it seems that the antecedents of caricature may without difficulty be traced back to the world of effigy magic.

We will confine ourselves to an aphoristic reference on the subject of the transition from this attitude to that of the caricaturist. The distortion of the image here, too, "represents" a distortion of its original. This hypothesis supports the view often held (we introduced it earlier in the form expressed by Bergson) that the pleasure gain in caricature is due to our imagination, as it were, forcing the features of the person caricatured to assume a grimace, and that we may infer the existence of annihilation tendencies behind comic gestures, "caricature by gesture." This seems to be confirmed and substantiated by sociological data: Whenever caricature develops to any great extent as a form of artistic expression, which apparently only occurs under quite definite historical

10 I may here mention the stimulus I owe to a repeated exchange of views with E. Bibring, whose clinical material promises extensively to clarify the very problem which I deal with here only in a cursory way. One of his observations which throws light on the connection between imitation and aggression may be cited here: a patient was only able to imitate certain persons (and then very faithfully) when aggressively disposed toward them.

11 See now for further discussion of this point and illuminating clinical illustrations Reich (1949).

conditions, we are invariably able to discover the use of effigy magic at some point in its development. Of modern caricature it can be stated with certainty that one of its roots reaches back to the insulting and derisive representations on which punishments were carried out (in a real sense *in effigie*) when the culprit had put himself beyond their reach.[12]

V

Once more we will revert to our comparison between wit, caricature and dreams and look for support from an idea of Freud's which contrasts wit as a consummately social product with dreams as a consummately asocial one. We already find an explanation of this contrast in the formula to which we are accustomed when evaluating the process of wit: a preconscious thought is committed *for a moment* to elaboration by the system Ucs—for a moment. Whereas in dreams, owing to the operation of the primary process, thoughts undergo distortion until they become quite unrecognizable; in wit—and, we may add, in caricature— the distortion is only carried through by half, and is subject to the ego's control; a thought is disguised rather than distorted, its distortion is pressed only so far as is consistent with its remaining intelligible to the firstcomer. Here of course we have again to think of the objection that we have been describing a process not confined to wit and caricature, but of general validity (Reik, 1929) ; nevertheless, since it relates to the social character of comic phenomena, it acquires a peculiar significance in the present context. For their social character is an essential quality of most forms of the comic: "A new joke runs through the town like the news of a recent victory." And to this simile of Freud's we might add: "A caricature *is* a broadside."

The primary social character of tendentious forms of comic expression appears to be conditioned by two factors; in the first place, another person's approval is used to justify one's own aggression, and furthermore wit and caricature can easily be recognized as an invitation to that other person to adopt a joint policy of aggression and regression. Accordingly, tendentious forms of comic expression (and with this we bring Freud's line of argument, which our last remarks have followed verbatim, into connection with the discoveries of other workers) assist the "conquest and seduction of the partner." Recently an opportunity has presented itself from an unexpected quarter of linking up these tendentious forms (and harmless ones too) with the realm of the infantile. I consider

[12] For a more detailed discussion see Chapter 7.

that we are entitled to look upon the social character of the comic as a survival, or better put, as a legacy from an infantile attitude which Dorothy Burlingham (1934) calls "the child's urge to communicate." The social character of the comic cannot, however, be said to reveal a fixation to a particular aspect of infantile reaction; it impresses us rather as a magnificent work of elaboration, by virtue of which an impulse active in childhood proves capable of adaptation to adult reality.

These considerations enable us to arrive at a fuller understanding of a fundamental characteristic of comic phenomena relative to their dynamic character. We might well begin with cases in which the comic intention fails of its purpose. This appears as a failure to evoke an appropriate response in the environment. Very often it gives rise to feelings of discomfort instead of pleasure, and this experience may be either painful or uncanny in tone; we can easily tell which of the two alternatives predominates in a given case. Since cases in which the failure of the comic process produces this result are accompanied by a reversal of their normal effect, I propose to speak of a double-edged character of comic phenomena. I have in mind a quality of the comic of quite general validity.[13]

In order better to understand this, let us present in schematic form a simple case where the comic intention fails of its purpose. The discomfort experienced affects everyone involved in the comic experiment—the person for whom it is meant and the person who carries it out. Thus in the case of tendentious wit we may suppose that the hearer has recognized the aggression behind its disguise and that his superego has called upon him to repudiate it; we may say that he has "misunderstood" the witty remark, or rather, misunderstood that it is a witty remark. This "misunderstanding" on the part of the hearer may correspond to a "mistake" on the part of the speaker; the "misunderstanding" may be a reaction to the "mistake." We might (in agreement with Reik, 1929) envisage the speaker as dominated by his compulsion to confess. He might be considered caught between the compulsion to confess and the urge to communicate (which is to be regarded as a "compulsion to confess" in the service of the pleasure principle, forming the contribution of instinctual life to the compulsion to confess).[14] We may suppose that the discomfort of the hearer is produced or intensified by the conflict between whether to approve or to disapprove of the speaker's aggression. The speaker's discomfort is intensified in turn by the hearer's disapproval,

13 For further discussion see Chapter 8.

14 For a closer investigation of similar situations on different lines see now Eidelberg (1945) .

which leaves him to deal with his conflict of conscience single-handed. The attempt to acquire pleasure by effecting a saving in expenditure on suppression miscarries and fresh cathexes are required.[15]

Though crude, this presentation follows directly on the views expressed by Freud and Reik. It enables us to appreciate that the comic originates in the conflict between instinctual trends and the superego's repudiation of them, and to grasp its position midway between pleasure and unpleasure. These are the roots of its double-edged character. Much the same seems to hold good for man's earliest attempts in comic expression. As its next relation in the household of man's mind we may accept play—first of all the play of adults which, like their comic invention, may be partially understood in terms of a "holiday from the superego." As its precursors we shall find the play and fun of childhood, which are required at a critical juncture to supply a bridge enabling instinctual satisfaction to take a form adapted to reality. Children's play performs two tasks in the interests at once of acquiring mastery over the environment and warding off unpleasure (mastering "painful" experience) ; but besides these, one may recognize that the promotion of pleasure in function furnishes an additional motive. We learn how the three interact when we turn our attention to precisely that aspect of play which survives in the comic word play of adults, the child's play with words. This phenomenon receives a partial explanation when one reflects that the urge to communicate (here again we would refer to Dorothy Burlingham's account) also at times finds expression in the child's play with words, or better put, playful experimentation with words; although it is evident that at a still earlier stage playing with words is aimed at securing the mastery over them.[16] If, then, the child's play is to be treated as originating beyond the pleasure principle, or as incapable of explanation without postulating for it a root beyond the pleasure principle,[17] we might easily be drawn to contrast it with the child's fun, as representing a form of behavior in the exclusive service of the pleasure principle, and something certainly to be understood in all respects as a reaction to the behavior of adults.[18] But attractive as it might be to distinguish the

[15] See the similar views of Waelder (1934).

[16] Observations of children in their second year over and over again confirm this point, which also finds support here and there in published compilation of data. See, e.g., D. and R. Katz (1928).—The argument here presented approximates that of Reik (1933).

[17] See Waelder (1933).

[18] We cannot here enter upon a discussion of the circumstance that children's fun —in contrast to their play—is a primary social form of behavior which promotes contact, nor of the conclusions to be derived therefrom for a differentiation of the functions of play and fun. For a further discussion see Chapter 8.

principal tasks of play and fun as the mastering of pain and the acquisition of pleasure respectively, there is little to be found in favor of such a division. For no clear line can be drawn between play and fun, and as early as the end of the first year both are expressed and understood. In order to illustrate the close connection between them, we may adduce the findings of a reliable psychological investigation, according to which the child's most "effective" means of comic expression consists in his latest discovery, his most recent intellectual acquisition of the moment (Herzfeld and Prager, 1929). The material which play chooses for its purposes could be described in identical terms. However, it does not require this analogy between play and fun to confirm what daily observation of children tells us, namely, that even in their second year and in fully developed form in their third, fun is over and over again favored as the chosen means of mastering aggression, or more correctly, ambivalence. Even the attitude expressed by fun plainly shows that it has to perform a task of mastery and defense; for it is treated—even in the usage of speech—as in every respect the antithesis of "being serious." Here again it differs from play, since "the opposite of play is not being serious, but reality" (Freud, 1908). But the opposition between fun and seriousness appears in the end to hold good for wide tracts of the comic. Adult comic invention, and certainly the comic in its tendentious forms, helps in obtaining mastery over affects, over libidinal and aggressive tendencies warded off by the superego; the ego acting in the service of the pleasure principle is able to elude them by taking the path of comic expression. The instinctual trends of the id are given their way, but this does not mean that they are gratified in their true and original form. Instead of a direct action, we have a reproduction, the half-measures characteristic of the comic.

It would be well once more to describe this process, although in a schematic and abbreviated form, as it applies to the field of caricature. Instead of disfiguring the face of an opponent in reality, the effect of this act is merely imagined and is then realized in relation to his effigy. As long as this process continues to be dominated by magical thinking, it cannot yet be said to have attained to the level of caricature. For while it is true that the method of action is changed, the intention remains unchanged; the action is performed in relation to an image which is regarded as identical with the person it represents. But where caricature is concerned, this belief no longer holds good in consciousness or in the preconscious. Caricature indeed also tries to produce an effect, not, however, "on" the person caricatured, but on the spectator, who is influenced to accomplish a particular effort of imagination.

This evolution of the process from a more primitive (magical) stage to a higher one is accompanied by decisive transformations in the image itself.[19] At the stage of magical thinking, the features of the image are of minor importance; at that which corresponds to caricature, this resemblance is a prerequisite of the social function of the image. It is the result of a definite, but not easily determined, measure of concern with the reproduction of reality; resemblance is a prerequisite of caricature.[20] It is the resemblance between a man and his image which really first gives caricature its specific character, namely, the distorted reproduction of a recognizable likeness. The comparison between a person and his caricature of which we spoke at the beginning causes a saving in expenditure on thought, and so produces an effect which in the narrower sense of Freud's definition is comic. But by means of condensation, displacement and allusion, certain elements in the distortion point to the existence of other ideas, the distorting ones, we might say; these are the elements which betray the *tendency*. We now acquire a deeper insight into a state of affairs to which we made passing reference at the beginning of this account. The comic effect produced by a comparison and the effect of an ingeniously concealed tendency react one upon the other. If in Freud's view the "comic" effect of wit can form a façade for the effect produced by its tendency, a very close alliance between the two appears to form the basis of the *specific quality* of caricature.

To sum up: if what we have described as the half-measures characteristic of the comic satisfy instinctual demands, its specific quality protects caricature against a censorship proceeding from two directions—both from the external world, from which we borrow the term, and from the internal world.[21]

19 See also Chapter 7.

20 This conception could be formulated in more general terms by saying that an activity designed to produce a magical effect is replaced by one concerned with a particular order of values. This formula, "value, not effect" appears, as we would further suggest, to enjoy a wider validity and to open one approach to the psychology of value in general. We have still to state explicitly that *complete* indifference in regard to the features of the image is not to be found, even among peoples whose thinking is still ruled by magic. In this matter, too, historical description in the widest sense can proceed only on the basis of conceptions worked out by psychology. The development of the child's attitude to pictures and the response of many insane patients to pictorial representations give us a clear notion of the "ontogenetic model" which psychological experience is in a position to offer to the historical social sciences. The view here indicated concerning the relation between effect and value may itself be deduced from the discoveries which we owe to this "model."

21 The Greek painter Ctesicles painted a scandalous picture of the queen, Stratonice, in the embrace of a fisherman. He had this picture exhibited publicly, and was obliged to flee the city. At first, in her anger, the queen wanted to have it destroyed,

Accordingly, if the comic process is to succeed, we may conceive of this as dependent on two factors. The claims of instinctual life are satisfied by its content, the objections of the superego by the manner of its disguise. When the ego is able so to master the tension between the two, pleasure can arise from unpleasure. The double-edged character of comic phenomena, however, is seen to be a quality conditioned by the conflict in which they originate; at times it succeeds in opposing the work devolving upon the ego, so that this impresses us as a failure.

One would be glad to learn the general conditions responsible for such a failure. It is difficult and perhaps impossible to formulate them, and there is only one we would make bold to indicate. Things which simply arouse anxiety or unpleasure cannot be adapted to comic expression—to attempt to do so may produce an uncanny effect—until they have been reduced in intensity and undergone some degree of working over. A measure of elaboration is a prerequisite of comic expression, and at the same time comic expression accomplishes a measure of elaboration. If this elaboration is not achieved, the quantity of affect still being too great for a working over in terms of the comic to be possible, there ensues a reversal of the effect produced by the comic from pleasure into unpleasure. Some important features of this process, its frequency and its occurrence at unexpected moments—we can never be certain that the comic process will be proof against failure—are capable of an explanation if we bethink ourselves once more of the social function of all comic expression and bear in mind the extensive differences and variations in the degree of liking and toleration shown for comic phenomena. For among the much-discussed and most constant qualities of the comic, we may include its dependence on historical and social conditions, which we are in the habit of describing as its "subjective" aspect. We know that every period and class of society and quite a number of local communities have their own peculiar forms of the comic, which often differ widely from one another, and are not readily amenable to a change of climate.[22] This peculiar feature of comic phenomena becomes intelligible when we reflect that the comic in its tendentious forms cannot really find a mark where indifference prevails; the kind of disparagement which it allows

---

but later she resolved that it should be carefully looked after and preserved. The work of art was too important to be consigned to destruction merely on account of its content.

[22] Many questions of structure could be discussed with reference to the varying degrees in which they can be "transferred" or "translated."—The recent literature has assembled much relevant material on this point; see, e.g., Arieti (1950). For experimental work in this area which tends to point to the limitations of cultural differentiation, see Eysenck (1944).

us to infer, however, rather suggests that in a similar way it can scarcely make the eternally forbidden its object (if it does, it is wont to produce a painful effect), but that this must be found in something which is even now held in esteem, *is even now represented in the superego*. I may express my meaning in a word by reminding you of the glorious figure of Don Quixote[23] and for the rest I will merely indicate that this point of view promises to render more intelligible to us a number of particularly obvious problems. Thus we are all familiar with the irresistibly comic impression created by certain fashion plates of earlier generations, one which has recently been much exploited in films. But it is remarkable that this holds true only for fashions of a certain type, for such, namely, as still retain connections with our own memories, with the impressions and experiences of our early years. Beyond this limit, our historical interest begins, and, we would add, the comic effect of such impressions is greatly reduced in scope.[24]

If now we try to summarize these remarks, we find that the comic in its tendentious forms also has its roots in the ambivalence conflict of adults and can at times represent the outcome of this; it may be regarded as a means of mastering simultaneously feelings of admiration and aversion, and by converting "unpleasure" into pleasure of lessening tension in the psychic apparatus, or speaking quite generally, of reducing psychic expenditure. With this, we have reached Freud's conclusion from which we started, and need now only examine one more question: How lasting is the success achieved by the comic process? We know its limitations; the conflict is not always resolved. The melancholic disposition of the typical humorist, who either displays a marked preference for this form of outlet or knows of no other, is a clinical fact which may be regarded as statistically proved. This fact especially merits our attention, for it brings mania, the great pathological parallel of the comic, into our field of view. We may regard it as the pathological correlate of the comic. We

[23] For a psychoanalytic interpretation, see Deutsch (1934).

[24] Attempted explanations of an analogous kind can often, it seems, be made to some purpose. Thus they enable us to understand the need of the modern theatrical producer to subject comedies of an earlier period to a more thorough adaptation—"modernization"—than other works of dramatic art of the same date. Again, other phenomena can evidently be explained from the immediate argument which declares that the comic for preference takes as its object something *even now* represented in the superego; such, for instance, as the *role* of certain typical figures of fun in general. See on the "distance" from the attacker, Murray (1934, 1935). This problem is particularly relevant for the understanding of the peculiar nature of Jewish jokes, which are recounted and popularized principally by the Jews themselves, by Jews who have partially broken away from their tradition; see, e.g., Hitschmann (1930 a), and Reik (1933).

know that it is distinguished by the triumph of the ego, in whose favor the superego renounces its power, and we perceive that in it is revealed on an enlarged scale what the comic attempts in a small way, namely, the equalization of tensions which constitute a menace to existence.[25] Finally I would refer to ecstasy, at the opposite pole to mania; it is distinguished by the triumph of the superego; the ego for the time being surrenders its independence, possibly in the interests of a "tendency to unification" (Deutsch, 1927) which controls the mental apparatus. This contrast between the two has a real significance beyond its purely formal implications. For if mania is to be regarded as the pathological correlate of the comic, we must look to the sublime for the experience which corresponds in normal life to ecstasy. But we know that the sublime is a "psychic greatness." And if the comic effects a reduction of mental energy, the sublime calls for a surplus expenditure of this. This aspect of the problem may throw light on another idea of Freud's, namely, the special position of humor,[26] the only phenomenon in the whole realm of the comic bordering on the sublime. This is not so much because it has passed beyond ambivalent levels (is postambivalent) and represents the superego's contribution to the comic, but first and foremost because it finds its fulfillment in relation to the subject himself and so has no need of others before it can offer an increased pleasure gain. It belongs within the mental economy of a single individual, and this may account for its near relation to the sublime. It seems that this variety of the comic is latest in developing in the course of a man's life; it passes as a sign of emotional maturity and is less dependent on restricted social and temporal norms than other forms of the comic. In this, too, it is more akin to the sublime.

The contrast between the comic and the sublime is an old *topos* of

25 See now Lewin (1950).

26 It would be worth while to define this special position with greater accuracy. Here we will confine ourselves to two observations. The remark made by the criminal on his way to the gallows, "Well, this is a good beginning to the week"—one of Freud's basic examples—can also be regarded as a form of self-irony. One is tempted to believe that humor too has a double-edged character, as when the irony implicit in the "humor of the gallows" dominates its effect. In this sense only am I able to understand a remark of Jekels and Bergler (1934) to the effect that humor serves the ego in its offensive tactics against the ego ideal. See now also Bergler (1937). One would like to think that humor could also be distinguished from other allied forms by saying that it has no technique or formal medium of its own. It seems to accord well with this that we seldom meet with it in a pure form, but most often in an alloy, supplementing or coloring other varieties of comic expression. The history of the term and of the concept it denotes, which has been sketched by Benedetto Croce (1923) —from the seventeenth century onward the English use of the term proceeds step by step to determine its conceptual content—points the way in which this conception might be supported.

aesthetics. Their position at opposite poles of the mental economy seems to pave the way for a new approach to old problems; indeed it may appear as premature to claim the comic as a subject for psychology, for it looks as if our own attitude to the problem would lead us once more to the gates of aesthetic theory. For the moment, we consider it better that they should remain closed.

We may, however, accept it as a favorable augury for closer relations in the future that our own findings accord well with those of the aesthetic tradition of the Greeks, the oldest that is known to us. We shall not allow ourselves to be misled by the contrast between the comic and the sublime into forgetting that they serve a common purpose: the mastery of an inner danger. Psychoanalysis soon came to recognize that ultimately tragedy and comedy,[27] the great twin dioscuri of art, may be regarded as alternative attempts to relieve the ego of a burden—let us say, of an obligation.

Plato's Symposium ends by telling that it was already daybreak, the cocks were crowing and all the others asleep or gone except Agathon, Aristophanes, and Socrates, who were still awake and drinking in turn out of a large bowl, "and Socrates made the others agree that the qualities requisite for writing tragedy and comedy were the same."

[27] See also L. Jekels (1926).

Chapter 7

THE PRINCIPLES OF CARICATURE

Written in Collaboration with E. H. GOMBRICH

I

It is a startling fact that portrait caricature was not known to the world before the end of the sixteenth century (Wittkower and Brauer, 1931). What seems so simple and even primitive an artistic procedure to our own days, the deliberate distortion of the features of a person for the purpose of mockery, was a satirical technique unknown to classical antiquity, to the Middle Ages and the High Renaissance. To be sure the artists of these former periods were well versed in many forms of comic art. We find the clown, the comic type, the satirical illustration, and the grotesque, in magnificent profusion, but portrait caricature was never practiced before the time of the brothers Carracci who worked in Bologna and in Rome at the turn of the sixteenth and seventeenth centuries.[1] Those who witnessed this invention—and we use the word in its full meaning—were quite conscious of the fact that a new form of art had sprung into being in the studio of these admired masters. The connoisseurs and critics of the period took pleasure in justifying and defining this mode of representation, and thus we find elaborate theoretical discussions of caricature in seventeenth-century writings on artistic theory by Agucchi (1646), Bellori (1672), and Baldinucci (1681). These theorists were well trained in formulation. They define *ritratti carichi* or *caricature* (literally "loaded portraits") as a deliberate transformation of features in which the faults and weaknesses of the victim are exaggerated and brought to light.

Caricaturing [reads the definition of Baldinucci (1681)] among painters and sculptors signifies a method of making portraits, in which they aim at the greatest resemblance of the whole of the per-

[1] Lodovico Carracci (1557-1602); Annibale Carracci (1560-1609). For the relation of these artists to contemporary art criticism see the recent publication of Mahon (1947).

son portrayed, while yet, for the purpose of fun, and sometimes of mockery, they disproportionately increase and emphasize the defects of the features they copy, so that the portrait as a whole appears to be the sitter himself while its component parts are changed.

The recognition of like in unlike produces the comic effect—comparison being the royal road to the comic—but beyond this purpose of fun it is claimed that the likeness thus produced may be more true to life than a mere portrayal of features could have been. A caricature may be more like the person than he is himself. This paradox, favored by the critics, should not only be read as hyperbolic praise of a new art form. It reveals a new creed which is essential to our understanding of the rise of caricature.

"Art" to the age of the Carracci and of Poussin no longer meant a simple "imitation of nature." The artist's aim was said to be to penetrate into the innermost essence of reality, to the "Platonic idea" (Panofsky, 1924). Thus it was no longer mere mechanical skill that distinguished the artist, but inspiration, the gift of vision, that enabled him to see the active principle at work behind the surface of appearance. Expressed in these terms the portrait painter's task was to reveal the character, the essence of the man in an heroic sense; that of the caricaturist provided the natural counterpart—to reveal the true man behind the mask of pretense and to show up his "essential" littleness and ugliness. The serious artist, according to academic tenets, creates beauty by liberating the perfect form that Nature sought to express in resistant matter. The caricaturist seeks for the perfect deformity, he shows how the soul of the man would express itself in his body if only matter were sufficiently pliable to Nature's intentions.

Malvasia (1678), a seventeenth-century biographer of the Carraccis, describes how these artists used to look for victims of their new art while on their leisurely walks through the streets of Bologna when their serious work was done for the day. Among the seventeenth-century caricatures that have come down to us there are sheets of sketches (now in Munich) by a Bolognese artist who obviously continued this tradition.[2] We can see how he circles round his prey before he pounces. The man with the crooked nose is first tentatively sketched from different sides (Figs. 62, 63). The features are altered several times till the finished caricature presents him as a comic type with an enormous hat and a pathetically grave expression.

[2] These sketches have sometimes been attributed to Annibale Carracci himself (Brauer and Wittkower, 1931) but they may belong to a later generation of Bolognese artists (Juynboll, 1934).

Others of these caricatures are even simpler (Fig. 64). A naturalistic portrait sketch of a vivid and fleeting expression suffices to produce a comic effect when placed on a dwarfed body. The victim has been transformed into a dwarf. We need hardly say that caricature since those days has never ceased to use this primitive but easy means of transformation. Even the greatest master, Daumier (1810-1879), did not refrain from employing it in his famous series of *Representents Représentés* where, for example, the portrait head of Louis Napoleon is fitted upon a dwarf-like body (Fig. 65). It may be emphasized again that it was not the form of such a picture that was new in the seventeenth century. The comic dwarf with an enormous head was known to Greek art as well as to that of later times (Fig. 66). But in those times it was only made to ridicule types rather than to reshape an individual as a type. Yet that is precisely what our caricatures may be described as doing.

II

There is one feature of these early portrait caricatures which demands our particular attention—their playful, "artless" character. True, highly finished caricatures do occur, but then as now the typical caricature had the appearance of a casual scrawl, "dashed off" with a few strokes. This feature, too, was recognized and described by a seventeenth-century critic. André Felibien, the influential member of Louis XIV's Academy, incorporates this trait in the very definition of the caricature which he calls a likeness done in a few strokes (1676). The caricatures he probably had in mind were those of the famous master of Baroque art, the sculptor and architect Giovanni Lorenzo Bernini (1598-1680), whose powerful figure dominates the religious art of Catholic Europe. We know from contemporary accounts that Bernini's magnificent portrait busts had their counterpart in caricatures of amazing virtuosity (Figs. 67, 68).

It is in the nature of caricature that not knowing the "victim" we can no longer estimate their successfulness but what survives of Bernini's drawings can be savored even without this element of comparison. The strokes of his pen show a sublime freedom. The dominant expression of a long-necked captain of the fire brigade (Fig. 67) is an inane grin, and this grin is produced by one scrawly line. The face of Cardinal Scipione Borghese (Fig. 68) with his double chin and his baggy eyes is boiled down to an easily remembered formula. In these simplifications the abbreviated style itself acquires its own meaning—"Look here," the artist seems to say, "that is all the great man consists of." It was the German painter Max Liebermann who expressed this feeling in the most drastic and succinct manner when he said of a pompous nonentity, "A face like his I can piss into snow."

It is not by accident, then, that simplification and reduction to a formula became part of the tradition of caricature. To Hogarth, in fact, this was the distinctive feature that separated the fashionable craze of *"caricatura* drawing" from the serious artistic pursuit of delineating "character." "I remember a famous caricature of a certain Italian singer," he writes, "that struck at first sight, which consisted only of a straight perpendicular stroke with a dot over it" (Hogarth, 1758). He points to the similarity between the "early scrawlings of the child" and the successful caricatures by amateurs which were then making the round in English political circles. His eyes, sharpened by the fear of competition which threatened to oust his generalized comic "characters" in the esteem of the public, had perceived another essential trait of caricature —the absence of "drawing," as he calls it, the deliberate or incidental renunciation of academic skill implied in the lighthearted simplifications of the mock portrait.

It was due to this mechanism of reduction that the portrait caricature could be assimilated to the older technique of cartoon symbolism. Just as the Lion may stand for England or the Bear for Russia the distilled formulae mentioned by Hogarth could stand for the protagonists of the political scene, for Lord Holland or Lord Chatham. The process has stood pamphleteers in good stead ever since. In Figure 69 David Low demonstrates how the caricaturist transforms a public figure into a formula, a "tab of identity," which is cartoon symbol and caricature at the same time. All you need know of Herbert Morrison, he seems to say, is that he cultivates a cocky forelock—this lock gives you the whole man.

III

Can all this really have been "invented" at so recent a date? Did people of earlier centuries really never use pictorial art for personal aggression and abuse? Were they content with the creation of innocent comic types without any malice aforethought? Of course they were not. Pictures were used in many contexts to give vent to aggressive impulses. But from these aggressive pictures precisely that feature is missing that constitutes the essence of portrait caricature, the playful transformation of the likeness. This aggressive imagery of propagandist art does not aim at the achievement of aesthetic effect. Unlike Bernini's caricatures it lies outside the realm of art. We do not mean to say that the quality of such products is usually low—though it is—but that the whole cultural context of these aggressive images precludes their being taken as "art" in our sense. This is, first of all, an empirical statement. Among the many works of art which have come down to us from earlier times there is not one which may be said to serve exclusively or even predominantly aggressive purposes. The very examples often listed in histories of caricature seem to prove this point. Take the so-called mock crucifix (Fig. 70), a sgrafitto probably deriding a Christian who is shown worshiping a crucified God with a donkey's head. Whatever the implications of this image may be, whether its author believed that Alexamenos rather worshiped an animal-headed God or whether he added the ass's head as a piece of vulgar abuse, whether he thought such a God funny or hateful, we are here clearly outside the realm of art. The clumsiness of the drawing betrays lack of skill, not deliberate simplification—it is an abusive scrawl, not a caricature.

There is one sphere in which the aggressive image had become institutionalized long before the invention of caricature—it is the custom of hanging in effigy and similar practices, frequent in the later Middle Ages. It was the custom of Italian cities to have defamatory paintings placed on the façade of the town hall commemorating the overthrow of the community's enemies. The rebel leaders or members of opposing factions were painted hanging on the gallows or hanging head downward, and, to add to the perpetual insult, their coats of arms were added turned upside down. We can call such paintings forerunners of caricatures. But they are forerunners only in a very limited sense inasmuch as they are portraits used to attack a person's dignity. Artistically they were far from being caricatures. The few examples, at any rate, which are preserved from Northern countries (Hupp, 1930), show no comic distortions of the face but probably crude attempts at giving a likeness. The figure shown on the gallows for having failed to pay a debt is a schematic portrait (Fig. 71). It is only the context of symbols, the gallows, the raven, which degrades the victim, not the artist's reinterpretation of the man.

The same reliance on pictorial symbolism rather than artistic transformation will strike anyone who studies the propagandist imagery which gained in importance after the invention of printing (Grisar and Heege, 1922; Blum, 1916). If Luther is represented in the form of a wolf, or if a seventeenth-century preacher is depicted as inspired by the devil (Fig. 72), wolfishness or devilishness is in no case expressed through a transformation of the victim's features. A wolf wears Luther's gown or the preacher's likeness remains unaltered in the degrading context which shows him with the attributes of madness and wickedness. These satirical prints, in other words, are again imagery rather than art. They rely on ideographic methods rather than on the artist's power.

We have seen how the caricaturist's abbreviation developed an affinity to the pictorial symbolism of these broadsides. It was, in fact, when the two traditions merged, when in eighteenth-century England *caricatura* portraits were first introduced into political prints, that the cartoon in our sense was born and caricature was given a new setting and a new function: From a sophisticated studio joke, thrown off for the amusement of the artist's intimates, caricature had become a social weapon unmasking the pretensions of the powerful and killing by ridicule.

IV

Why was it really that such an obvious and apparently simple means of ridicule made its debut at so late a date? Two possible explanations would immediately suggest themselves but both of them seem inadequate. The historian of the visual arts might be tempted to look for a solution simply in the development of representational skill. Such an explanation might be superficially plausible for he could argue that the portrait, too, only acquires its full dimension of physiognomic veracity at the time in question. The century of Rembrandt, Frans Hals, and Bernini, had mastered the rendering of play of emotions on the human countenance to a degree unknown even to a Raphael or a Titian. But in a way such an explanation only shifts the problem without contributing to its solution. That the portrait, too, undergoes a profound change in the century in question need not be denied, nor that the interest in expression which manifests itself in these changes was also at play in the invention of caricature. What is questionable is, whether we have a right to speak of skills in these contexts. The manual dexterity needed to create the interlace patterns of Anglo-Irish art or of Gothic scrollwork is surely as great, if not greater, than the skill applied in Bernini's caricatures. Within the history of art alone the question cannot be answered. Recognizing this fact Brauer and Wittkower have turned to social history for an explanation of the rise of caricature (Brauer and Wittkower, 1931). They think that the emergence of the individual on the one side, the spirit of ridicule and mockery on the other were responsible for this invention of mock portraiture. Again the explanation throws light on one aspect of the matter. The climate of an age that created the immortal figures of Falstaff and of Don Quixote was certainly conducive to an art that revealed the comic side of man. But as an explanation this observation is hardly sufficient. Does the Renaissance lack this sense of the individual or the sense of humor that unmasks pretensions?[3] Was the age of an Erasmus (1465-1536) or an Aretino (1492-1556), or was the time of Aristophanes, of Lucian, unable to spot the chinks in the armor of the mighty? The art historian is often tempted to fall back on literature, the literary historian on art, and both on philosophy when they are unable to provide a solution within the realm in which their problem arose. Stimulating as these cross-fertilizations may be, they should not blind us to the methodological problem of "explanation" in history.

V

As far as history records unrepeatable events the concept of explanation has to be used with caution. But caricature is not only a historical phenomenon, it concerns a specific process and this process is repeatable and describable, for here we are in the field of psychology. Let us look once more at one of the sheets in the Munich sketchbook from the early period of caricaturing (Fig. 73). It contains a purely emblematic sketch of a man devouring gold coins, but also attempts at transforming a human head into that of an animal, an ape. This game of transformation too stands in a definite cultural context. It was a widespread belief, codified in a text attributed to Aristotle himself, that to read the character of a man one only had to trace in his physiognomy the features of the animal which he resembled most. The man with the fishlike stare would be cold and taciturn, the bulldog face would betray stubbornness. During the lifetime of the Carracci a book by Giovanni Battista Porta (1601) expounding this old theory was published for the first time with woodcuts illustrating the similarity between human types and animals (Fig. 74).[4] That caricature received an impetus from this doctrine is likely. But it is not this historical fact we want to stress in our present context but the art of transformation which has remained a

---

[3] In the polemics of the Humanists we find passages which read exactly as written caricatures. When the great scholar Filefo (1398-1481) pours out his hatred against the elder Lorenzo Medici, he writes: "Aspice Laurentii latera, aspice palearia, incessum considera! Nonne cum loquitur mugit? Os vide et linguam e naribus mucum lingentem. Caput cornibus totum insigne est!" ("Look at Lorenzo's sides, at his head, at his gait! Does he not know when he speaks? Look at the mouth and the tongue, the mucous slipping out of his nostrils. The head boasts its horns."--Voigt, 1880.) The parallel to caricature is obvious, yet the first one was not created until a century and a half later.

[4] See p. 138.

favorite trick with caricaturists revealing much of the rules of the game. There is nothing astonishing in that, for the process revealed in these transformations rounds off the achievement of the caricaturist as it was postulated by Baldinucci in the seventeenth century—"the portrait as a whole appears to be the sitter himself and yet its component parts are changed."

Perhaps the most celebrated example of such a transformation is the series of drawings showing the metamorphosis of Louis Philippe, the Roi Bourgeois (1830-1848), into *poire* (a slang term for fathead) (Fig. 75). The idea came from Philippon, the editor of *La Caricature,* the first comic weekly ever to appear (Davis, 1928). Philippon was accused of seditious libel but undeterred by his conviction to a heavy fine he published the famous sheet, which, as the caption says, might have constituted his defense. It is not my fault, he argues with mock seriousness, if the King's likeness has this fatal resemblance to the incriminating symbol of fatuity. And so skillful is the play on features that the transformation really seems to happen imperceptibly in front of our own eyes. The proof is given, the King *is* a *poire.* As the pear became the mocking symbol in countless caricatures and cartoons, we witness once more the reduction of the portrait caricature to the stereotype for political imagery.

VI

The psychologist has no difficulty in defining what the caricaturist has done.[5] He is well acquainted with this double meaning, this transformation, ambiguity, and condensation. It is the *primary process* used in caricatures in the same way that Freud has demonstrated it to be used in "wit." If we fall asleep and our waking thoughts are submerged by our dreams, then the primary process comes into its own. Conscious logic is out of action, its rules have lost their force. One of the mechanisms now in action can cause, in a dream, two words to become one, or merge two figures in one. This peculiarity of the psychic apparatus is sometimes exploited in jokes. If, for instance, we describe the Christmas vacations as "Alcoholidays,"[6] we understand that the new word, the pun word, is obviously composed of two parts: of "alcohol" and "holidays": they are united or—as we say—"condensed." An analogous condensation could also have arisen in a dream. But unlike the dream, the pun is thought out, created. We make use intentionally—which is not

[5] For the following see Chapter 6.

[6] One of the examples used by Brill (1916) in his translation of Freud's *Wit and Its Relation to the Unconscious* (1905 a).

synonymous with consciously—of a primitive mechanism in order to achieve a particular aim.

Like words in a pun, the pictures in caricatures are subjected to such readjustment. The confusion that strikes one as a defect in dreams as against the precision of clear thought here becomes a valuable achievement. Of course, the primary process must have an instrument to play on. It cannot produce a pun which is not hidden in the language. Neither can the caricaturist entirely follow his whim. He is bound by the grammar of his language, which is form; a grammar, we may add, that differs widely from the grammar of spoken languages, and that still awaits analysis.

Sometimes a picture is used merely to stress or underline a verbal pun. If, for example, Fox is represented in the form of a fox (and jokes of that kind have appeared in satire ever since the Middle Ages) an infantile attitude toward words is used which is related to all wit. It takes metaphors literally, as does the child. This is not the only case in which wit revives infantile pleasures. In fact—as Freud has shown us—in all play with words, in puns as well as nonsense talk, there is a renewal of the child's pleasure when it just learns to master language. It is easy to understand that in play with pictures the case is slightly different. Not everyone acquires the mastery of pictorial construction at all. Yet at bottom caricature, too, renews infantile pleasure. Its simplicity (as Hogarth knew) [7] makes it resemble the scribbling of the child. But we have learned to see it in a wider context. We have learned to define caricature as a process where—under the influence of aggression—primitive structures are used to ridicule the victim. Thus defined, caricature is a psychological mechanism rather than a form of art, and we can now easily understand why, once having come into existence, it has remained always the same in principle. Caricatures like those of Louis Philippe as a pear are at bottom nothing but visual puns and the taste in puns may change but their mechanism remains the same.

VII

Perhaps we are now better equipped to approach the historical problem of the application of this mechanism in the visual arts. Seen in the light of our analysis the emphasis on skill, for instance, acquires a new meaning. Certainly the controlled regression that is implied in the scribbling style of the masters is only possible where representational skill determines the ordinary level from which the virtuoso can let him-

[7] See p. 192.

self drop without danger. The pleasure in this sudden relaxation of standards demands a certain degree of security which we can observe in individual instances in such acknowledged masters of draftsmanship as Michelangelo and Dürer[8] but which the public learned to appreciate only when ordinary naturalistic imitation had become commonplace. To explain the significance of transformation, however, the controlled use of the primary process, that is, the essence of the caricaturist's power, we must view the historical position in a somewhat wider perspective.

Once more the first theoretical formulations on the caricaturist's art may provide us with indicators. These theories, it will be recalled, were couched in terms of neoplatonic aesthetics. The successful caricature distorts appearances but only for the sake of a deeper truth. In refusing to be satisfied with a slavish "photographic" likeness the artist penetrates to the essence of a person's character. We do not believe that this insistence on the artist's power is accidental. It is symptomatic of a complete change in the artist's role and position in society which marks the sixteenth century, the century of the Great Masters.

This refers neither to the artist's income nor to his prestige as a member of a concrete social group, nor to whether or not he carried a sword—but to the fact that he was no longer a manual worker, the *banausos* of antiquity; he had become a creator. The artist was no longer bound by fixed patterns, as in the Middle Ages; he shared the supreme right of the poet to form a reality of his own. Imagination rather than technical ability, vision and invention, inspiration and genius, made the artist, not merely the mastering of the intricacies of handicraft. From an imitator he became a creator, from a disciple of nature its master (Schlosser, 1924; Panofsky, 1924). The work of art was a vision born in his mind. Its actual realization was only a mechanical process which added nothing to the aesthetic value and indeed often diminished it. This state of mind is best illustrated by the paradoxical remark of a guidebook to Florence published in the late sixteenth century, which expressed the opinion that Michelangelo's unfinished marble blocks of the "Slaves" are even more admirable than his finished statues, because they are nearer to the state of conception (Kris, 1926). It is not difficult to formulate this aesthetic attitude in psychological terms. The work of art is—for the first time in European history—considered

8 Vasari (ed. Milanesi, Vol. VII) tells us that Michelangelo surpassed his competitors when a group of them playfully attempted to imitate drawings by unskilled people. The drawings accompanying the grotesque sonnet on the torturous labor on the Sistine ceiling may give us an idea how these scribbles may have looked. In a letter by Dürer from Venice a childish scrawl occurs allegedly representing his latest work.

as a projection of an inner image. It is not its proximity to reality that proves its value but its nearness to the artist's psychic life. Thus for the first time the sketch was held in high esteem as the most direct document of inspiration. Here is the beginning of the development which culminates in the attempts of expressionism and surrealism to make art a mirror of the artist's conscious or unconscious.

VIII

There are many fields in which the artists of the period sought to assert the priority of imagination over slavish imitation. The *capriccio*, the whimsical invention, became the sure means of impressing the connoisseur and arousing the envious admiration of fellow artists. From a wide range of examples we select one in which the role of the primary process is most easily demonstrable—the fashion in ornaments. In many periods of the past the ornamental border had given most scope to the artist's free play of imagination. In the late sixteenth century, however, this free play itself becomes emancipated from its shadowy range on the margin of the book or under the seat of the choir stall. Series of engravings or woodcuts proudly displayed the artist's power of creating grotesques (Fig. 76). The affinity of these creations with the dream was recognized. "He who wants to create dreamwork," says Albrecht Dürer, "must make a mixture of all things." Often the play with meaning, the ambiguity of form, becomes a predominant feature in these fantastic works. Even the traditional monsters of medieval demonology are now transformed into a mere exercise of wit and formal ingenuity. A characteristic example of this development is a series of woodcuts which appeared in 1569 under the name of Rabelais (Figs. 77, 78). In this series the ambiguity of form is used with much virtuosity. Implements are transformed into human beings, the world of the inanimate has come to life. It is instructive to look at the prototypes. These Rabelaisian monsters are escaped from Hieronymus Bosch's hell (Fig. 79). But the change of context results in a change of meaning. The uncanny has turned comic, confirming what we know of the character of the comic phenomena[9]—at the same time this ancestry in the sinister world of Bosch explains the double-edged character of our experience of the grotesque.

We seem to have moved far from the sphere of caricature, but the affinity of these creations of the primary process to the mock portraits of the Carracci is greater than might at first appear. In the Rabelais wood-

[9] See Chapter 8.

cuts, implements, pots, pans, and bags, are turned into human beings. The Carraccis—so their biographers tell us—loved to transform human beings into pots, pans, or cushions. The play with form, the controlled primary process, had found a new outlet in the most striking of *capriccios*, in the *ritratto carico*, the portrait caricature.

IX

The psychological analysis of the caricaturist's procedure has thus given us the tools to describe several aspects of a historical development in terms which bring out their essential coherence. The new role assigned to the artist's fantasy life manifests itself in caricature no less than in other spheres of art. But this finding alone would not be sufficient to account for the late occurrence of these phenomena in history. Human fantasy, after all, is universal—why was it kept so long within strict bounds? Formulated in this way our problem becomes, perhaps, even more puzzling. For in the realm of words we know of no such restrictions. Play with words, punning and nonsense talk is one of the most beloved tools of comic creation in many civilizations. How should we account for the fact that play with images requires apparently a much higher degree of sophistication? Why is the visual image as an artistic mode of expression so much more resistant to the free play of the primary process than is the word? If there is an answer to this question it must certainly throw light on the role that the visual image plays in our mind. It was for this reason that we started this investigation. We believe that here, too, psychoanalysis can furnish the answer.[10] We know from clinical experience that visual images do in fact play a different part in our mind from that played by words. The visual image has deeper roots, is more primitive. The dream translates the word into images and in heightened states of emotion the image may impose itself upon the mind as hallucinatory perception. No wonder that the belief in the special power of the visual image is particularly deeply rooted. Image magic is one of the most ubiquitous forms of magical practice. It presupposes a belief in the identity of the sign with the thing signified—a belief which surpasses in intensity the belief in the magic potency of the word. Time and again it is found that the word is more easily understood as a conventional sign that can be distorted and played with, without ulterior effects,

10 On reconsidering this passage written some fifteen years ago we now (1951) find our answer incomplete. A good deal of further investigation concerned with the relation of word and image in ontogenetic development and in historical contexts may prove rewarding. We hope to return to this question jointly.

while the visual image—and most of all the portrait—is felt to be a sort of double of the object portrayed. The one must remain inviolate lest the other come to grief. We need not look far for evidence of this universal feeling with regard to the image. The lover who tears up the photograph of his faithless love, the revolutionary who pulls down the statue of the ruler, the angry crowd burning a straw dummy of a hostile leader—all testify to the fact that this belief in the magic power of the image can always regain its power whenever our ego loses some part of its controlling function.

It is precisely this belief which explains the secret and the effect of the successful caricature. Under the surface of fun and play the old image magic is still at work. How otherwise could we account for it that the victim of such a caricature feels "hurt" as if the artist had really cast an evil spell over him? Nor is such a feeling confined to the self-conscious victims of pictorial mockery. If the caricature fits, as Philippon's *poire* obviously did, the victim really does become transformed in our eyes. The artist has taught us how to see him with different eyes, he has turned him into a comic monstrosity. He is not only abused as a fathead or unmasked as a stupid man—he simply cannot shake off the *poire*. He carries the caricature with him through his life—even through history. Great satirists have been very well aware at all times of their magic power to cast this spell of transformation on the memory picture of their butts and victims. The great poet Ronsard (1524-1585) calls out to his opponent:

Qu'il craigne ma fureur! De l'encre la plus noire
Je lui veux engraver les faits de son histoire
D'un long trait sur le front, puis aille où il pourra
Toujours entre les yeux ce trait lui demeurera.

When these verses were written, every reader understood that they were meant metaphorically. And yet the same threat which here applies to verbal satire had not yet been translated into the realm of pictorial art.

X

The conclusion that is forced upon us is this: Caricature is a play with the magic power of the image, and for such a play to be licit or institutionalized the belief in the real efficacy of the spell must be firmly under control. Wherever it is not considered a joke but rather a dangerous practice to distort a man's features, even on paper, caricature as an art cannot develop. For here as in the other spheres analyzed before, the caricaturist's secret lies in the use he makes of controlled regression. Just as his scribbling style and his blending of shapes evokes childhood pleasures, so the use of magic beliefs in the potency of his transformations constitutes a regression from rationality. This very regression, however, presupposes a degree of security, at distance from action that we can certainly not expect in all periods. The absence of caricature in earlier times indicates to us that this security, or distance, was absent. This does not mean that a belief in image magic was always consciously held in classical antiquity or in the Renaissance but it does mean that a free play with the representational image would not have been experienced as funny. For this to happen the pictorial representation had to be removed from the sphere where the image stimulates action.[11] Once the artist's prerogative as a dreamer of dreams was asserted the sophisticated art lover of the seventeenth century would be flattered rather than hurt to look at his countenance in the distorting mirror of the great artist's mocking mind. The birth of caricature as an institution marks a conquest of a new dimension of freedom of the human mind, no more, but perhaps no less, than the birth of rational science in the work of Galileo Galilei, the great contemporary of the Carraccis.

But even though the world of art admitted caricature as a sophisticated joke it remained quite aware of the element of regression it presupposes. "C'est une espèce de libertinage d'Imagination," says the *Encyclopédie* on Caricature (Vol. II, 1751), "qu'il faut se permettre tout au plus que par délassement." Caricature is relaxation because in its style, in its mechanism, and in its tendency, it relaxes the stringent standards of academic art.

Perhaps it may be legitimate to see in this aesthetic verdict, often repeated, a last remnant of the taboo which had once forbidden the play with a person's likeness. This explanation does not imply that no problem of artistic values is here involved. The license of humor is one thing, the relation of the comic to the sublime another. The best caricatures cannot and do not claim equality with great portraits. The effect of caricatures is sudden, explosive, and tends to evaporate. The great portrait has more dimensions; it continues to stimulate responses, reinterpretation, and thus processes of re-creation.

XI

Looking back on the ancestry of caricature we may, perhaps, con-

---

[11] For the psychological implications of this formulation see pp. 26ff., and 39.

veniently distinguish three stages which correspond to three possible mental attitudes toward image magic.

In the most primitive stage of witchcraft and sorcery the hostile action that is done to the image is meant to harm the person represented. Image and person are one. To pierce the wax dummy means to destroy the enemy.

There is another frequent stage in which the hostile action is carried out on the image *instead* of on the person. In hangings in effigy or in defamatory paintings not so much the person as his honor is the target. The image here serves to perpetuate and promulgate in graphic form a hostile action, injury or degradation. It serves communication rather than immediate action.

In the third stage, to which caricature belongs, the hostile action is confined to an alteration of the person's "likeness." Thanks to the power of the artist the victim appears transformed and reinterpreted and only this interpretation contains criticism. Aggression has remained in the aesthetic sphere and thus we react not with hostility but with laughter.

In comparing these conclusions with the clinical experiences of psychoanalysis, we open a wide field for further research. One thinks of patients to whom caricature and satire are dangerous distortions; the feeling of magic about these comic achievements destroys for such patients their aesthetic value. One is reminded of persons to whom the comic in general is unknown; they fear the regression in all comic pleasure, they lack the faculty of "letting themselves go." One finds in analysis that this is due to a lack of strength in the ego. If patients of this type acquire or reacquire the faculty of humor in analysis, it is only after the dominating power of the ego has been restored, and thus regression to comic pleasure has lost its threatening aspect. We might then say that the patient has made a new step toward freedom in his attitude to life.

The mechanism of artistic creation itself may be illustrated by other cases, in which the faculty of projection is disturbed. A painter whose interest in caricature is evident is unable to make convincing caricatures so long as he distorts his own personality. Unconscious self-distortion has taken the place of the distortion of his models.

Chapter 8

EGO DEVELOPMENT AND THE COMIC

Life gives us many different aspects of the comic, and it is linked up with various kinds of human activity. We may begin our classification by introducing a simple distinction. The comic which we find in life can clearly be distinguished from the comic which men deliberately call into being. The first, the perception of the comic, requires the activity of two people, one to observe and one to be observed. It is a well-established fact that wherever the comic occurs in connexion with nonhuman beings, this effect is due to an analogy with some human form of activity. The comic which we invent or call into being, in a word the comic which we act, is usually based on three persons, the spectator, the actor and a passive agent against whom the jest is directed. It is thus a process in which the social character predominates. To complete this rapid summary we may mention an analogous problem connected with humor. Humor can be completely expressed in one person: The play can be acted between the ego and the superego.

Naturally enough the connexion between the phenomena which we can assign to these groups is only a slender one. The sight of a clumsy waiter, who lets fall a pile of plates, the effect upon us when somebody makes a tendentious joke, or the monologue of Falstaff on the nature of honor resemble each other neither in kind nor in value. Freud has taught us to draw a sharp distinction between the characteristics which are common to these phenomena and those in which they differ. May I remind you of the well-known formulae: "The pleasure of wit originates from an economy of expenditure in inhibition, that of the comic from an economy of expenditure in thought and that of humor from an economy of expenditure in emotion."

For the present we can neglect these differentiations, as well as the fact that in his formula Freud uses the term "comic" in a limited sense, that of the comic which we find in others. We shall use the term in a more general sense (Freud also uses it thus) to designate the various peculiarities and characteristics which are common to phenomena generally characterized in speech as "comic." And now we shall try and see

204

how far the understanding of the "economy" of psychic expenditure in the comic can lead us.

Evidently it does not adequately specify pleasure at the comic. We may say—quoting a later statement of Freud's—that we cannot refer to "pleasure" and "pain" merely as a quantitative increase or decrease in what we call stimulus tension, although they have a great deal to do with this factor. They appear to depend not only on this quantitative factor, but also upon a characteristic which we can only describe as qualitative.

In our search for such a qualitative element in the economy of the comic, we might easily be led to confine our attention to the importance of time, or rather of the tempo in the saving of psychic expenditure, or more generally the speed at which tension is relieved. One might suggest that the element of suddenness in this economic process is responsible for the nature of comic pleasure.

We know what happens if sudden relief occurs: The energy held in check by the inhibition suddenly becomes superfluous and is ready to be discharged in laughter. But the comic and the laughable are not identical. Much laughter has nothing to do with the comic. The laughter of children at play, the laughter of flirtation or the laughter of intoxication may each be considered as due to some saving in psychic energy, but they are not always caused by the perception of the comic. On the other hand, the comic includes more than laughter. We often express our pleasure at humor not in laughter but in a quiet smile.[1]

We may remark in passing that the specific quality of humor seems to be bound up with the fact that time plays no part in the psychic economy; thus its achievement is more lasting.

But Freud did not confine the essence of the comic to its economic function. He recognized another of its properties in what he calls the relation to the infantile, to the pleasures and pains of childhood, to childhood itself. Now Freud simply indicated this relation without developing it any further, and later writers have only touched upon it occasionally. So I want to give it special attention in this survey.

If we consider its frequency in psychic life, the most important or rather the clearest relation of the comic to childhood is what we might call the regressive character of the comic. Under the influence of the comic, we return to the happiness of childhood. We can throw off the fetters of logical thought and revel in a long-forgotten freedom. The perfect example of this type of behavior is pleasure in talking nonsense; here we handle words as we did when children.

[1] See Chapter 9.

But this behavior is not characteristic of the comic only. It occurs if the ego has renounced some of its functions and does not exercise its full power. In dreaming, in neurosis and finally in psychosis the ego has been overwhelmed by the primary process. Logical thought is invalidated by elementary forces.

The way in which the primary process directs word pleasure in the comic is evidently very different. We are actually in search of this pleasure and the primary process works creatively. This becomes especially clear when we study the pun. We all know, of course, Freud's explanation: A preconscious thought is committed for a moment to unconscious elaboration or, as Freud also put it, the *pre*-conscious thought is submerged for a moment in the *un*-conscious. Both expressions seem to me to contain the idea that in this case the ego dominates the primary process. There is no contradiction between this statement and the fact that although we "make a joke," wit has the character of involuntary inspiration, of a sudden "flash of thought." Making a joke belongs to the preconscious, not to the conscious activities of the ego.[2]

Pleasure over words—to come back to our original example—which is the basis of our understanding of wit, develops out of a complicated process. For the sake of brevity, I shall leave out the teaching of the history of human language on the phylogenetic part of this problem and refer only to a few well-known facts in the ontogenetic process. The child acquires its understanding of wit or pun only when it has mastered speech.

According to Kenderdine's (1931) observations the earliest case of a child laughing at a pun is between the age of three and five.[3] If before this a child seems to find pleasure in talking nonsense, it must be a different kind of pleasure from that experienced by adults, and it is easy to see where the difference lies. For a child nonsense talk need not be a product of voluntary regression to an earlier stage of mental development, it is simply the actual handling of words at this early stage, the stage of playful experimentation with words. The child tries to understand words and their meaning, and it is an arduous process. Children are not at home in the world of words, yet words are indispensable for they serve to establish contact. The child's first belief in the omnipotence of thought disappears once it becomes conscious of an objective, yet

[2] For an elaboration of this point see pp. 312ff.; for a formulation on the relation of automatic to preconscious ego functions see now Hartmann (1939 a).

[3] For further observations see now Brill (1941), and Wolfenstein (1951), whose illustrations apparently, but probably not actually, contradict Kenderdine's findings (1931).

changing reality, and in normal cases the process of acquiring words begins at the end of the first year of its life. We know a few of the attendant
phenomena of this process, some of which seem to have an especial importance for analytic problems; for example, the child's anxiety when he
comes across a new word, his attempts and experiments until he has really
learned to deal with it correctly. Or again the child's exasperation if he
cannot find words for what he thinks, if his speech does not give his
meaning, or if grownups do not understand.

I certainly shall not try to describe these phenomena. I only want
to point out that we can follow not only the dramatic prelude of this
.process, but its triumphant conclusion, the child's delight when using
newly acquired words, its repetition of them in a sort of rhythmical
chant, its happy experiments with sound and meaning before the difference between them is finally grasped.

The child's joy at playing with the language it has just mastered
lives on in the pleasure which adults find in words and is a pleasure
which wit justifies before the superego. Morevoer the sovereignty of the
ego over the primary process is pleasurable in this case because something is desired which would otherwise happen against the will of the
ego and a passive experience is reproduced actively.[4]

We will leave the problem of regression in the comic represented
schematically in nonsense talk (we could equally well have chosen the
language of comic gesture or expressions of the comic in plastic art)
and, instead of the man-made comic we enjoy when we indulge in or
listen to jokes and nonsense, let us take an example from the comic we
find in others.

I should like to suggest three different examples and try, with a slight
deviation from Freud's formula, to discover a common characteristic
underlying the dissimilar circumstances. If we laugh at naïveté—that is
to say at the unintentional comic of the child, or at a person who makes
a clumsy movement, the waiter, for instance, when he drops a pile of
plates, or at a display of stupidity on the part of someone—common to
all these cases is an insufficient or unsuccessful adjustment to reality.
Now from the very beginning psychology has suggested that our reaction
to such experiences is connected with a feeling of superiority which takes
hold of us at the sight of another's failure.

Classical antiquity taught this. Quintilian wrote: "Non procul a
derisu est risus." Thomas Hobbes, one of the founders of psychology
in modern times, reformulated this idea with greater precision in the

4 See for an elaboration Kris (1951 b) .

middle of the seventeenth century—even before Descartes: "The passion of laughter is nothing but sudden glory arising in ourselves from sudden conception of some eminency in ourselves by comparison with the inferiority of others *or with our own formerly.*" Hobbes, in my opinion, is more akin to Freud than any later psychologist, although Freud takes economy in expenditure not superiority to be the decisive element in comic comparison. To discuss this theory I shall employ a well-tried method in which the crucial point is not our reactions to the comic but those cases in which we fail to react, in which the comic effect is disturbed. Our preoccupation with something else, the fact that our attention is diverted can be taken as a frequent cause of this failure. The disturbance lies in an ego which has lost interest in the very basis of the comic, the comparison between successful and unsuccessful adjustments to reality. To take an example used by Freud: the dancing master who points out the mistakes of a bad dancer will not find his pupil's clumsy steps funny. The preconscious automatic activity of the ego is disturbed by the conscious activity of attention.[5] Here, then, we are justified in saying that the comic effect is absent, but there are other cases in which just the opposite effect is produced, and it is these cases which we can expect to throw light upon our problem. I choose the case of a patient who is a successful teacher and shows a marked degree of psychological insight when dealing with her pupils. She is incapable of experiencing the comic pleasure which is usually aroused in adults by the naïveté of a child. She is incapable of "laughing at the child." Here, as in the case of the dancing master, we might think that it is a question of the typical attitude of the teacher, and so consider the case normal, yet what appears as praiseworthy pedagogic restraint is in fact the expression of a far-reaching disturbance. The restraint is not voluntary but compulsory. The teacher simply cannot enjoy the comic. The disturbance itself is connected with a particular dramatic situation in her childhood. As a child she had the misfortune to be laughed at and now in cases where an adult would normally experience comic pleasure, she unconsciously identifies herself with the child who is laughed at. Once we have learned to recognize this disturbance (we might well describe it as "identification with the person laughed at") we find it repeatedly, even regularly. It is not simply pathological; in fact, we can hardly consider it apart from normal human activity, for we do not feel like laughing at every slip made by another person nor does our social code permit us always to laugh. I do not intend to go into further detail and should like

[5] For theoretical formulations in this area see Chapter 14.

to try instead, in a schematic survey, to pick out the factor common to those cases in which identification with the person laughed at prevents the comic effect from being experienced and often causes a disagreeable sensation. I believe that in all these cases it is a question of our inability to dissociate ourselves fully from the experience, and such a dissociation or, in other words, such a relative detachment is certainly a preliminary condition for comic enjoyment. But we can find a better and more general definition for this condition and one which will be more useful for the development of our *exposé* when we say that enjoyment of the comic entails a feeling of complete security from danger.[6]

Let us turn once more to the genetic standpoint and ask ourselves when in fact does a child find an experience funny? The answer is borne out by a wealth of observation. A preliminary condition is complete control over the function in question. An absurd movement on the part of another person will seem funny to a child *only* when it has itself mastered the movement. At a later stage of development it will laugh at a mistake in thinking only when its own powers of thought are firmly established. Here one may ask whether the comparison between the other person's irrational expenditure (of energy) and one's own always releases a feeling of superiority, if this laughter, in Hobbes' words, "points out some eminency of our own." Laughter may denote superiority, but it denotes something else as well. Not so much *"I can do it better"* as *"I can do it."* If we could see it as a slow motion picture we should realize that our sense of the comic is preceded by an experience which can be compared to a kind of examination, to a resistance test if you like. We do not necessarily relive the entire former situation in our infantile development; a fear signal, however faint, may take its place. A feeling of anxiety over our own powers of mastery, or more accurately, the memory of an averted, superfluous anxiety, seems to accompany the comic.

At first sight this appears paradoxical. How can the increase in and search for pleasure which find their expression in the comic originate "beyond the pleasure principle"? Yet this is the logical result of a generation of psychoanalytic research leading us to supplement Freud's original statements.

The immediate point of contact lies in our conception of children's play. This conception as a whole need not be considered here: I do not wish to refer to that domination of symbolism in play which gives a unique insight into the mind of the small child; nor to the manner in

[6] In two impressive case histories Jacobson (1946) has recently demonstrated how this feeling of security develops.

which the pleasurable character of play is dominated by fantasies which set it in motion.[7] No, my intention is to pick out some points connected with the psychic achievement of the child at play, without referring to anything pathological and dealing exclusively with the normal.

In the first phase of a child's development, play serves to master the plaything—and at the same time or even earlier, to master the body. In a later phase the active repetition of passive experience dominates play, and permits—in the words of Isaacs (1933)—the active dramatization of the inner world of imagination as a means of maintaining psychic equilibrium. In both cases we are justified in saying that play serves to overcome the outer world and anxiety.

But now, if we watch the child himself at play one observation is forced upon us: He carries on with the game until every difficulty is overcome, all apparent fear mastered.

We might, of course, imagine that the defense is continued because all trace of pressure has not completely disappeared, but this is contradicted by the impression of pleasure, of enjoyment given by a child at play. It seems to me to be a question of something else. When a small boy who has been to the dentist plays at being a dentist for days on end, he does so not only because he is still afraid but because the pleasure he finds in dominating his fear gives real enjoyment. And yet it need not necessarily be the activity of the dentist which appeals to him; naturally this can be an additional factor, but to my mind it is accessory, for the pleasure of repetition is genetically older. We need only to remember how even a small child will play a game of hide and seek over and over again. I do not want to discuss pleasure in repetition, but merely to draw your attention to one element: Repetition means a return and a rediscovery. Its permanent pleasure content seems to me to be decisively influenced by a permanent delight at the harmlessness of what has once been dangerous; here too pleasure springs from economy, an increase in pleasure from a difference in expenditure. However, this gain in pleasure has nothing to do with the comic, but forms—as I am inclined to assume—the foundation for an attitude which some psychologists take to be an ultimate biological condition in the psychic life of man. I refer of course to *functional pleasure*, which has gained considerable prestige and wide application in modern literature.[8] I do not doubt that this problem

7 See particularly Klein (1929) and Searl (1933).

8 Following Herbert Spencer and Groos, Utitz (1911) and Jerusalem (1921) introduced the term into aesthetic theory; see also Bühler (1927). For the role of functional pleasure as nuclear phenomenon of the counterphobic attitude see since the publication of the present paper (1938) Fenichel (1939 a, and 1946 pp. 13, 45, 480).

has been observed correctly, and it is quite possible that one of its roots can be traced back to biological conditions, nevertheless observation of the child seems to me to show definitely that the *functional pleasure itself* is to a great extent the pleasure we have just described—pleasure arising from a sense of mastery.[9]

Functional pleasure as a phenomenon is clearly distinguishable from comic pleasure. If I attempt to suggest a line of demarcation, I do not wish to compare the extent of each phenomenon but merely to point out the one decisive difference, which lies in their relation to time. Pleasure in mastery *plays itself out in the present*, and is experienced as such. Comic pleasure, according to this hypothesis, refers to a past achievement of the ego which has required long practice to bring it about. We experience not only the success of the achievement itself but the whole process by which we gradually attained this mastery.

Freud recognized children's play as the forerunner of the comic; to my mind it is the starting point for the comic we see in others, for the realization of the comic impression.

In childhood we pass through another preliminary phase of the comic, namely fun, and a child begins to understand the nature of fun at a very early age. It is a great moment in the life of a child when for the first time it understands a joke made by an adult, or when it makes its own first joke. Illusion takes the place of reality—and in this world of make-believe forbidden things are suddenly permitted. Freud admitted as much and we can now add that all fun is directed toward a second person. Play can be solitary, fun is sociable. By its play the child tries to dominate the outer world, and in fun it is looking aggressively or libidinously for a companion. In fun the child is trying to seduce the surrounding world, fun is the frame within which this instinctual drive is indulged. Now just as our childish experiences live on as an undercurrent to the pleasure we find in a comic object, so the tendentious joke of the adult has its roots in the child's notion of fun. Fun is founded on the approval of those in authority and this is true of tendentious jokes as well. As we shall see later a situation in which an audience does not laugh at a daring joke, in which instead of general amusement (the pleasurable experience aimed at) a painful silence follows, this situation preserves some definite features of childhood: the unfortunate who told the joke feels very like a child whose parents express their displeasure at its rowdiness or exhibitionism, who has been told "That's going too far."

---

[9] For observations in support of this assumption see now Hendricks (1942, 1943 a, b). Hendrick's views on an "instinct to master" seem to me not to add to his brilliant exposition.

And now perhaps we are ready to discuss a thesis of Freud's which has been the subject of much criticism. He maintains that the experience of the comic is unknown to the child, with more reason to the small child. We are inclined to supplement this statement by actual observations of children and so far as such observations are available, they seem to confirm our hypothesis.[10]

In 1929 Herzfeld and Prager published the results of experiments they had made to test children's understanding for fun and the comic. The results are impressive when they refer to the "comic" productions of children in their early years of latency. When we examine the contents of children's drawings which are intended to express something "funny," we gain the impression that what the child represents are objects of the surrounding world which it has just learned to comprehend and to master. Graber's (1931) psychoanalytic observation in a similar case seems to reveal that the deepest problems in the child's life—in Graber's case the repressed fear of castration—may come to be expressed in what the child calls "funny."

This theory is not confined to the child's comic productions. It is also true of cases in which the child learns to appreciate the comic.[11] Various protocols show that a child of one or two years only gradually becomes aware of the comic impression created by the jerky movements of a puppet or a cat. The child's reactions seem to pass from fear to interest and only very slowly from interest to pleasure, which is the last phase of this triple process. To be sure, it is impossible to gain more accurate and detailed information from this study—to my knowledge the only one dealing with this particular subject—but then we must remember that it is carried out by observers who make no effort to understand the dynamic character of man's mental life. For this reason their observations are only of limited value for our discussion. On this basis, I should like to attack a more general problem in the psychology of the comic one which to my mind has been insufficiently appreciated: It concerns the part played by the comic in overcoming emotion, especially when this is roused by strange and terrifying things. Here I think the following formula suggests itself: The comic alone cannot overcome emotion for it presupposes a certain control over anxiety before it can become effective. Once it has come into being, however, it combines a sense of mastery with

[10] See now Grotjahn (1940, p. 40) who assumes that the harmless shock is the only form of the comic about which the child is able to laugh during its preoedipal development.

[11] Recent studies by Gellert (1950, 1951), under the supervision of del Solar at Yale University, seem to confirm a number of assumptions here offered.

a feeling of pleasure. The German Jean Paul (Richter), one of the greatest of poet psychologists, had this psychic fact in mind when he said: Wit brings freedom, and freedom wit. All branches of psychology help to confirm this thesis and some examples already discussed could be used as further proof, but I only want to add one or two other examples which refer to historical problems.

We are all familiar with the great company of comic figures which are to be found in the art and literature of all civilized peoples. We can often discover their genealogy and trace it right back to the antique satyr play, or even further. It is a fact that as a general rule, we can perceive behind them another more sinister shape once feared or dreaded. Satyrs who at first were goat demons, the pulcinella of South-Italian comedy, descendant of the cock dancers, the comic devils of the mystery plays, even the lovable Mephisto in Goethe's *Faust*, are the best-known examples of such ci-devant demons now travestied as fools.[12]

Although the grinning gargoyles on Gothic cathedrals are intended to turn away evil, they look terrifying enough perched high up among the gables and gutters. Their development is interesting. In the thirteenth century these figures of an apotropaic magic are still terrifying. In the fourteenth, they tend to become mere comic masks; by the fifteenth century the process is complete and, instead of threatening, they are only intended to amuse. This observation is not inconsistent with older psychoanalytic knowledge. The mechanism which determines this functional change of the object is a general one, and for obvious reasons I do not wish to go into its origin. Jekels (1926) attempted to explain the secret of comedy as a displacement of the tragic guilt from son to father, and we may add the aphorism: When we laugh at the fool, we never forget that in his comic fancy dress, with bladder and cap, he still carries crown and scepter, symbols of kingship. And is it not possible that the freedom exploited by the fool is a direct inheritance from the omnipotence of his demonic predecessor? If we look at the peculiarity of comic experience from this angle we may say that what was feared yesterday is fated to appear funny when seen today. The intermediate position of the comic between pleasure and the warding off of emotion, especially fear, even finds expression in our speech. The French word *drôle* has undergone a transformation in meaning from the uncanny to the comic.

12 For the relation of the clown to the devil see now Tarachow (1951) who discusses the meaning of the clown in various contexts; for the devil as comic figure see Tarachow (1948). Material presented in this latter paper throws additional light on some of the points made below.—For other aspects of the problem see now also Moellenhoff's (1940) discussion of the popularity of Mickey Mouse.

The word *komisch* in German, as well as the French word *drôle* can be used even today to denote anger or surprise, for example, when we say, *C'est drôle,* or, *das ist komisch;* and the English word "funny" can be used in a similar way. But such examples are hardly necessary to prove the intermediate position of the comic, a character which seems to be common to all comic phenomena.

I cannot avoid referring here to suggestions which I have already made elsewhere. I suggested calling this peculiarity of the comic the double-edged character of comic phenomena.[13] By this is meant the characteristic fact that these phenomena under certain conditions can cause displeasure or even pain instead of pleasure.[14]

The cases we mentioned of unsuccessful dissociation can be considered from this point of view. If we identify ourselves with the person laughed at we feel discomfort instead of pleasure. We do not receive a comic, but a painful impression. Sometimes it is as if our old fear, the mastering of which is a necessary precondition of the comic, were suddenly strong enough to overwhelm our actual experience.

As the clearest example of such cases I may allude to the technique familiar to all those who know anything about certain films. In some of these pictures—I refrain from giving examples—the mechanism latent in all comic is openly exploited. Relief is achieved by a previous increase in tension. However, this technique is dangerous, for all are not equally suitable subjects for this species of psychic manipulation. Some people get no further than the preliminary tension and are unable to forget their fear in the pleasurable release which follows.[15]

However, a deeper psychological interpretation of this technique belongs to the psychology of the grotesque rather than to that of the comic; it is largely based on the sudden and surprising relief from anxiety which leads to laughter.[16]

What is true of the comic that we find in others holds good for "manufactured" comic as well. The double-edged character of the comic is apparent when, for instance, an audience listening to a joke rejects the implication and does not respond to the appeal for common aggression

[13] See Chapter 6.

[14] Fenichel (1946) has since pointed also to the double-edged character of children's play. I doubt that he uses the word in the sense I do, though a similarity exists between the phenomena he has in mind and those which originally suggested the term to me.

[15] The reference to the circus supplies better and, it seems, more illuminating examples; see now Tarachow (1951), who has treated this subject in a wide context.

[16] For other aspects of the grotesque see now Reich (1949).

or common regression. In identifying ourselves with the audience, we hear the severe voice of our own conscience. The pleasurable experience which should have arisen from a compromise between the tendencies of the id and the superego remains unrealized. A similar process takes place in the listener. He accepts the proffered invitation tentatively, feels for an instant the aggressive impulse which the joke ought to satisfy; but the joke is only successful in removing existing inhibitions and fails to prevent a new cathexis from which springs an unpleasurable and painful impression.[17]

I am afraid some confusion has crept into our survey. Let us therefore summarize the results: Our starting point was Freud's idea of the economic and genetic conditions in the comic. We thought it necessary to point out an additional element, the fact that most comic phenomena seem to be bound up with past conflicts of the ego, that they help it to repeat its victory and in doing so once more to overcome half-assimilated fear. From this essential peculiarity of the comic experience arises its double-edged character, the ease with which it passes from pleasurable success to unpleasurable failure. Certainly we have treated the comic unfairly in concentrating on comic phenomena as a compromise in psychic life and neglecting the pleasure produced by these phenomena, but this is due to the intentional onesidedness of this paper.

The compromise achieved by the comic is the foundation of a phenomenon well-known to psychoanalysts: The comic as a mechanism of defense. We know it from clinical experience: Here it can appear in various guises to master and ward off emotions, above all anxiety.

At the beginning of an analysis a patient spoke about a sexual habit which played an important part in her life. She was unable to control her laughter, which had to camouflage her repressed fear of permanent damage through masturbation. In such a transitory form the comic as a method of defense is completely normal but we also come across it as a permanent state which stigmatizes the whole personality. I should like to describe this clinical picture as that of "the typical clown." So far as I can see the strongest incentive to playing the fool is exhibitionism. The connection between exhibitionism and comic pleasure is now well known and was noticed as early as 1912 by Ernest Jones. I was able to follow the fate of this character type in a young man, a scoptophiliac, and an ex-

---

[17]An experimental verification of this hypothesis and others here developed is implicit in the findings of Redlich, Levine, and Sohler (1911). Through a skillful variation of experimental procedures applied by Sears (1934), Murray (1934, 1935), Eysenck (1942, 1943), Cattell and Luborsky (1947 a, b), they studied the reaction of subjects to a series of cartoons with the intention of developing a test procedure, the Mirth Response Test, which promises to produce interesting data.

hibitionist, who had early been outrivaled by his brother, and thereafter saw himself condemned to be the humorist, the clown. When in some political argument the others were absorbed in a fierce discussion, he, the buffoon, had to be content with an occasional joke. His wit could be spiteful and aggressive; it served as a defense against a passive oral fantasy, it took the place of his desire to seduce with words. For a time his post as contributor to a comic paper gave him a certain balance. But the distortions which he inflicted on his personality by his perpetual joking were due to his desire to avoid competition with a stronger rival.[18]

Psychoanalysis teaches us the outcome of such an attitude. The clown will not remove his cap and bells until he has conquered his anxiety.

The intimate connection between the comic on the one hand, anxiety and instinct on the other, helps us to understand the limits of its influence. It cannot approach sacred things without appearing blasphemous— a form of double-edged effect. It cannot bring permanent relief for, as in mania which is to some extent the pathological enlargement of the comic, the victory of the ego is transitory, the pleasure gain of short duration. But this is not necessarily the case; in a particular form the comic relief is permanent, for here it is not an often-repeated attempt of the ego to find a solution, but a permanent transformation of the ego. We begin to realize the value of the humorist's achievement, for he banishes man's greatest fear, the eternal fear, acquired in childhood, of the loss of love. The precious gift of humor makes men wise; they are sublime and safe, remote from all conflict. According to Freud's outline of the libidinal types (1931 b), humor can be most readily conceived as a composite type, in which elements of narcissism are prominent; but how few people possess humor in the Freudian sense!

Humor too has a counterpart; there is also a double-edged phenomenon of humor. Freud's criminal as he is led to the gallows on a Monday morning remarks: "Dear me, this week's beginning well!" It seems to me that Freud's interpretation is doubtful: This is called, and rightly, "grim humor," and I think we are justified here in recognizing a particular form of rebellion against fate: *Self-irony,* a form of the comic which is related to cynicism and sarcasm and bears the stamp of aggression.[19] This difficulty in drawing the boundary between humor and self-irony reminds us again how imperfect is any happiness which the comic can offer us. We see man as an eternal pleasure-seeker walking on a narrow ledge above an abyss of fear.

18 For a case with similar personality structure see now Tarachow (1949).

19 See also p. 187. Continued clinical observations suggest to me now (1951) that Dooley (1934) was correct in pointing to the frequent correlation between humor and self-criticism of a masochistic type.

Chapter 9

LAUGHTER AS AN EXPRESSIVE PROCESS

Contributions to the Psychoanalysis of Expressive Behavior

I. FORMULATION OF THE PROBLEM

It is possible to distinguish two formulations of the problem in regard to the psychology of laughter. One examines the occasion and cause of laughter and the underlying question runs: "When does one laugh?" The other examines laughter as a physical process and the underlying question is: "How does one laugh?" The first question has as its focus the psychology of the comic,[1] and the second the facts of physiology and anatomy. Laughter as a physical process, and more precisely as an expressive process, will form the starting point of this essay, but a choice must be made of the problems in this field and some things must be omitted which would otherwise stand in the foreground. For our aim is to examine, by means of this example, what contribution psychoanalytic considerations can make to the understanding of expressive processes; it is clear that the scope of those considerations is only a limited one and cannot cover the whole subject.

The expression of the human countenance and its play of feature have a mysterious power. They play a decisive role in the contact between man and man, always confronting us with the riddle: what is the relation between man's appearance and his personality?[2] In every field of psychological research approaches to this question have been sought. Psycho-

---

[1] For purposes of definition: not everything that is comic is laughed at, not all laughter is a reaction to something comic.

[2] In the scientific study of expression, "expressive behavior" or "pathognomy" (from the Greek *pathos*-feeling) —and I employ these terms indifferently—must be distinguished from "physiognomy," which is based upon the physical framework of the face. The antithesis between the two points of view was brought out as early as the eighteenth century in Lichtenberg's polemic against the physiognomy of Lavater. The doctrines of physiognomy have persisted to a certain extent in the science of bodily build; pathognomy or expressive behavior is a part of the branch of psychology first studied scientifically by Bell and Darwin, namely the psychology of expression. See Lersch (1932), and a more recent compendium of wider appeal by Herland (1938). For historical references see Pollnow (1928) and Bühler (1933).

analysis too has contributed to such attempts: the countenance of a predominantly anal or oral person has been described by a successful use of intuition (Abraham, 1921; Gero, 1939). But we do not intend to pursue such attempts here; what we shall deal with is not the characterological side of expressive behavior, but expressive activity itself and the course it takes.

When seeking orientation with regard to the expressive behavior of another person, one uses two kinds of data: his unintentional reactions to stimuli and the signals he makes to his fellow men, because only a part of his expressive behavior is directed toward the other person, whereas the whole of it is perceived by the latter and serves the purposes of social contact.[3] Expression as a means of contact is called "the speech of the human countenance."[4] We venture on such a comparison not in order to demarcate the line between the verbal and the pathognomic giving of information, but because this comparison offers a useful approach for a survey of the problems which pathognomy presents to science and the scope of our limited subject can be defined with its help.[5] We distinguish at the outset between linguistic questions and those concerning the history of speech. We may ascribe to the latter the researches of Darwin, who tried to discover how pathognomy had developed in the course of human evolution as a medium of communication, a question concerning the prehistory of expressive behavior. But even since its establishment the speech of the human countenance has certainly not been without its history. It became differentiated according to age, social position, race, and period, in the same way as speech through human gesture, of which it is regarded as the most universal part. Compared with these questions of prehistory and history, those of the linguistic branch of research

[3] See Buytendijk and Plessner (1925-1926), and for another aspect, Bernfeld (1929). If one thinks of the contact achieved through expressive behavior as a "transmitter-receiver system," one may look for disturbance at both ends if the contact is disturbed. Disturbances relating to the transmitter will be dealt with later. Concerning those relating to the receiver I shall only say this: people who interpret the expressions of others with considerable uncertainty and whose understanding of them is to a high degree unstable are usually disturbed themselves, or can easily be disturbed, with regard to their own expressions. But the converse does not seem to be true: "Good" interpreters need not be themselves good communicators.

[4] Lange (1937). This kind of speech extends far beyond the species *homo sapiens*— but of course the trustworthiness of communication varies. We understand animals, too, and we can even "understand" some things in plants. (See Buytendijk and Plessner, 1925-1926, p. 108). In this sense the limit of understanding is set by bodily experience.

[5] Bühler (1934) has examined the history and significance of such a comparison between the speech of expression and verbal speech. A discussion of Bühler's point of view regarding the psychology of expression cannot be attempted here.

would seem somewhat more modest. One can direct one's research to the vocabulary of pathognomic speech, to the types of pathognomic expression, and, in the case of laughter, to types and subtypes of laughter; the answering of these questions falls into a descriptive or classifying field of work. A further investigation can be made of the grammar of pathognomy, where the question is one of the method of formation of each separate pathognomic act, and in the case of laughter, the method by which it arises as a bodily, and, in particular, as a pathognomic process, which concerns the anatomy and physiology of pathognomy. Finally one can investigate the syntax into which the vocabulary and grammar of pathognomy are fitted. This question, which relates to the central regulation of the pathognomic processes, will be in the foreground of our discussions, while others can only be incidentally touched upon.

If we attempt to estimate, in regard to laughter, the scope and importance of this formulation of the question, we must first refer to the extensive field of work which has been opened up by neurological research, such as the work of Oppenheim, Bechterew, Brissaud, Dumas, etc., on the pathology of laughter in cases of disease of the brain. In comparison with this imposing trend of research, a more modest task falls to the hypotheses at which we are aiming; they deal with the problem of the central regulation of expressive behavior as a problem of psychoanalytic ego psychology.[6]

We can make a connection with psychoanalytic research if we start from the fact that the human body as an apparatus for movement constitutes a unit, in which expressive and motor activity cannot be separated from each other. The fact that the system Pcs., "the last system at the motor end," controls motility, gives us sure ground to stand on. We are concerned with a preconscious, automatically discharged ego function.[7] Since he introduced the theme in *Studies in Hysteria*, Freud formulated the problem in this way, and on this foundation Abraham, Ferenczi, Landauer, Fenichel, and others, have based their considerations.[8] It is not our intention to add anything new to these researches. What is new in psychoanalytic research always arises out of analytic experience; but by glancing over one's analytic material, which anyone can do, as well as by reviewing psychoanalytic literature, the impression is

[6] I make no attempt here to prove the correctness of this formulation of the question, as opposed to a neurological one, or to mark off the one from the other; see now Davison and Kelman (1939), and Migliorini (1939).

[7] For a similar approach see Schilder (1931). See also Rapaport's (1951, pp. 527 f.) comments. For a divergent approach see Maslow (1949); for the theory of automatic ego functions see Hartmann (1939 a).

[8] See particularly Landauer (1927); Fenichel (1928).

confirmed that only rarely and in special cases (as in cases of tic) does one have the opportunity of bringing into the foreground of analytic discussions the questions referred to here, namely, the "slighter" psychological disturbances of the apparatus controlling expressive and general movement. Our observation is mostly limited to chance occurrences which appear on the periphery of the field of treatment. To some such observations I am indebted for whatever understanding I bring to the questions to be discussed in what follows. They have given me the opportunity of relating together, in a way that I shall try to present here, reflections which have occupied me in another connection for a long time. My aim is to give an exposition of the operation of the ego in the phenomenon of expression and this will be exemplified by reference to the process of laughter.

II. THE EGO AND LAUGHTER

Laughter as a Social Act

Let us consider first a concrete situation, by analyzing which we shall try to proceed step by step to a more general understanding. Some people are in a room together and in one part of it laughing begins; it spreads and becomes a social act. We then look for an explanation of the phenomenon; we shall try to give it step by step, without avoiding detours, and yet without being able to complete it in one important point.[9]

Laughter breaks out, according to one of Freud's theories which has been confirmed again and again, when a sum of psychic energy which has been employed for the cathexis of certain psychic trends suddenly becomes unusable.[10] What use can we make of this theory for our problem?

Let us start with a special case, that of some kind of occasion which provokes a common outburst of laughter among some people whom we are watching—the telling of a joke perhaps. This is a familiar example which we know from Freud's description: the communication of an experience or the mutual experience of the comic through the telling of a joke affects the listener like "an invitation to common aggression and common regression." One part of the psychic energy which is freed—if we consider an aggressive joke for instance—comes from the saving of an expenditure of energy for repression, the other part, the pleasure gain, comes from a common regression and common utilization of infantile

[9] See below, footnote 23.

[10] In Freud's formulation the word "suddenly" does not occur. It seems to me that the word is essential since it is precisely the "shock nature" and suddenness of the discharge which is the specific precondition of laughter. See also p. 205.

modes of thought. The pleasure gain from regression shows us that the adult requires a certain cathexis, i.e., expenditure of energy, to curb in himself the working methods of the primary process, which breaks through in the infantile modes of thought contained in the comic of adults.[11] And so laughter indicates in a double sense mutual understanding and mutual guilt.

To apply this to our example: the united action which takes place within the human group, the group formation in laughing, is to be understood as a joint way of reacting. This seems to be in accordance with the fact that when someone joins a laughing group, as a stranger to it, he becomes acutely conscious of being an outsider.[12] He cannot join in the laughter when the others laugh; for them anything is good enough to laugh at, everything adds to their mirth; to him, the things that amuse them seem senseless and stupid; he has not made the intellectual regression with them and it will be some time before he can adjust himself and then, in laughing, become part of the laughing group.

But how does it happen that an alliance is formed between those who laugh—that laughter becomes a group situation? Can we hope to find an answer that will satisfy us by means of this illustration of telling jokes? An argument against this is provided by simple observation: in a group situation one may join in the laugh without quite knowing what the laughter is about, in fact without even knowing anything about it at all. At this point laughter is not necessarily a reaction to a common stimulus. The laughter of the group no longer requires a "butt" to laugh at, it can itself represent both content and sealing of the pact. The motive for laughing will sink into the background in this way, as the mass tie becomes sufficiently strengthened, at the same time that the controlling and inhibiting function of the individual becomes restricted. Every weakening of the ego can hasten this condition, a slight intoxication being the most certain method.

At this point let us consider once more our illustration, the telling of a joke. Here too the aim is the creating of a group, the establishing of a community, schematically a "group of two." But the weaker the identification secured by the group situation, so much the cleverer must

---

[11] Strictly speaking we ought to speak here of an expenditure for suppression. In the first case an instinctual impulse is suppressed and in the second a method of behavior.

[12] See Bergson's description of this situation which is not only valid for laughing: "Un homme, a qui l'on demandait pourquoi il ne pleurait pas a un sermon ou tout le monde versait des larmes, repondit, 'Je ne suis pas de la paroisse.'" This "not being able to join in the laugh" is met with as a symptom in obsessional neurotics; see Jones (1912).

the device be and so much the better the joke; conversely, these stand-ards are lowered if the collectivity is firmly established, until laughter, apparently without cause, or easily provoked, leaps from one person to another. But what is the source of the "freed psychic energy" in this case?[13]

For an explanation we must focus our attention on the fact that laughter is a bodily process, which may be distinguished by two charac-teristics: by the coming into prominence of a rhythmic movement, pri-marily depending on an interference with outward breathing brought about by the intercostal muscles,[14] and by an accompanying excitation of the whole body, which is clearest in an attack of laughing: one is con-vulsed with laughter.

Instead of any description I will introduce here a quotation from the best psychological tradition. Cicero declares: "Ore, vultu denique ipso toto corpore ridetur."[15] Laughter begins with the mouth, gradually spreads over the whole face, and finally indeed over the whole body—i.e., a pathognomic act is changed into or, more exactly, changed back into a motor one. Here also it is a matter of regression, the reduction or re-nouncing of functions which the ego otherwise carries out. These condi-tions also—no matter whether of reduction or renunciation—are to be understood as regression to an earlier level of behavior, if we think along the lines of the ontogenesis of human motor activity.[16] The motor activ-ity of infants has rhythmical muscular actions as its principal character and these become coördinated in the course of cortical development.[17] The acquiring of bodily control culminates, from four to six years of age, in a phase of development distinguished by the grace with which individual movements are carried out and it has been described as the period of "luxury of movement" in children. One can observe something analogous in the expressive behavior of childhood. At first there are strong but undifferentiated reactions to pleasure and unpleasure;[18] differ-entiation takes place by a gradual acquisition of newer forms of com-

---

13 See now also Ferenczi (1913, posthumously published).

14 See Dumas (1931, p. 244).

15 *De Oratore*, IV, 441.

16 See Homburger (1922). Homburger's views, as Landauer (1926) has pointed out, approach those of psychoanalysis in several important respects. For example, he distinguishes in the historical development of human motor activity a dichronous onset, which corresponds exactly to the dichronous onset of sexual development, in the Freudian sense.

17 For the relation of (autonomous) ego development to the control of rhythm, see now Kris (1951 b).

18 See Drommard (1909, p. 3).

munication and by a toning down of the older ones. Let us visualize the face of an infant at the moment when it begins to be contorted: we do not know whether he is going to laugh or cry. (Anticipating what comes later, I may add that it is possible for an adult also at the peak of an emotional experience to say that he does not know whether he feels impelled to laugh or to cry.) It is only the continuous development of the pathognomy of the child which leads gradually to an ability to supplement involuntary reactions to stimuli by signals to the environment which show differentiated mental processes. Considering the two lines of development together, we may say that a generalized periodic and undifferentiated process of expression is developed in the service of the reality principle in two directions not previously differentiated, toward purposive movements and expressive as well; a person's walk, the way in which he performs a purposive movement can tell us something about his nature, what sort of a person he is. The converse does not hold; not all expression is purposive.

What has just been stated in the terminology used by contributors to neurology, particularly Homburger, may now be expressed in psychoanalytic terms (Freud, 1911 a). The musculature was originally used in the service of the pleasure principle for the relief of the mental apparatus from situations of stimulation, by discharging uncoördinated stimuli in movement and by sending innervations to the interior of the body, which set going pathognomy and general movement. Only when the reality principle was introduced did the uncoördinated movements become "purposive actions," or—and this is my insertion—appropriate signals, i.e., they were used for an effective mastering of the outer world and—by the same token—for making contact with the environment.

And now another statement of Freud's, to the effect that the necessary restraint of motor discharge is provided by means of the process of thought. We shall not proceed with a direct recapitulation of Freud's train of thought; everything seems to point to a familiar formula: the language of the body is replaced by the language of words. Thereby a state of affairs arises which is of fundamental importance for the development of motor acts: the acquisition of speech was the event which determined the fate of one branch of general movement, namely, movements of expression; that branch is the more archaic means of expression, and its "plasticity" is lessened through verbal language. Experimental research confirms this. In the case of children of normal intelligence the capacity to use expressive movements for purposes of making themselves understood gradually diminishes and for early latency it is true to say that the higher the level of intelligence, the less the capacity to use the body as an apparatus for expression. It is well established that this experimental finding depends on the acquisition of speech, since the capacity remains latent in normal cases and is regained by people who become deaf and dumb after organic illness.[19]

The phrase "language of words instead of language of the body" requires nevertheless some modification. Bodily processes of expression are not completely replaced; certain forms of expression—"gestures" and the whole field of pathognomic expressions—remain. The amount of what remains varies according to social position and the level of culture, but for the normal person expression *toto corpore* is eliminated. This elimination, which among civilized peoples certainly does not take place only under the pressure of education, is subject to considerable cultural variations. Expressive movements shown by less complex cultures are more lively and various than our own.[20] But even primitive society recognizes limitations, as well as conditions under which special freedom is permitted to expressive movement: these considerations are part determinants of orgy and dance as ritual customs.

To complete our review let us turn our attention to the animal species. A quotation will help us here: "Animals have not shared in the transformation of grasping into pointing movements" (Cassirer), which for the first time posit an object. An animal lacks the capacity to point things out; in short, an animal has no index finger, its whole body being its apparatus for expression.[21] This anthropological approach marks out a field which includes the development from autoplastic to alloplastic

[19] See Schäfer (1934). This stimulating paper also deals with expressive behavior in the latency period and the conclusion is reached that the average capacity for expression is low in this phase. I have not been able to convince myself that these findings are sufficiently well established.

[20] That is particularly true of the free uninhibited laughter *toto corpore*: "The aborigines of Australia express their emotions freely, and they are described by my correspondents as jumping about and clapping their hands for joy, and as often roaring with laughter. . . . Mr. Bulmer, a missionary in a remote part of Victoria, remarks, 'that they have a keen sense of the ridiculous; they are excellent mimics, and when one of them is able to imitate the peculiarities of some absent member of the tribe, it is very common to hear all in the camp convulsed with laughter'" (Darwin, p. 218). An analogous observation was kindly put at my disposal by Roheim. A central Australian who listened to a gramophone record of Roheim's, which he could not possibly have understood, began to laugh unrestrainedly when laughter began to come from the record; he threw himself on the ground as he laughed. Many ethnologists referred to by Sully (1904) think that the free laughter of primitives can be distinguished from the restrained laughter of those who have been in contact with missionaries. Experienced field workers dispute this statement.

[21] See Witte (1930). With regard to the disturbances shown by psychotics, the behavior may be such that the whole body suddenly becomes the vehicle of expression; for a descripiton and evaluation of this see Nunberg (1920).

behavior and allows us to recognize pathognomy as the "legitimate residue" of what was once a more universal method of behavior. The more archaic methods of expression, however, have not lost their power of attraction; we recognize them in various phenomena of human behavior and may ask under what conditions civilized man is inclined to turn again to the archaic type of expression, namely *toto corpore*.

A survey of these conditions is not difficult: if we disregard cases of pathological damage to the central nervous system, it is always a matter of alteration in the extent of the ego's power, of the limitation of one or more of its functions on the part of or in favor of the id. The clearest cases are those in which the ego is overwhelmed by instinctual claims or affects. The role of the instinct can be seen at once: in states of sensuous excitement everything presses forward with a different rhythm. And, as Edward Glover (1924) has pointed out, the motor apparatus functions in many ways that remind us of the movements of an infant.[22] Something analogous is true of facial expressions: what would be regarded as normal in the "speech of the countenance" is overstepped in states of physical excitement. One speaks of an expression of animal greed. What is still more evident—though it can only be noted aphoristically here—is that no fixed pattern of expression has been evolved for orgasm. The id has no expressive behavior. A state of violent emotion has similar characteristics: in a furious temper the human countenance can become a grimace, at times of the keenest despair there is a breaking through of rhythmical movement in attacks of uncontrollable sobbing and crying. Something similar happens in the act of laughing and it enables us to see how narrow the dividing line is which separates the expressions of opposite affects. But we are now concerned with the differences and not the likenesses. The rhythmic shaking of the body in laughter is marked by the positive and not the negative sign. It is pleasurable, it serves to discharge mental energy in the service of the pleasure principle. In laughter the whole body becomes, to a varying degree, an "apparatus for expression"; archaic pleasure in movement is reactivated and is socially permissible.

Let us return once more to our starting point. Group laughter, as shown in infectious laughter, is to be understood as regression in common. It requires no or only a slight "occasion"; what is tolerated in this case need not be some special way of thinking, or aggressive thoughts, but the behavior itself, namely laughter. But according to this theory some part at least of the energy set free for laughing comes from a

22 See also Vanlar (1903).

diminution of expenditure, which would otherwise be used to safeguard our "adult behavior," making it appear that we are "in complete control" of our motor and expressive behavior.[23]

The Control of Laughter

That laughter holds a unique position is made very plain by the fact that we can seek out laughter. We are inclined to give in to it and long for the relief it brings. "I should like to laugh today!" we say, and we often succeed. Looked at from this point of view laughter belongs to the extensive group "enjoyments," the tame descendants of primitive orgies, which are characterized by the same relief and the same voluntary sinking below the wearisome high level of adult everyday behavior. But this is not the only conceivable case and perhaps not even the most frequent.

We may also start laughing without meaning to; it can also happen in opposition to the ego and it can attack us quite suddenly. We become weak with laughing; he who laughs is defenseless. When laughter overcomes us and disarms us, we speak of an attack of laughing; it has been repeatedly compared to an epileptic attack. An attack of laughter is often very difficult to stop; it is much easier to prevent it starting, to control it before it develops. This is best done, as everyone knows, by diligently turning our attention to something else: the ego function of attention is called upon to check a threatened process which would otherwise be uncontrollable.[24] This method of procedure is universally valid for the function of attention. It is characteristic of this function that it lays claim to the whole of us; any other activity interferes with it; we hold our breath when we pay attention. On the basis of this theory we assume that a close relation exists between many automatic actions of the body and ego functions. Let us return once more to the suppression of laughter by a voluntary diversion: the ego acts here (as Ferenczi has said) like a railway pointsman.[25] But how does this switching-over work in the case of laughter? Two extensive groups of substitute actions are observable in the pathognomic apparatus. It is possible to make a serious face instead of laughing; the laughter is suppressed, but a somewhat artificial expression persists. This artificiality can be described as a special

[23] The discussion of laughter as a social activity is not pursued here beyond what is useful for our special purpose. For instance, an important problem concerning the nature of contagion in pathognomic-motor activity demands separate treatment, such as that given in the special contributions to this question by Schilder (1935).

[24] See Suter (1912), Fenichel (1931), and Ferenczi's highly condensed formulations (1919).

[25] See Ferenczi (1922) for further formulations; see also p. 313.

kind of rigidity. The approach to motility is shut off and is anxiously kept shut; all play of the facial muscles is stopped in order to prevent their being seized by laughter. The other way out is more remarkable: if one can call the first a complete turning away of the ego, the second strikes one as victorious fight, in which the desire to laugh is subjugated and becomes reduced to a smile. A movement producing sound and spreading to all parts of the body is reduced to a play of the muscles around the mouth; in the words of Cicero: *ore* instead of *vultu* and *toto corpore*. This is the way out which polite manners recommend. In the West it goes back to Plato and Seneca, but it has been constantly in force outside the bounds of Mediterranean civilization; the most famous instance of this is well expressed in the 144th letter of the Earl of Chesterfield to his son, in which he says: " . . . and I could heartily wish, that you may often be seen to smile but never heard to laugh while you live." But what was taught as a model of behavior for an English gentleman in the eighteenth century has a general currency, though with varying intensity: for us too smiling is "higher" than laughing, we regard it as the humanization of laughter. But however indisputable this theory seems to me, it still requires some comment, because if we test our theory that the smile is a restricted and more civilized form of laughing by applying it to the development of the individual, to the "ontogenetic model," it does not fit. The smile of the child is older than his laugh and not the product of later development.[26]

The smile has just as many riddles as the laugh. Just as we do not intend to touch on all the questions relating to laughter, so we have just as little hope, or even less, of contributing anything new to the "riddle of the smile." By a few remarks only shall we attempt to establish its connection with our subject.

To paraphrase Aristotle, it may be said that mental life begins in a human being on the fortieth day,[27] because the smile of the satisfied infant, free from want and anxiety, is the expression of the first contact —outside the sphere of vital needs—the first mental contact between one human being and another. We can only surmise what it is in the behavior of the infant that releases precisely a smile; a theory of Freud's deals with this question. He is of the opinion that the position of the lips which is characteristic of the smile represents, so to say, "Enough"

[26] The existence of a genetic connection between laughing and smiling is a disputed point in the literature of the psychology of laughter; many authors (McDougall, for instance) deny it. For experimental work on smiling see Kaila (1932), whose findings have been confirmed by Spitz and Wolf (1946).

[27] As a matter of fact, the smile can appear much earlier.

or even "More than enough" (1905 a). The smile, however, becomes detached quite early from this situation, from which it may derive its shape, and becomes a reaction to what is familiar, the human face in particular. If we adopt Freud's line of argument, we may then say that the expression which first denoted repletion becomes the expression of friendly psychological contact in general.

The smile retains the privileged place of the first-born in pathognomic functioning. One can say that it appears everywhere as a substitute expression, to bring about a moderation of any pathognomic situation which was of a contorting kind: Anger that has been repressed, fright that has been assimilated, crying that has been overcome can turn into a smile. If we also think of the smile in all these cases as an earlier form of laughing we may be inclined to attribute to it a function of discharge. We could put forward some such view as the following: that in all these cases the smile expresses a "relief of tension," a discharge of very small amounts by the ego. It would be very difficult, however, to verify such a connection by observation. For the use of the smile as a substitute act of the pathognomic apparatus extends still further: the "keep smiling" custom of the West, the unvarying smile of the Oriental which is imposed by social custom and ritual, the stiff, compulsive smile of many people who are to a greater or lesser degree mentally disturbed and smile in order to hide an affect, chiefly anxiety—all these show the smile being used as a mask, in a series extending from the normal to the symptomatic.[28]

If we place alongside this what we know of the slight smiles, or the occasionally distorted ones, in archaic works of art, in Greek art of the seventh and sixth centuries B.C., in the art of the Middle Ages from the late twelfth to the fourteenth centuries, then the field of our problem is amplified very considerably. It seems that in Greek art, as in the art of the Middle Ages, the smile serves the general purpose of representing pictorially psychic animation; in this sense it emerges again at a higher level in which "animating" has acquired a new meaning, pictures no longer the psychic activity of mankind in general but that of a particular human being: for example the smile of Leonardo da Vinci's women.

Now it is my opinion that the smile in these works of art is nothing

[28] In a discussion of part of the views here developed and of those discussed later in this paper Spitz and Wolf (1946) suggest an alternative formulation. They stress that "smiling is the first structured (and also mastered) of those pathognomic-motor manifestations which characterize the discharge of emotional tension. For this reason smiling becomes also the first mastery of pathognomic manifestations, which is appropriate for the purpose of social reciprocity. On the other hand, it is also the first mas-

else than a pathognomic expression of mental activity. And as the smile is the first pathognomic expression by means of which a human being makes contact with another, it remains the most universal, which sometimes expresses no more than: "here is some psychic activity taking place." So the smile would be the first pathognomic constellation which plastic art copies from life, if such copying may be assumed to be its aim, and so the smile would come to be, on the other hand, the representative of those pathognomic constellations which are prohibited as being major distortions of the countenance and have therefore to be suppressed. They are replaced by a signal which we are accustomed to interpret as indicating a friendly and contented state of mind and also as a good omen for emotional relationships. But besides this there is undoubtedly still another special relation between smiling and laughing: it expresses moderate joy, a controllable quantity; it stands as evidence of the triumph of the ego.

III. Some Typical Disturbances of Pathognomic Activity

So far we have represented in a very one-sided way the contribution which the ego makes to expressive behavior, in that we have ascribed to it, first and foremost, the inhibition of primitive pleasure in movement. It is now time to proceed to a wider examination of the subject.

To begin with, there is a statement from Freud to the effect that the ego's control over motility is so firmly rooted that it regularly withstands the onslaught of neurosis and only breaks down in psychosis[29] (1915 b). This statement can obviously be valid only within certain limits; even if the ego's control over motility breaks down only in a psychosis, limitations of this control certainly exist within the spheres of both normality and neurosis. I should now like to discuss a few examples illustrative of such limitations in the control of the pathognomic apparatus. They will be arranged in a scale extending from the normal to psychotic behavior.

We start with the fact that two fundamental functions of the ego are liable to disturbance. The first concerns the integration of the separate pathognomic impulses—it is bound up with those tendencies of the ego which strive toward synthesis; the second is related to the temporal sequence of the pathognomic procedure.

---

tery in the field of pathognomic expression which is used indiscriminately in the beginning of the infant's ego development for the expression of all positive emotions."

29 Restrictions similar to those which are about to be discussed have been considered by Fenichel (1928). He distinguishes gross alterations from slight modifications.

Let us consider the first kind of disturbance. The examples used to exemplify it relate mostly to laughing or smiling.

(1) Often the integration of an individual pathognomic impulse cannot take place because the ego "hinders" it; the inhibition may be intentional. The suppression of an expression, the stifling of physical pain, and in fact all those cases in which we mean to hide what goes on in us, belong to this group. It is clear how near we are here to the border of the pathological; it is obviously already crossed when "not to reveal oneself" becomes an instinctual aim. But in pathological cases the process in relation to the pathognomic apparatus itself can be described in a simple way: we will make use of an example chosen for its transparency.

One frequently observes that dancers and acrobats have a particularly artificial and empty smile (Toulzac, 1901); it is directed toward the audience and is supposed to heighten the effect of their performance by giving the impression that it is effortless. Here also the smile is a mask, i.e., a pathognomic substitutive act, which is recognizable as it forces aside another expression. This is an attractive example because we are able to say why this smile is not a convincing one. Examination of the pathognomic position shows that we get the impression of an "artificial, empty smile" because there is a "false innervation" either of a branch of the zygomatic muscle—which is manifested by the position of the lips—or, more frequently, of the orbicular muscle, which is contracted instead of relaxed. It is easy to understand how just this grammatical mistake arises—this refers to the introductory observations which I made in reference to a grammar of pathognomic speech. The contraction of the orbicular muscle is known to be a reaction to exertion, which one may surely ascribe to the dancer who has to perform a difficult step correctly, or to the athlete attempting some physical feat. The artificiality of the smile is thus caused by the fact that only the mouth smiles, that the smile is not echoed in other parts of the face.[30] In short, it is a case of failure of integration of differently directed pathognomic impulses. One can describe the disturbance from two points of view. Either an

[30] Instructions to be found in textbooks on art from ancient times onward lend support to this point of view. "If the mouth smiles while the rest of the features contradict its mirth, a distortion arises, a sneering smile . . . A smiling expression must be put on from the very start; the cheerfulness must spread equally to all parts of the face. The mouth must smile; but also the eyes, and the forehead, the whole countenance" (Sonnenfels, 1768, p. 57). "Dans une tête qui rit, non seulement l'oeil rit, mais encore le nez rit, les lèvres, le menton, les joues rient aussi" (*Magasin Pittoresque*, Paris, 1872, p. 267). There is an old French proverb: "Ne crois pas au sourire de la bouche que n'accompagne pas le sourire des yeux."

expression of something artificial arises because the appropriate pathognomic expression—it would be one of exertion—has to be withheld, or the expression of a smile has failed because all the different facial muscles do not vibrate together correctly, all the pathognomic impulses in the direction of smiling have not been integrated.

(2) The example I shall now use is one mentioned incidentally by Freud (1909). It concerns the laugh or smile of a condoling person and represents an actual derailment of the pathognomic act, a parapathognomy. We enter a room with a sympathetic face, we are filled with "compassion" or "fellow feeling" and are about to press the hand of the afflicted person in order to show our sympathy, when a smile intrudes itself on our features which we are not able to deal with pathognomically and which gives our face an awkward and embarrassed expression, or else we feel that we want to laugh and fear we may do so; compulsive laughter does actually occur in pathological cases.

We all know what is generally accepted as the explanation of this phenomenon: a repressed, condemned, and usually aggressive thought has presented itself, has disturbed the pathognomic activity and has turned it into parapathognomy. The topography and dynamics of the process are easily discernable: it is a matter of pathognomic parapraxis. There has been a failure to integrate contradictory impulses, the intended impulse and the one which breaks through. This is as far as we can go in the description of the process, since any attempt to pursue it further into its pathological ramifications would lead us away from our subject. We may, however, state briefly that we have touched here upon one of the origins of the grimace, because the way in which anger produces facial distortion is not fundamentally different from that of a parapraxis. If in one case it is a matter of the sudden upheaval of a suppressed impulse, in the other it is a storm of affect, the control of which is unsuccessful: the result can be the same in both cases—distortion resulting in a grimace. Failure to integrate emotional expressions may be brought about not only by instinct and affect, not only by aggression, anger and doubt—by the passions, that is to say—but also by a disturbance in the ego itself, such as fatigue occurring in certain states of exhaustion; the victorious athlete occasionally makes a grimace of this kind.[31]

(3) We have so far considered examples of inhibition of function and

31 I come to no conclusion here as to how far the intelligibility of the expression is retained in the distortion; the empirical side deserves exhaustive examination by the psychology of expression. But the theoretical approach from which we started out is still too simplified to be fully useful in empirical investigations, because passionate

unsuccessful purposive acts within the field of expressive phenomena, without crossing the borders of pathology; what now follows refers to an extremely large group of phenomena which can be roughly described as neurotic disturbances. For this purpose, phenomena are grouped together which range from simple hysterical conversion symptoms—such as frequent blushing, increased perspiration of the face—to such things as tic. The theoretical aspect calls for no special discussion; much light has been thrown on the clinical aspect by the exhaustive researches of Ferenczi and Abraham which were amplified by Deutsch, Klein, and Kovacs, from different points of view.[32] A discussion of their findings and theories—they are concerned with the autoplastic and magical significance of tic, its relation to aggression, or its genesis in specific infantile situations—would take us outside the general plan we have in mind in this paper.

An example may be introduced instead, the case of a young man suffering in a mild degree from psychogenic compulsive laughter. I will enumerate the determinants and the meanings of his laughter in the order in which they occurred in the psychoanalytic sessions. One of the very early meanings which lay very near consciousness was superiority; it always appeared in his ordinary life when he felt in fantasy that an opponent was defeated or could be defeated, and in the transference when he had seen through the analyst: "You are not omnipotent, you are a man like me, I can defeat you." Already in this setting one cannot fail to see a close relation between laughter and anxiety, the attitude of superiority striking one as a defense against anxiety as well as a mastery of it.[33] This function of laughter rests upon the formula: "I need not be afraid; it is laughable"—and, in the language of denial: "I laugh, so I am not afraid, for he who laughs is powerful, strong and superior."

---

feelings are not simply or invariably foreign to the ego. We must admit that all we can do at present is to point to some general principles. (Addition 1952: Recent advances in our theoretical equipment may here prove to be useful; reference to varying degrees of neutralization of the energy at the disposal of the ego would permit us to account for its failure to control expression in both inter- and intrasystemic conflicts. See Chapter 14.)

[32] See the comprehensive presentation of the problem and its literature by Fenichel (1946) ; for recent approaches see Mahler (1949) .

[33] It seems that the relation of laughter to anxiety forms a central theme in the psychology of the comic; see Chapter 8. In the process of laughter itself we can scarcely overlook the phenomenon of increased activity of expiration, which reminds us of the reactions to experiences of anxiety; all the respiratory accessory muscles participate in the same way as in attacks of suffocation; see Hecker (1873). E. Bibring has many times referred in discussions to similar observations.

In a deeper layer laughter has a still closer and more direct relation to defense against anxiety: "Look at me and see how I laugh; a fool like me who is always laughing is a very harmless person"—and by this means he thinks he is able to evade the responsibility which he so much dreads in connection with his aggressive wishes.

Just as in this sense laughter serves the purpose of autoplastic representation—debasement to the level of the laughable buffoon—so on another level there is an even clearer indication of an autoplastic and double meaning in the opened mouth in the act of laughing: the showing of the teeth in the laugh serves an aggressive purpose in that it is meant to be an aggressive grimace, still full of that secret significance which attaches to all the masks used by primitive cultures;[34] at the same time the mouth opened for laughing is in the service of homosexual and feminine instinctual tendencies, and is used to seduce the dreaded and ridiculed object in a feminine way.

This example was inserted here to make clear how extraordinarily rich in meanings the process of laughter is. All possible overdeterminations of clinical material—in which, however, though we have not explicitly mentioned it, they are not all of equal importance—are represented independently in the field of normality; it is obvious that all these and many other meanings belong to laughter and can be expressed and conveyed by it. It is easier to prove this theory in relation to the role which laughter plays in cult and myth than by observation itself: it represents aggression and seduction simultaneously, is associated with birth or rebirth and procreation, is the sign of godlike strength and so of godlike privilege, but is also the sign of the rebellion of the human race,[35] and one feels continually forced to the conclusion that ultimately defense against anxiety, mastery of anxiety, and pleasure gain, are compressed together in the one act.

I must forego any detailed discussion of this hypothesis, which leads to the heart of the psychology of the comic, and return once again to our example. The young man, from whose analysis we selected a part, finds it very difficult to control his laughter. An attempt to suppress it produces

[34] Herland has given a consistent account of the derivation of laughter from a position in which it was an attack, making it possible to distinguish two kinds of laughter, a primitive one nearer to this position and a higher, more intellectual form, in which "inhibitions against the tendency to attack are brought into play" (1938, pp. 209 ff.). The "phylogenesis" of the smile has a similar origin: it is derived from the apotropaic grimaces of masks; see also Pottier (1916) who has shown that a defensive threatening attitude persists in the smile of Bes.

[35] See Reinach (1911), Luquet (1930), Fehrle (1930/1931), and for clinical examples now Grotjahn (1949).

a fixity of expression or a slight distortion of the features. The integration of the pathognomic impulses continually miscarries, a piece of the pathognomic apparatus is sexualized. The laughter itself functions as an assault which is passively experienced; the attempt to get control of the laughter—by means of a plausible occasion, by voluntarily laughing it off—serves the purpose of a defense against the passive experience. The symptom has become libidinized and has the full value of a satisfaction. Here also the language of the body has replaced the language of words, autoplastic movement has ousted every other method of elaboration.

(4) We choose as our final example disturbances of pathognomic behavior which are met with typically in schizophrenics. It is not convenient to discuss this class of disturbance in any complete way, but we shall instead bring forward some descriptions from psychiatric literature which are trustworthy. For a starting point it is useful to compare the motor behavior of a schizophrenic with that of a normal adolescent. Homburger (1922), who has discussed this relationship exhaustively, refers to the fact that the phenomenon of the motor behavior of adolescents oscillates between two extremes. One of these is characterized by the utmost control of the motor apparatus—it is kept in hand to such an extent that the effort expended in control exceeds what is necessary; in the other type of behavior the effort made is not as great as the demand and the motor apparatus is only partially under control. Affectations, with the accompanying false innervations and stiffness of behavior seen in the movements of adolescents, belong to the first type of disturbance, while to the second belong their lazy and clumsy movements. The comparison which neurologists make between the motor movements of adolescents and those of schizophrenics gains fresh and additional support from the psychoanalytic standpoint. In both types of behavior the disturbance lies in the relation of the ego to the outer world. "The heightened libidinal cathexis of the id"—brought about in puberty by the biological processes of maturation and their psychic elaborations, in schizophrenics by the withdrawal of libido from the environment—"in each case adds to the instinctual danger, causing the ego to redouble its efforts to defend itself in every possible way" (Anna Freud, 1936). In the case of schizophrenics, contact with the outer world is endangered by withdrawal of interest; but it is precisely expressive movements which further that contact. That makes it seem understandable that disturbances of expressive behavior stand out in bold relief while normally all purposive motor acts remain undisturbed.

One might suppose that one could understand many pathognomic disturbances of schizophrenics by the application of Freud's theory of attempts at restitution. The loosened contact with the outer world has to be reinstated, a certain apathy in the pathognomic processes has to be overcome. This attempt miscarries; a natural behavior is not achieved, but instead artificial ways and mannerisms appear, which produce a pathognomic effect. How this struggle can shift from one expressive pattern to another, I endeavored to show in relation to the self-portraits of the sculptor Messerschmidt.[36]

But the disturbances of expression of many schizophrenics explained in this way as attempts at restitution—attempts to "make a face" in order to retain contact with the outer world—lead us to new problems. Psychiatrists know that the impression of something strange and affected in the behavior of the patients is only gained after some observation; the impression is acquired gradually. It might be supposed that this was so because a certain period of time is required for the observations accumulating in the preconscious of the psychiatrist as observer. But it seems that what is most important is not the time at the disposal of the observer, but the temporal sequence of the behavior itself—in our case, in the pathognomic phenomenon—which he is observing.

Certain knowledge empirically gained lends support to this hypothesis: if snapshots of schizophrenics are cleverly selected they are often not recognizable as those of mental cases.[37] Now I am of the opinion that this impression is not due to any success in the expressive act itself but to the conditions of photographic portraiture; the point discussed here first became clear to me owing to another experience. Most of the busts of the sculptor, Messerschmidt, when seen singly, had sufficient effect to cause the observer to try to puzzle out the "meaning" of each one as an expression. He would put the question to himself: "What is it that is represented here? What does this expression mean?" But when looking at many of the busts, or perhaps the whole series of more than forty pieces, he would become impatient and recognize the pathological element in the stereotypy of the expression. The fact that is decisive for the observer is just his awareness of what is empty and artificial in the expression, his awareness that "there is nothing behind it." Now the analysis of individual pathognomic situations in most of the cases which we have in mind here leads us to discords recognizable as disturbances in integration. Bleuler, according to the accounts of his fellow workers,

36 See Chapter 4.

37 I was able to make a cursory examination of the material referred to here in the Heidelberg Clinic in 1931. H. W. Gruhle used it in lectures (1930) and drew the conclusion that a diagnosis based on expression should receive a skeptical judgment.

sometimes attempted to confirm a diagnosis of schizophrenia by shutting off one half of the patient's face from his field of vision, so that he could see the upper and lower halves in turn, separated. But I am inclined to think that this method of approach is only applicable to certain cases. In others, and in a much clearer way, the disturbance in expression reveals itself not in lack of unification of individual impulses but in another attribute of expressive behavior.

At the beginning of this section of the paper we mentioned a second function of the ego concerned in the regulation of expressive activity, which has not yet been given further attention. It is now time to bring it forward. All motor activity is composed of movements and in all movement sequence plays its part.[38] If one follows the example of Monakow and Uexküll one speaks of the melody of movements, or, according to others, the temporal form of motor processes. In the same way, we may regard the temporal form of an expressive act as an important factor and we may ascribe the regulation of this expressive act to the ego. In every disturbance of expression—so I am inclined to think —something has been disturbed in the curve followed by the process. We find this supposition confirmed if we review the types of disturbances which we have distinguished. In the first type, which is represented by the *risus artificialis* of the athlete, as in every other analogous case, it is the fixity of the expression, the fact that there is no pathognomic melody and no change of expression, that is partly responsible for betraying the failure. In the second case, that of a parapraxis of expression, the repressed smile intrudes itself on features which are attuned to grief, it disturbs a process by interrupting it. In the third case, that of psychogenic compulsive laughter, the situation is clearest. The laugh which appears here like an attack can only gradually be brought under control, and turned from a grin into a smile and be "laughed off." In those stilted poses which are the pathognomic characteristics of attempts at restitution, single solutions may be "correct"; in a static picture, and therefore in a photograph, which shows one section of the curve of the process, the difference may be blurred; over a long period of observation the stiffness of the process, the disturbance in the pathognomic melody may attract our attention. What I have brought forward here as a theory can be tested by making a comparison of a film strip with a photograph; many new aspects to the problem would thereby be opened up, which must be omitted from this sketch.[39] But a macroscopic impression supports the

---

[38] See Brugsch-Levy (1926), Flach (1928, 1934), and Kauders (1931).

[39] Buytendijk and Plessner (1925/1926) emphasize the small degree of certainty pertaining to an interpretation of an expression in a static picture. The interpretations,

point of view put forward here. The disturbances of expression which have been described here are part of a series, at the end of which are placed those cases where, according to Freud, the ego's control over motility breaks down, and we have the picture of catatonia. Here the process has disappeared. A single motor situation has escaped from the curve of temporal sequence and become immobile.

The two disturbances of the pathognomic apparatus which in our description have been treated in succession, disturbance in synthesis and disturbance in the temporal sequence, are in reality very difficult to separate from each other. They interact, and indeed one may be continually in doubt to what extent they exist independently. It must often remain uncertain whether one distinguishes a grin from a smile on account of its inharmoniousness, whether one regards a smile as compulsive because of its fixity, or because only part of the face is involved. Moreover, the development of both functions extends far back into the individual's early childhood. For we may connect the capacity to organize and shape the pathognomic-motor process with the most archaic function of the ego, with its task as an apparatus to subdue the primordial rhythmical movements and to mold them into the temporal forms of

---

according to them, are uncertain because the expressive pictures belong simultaneously to more than one situation. A bad taste in the mouth and loathing, listening and reflection, scorn and irritability, are mixed up and "still stronger contrasts are to be found in the interpretations made"; and thus both Darwin and Klages are contradicted. They believed that one meaning at a time belongs to one expressive picture, though it is obvious that more than one meaning may fit it, and the decision of which meaning is correct can only be obtained from the situation as a whole. Buytendijk's and Plessner's views have, as far as I can see, not been invalidated and possibly been at least in part confirmed by experimental evidence. For a summary of this evidence see Kanner (1931). The material used by Kanner and other experimentalists is of so specific a nature that one wishes to see these experiments repeated, which would allow for a closer comparison with the statements by Buytendijk and Plessner. Their theory is the basis of unpublished researches by Ruth Weiss (at the Psychological Institute in Vienna) under the supervision of K. M. Wolf. I am permitted to use one result of this enquiry, which coincides with my own observations. If one covers up everything in the photograph of a group except the expression of one face, people's guesses as to the situation in the photograph vary enormously. The statements are astonishingly correct when they relate to behavior which is strictly regulated and intentional; thus, one recognizes with a high degree of certainty a spectator at a sporting event, but only with difficulty a mourner at a funeral. Perhaps the further development of this line of research will confirm a conclusion suggested to me again and again by casual observations. The more complete the ego regulation of the expression, the clearer will be the understanding of it in a snapshot without any need of a context. It seems that the more the ego is engaged in working over affects and the more full of conflict the situation is which the pathognomic activity expresses, the less unequivocal does the expression seem to be. Only when there is an irruption of affect does the expression once again become unequivocal. According to Buytendijk and Plessner laughing and crying are clearly recognizable.

pathognomic activity:[40] when we try to control an attack of laughter, and when a convulsive type of laughter is turned into free and voluntary laughter, the ego has reconquered a position which was threatened.

One further reflection. If we review the whole field of phenomena in which laughter occurs as an expression of mental activity, we find that one and the same physiological and muscular process—it has been appropriately described as "a mechanism prepared in advance"[41]—can range from "scorn to humor" (Reik), and from pleasure to sadness. How is this possible? How can such a thing come about?

I am of the opinion that it is the central function of the ego which controls our pathognomic apparatus and supervises the shaping of expression. We hear a laugh in the next room and listen to it at first with uneasy surprise, but soon we get our bearings and feel at ease about it: it was the gay laugh of a happy person, or the ironical laughter of someone who has been offended. In this case too the temporal course of the process is not the least important factor in our recognition.

The shaping which the physiological act of laughter undergoes through the agency of the human ego is a clear and impressive example of the fact that everything which we recognize to be a process of giving form and shape to psychic material is to be regarded as an ego function.

Let us return once more, in view of this theory, to the analogy we used when seeking to present the problems to be dealt with in a scientific examination of expressive behavior. The speech of the countenance is limitless and capable of great variety of expression; vocabulary, grammar, and syntax are astonishingly copious, and this richness is all the more impressive precisely because pathognomy is remarkably poor in what would correspond to verbal roots, to *etyma,* in speech. Let us not bind ourselves to a comparison with speech which threatens here only to hinder our understanding; let us try to account for the fact that all the various manifestations of the expressive function are closely related at the start. In the illustrations which are to be found in old textbooks on facial expression, one notices how easily and through how slight an alteration in the illustration the whole of the expression changes. Here also it is only a step from laughing to crying. Or again, if photographs are covered so that only a part of the face, mouth and lips, or eyes and forehead, show, we can complete each one in our mind into very different expressive situations.[42] Only when we see the complete face with its

[40] See on this point now Spitz and Wolf (1946), and Kris (1951 b).

[41] See Johannes von Kries (1925), who follows Spencer.

[42] See Wundt (1900, p. 114). A good empirical investigator of expressive behavior describes such similarities in different expressive movements somewhat as follows:

temporal changes do we get "the expression." This view of things seems banal and self-evident if one is relating it to one's own perception, since no one has ever doubted that the expression of the human countenance is a question of Gestalt in the sense used by Gestalt psychology. But I do not plead for this point of view here as a contribution to the understanding of pathognomy but for its creation, not as an attribute of our perception but as an achievement on the part of the body, by whose agency this entity is brought into being. In regard to disturbances of expression, in cases, for instance, in which what is usually automatic about the function becomes conscious, everyone can experience in himself, can "feel" in his own motor actions, how "integration" and temporal regulation may fail. It is, however, only these functions that ensure the richness and fullness of the "speech of the human countenance."

And laughter too, which lies on the border between expressive and purposive motor behavior, only acquires its meaning as an expressive action through undergoing this formative process in its nature and the course it takes. Only because of the wide scope of its significance does it become human and in the Aristotelean sense peculiar to man.[43]

"Laughter is only a facial movement of extension and is effected principally by an extensor muscle. Hence in mirth the nostrils and forehead are placed in horizontal folds and the teeth are shown, as in anger. So it is possible for two different affects to correspond with each other in respect of their types of movement, whether in one sense or the other, i.e., because they move in the same direction. One only has to picture to oneself the teeth bared in wrath, in strong sexual desire, and in laughter, or the staring eyes of a snake inflamed with greed and those of a man in both fear and hope" (Huschke, 1821).

43 *Bibliographical note*: The problems dealt with in this paper refer to different fields of research and therefore the relevant literature cannot be presented in any comprehensive way. In the following I give at least a brief indication of the bibliographical resources employed. Lists of the more recent literature on the problems of expressive behavior will be found in the works by Bühler (1933) and Dumas (1933) ; with regard to the earlier literature, in which the postclassical tradition survives, reference may be made to Orbilio Anthroposco (1784). For the literature which deals with the psychology and physiology of laughter see s. v. "laughter," *The Index-Catalogue of the Surgeon-General's Office, United States Army* (First Series, Vol. VII, Washington 1886, p. 878; Second Series, Vol. IX, Washington 1904, p. 314; Third Series, Vol. VIII, Washington 1928, p. 408).

Part Four

Problems of Literary Criticism

Chapter 10

AESTHETIC AMBIGUITY

Written in collaboration with ABRAHAM KAPLAN

I

One of the most influential contributions in recent times to the analysis of poetic language is William Empson's treatment of ambiguity (1931).[1] Empson has shown, not by precept alone but by his own practice as well, how the aesthetic experience is immeasurably enriched by close attention to the multiplicity of meanings encompassed in the poetic use of language. Difficulties in Empson's account arise, however, in three crucial areas: the concept of ambiguity, the theory of the aesthetic experience, and standards of interpretation.

(1) Empson describes his subject matter, ambiguity, as "any consequence of language, however slight, which adds some nuance to the direct statement of prose" (p. 1). Clearly "prose" includes an enormous variety of forms of discourse; and though one can analyze poems without an analysis of poetry, it is relevant to ask whether and in what ways the "consequences of language" with which Empson deals differ in the different forms and functions of language. Accordingly, we shall attempt to differentiate more closely the kind of ambiguity characteristic of poetry from that found in nonpoetic language.

(2) In particular, the differentiation will be made in terms of the functioning of ambiguity in the process of creation and interpretation of poetic language. For Empson, ambiguity has largely the status of an empirical finding only: when any poem is subjected to analysis, ambiguities are disclosed. We wish to relate this finding to a theory of the poetic process. Hence we shall develop the conception of art as a process of communication and re-creation, in which ambiguity plays a central role.[2]

[1] This essay refers to the first edition of Empson's *The Seven Types of Ambiguity* (1931). The additions to the second edition (1947) seem to have no immediate bearing on our discussion.

[2] In doing so we are elaborating a common assumption which Empson also makes but does not justify: ". . . the purposes of getting to understand a poet is precisely that of constructing his poems in one's own mind . . ." (1931, p. 79).

(3) The process of re-creation presupposes standards of interpretation. Empson's own practice seems generally unexceptionable, but he does not concern himself with the standards that keep him from constructing what he calls "the wrong poem." We shall therefore attempt to make explicit the standards of interpretation of ambiguity.

Throughout, we shall be dealing only with the art of poetry, but similar considerations are, we believe, applicable to at least those of the other arts (e.g., painting) in which meanings in a straightforward sense are plainly involved.

II

For present purposes we may analyze meanings in terms of verbal (and other) responses. The meanings of a word (phrase, sentence, set of sentences) to a particular person may be characterized by describing the responses he makes (or would make) when asked for its "meaning." (If we are interested in unconscious meanings as well, we can require special conditions for the response—e.g., the conditions of the psychoanalytic interview) A set of such responses will be said to constitute a *cluster* in the degree to which each response word, when acting as stimulus, in turn evokes the other members of the set in response. The meanings of the original stimulus word are describable in terms of these clusters.[3]

Obviously the clusters evoked by a word in actual usage will be considerably affected by the context in which the word occurs. We may distinguish between *codes* and *symbols* according to the degree of their response constancy in varying contexts. A code word has a single fixed meaning regardless of the words accompanying it or the situations in which it occurs; the meaning of a symbol word varies according to the context in which it is construed. Hence a dictionary in the strict sense can be constructed only for codes; for symbols, the "dictionary" provides only cues for contextual interpretation. We may refer to rigidity of response in varying contexts as *interpretation on the dictionary principle.*

Clearly all words exhibit the symbolic character to a greater or lesser degree. All occur in multiple contexts in which differing responses are evoked; and previous meanings persist as components or determinants of present response. The symbol is neither learned anew in each case, nor like the code determined once for all. One cannot speak, therefore, of *the* meaning of any symbol, but can only specify its range of responses and the clusters into which these tend to be grouped.

---

[3] Compare the definition of "proposition" as, not what is designated by a given sentence, but the set of sentences logically equivalent to the given one. We construe "equivalence" here not in a logical sense but in terms of association responses.

We refer to this general characteristic of language as *ambiguity*. The word "ambiguity" is usually given a narrower reference, being in fact restricted to one or perhaps two of the types of ambiguity discussed below (disjunctive and possibly also conjunctive ambiguity). A word to which the responses are diffused—i.e., not grouped in sharply distinct clusters—is often described as "vague"; and a word evoking multiple clusters simultaneously is sometimes said to signify unambiguously a "complex" meaning rather than to be ambiguous. (These cases roughly correspond to what we shall call below additive and integrative ambiguities, respectively.) In their bearings on problems of communication and interpretation, however, particularly as these occur in poetry, these various characteristics of language can be treated as generically identical. In comprising them all under the concept of ambiguity, we have reference, not necessarily to uncertainty of meaning, but to its multiplicity. Thus conceived, ambiguity is not a disease of language but an aspect of its life process—a necessary consequence of its adaptability to varied contexts.

Now the multiple clusters that constitute an ambiguous meaning may in any concrete case of interpretation be related to one another in various ways. There is a continuum from the extreme in which the clusters are completely dissociated and inhibit each other to that in which they are scarcely discriminable and reinforce each other. Demarcations within this continuum may be taken to specify·various types of ambiguity, further distinguished by the forms of discourse in which they characteristically occur.

We call an ambiguity *disjunctive* when the separate meanings function in the process of interpretation as alternatives, excluding and inhibiting each other. Usually the meanings are far enough apart for the ambiguous symbol to be construed as consisting of several distinct words—homonyms. This is the type of case most commonly referred to as involving "ambiguity."

Perhaps the most familiar sort of discourse in which disjunctive ambiguity characteristically occurs is the oracle. Here the ambiguity usually depends on an equivocal construction—amphiboly. "The Duke yet lives that Henry shall depose" may be interpreted in two ways, but each excludes the other.[4] This is the defining feature of the disjunctive type.

Another type of discourse in which disjunctive ambiguity characteristically occurs is political discourse whose content is severely restricted

---

[4] Closer psychological analysis suggests that the interpretations of the oracle, though antithetical, are yet not exclusive, but jointly operative to sanction a guilty wish. In this case we should classify it as an instance of conjunctive ambiguity shortly to be discussed. See Fenichel (1943, and 1946, pp. 302-303).

by the power structure. Disjunctive ambiguity then becomes a technique of evading censorship or the penalties of subversion.[5] Sophocles' *Antigone* was staged in occupied France in a production that obviously lent itself to an alternative interpretation of Creon's tyranny.

The concept of disjunctive ambiguity is used in practice in the preliminary stages of dream interpretation, though another type is disclosed in fuller analysis of the dream (conjunctive ambiguity), and still another—contrary to loose generalizations about poetry, dream, and fantasy—in the arts. Freud (1905 c, p. 79) has spoken in this connection of "switch words":

> In a line of associations ambiguous words (or, as we may call them, 'switch-words') act like points at a junction. If the points are switched across from the position in which they appear to lie in the dream, then we find ourselves upon another set of rails; and along this second track run the thoughts which we are in search of and which still lie concealed behind the dream.

The separate "set of rails" characterizes the ambiguity between manifest and latent content as disjunctive. The latent content is an alternative meaning which in a given interpretation excludes (initially, at least) the manifest. The image of a wheel in a dream may be taken to symbolize, not a vehicle, but a revolver; the ambiguity of the image is thus disjunctive.

In *additive ambiguity* the separate meanings, though still alternative, are no longer fully exclusive but are to some extent included one in the other. Rather than several distinct clusters, we have a set of clusters of varying range and with a common center. Thus a symbol is additively ambiguous when it has several meanings differing only in degree of specificity, or in what they add to the common core of meaning. The word "rich," for example, may be interpreted in terms of "abundance" or "value" or "excellence"; but the response clusters which these indicate are not fully distinct and exclusive, but overlap and merge into one another.

The ambiguities that occur in scientific discourse—for instance, in the language of social inquiry—are characteristically of the additive rather than disjunctive type. Terms like "oligarchy," "depression," "culture pattern" are additively ambiguous in allowing multiple interpretations differing from one another chiefly in how much or how little they include. (By contrast, the perfectly distinct meanings of "depression" in

[5] See Strauss (1941).

geology, economics, and psychiatry give to the isolated word a disjunctive ambiguity.)

Again, the repetitiveness characteristic of much legal discourse is an attempt to minimize latent additive ambiguity, as with the sequence "mar, deface, damage, injure, or destroy" in the wording of an ordinance. Each word separately includes elements of the others by additive ambiguity; the sequence as a whole minimizes uncertainty as to the intended scope. Diplomatic language professionally exploits additive ambiguity; the commitment to "support" a given policy lends itself to multiple interpretations ranging from sending troops to formal expressions of sympathy.

We may note that the distinction between disjunctive and additive ambiguity is not a sharp one. Cases may occur where the alternative meanings of the ambiguous symbol are neither completely distinct nor yet so closely related that one is but an extension in certain directions of the other. The word "cat" may be taken to refer to a tabby or tiger: for the layman these alternatives are disjunctive; a zoologist would construe them as additive.

An ambiguity is *conjunctive* when the separate meanings are jointly effective in the interpretation. Rather than overlapping of clusters, there is but a single cluster consisting of paired (or multiple-linked) responses, each member of the pair (or n-tuple) corresponding to a different partial meaning. The understanding of irony, for example, involves the recognition of two distinct (indeed, opposed) meanings, which are, however, responded to conjointly. This type of ambiguity is especially suited to the expression of ambivalent attitudes, and in this use has long attracted the attention of psychologists and linguists who have noted the frequent occurrence in many languages of such words as the Latin *sacer*, which means both holy and accursed.[6] These exemplify conjunctive ambiguity in so far as both the antithetical responses tend to be evoked simultaneously.

The ambiguities that characteristically occur in the epigram and joke are also conjunctive. The wit and humor arise only if the several meanings are simultaneously responded to. The play on words is "playful" precisely in its compounding of meanings, not in its choice between them.

Empson in *Some Versions of Pastoral* (1935) deals with thematic

---

[6] See Freud (1910 b, pp. 184-91). Conjunctive ambiguities also occur characteristically in the dream, as so-called condensations. A compound image may be formed of several persons to whom the dreamer has similar emotional responses; the resultant figure is obviously ambiguous, but its significance lies precisely in the conjunction of the multiple references.

ambiguities characteristic of a certain literary genre. Character, plot, and treatment exploit the antitheses of the comic and heroic, simple and wise, ridiculous and admirable, and those involved in various social stratifications. The resultant ambiguities are for the most part conjunctive; the particular quality and effectiveness of the genre, Empson points out, lies in the conjunction of these antithetical responses.

It is clear that with conjunctive ambiguity we approach the realm of the aesthetic. The qualities of fantasy and wit clearly approximate those of literature much more closely than do those of the political, legal, or scientific discourse in which we found the disjunctive and additive ambiguities. And Empson's *Pastoral* provides cases which are unquestionably aesthetic. (Empson, indeed, introduces in this connection a concept of "dramatic ambiguity" which involves compounding "the possible reactions in the right proportions.") But though conjunctive ambiguity occurs frequently in aesthetic discourse—Shakespeare provides hundreds of examples—it is not in itself aesthetic in substance, but is superimposed on an underlying ambiguity of a different type.

A word might be added on the continuity of conjunctive with additive ambiguity. The multiple meanings effective conjointly may themselves be more or less closely connected, as in the purely additive case. " 'How goes it?' asked the blind of the lame one. 'As you see,' was the reply." Here the conjunctive double meanings can be easily construed as extensions from a common core, indicated by "proceed" or "progress" for the first ambiguity, and by "awareness" for the second.

We call an ambiguity *integrative* when its manifold meanings evoke and support one another. There is a stimulus-response relation between the clusters as well as within them. They interact to produce a complex and shifting pattern; though multiple, the meaning is unified. To speak the language of Gestalt, in disjunctive ambiguity there are several distinct and unconnected fields; additive ambiguity consists in a restructuring of a single field to reveal more or fewer details; in conjunctive ambiguity several fields are connected though remaining distinct; with integrative ambiguity, they are fully reconstituted—integrated, in short, into one complex meaning.

We shall consider but one example, from T. S. Eliot's *Sweeney Among the Nightingales:*

> Gloomy Orion and the Dog
> Are veiled; and hushed the shrunken seas;

Confining ourselves to the ambiguities in just the word "shrunken" we may note the following.[7] Most directly, the reference is to the state of the tides, the moon having been mentioned in the preceding stanza. But shrunken is also withered and old, and especially in the case of the seas, dried up: there is a suggestion that we are present at the end of a world. To shrink is to contract, huddle, cower; hence we find an attitude of fearful expectancy appropriate to impending death (the image of adulterous murder runs through the poem). To shrink is thus also to recoil in horror and detestation. Again, the shrunken sea is at its most vulnerable, smallest, and weakest, and indeed has already to some degree been awed and overpowered; the crashing waves have been hushed. And the vulnerability extends perhaps to the land on which the murderous action is to take place: the seas have withdrawn, leaving the land naked, exposed, forsaken. This brings us back to the literal reference to the tide at its lowest ebb, the intermediate interpretations reinforcing the response to shrinkage as symbolizing a decline or decay, the falling off from past glory embodied in the figure of Sweeney.

To what extent all these meanings are conscious in the reading (or writing) of the poem need not here detain us; it is clear that they can enter into the poetic response without appearing at the focus of attention. The point is that a number of meanings are operative, and not merely conjointly but in interaction with one another. No one of them is "the true meaning" of the phrase. We may speak here with Kenneth Burke of the "proportionalizing" rather than "essentializing" strategy: the phrase does not "essentially" signify this or that, but all of the meanings in varying "proportions." And even this locution does not sufficiently emphasize the integrated quality of the complex. This quality does not, as in the case of additive ambiguity, consist of a core of meaning common to the various clusters discriminated, but emerges in the process of interpretation by which each response evokes and sustains the others. In the next section we shall deal with this process as that of aesthetic creation and re-creation.

Again the continuity of integrative ambiguity with the types previously discussed may be noted. When multiple meanings are jointly operative they may be more or less interactive, and dispose us to regard the ambiguity as integrative or merely conjunctive accordingly. The parody exploiting only style exemplifies, perhaps, this intermediate type, ambiguities partially integrative falling apart into the conjunction of original and parody content.

[7] For the purposes of the example it is unimportant whether the analysis is "correct"; the problem of "correctness" will be considered below. Other examples, of varying degrees of complexity and perceptiveness, are to be found throughout Empson's *Seven Types*.

We shall speak of an ambiguity as *projective* when clustering is minimal, so that responses vary altogether with the interpreter. The term is in such cases said to be "hopelessly" vague, the meanings found being in fact imposed—projected—by the interpreter. This type of ambiguity (if, indeed, it is to be called such) will obviously be of importance in connection with the problem of standards. For the present, it is introduced only to set in relief the "objectivity" (intersubjectivity) of the other ambiguities. The multiplicity of meanings of the types previously discussed are not "read into" the symbol, but belong to it precisely by virtue of its symbolic status. We do not say that ambiguous symbols are all things to all men—this is just the defining characteristic of projective ambiguity—but only that they are more than one to most men. An ambiguous meaning may be just as objective as a precise and univocal signification.[8]

The distinction of these various types of ambiguity suggests that the common dualism between scientific and poetic language (as developed by I. A. Richards, for instance) has been overemphasized. For the difference between them is not one of absence and presence of ambiguity, but rather of the form and function of the ambiguities to be found in both. They occur in what Morris (1946) calls different "modes of signifying" and serve different purposes. Disjunctive and additive ambiguities are more common in the designative mode, and arise when language is used as an instrument of discrimination and generalization; conjunctive and integrative ambiguities emerge in language embodying syncretistic and autistic thought. In the former case, where discourse is primarily "informative," ambiguity is a necessary evil; in the latter, where the functions of language are predominantly "valuative" and "incitive," a virtue is made of that necessity.

But the characteristics of both science and poetry are obscured when they are loosely contrasted as "definite" and "indefinite" or "assertive" and "suggestive." In both cases, language communicates by evoking responses in the interpreter, and such responses do not occur as neatly demarcated and independent atoms of meaning. As Edmund Wilson observes (1945, p. 245):

> Speaking accurately, it is impossible to say that one kind of writing suggests, whereas another kind proves or states. Any literary work, if

8 Compare Empson (1931, pp. 102-3): ". . . It is assumed, except when a double meaning is very conscious and almost a poke, that [the poet] can only have meant one thing, but that the reader must hold in mind a variety of things he may have meant, and weigh them, in appreciating the poetry, according to their probabilities. Here as in recent atomic physics there is a shift in progress, which tends to attach the notion of a probability to the natural object rather than to the fallibility of the human mind."

it accomplishes its purpose, must superinduce in the reader a whole complex of what we are accustomed to call thoughts, emotions and sensations—a state of consciousness, a state of mind; it depends for its effectiveness upon a web of associations. . . .

Nor is this state of affairs altered by the use of mathematics in science. It is common to contrast the precision of mathematics with the vagueness of poetry. But mathematics is free from vagueness only when it is purely formal, and thus lacking reference altogether. As used in science, it is descriptive, and no more precise than the terms which give it empirical reference. We can give an absolutely exact count of the number of objects in a class only if the class itself is defined with absolute precision.

The point is, not that scientific discourse is free from ambiguity, but that the operations of inquiry enable us to deal with it whenever it becomes problematic.[9] When discourse purporting to be informative is no longer operational, then indeed ambiguities are recalcitrant. Poetry requires no operational specifications of its denotata because its purposes not only tolerate but may even require ambiguity.

Thus the frequent view that the flourishing of scientific discourse in our culture is inimical to poetry seems to us without foundation. Whether the scientific world outlook interferes with the production or enjoyment of poetry is not here in question. What seems doubtful is that the characteristics of scientific *language*—its abstractness, technicality, logicality— is working changes in our linguistic habits antithetical to those required by poetry. For any language adaptable to varied and shifting contexts— any system of genuine symbols, in short, not a code—will inevitably involve shades and overtones of meaning which can serve as the raw materials for poetic creation and re-creation.[10]

III

Aesthetic creation, as Dewey has convincingly set forth in his *Art as Experience,* may be looked on as a type of problem-solving behavior. The contrast between scientist and artist as "man of thought" and "man of feeling" has no more merit than the parent dualism between "reason"

[9] For an account of the logical aspect of these procedures, see Kaplan (1946).

[10] Compare the conclusions of the linguist Vossler (1932, p. 94): "The language of prehistoric times was no whit more naïve, not a particle more natural, neither more poetical, nor more pious, nor less logical, nor less practical than the most developed literary languages of art or intercourse of the present day. The opinion of sentimental Philistines, that the poetical and the natural are gradually dwindling away in favor of the intellectual and technical, should find no further encouragement in science."

and "emotion." Ratiocinative processes are embedded in a manifold of feeling of various degrees of intensity. Emotions, as they are embodied in aesthetic activity, are not blind, but incorporated in structures of a complex patterning which result only from taking thought.

But problem solving in the arts differs characteristically from its counterpart in scientific inquiry. For one thing, the artist works in a medium consisting of sensory materials, not the intellectualistic concepts and propositions of the scientist. The poet, to be sure, employs, like the scientist, linguistic symbols. But for the poet, language itself has a sensory form, a sound and rhythm; and he exploits the full range of responses to language, including imagery and excitation, not some operationally limited area of abstract significance.

A problem can be constituted as such only by the existence of conditions in terms of which it is to be solved. We shall refer to these conditions in a general way as *stringencies*: they restrict the possible modes of behavior by which the problem is "legitimately" dealt with. These stringencies further differentiate the problems of aesthetic creation (and recreation) from other sorts. In mathematics, the stringencies are maximal; the permissible operations on given symbols are rigidly specified by what Carnap calls rules of formation and transformation. A derivation or demonstration is valid or invalid in terms of its strict adherence to such rules. In the inductive sciences, stringencies are not so extreme. At a given stage of inquiry, various hypotheses may be equally warranted by the data and known laws. Stringencies themselves emerge in the process of inquiry, and are subject to modification according to their workings in inquiry.

In the arts, stringencies in this sense are minimal. A given aesthetic problem may be solved (and indeed, even formulated) in a wide variety of ways. Hence arises the possibility of art as a means of expression. Two mathematicians, two scientists, will deal with their respective problems in much the same ways; but aesthetic solutions bear to a much higher degree (at least in many historical periods) the stamp of the solver, his individuality—his style.

Stringencies are minimal in the arts, however, only as compared with other sorts of problem solving; in themselves, they are not inconsiderable. Materials have their own properties, and the transformation of physical material to aesthetic medium requires recognition of and adaptation to these properties. And of equal importance (greater, in the case of poetry) are a set of stringencies more or less independent of the requirements of the material: the *conventions* of the particular art form at a given period. Here is the point at which ambiguity enters into aesthetic creation—it is a means of expressing style within the limits of the conventions.

For rigid adherence to stringencies defines the academic in art, as will be elaborated below. And the extreme of stringency domination carries us back from art to ritual. In ritual, form and content are strictly patterned, and repeated again and again with minimal deviation, on pain of losing the ritualistic efficacy. The ritualistic act is one of *participation* rather than creation: the response which the members of the group are required or expected to have is rigidly limited. As ritual becomes secularized, the priest gives way to the bard or poet. Conformity of reaction vanishes: interpretations are not rigidly confined to the institutional or doctrinal requirements, but proliferate in accord with the creative impulse of the individual artist. Poetry becomes ambiguous concomitantly with its emergence from ritual.[11]

Art, in short, is a product of inspiration as well as skill. The satisfaction of stringencies provides only for the element of skill, which culminates in mastery of technique. Expressiveness, as contrasted with mere technical excellence, lies just in what is not determined by the stringencies, and involves the workings of a distinctive psychic process in which ambiguities frequently play a central role.

A detailed discussion of inspiration is outside the scope of this essay.[12] What is relevant here is its relation to external stringencies and internal ambiguities. The psychic activities or functions devoted to the adaptation to reality are comprised in the psychoanalytic concept of *ego*. Central to artistic—or indeed, any other—creativeness is a relaxation ("regression") of ego functions. The word "fantasy" conveys just this disregard of external stringencies in its reference to the process and product of creative imagination. In fantasy and dream, in states of intoxication and fatigue, such functional regression is especially prominent; in particular, it characterizes the process of inspiration.[13]

But the regression in the case of aesthetic creation—in contrast to these other cases—is purposive and controlled. The inspired creativity of the artist is as far from automatic writing under hypnosis as from the machines recently marketed for "composing" popular songs. The process involves a continual interplay between creation and criticism, manifested in the painter's alternation of working on the canvas and stepping back to observe the effect. We may speak here of a *shift in psychic level,* con-

[11] For a fuller account of the relation between art and ritual from this viewpoint, see here, pp. 40ff.

[12] See Harding (1940) and here Chapter 13.

[13] See Kris (1944) and Chapters 3, 6 and 14. The term "functional regression" is here and in the following used equivalent with topographical regression.

sisting in the fluctuation of functional regression and control. When regression goes too far, the symbols become private, perhaps unintelligible even to the reflective self; when, at the other extreme, control is preponderant, the result is described as cold, mechanical, and uninspired. Poetry is, to be sure, related to trance and dream, as aestheticians since Plato have never tired of observing. But it is also related to rigorous and controlled rationality. No account of the aesthetic process can be adequate without giving due weight to this "intellectual" component.

It is the other component, however—the well of inspiration or so-called "primary process"—that is of most immediate interest. For it is in this aspect of aesthetic creation that ambiguity is most prominent. The symbols functioning in the primary process are not so much vague and indeterminate as "overdetermined," loaded down with a variety of meanings. An action (including an act of producing symbols) is said to be overdetermined when it can be construed as the effect of multiple causes. Such overdetermination is characteristic of almost all purposive action; but it is especially marked when the psychic level from which the behavior derives is close to the primary process. Words, images, fancies come to mind because they are emotionally charged; and the primary process exhibits to a striking degree the tendency to focus in a single symbol a multiplicity of references and thereby fulfill at once a number of emotional needs. This is most clearly exemplified in the dream, but can be traced as well in the production of poetry, as was shown, for instance, in John Livingston Lowes' *Road to Xanadu*. Overdetermination and consequent ambiguity is central to the understanding of poetry as self-expression—i.e., as the distinctive product of an individual artist. But it is equally important when we transfer attention to the reader of poetry.

Aesthetic creation is aimed at an audience: only that self-expression is aesthetic which is communicated (or communicable) to others. This is not to be taken as implying the existence of a content separable from the aesthetic form—a message, in other words—which the work of art must get across. To speak of art as communication does not involve a commitment to such positions as Matthew Arnold's, where poetry is valued for precisely what is *not* characteristic of it, i.e., what can be translated into prose. What is made common to artist and audience is the aesthetic experience itself, not a prëexistent content. Dewey's warnings of the confusion between eventual function and antecedent existence are very much to the point. Communication lies not so much in the prior intent òf the artist as in the consequent re-creation by the audience of his work of art. And re-creation is distinguished from sheer *reaction* to the work precisely by the fact that the person responding himself contributes to the stimuli for his response.[14]

What is required for communication, therefore, is similarity between the audience process and that of the artist. But it is clear that only certain aspects of the artist's process are relevant to this comparison. As T. S. Eliot has observed:

> Impressions and experiences which are important for the man may take no place in the poetry, and those which become important in the poetry may play quite a negligible part in the man, the personality.

We cannot, that is to say, simply assume that what is emotionally charged for the artist will evoke a comparable response in the audience. Effect is a function of intent but not of intent only; it must be separately considered.

Accordingly, we may introduce the concept of the *potential* of a symbol as the obverse side of its overdetermination: a symbol has a high potential in the degree to which it may be construed as cause of multiple effects (rather than being taken as effect of multiple causes). While the two are obviously related to one another, potential does not *necessarily* correspond to overdetermination. The tyro may have an intense experience and employ for its communication symbols which—for him— are highly charged with multiple significance. But in fact this overdetermination may be purely private; the symbols lack potential and communication fails to take place. Conversely, symbols may have a higher potential for a particular audience than was involved in the artist's intent; Virgil, for instance, was for some centuries read as being in effect a Christian author—a particular religious significance was *projected* into his writings.

Now the potential of a symbol contributes to a specifically aesthetic experience only if the interpretation of the symbol evokes the resources of the primary process. It is a commonplace that communication, of whatever sort, requires a sharing of interests, knowledge, and experience. What is being said here is that aesthetic communication requires as well a sharing of *psychic level*.

A few pages earlier we indicated the effect on artistic creation of the extremes of psychic level: on the one hand the unintelligible, on the

[14] In so doing he reduces the ambiguity of the original stimulus: we say that the work has "become" clear or intelligible, i.e., it has become so as a result of his work of interpretation. But a rich core of ambiguity remains as constitutive of the poetic substance. See below, pp. 258f.

other the uninspired. The process of re-creation exhibits a corresponding effect if the interpretation does not involve shifts in level. Where ego control in the audience is high, the result is not re-creation but reconstruction. The experience is, in the common locution, "intellectualized." The aesthetic response is replaced by pedantic connoisseurship or historicism, and the trained incapacity which knows all about art but doesn't know what it likes. It is not without reason that A. E. Housman cautions in his *Name and Nature of Poetry* that "perfect understanding will sometimes almost extinguish pleasure."

On the other hand, when the psychic level of interpretation involves too little ego control, the meanings responded to are projective and lacking in integration. The aesthetic response is overwhelmed in blind raptures, the ecstasies of the "art lover." At best, the experience may be characterized—in terms of Dewey's useful distinction—as one of enjoyment rather than appreciation.

While shift in psychic level is a necessary condition, it is not a sufficient condition for aesthetic communication to take place. The response is not aesthetic at all unless it also comprises a shift in *psychic distance,* that is, fluctuation in the degree of involvement in action (Bullough, 1912). The aesthetic illusion requires, as was emphasized by Kant, a detachment from the workings of the practical reason. In the drama and novel failure to attain such detachment is manifested in that extreme of identification with the characters which focuses interest and attention solely on "how it all comes out." In poetry, the Kantian emphasis on detachment can be expressed by Coleridge's formula of "willing suspension of disbelief." More generally, when distance is minimal the reaction to works of art is pragmatic rather than aesthetic. Art is transformed to pin-up and propaganda, magic and ritual, and becomes an important determinant of belief and action. The ambiguities with which interpretation must deal are disjunctive and additive: meanings are selected and abstracted in the service of practical ends.

When psychic distance is maximal, the response is philistine or intellectualistic. At best, the experience is one of passive receptivity rather than active participation of the self. No contribution comes from the side of the audience because the interpretation follows the principle of the dictionary, as determined by the current conventions of the genre. Or, indeed, there may be no effort at interpretation at all, and the work rejected out of hand as unintelligible and worthless.

Shifts of both distance and level are, of course, matters of degree. There is nothing fixed and unalterable in the patterns of aesthetic response. Instruction, even though it is itself operative at a high ego level, may succeed in facilitating a relaxation of ego controls. Technical understanding may release energies otherwise employed in the reconstruction of the art work. Similarly, familiarity may serve to increase distance, liberating attention for other aspects of the work than its outcome or its practical applications. The function of criticism may be characterized concisely as that of contributing to such instructed familiarity, so as to induce the requisite shifts of psychic distance and level.

We are now in a position for a more adequate statement of the role of ambiguity in the aesthetic process. A distinction can be drawn between the decorative and expressive occurrences of ambiguity in the arts. Ambiguity is *decorative* when its interpretation is relatively independent of the psychic shifts just discussed. It is embodied in specific devices interpretable as such from a distance and in intellectual terms—the explicit pun, conceit, allegory, and similar artifices of style. The multiple meanings thus signified are limited in scope, having no bearing beyond the immediate context of occurrence—as is true, for instance, of so many of Shakespeare's plays on words. Or if, like the allegory, they extend throughout the work, they apply to it as a whole, rather than distributively in each of its parts, and so fall short of full integration.[15]

Ambiguity is *expressive* when shifts of psychic level and distance are involved in its interpretation, i.e., when it is distinctively aesthetic (in psychological, not valuational terms). Expressive ambiguity provides a good instance of what Allen Tate (1941, p. 72) has called the "tension" of poetry:

> . . . the full organized body of all the extension and intension that we can find in it. The remotest figurative significance that we can derive does not invalidate the extensions of the literal statement. Or we may begin with the literal statement and by stages develop the complications of metaphor: at every stage we may pause to state the meaning so far apprehended, and at every stage the meaning will be coherent [integrative].

This "tension" may thus be equated with what we have called the potential of poetic symbols; it is the richness of integrated significance emerging in the process of aesthetic re-creation. The distinction between "classicist" precision of language and "romantic" exploitation of vagueness and symbolism has reference, therefore, only to the extent to which decorative ambiguities are employed. Expressive ambiguity is less limited to the style of a particular school or genre, though it, too, of course, is subject to variations of degree.

15 For an extensive discussion of the decorative style, see for instance Kane (1928).

One function of poetic form may now be considered as that of pointing to the existence of latent ambiguities. Metre, rhyme, and poetic construction indicate that the symbols are to be construed as aesthetic, i.e., responded to at shifting distances. And they also constitute stringencies that force language from the channels of the prosaic, and in so doing create a problem of interpretation and hence a possibility of re-creation.[16]

The role of metaphor in poetry may be analyzed, we suggest, in similar terms. Metaphor serves as a stimulus to functional regression because the primary process is itself metaphoric and imagistic. The dream life, for instance, is predominantly visual, and shows a marked tendency to note similarities (especially by way of similar emotional responses) that escape the practical orientation of waking life. Metaphor serves, not to bring poetry close to the dream, but rather close to the psychic processes underlying both art and fantasy.

More specifically, metaphor may also serve as an instrument for multiplying ambiguity: the relation between elements themselves ambiguous to some degree generates a new and larger range of significance. And the relation serves at the same time as a mechanism of integration, indicating the direction along which unification of the multiple meanings is to be achieved. For example, Donne's simple metaphor "Find / what wind / serves to advance an honest mind" (in the poem "Go, and catch a falling star") not only admits of multiple interpretations within the main purport of an impossible task—the honest man is continually buffeted by adverse winds; the honest man finds no advancement on the seas of life; honesty already represents the highest level of advancement; there are paths of advancement open to the honest, but the difficulty is in finding them; etc., etc.—but these various meanings, centering around the idea that "advancement" depends on forces external to man and controlled by the gods, provides a focal point for integration of the poem in terms of a contrast between sacred and profane love, between the supernatural world of mandrakes, mermaids, and Faith, and the mundane realm of the purely human and inconstant.

In short, ambiguity functions in poetry, not as a carrier of a content

16 Compare Empson (1931, p. 39): "The reason that ambiguity is more elaborate in poetry than in prose, other than the fact that the reader is trained to expect it, seems to be that the presence of metre and rhyme, admittedly irrelevant to the straightforward process of conveying a statement, makes it seem sensible to diverge from the colloquial order of statement, and so imply several colloquial orders from which the statement has diverged." Here we construe poetic form not as the "reason" but as one condition of poetic ambiguity; the "reason" we have sought in the nature of the aesthetic experience.

which is somehow in itself poetic, but as the instrument by which a content is *made* poetic through the process of re-creation.[17]

We must emphasize, on the other hand, that ambiguity is only one of the resources of poetic effectiveness, on which more or less reliance may be placed. The "music" of poetry, for instance, would have to be given as much weight as its ambiguity in a full analysis of poetic effectiveness.[18] We are not saying, therefore, that the enjoyment of the aesthetic experience is altogther traceable to the pleasures of interpreting ambiguities, to what Mallarmé calls "the satisfaction of guessing little by little." But ambiguity is a frequent and important, though not the sole stimulus, to aesthetic response—the re-creation, at shifting psychic levels and distances, of the work of art.

IV

In so far as poetry is taken to emerge in the process of re-creation of artist's work, there arises the problem of the standards of interpretation to which this process is subject. But first a word of explanation to avoid a possible misunderstanding. As has been said earlier, it is not to be supposed that the multiple meanings of which we have been speaking are clearly and distinctly present to the mind of either artist or audience. For the most part they remain "preconscious"—i.e., though not conscious they can become so with comparatively little effort if the interpretation becomes problematic at that point. It is just because they are in the "back of the mind" in this sense that they contribute so much to poetic effectiveness.[19] Hence a concern with the problem of standards must not

[17] Just this is the function assigned to the language of poetry by Abercrombie (1926, pp. 82-83) : "Language is not the vehicle of inspiration in the sense of being a receptacle into which the poet pours his mind for purposes of transmission, and out of which the reader then extracts what is contained. Language in poetry is a transmission of energy rather than of substance. It sets the reader's mind working and directs the tendency of the work. It urges us to live for a time in a particular style of imagination—the style of the poet's imagination: but it is our own imagination that really does the business of poetry. In other words, the symbolic nature of language in poetry means just this: that it is a *stimulus* for our minds, though a stimulus of a very determining character."

[18] Empson suggests, however, that even here ambiguities are operative: "Apart from the ambiguities in the fully-developed language . . . , one would have also to consider the ambiguities (of the same sort, but entirely different in their details) which are always latent in the fundamental symbolism of the sound" (1931, p. 20).

[19] Compare Empson (1931, p. 74) : "I do not think that all these meanings should pass through the mind in an appreciative reading . . . ; what is gathered is the main sense, the main form and rhythm, and a general sense of compacted intellectual wealth, of an elaborate balance of variously associated feeling." An analysis of the effectiveness of poetry must also take into account the proximity of preconscious mentation to the high potentials of unconscious, repressed materials.

confuse the aesthetic experience with an intellectualistic reconstruction of the poem. The artist and audience are not themselves preoccupied with such standards. But standards are nevertheless important for a subsequent appraisal of the content of the experience.

One reason for their importance is the variation from person to person in the interpretation of the poem. Often, however, the varying interpretations correspond to equivalent effects in the respective readers; and again, the variation may be due, not to incompatibilities in the interpretations, but to the fact that each is only partial, and supplements the others. A more fundamental difficulty which requires consideration of standards is the possibility of projection, of reading into the poem meanings not present to others. This difficulty is brought into prominence by the art of the psychotic, and by the occasional success enjoyed by "fakes." Max Eastman, in his *Literary Mind,* quotes a sample of "Gertrude Stein's prose" which he then reveals to the unsuspecting reader as in fact having been written by a psychotic. And the Australian literary magazine *Angry Penguins* recently published with enthusiastic praise the work of a new "poet" which was in fact concocted in jest from a miscellany of reference works. Cases of this kind bring to a focus the question whether poetic re-creation is not in fact simply a form of "recreation," a game like finding shapes in the clouds and stars.

Interpretation, therefore, must have its stringencies just as does the original creation of the art work. Most obvious are the stringencies of subject matter, or, as we may call them, *standards of correspondence.* T. S. Eliot's reference to Agamemnon in the poem from which we previously quoted provides warrant for certain interpretations on the basis of knowledge about the myth in question. In the Donne example, a knowledge of the relation of inconstancy, in the poetic tradition of the seventeenth century, to the theme of sacred and profane love substantiates the re-creation of the poem along certain lines rather than others.[20]

Another set of stringencies of interpretation have reference to the genesis of the art work, and so may be called genetic standards or *standards of intent.* Here knowledge about the artist—whether directly in the form of biographical material or indirectly in terms of his society—

---

[20] Of special interest is the case where the subject matter gives rise to psychological considerations (about the reactions of the characters or of the poet himself). Examples of this type of check over interpretations could be multiplied endlessly; a particularly striking one, perhaps, is Ernest Jones' (1949, 1950) famous essays on *Hamlet* from a psychoanalytic viewpoint. It is to be understood that the standards of correspondence with psychological fact do not necessarily involve technical scientific knowledge, but may rest on the sort of understanding of motivation which is directly available to the perceptive reader or critic, as it was to the insight of the poet.

serves as a test of adequacy of interpretation. Here the familiar materials of literary history play their part. It must be pointed out, however, that interpretation resting chiefly on application of the standards of intent assumes an underlying similarity between the artist's basic desires, beliefs, values, and our own; or rather, the adequacy of interpretation depends on our adopting his standpoint. Where cultural differences are too great to make this possible, therefore, interpretation based on standards of intent is largely projective. This is true, for instance, of many parts of the Bible "viewed as literature."

A third set of stringencies has reference to the interrelation of the elements of the interpretation. We may refer to these as *standards of coherence:* an interpretation of a particular part of the work is tested by the coherence with the rest of the work it gives to this part. Whereas the standards of intent limit potential to known determinations, the coherence standards expand potential to include all possible determinations —whatever "fits in" is assumed to have been intended. This does not imply that the intent was fully conscious, but only that it was not wholly private: the genius characteristically "builds better than he knows."[21]

These three types of standards—others could perhaps be distinguished—are interactive. An interpretation may begin with any of them and seek confirmation from the others. Some fact about the subject matter may suggest a particular interpretation, which can then direct a search for evidence of such intent, or which can be further tested by its degree of integration with the rest of the work. Data about intent are checked by subject matter correspondences and internal coherence. An interpretation arrived at by considerations of coherence may be verified by knowledge about intent or subject matter. Thus the three sets of standards are jointly operative in the appraisal of a particular interpretation—as in the case of the coherence, correspondence, and pragmatic conceptions of truth, to which, indeed, these standards could perhaps be related. The more clearly an interpretation is substantiated by one sort of consideration, the less confirmation is required from the others, and conversely.

In effect, the standards discussed test an interpretation by its *completeness,* the degree to which it takes account of all the elements of the work, and its *power of synthesis,* the degree of integration which it

[21] The matter may be reformulated in terms of Croce's (1922) distinction between the "empirical" personality of the artist, with which standards of intent are concerned, and his "aesthetic" personality—what is manifested in and accessible through the art work considered in itself and not as a fact about the artist as a person. It is the aesthetic personality with which the standards of coherence deal.

gives these elements—in classical terms, by the "unity in variety" disclosed in the work by the interpretation. Cases where the ambiguities are primarily projective usually fail in both respects. Even if the work of the psychotic contains some intelligible elements, these are ordinarily integrated only in the psychotic's delusional system, and there must be recognized besides the presence of other elements having no public significance at all; similar considerations apply to the "fake." It must be said, however, that the aesthetic can sometimes occur without an aesthetic intent; work created in the service of magic and religion, for example, may regularly evoke in another culture aesthetic responses. But generally speaking, where such a response is frequent and widespread, the three sets of standards tend to converge: the meanings achieving coherence in terms of subject matter are those intended.

We conclude with a brief consideration of the social setting of ambiguity; the following remarks are to be viewed only as hypotheses in the sociology of art. The level of stringency in works of art—their degree of interpretability—varies markedly from period to period. In some cases ambiguity is fully exploited, and correspondingly great demands are made on the audience; in other cases, there is no more ambiguity than is involved in the work's being aesthetic at all; the demands on the audience are minimal; the interpretations called for are rigidly limited. We may suggest that art is likely to be characterized by low stringency (i.e., high ambiguity and interpretability) where systems of conduct ideals are in doubt or social values are in process of transition.[22] Poetry produced under such circumstances will perhaps reflect in its own high ambiguousness the uncertainties and equivocations in the culture of which it is a part. Such poetry is at the same time more likely to evoke a favorable response in the culture.

When stringencies are very high the art form either approximates ritual or may be spoken of as academic. Artistic achievement may consist in solving the traditional problems of the genre in traditional ways. Or the great artist may be revolutionary, working on the basis of new stringencies. Initially, his work is obscure; gradually, hovever, it becomes intelligible in terms of the new stringencies. Obscurity gives way to ambiguity; what was formerly unclear now appears richly significant. In turn the ambiguities become more and more stylized; works of the

---

22 The present period seems to be of this kind. It is perhaps for this reason that there is today such a widespread interest in the art of children and psychotics, and such striking successes of "fakes." The predisposition to deal with high ambiguity dominates over stimuli from the work itself, so that projective interpretations are the more likely to occur.

new type become increasingly interpretable on the dictionary principle; the revolutionary becomes conventional and the academic once more flourishes. This cycle in the history of art has been frequently commented on. We are suggesting that it might fruitfully be investigated in terms of the changing role and character of ambiguity.[23]

Such an approach, finally, might also have important bearings on the problem of survival. This problem is of especial interest because of its putative relevance to aesthetic merit. Survival has been frequently invoked as an index of aesthetic merit ever since Longinus's enunciation of the maxim that "that is truly great which bears repeated examination." Regardless of the weight of this principle of criticism, the question of what characteristics of the work of art make for its survival as an object of aesthetic value is of independent interest.

Among these characteristics ambiguity would seem to be not the least important. For one thing, high ambiguity allows for a wide range of interpretation, so that the work may be prized throughout various changes in cultural interests and values by being interpretable in a corresponding variety of ways. More important is the fact that ambiguity stimulates, as we have seen, the workings of the primary process. Now the primary process has been considered so far only in its bearings on the form of poetry rather than its content—i.e., on the occurrence of ambiguity, imagery, metaphor in poetry, rather than on the subject matters with which poetry most frequently deals. But the subject matters of poetry are as closely related to the primary process as the form of poetry; for they may be traced—in large part, if not solely—to the fundamental needs and desires of the personality, to the "id" in Freud's sense. Functional regression makes available as poetic material themes, like love and death, which are directly related to basic needs and desires, and which approach cultural universality far more closely than the patterns of satisfying such needs or the value structures controlling these satisfactions.[24]

[23] In particular, this approach could account for the changes in stringencies on the basis of its bearings on the process of re-creation, which is impossible if conventions are too rigidly adhered to. This is to be contrasted with such metaphysical positions as that of, say, Bergson, for whom art "has no other object than to brush aside the utilitarian symbols, the conventional and socially accepted generalities, in short, everything that veils reality from us, in order to bring us face to face with reality itself." From the present standpoint, it would be more correct, perhaps, to say that art brushes aside the conventional in order to bring us face to face with the artist—and with ourselves.

[24] Similar viewpoints are presented, for instance, by Muschgg (1933), Read (1938), and others.

The effectiveness of ambiguity for survival is limited, however, by the dependence which it involves on knowledge of subject matter and of intent as conditions of coherence. The less ambiguous work is correspondingly less dependent on such external knowledge. Survival may thus be presumed to be maximal for those works which have as high a degree of interpretability as is compatible with containing within themselves their own sources of integration. Other factors than ambiguity, of course, are also important for survival—e.g., the range of experience with which the work is concerned. And still others are to be taken into account in appraisals of aesthetic merit.

Chapter 11

FREUDIANISM AND THE LITERARY MIND[1]

When in 1895, Breuer and Freud published their *Studies in Hysteria,* reviewers in medical journals were noncommittal. Doubt and approval were equally balanced. Many reviewers were interested in a new therapeutic approach; some were more encouraging than others, but none recognized the importance of the publication as the herald of the new psychology.[2] One review only made this point—one published not in a medical journal, but in a daily newspaper under the title, "Surgery of the Soul." Its author was a poet, literary historian and dramatic critic of some merit. From the extensive writings of Alfred von Berger, director of the Imperial Theater in Vienna, who died in 1912, it may well be that this one review will survive longest. Berger (1895) followed the authors with deep admiration through their lengthy case histories which reported "how experience and memories are structured in the mind of the individual" and added that "we dimly conceive the idea that it might one day become possible to approach the innermost secret of the personality of man. The theory itself [Berger continued] is in fact nothing but a kind of psychology used by poets." Not only, he observed, had Shakespeare expressed thoughts similar to those of the authors; he had even based the psychological development and the catastrophe of Lady Macbeth upon concepts similar to those suggested by them. Lady Macbeth suffers from a regular defense neurosis from forcefully banishing from her awareness the affects of horror and anxiety at the murder of Duncan and at Banquo's apparition.

Through this, and other examples, Berger indicated the possibility that some of the dynamic principles developed in Breuer and Freud's study might serve to explain action and demeanor of characters in fiction; thus he was the first to sketch the possibilities of what was later to become a field of extensive studies. It is meaningful that a writer and not a scientist should have been the first correctly to appraise the greatness of the Freudian discovery from its initial and tentative presentation.

[1] Review of the book with this title by Frederick J. Hoffman (1945).
[2] For reviews see now my notes to Freud (1950, p. 167).

265

Freud's predecessors in the study of man were not the neurologists, psychiatrists, and psychologists, from whom he borrowed some of his terms, but rather the great intuitive teachers of mankind. When writing the *Studies in Hysteria,* Freud suddenly became aware of this ancestry:

> I have not always been a psychotherapist, but like other neuropathologists I was educated to methods of focal diagnoses and electrical prognosis, so that even I myself am struck by the fact that the case histories which I am writing read like novels, and as it were, dispense with the serious features of the scientific character. Yet I must console myself with the fact that the nature of the subject is apparently more responsible for this issue than my own predilection. Focal diagnosis and electrical reactions are really not important in the study of hysteria, whereas a detailed discussion of the psychic processes, as one is wont to hear it from the poet, and the application of a few psychological formulae, allows one to gain an insight into the course of events of hysteria [Breuer and Freud, 1895, p. 114].

Long after the few psychological formulae had been developed into an intricate system of propositions tested and retested in more than thirty years of clinical work and verified by manifold types of experimental procedures, Freud returned to a comparison between psychoanalytic findings and the poetic mind, or, more generally speaking, intuitive psychology.[3]

In the early days when clinical experiences were scant and workers few, the testimony of established genius and the psychoanalysis of fiction helped to establish the ubiquitous validity of some hypotheses, thus contributing to the elimination of the frequently spurious distinction between normal and abnormal in matters psychological. At no time since have psychoanalysts ceased to turn gratefully, from time to time, to great creators in literature. When drafting a somewhat utopian curriculum for students of medical psychology, Edward Glover (1934) included the reading of selected works of fiction among the essential prerequisites. Others point to characters in fiction to illustrate the meaning and general validity of clinical findings. Helene Deutsch recently incorporated a rich selection of examples from older and more recent novels in her extensive and detailed clinical compendium of *The Psychology of Women* (1944-1945). The vision of the novelist is, one might say, sometimes more to the point than life itself, as it is accessible to the clinician. The writers' vision has sifted what at first appears to the clinical observer to be an overwhelming mass of data; the writer gives the problem in a simpler but also in a purer version. While this is particularly

[3] See pp. 22f.

suited for the purpose of illustration and demonstration, in its present stage of development psychoanalytic clinical research can only in exceptional cases be based on any evidence other than clinical data, preferably obtained in the psychoanalytic interview, because it alone gives access to the full detail of interacting dynamic and genetic factors toward which the most essential part of current psychoanalytic research is directed.[4]

In marginal areas, however, there are problems of research which might well be presented in better perspective were the testimony of the literary mind to be taken fully into account. Some of the propositions of "culturalism," for instance, pay little attention to the survival of literary values in the widest sense, and more specifically to the spread and variety of literary patterns through time and space, factors which seem to stimulate the quest for a more detailed differentiation of relatively constant from relatively less constant character traits.

Touching thus in passing on the question of what psychoanalysis owes and may owe in the future to contact with the literary mind, interest is centered here on what the literary mind owes to the scientific discourse on men's motivation. How has the literature of his age been influenced by the work of Freud and his pupils? The question is obviously broad. The influence of psychoanalysis has permeated Western civilization at various levels. In medicine the psychosomatic approach has reëstablished the unity between body and mind, and psychoanalytic treatment itself has made curable what at no previous time had been classified as illness—deformities of character, proclivity to unhappiness. In social welfare and education, techniques have been developed which, though not always explicitly credited to the influence of psychoanalysis, are clearly derived from its correctly or incorrectly interpreted hypotheses. Variegated as it is, the influence reaches down into our daily life, into our everyday parlance, or to our everyday dealing with our fellow man, where common sense has added to its equipment some of the more obvious connections established by the clinician. The writer who depicts this world is naturally tempted to refer explicitly to the colors which psychoanalysis has thus added to the picture, and the psychoanalyst has become a fixture on the stage, on the screen, in the novel, and in the thriller.

All this is superficial. The more important questions arise from the challenge of Freud's discovery of a scientific method for uncovering the essential problems of mental life to writers and critics. A detailed or comprehensive investigation of this complex question is, as yet, lacking.

---

4 See in this connection, Greenacre (1945).

It should indeed be a task for the student of comparative literature, since writers of all nationalities and all schools have responded in various ways to this challenge. While a number of essays and general discussions have been devoted to the subject, frequently linking Freud and Marx as sources of stimulation for writers, it seems significant that of two monographs devoted to the subject, one dealing explicitly, the other predominantly, with writers in the English language, American, British and Irish.

One monograph is the subject of this review. The second of them has passed unacknowledged in psychoanalytic literature. A German doctoral dissertation published in 1934, but written before the National Socialist accession to power, it enumerated at great length, and with the care incumbent upon the candidate at that solemn occasion, those British poets of the twentieth century who referred in any sense to Freud. The author, Dr. Hoops, tried to establish the length of time they remained under Freud's influence. He assumed, at the time of writing, that the psychoanalytic "wave" was declining, and wrote as one who dealt with an outmoded literary fashion. He discussed the works of authors as divergent from each other in level and performance as May Sinclair, D. H. Lawrence, J. D. Beresford, Hugh Walpole and W. Somerset Maugham; also Joyce, Virginia Woolf, Rebecca West, Rose Macaulay and Aldous Huxley. Hoops wrote to many of these authors. Some of their replies are significant. Aldous Huxley preferred "Professor Jung, who seems to me much the best as a psychologist—good enough to be a novelist." Others disclaimed any familiarity with psychoanalytic writings, and the careful author concluded that they were not therefore "influenced" by Freud. A case in point is Virginia Woolf, who stated she had become familiar with psychoanalysis only through ordinary conversation. Dr. Hoops overlooked the fact that Leonard and Virginia Woolf were Freud's publishers in England. But neither this, nor the fact that Virginia Woolf's brother was one of England's most distinguished psychoanalysts, need be quoted to understand that the "ordinary way of conversation" to which Virginia Woolf referred had some considerable influence on the formation of one of the great literary minds of Freud's century.

The present contribution by an American scholar, which strangely enough does not refer to Hoops's previous publication, covers somewhat similar ground. The author, Dr. Hoffman, of the English Department of Wisconsin University, has presented a serious and valuable effort. The book starts with a summary of Freud's main theories. It is carefully phrased, cleverly compiled, and based on the whole of Freud's published work. Hoffman is aware of the fact that so formidable a task as a summary of Freud's views is unusual among experts in other fields. In discussing the widespread misunderstanding of psychoanalysis, Hoffman refers to those who misuse psychoanalysis by glancing at one or several of Freud's writings which they misleadingly quote out of the theoretical context. He stresses the fact that most popular views on psychoanalysis are still based on Freud's earlier clinical writings. "A person who comes to a man's writings some years after they have been completed," Hoffman says, "has an advantage which a contemporary rarely enjoys." Dr. Hoffman has availed himself of this advantage. However, he is not satisfied with presenting Freudian theory as developed in Freud's writings as a basis for his investigation. Rather, he proceeds to analyze in detail the spread of psychoanalysis among the American lay public, and especially its dissemination among literary people.

Walter Lippmann's early homage to psychoanalysis in the *New Republic* of 1914, his reflections on its importance in his *Preface to Politics,* are woven into a vivid picture of American intellectual life, of Greenwich Village, where, invited by Lippmann, Dr. Brill appeared in Mabel Dodge Sterne's drawing room. The subsequent reaction of the "little magazines" is discussed, and it appears that as a convenient device, Hoffman consulted the index of the *New York Times* to quote from letters to the editor and other source material, thus offering a stimulating account of the reaction to psychoanalysis in the nineteen-twenties, with all the misunderstandings which, to quote Lippmann, "are all concomitant of drawing-room psyching."

Bloomsbury, no less than Greenwich Village, reacted to the challenge of Freudian thought. Hoffman's information on this response is fragmentary. He omits any reference to Ernest Jones's extensive publications which, by their very topics, were bound to influence the "literary mind," and to the work of Jones's early collaborators and students who presented psychoanalysis to the intellectual public in Britain.

Hoffman's attempt closely to establish the way in which psychoanalysis was spread among the lay public deserves special attention. He is not satisfied to demonstrate that the influence existed, but carefully establishes the media which transmitted psychoanalytic insight and the distortions to which it was exposed.

Thus *repression* as Freud defined it lost much of its original meaning in a discussion; but it gained new cultural ingredients from the particular area in which it found an audience. The single term repression, therefore, suffered a variety of changes, which may be formulated as follows: Freud's definition of the term: *Repression, minus* what has been lost through hasty generalization or inadequate knowledge of its source-meaning, *plus* cultural ingredients which have been attached to the already altered concept, *equals* repression as American convention imposed upon free sex expression, or *neo-Puritanism*.

The factor of metaphor must also be considered. Hence the *mechanism* of repression was often replaced by the picture of a *repressed person,* or a repressed people. In the matter of an amateur or aesthetic usage of a term, the example is more important than the term it is designed to illustrate; and the term acquires the qualities of its illustration, and loses its original accuracy of "abstract purity" [pp. 86-87].

Hoffman does not overlook that the historian's task is not limited to the surface. However valuable it is to know what books on psychoanalysis Dylan Thomas, Ludwig Lewisohn and Conrad Aiken have read, or with what psychoanalysts they had contact, these are only part of the historian's data. Freud's discoveries did not, as it were, hit the trends of literary development from the outside. Their influence on "the literary mind" would be inexplicable had not the previous development of literature turned in a direction which created favorable predispositions for this influence.[5] Hoffman devotes a brief chapter to this problem. Following Thomas Mann's lead, he considers Schopenhauer, Nietzsche and Dostoyevski as "Freud's precursors." One misses, however, references not only to the traditions of German romanticism, and to the widespread interest in the unconscious in its philosophy and science, but also to precursors in other countries of Western civilization. Among English writers, one might have expected to find at least a discussion of Samuel Butler. Preëminent among his contemporaries, he anticipated many of the ideas of C. G. Jung, with no less fantasy but surely with greater charm.

No historical account of forebears of psychoanalysis can possibly be complete without reference to France, the mother country of modern psychiatry. It can hardly have been an accident that the literary expression which by its essence comes closest to the method of free association stems from France: the "stream of consciousness" novel, in which the preconscious reverie becomes the paramount way of expression. It was introduced by Eduard Dujardin in 1887, in his novel, *Les Lauriers sont Coupés*. It might be worth mentioning that early in the twentieth century this technique was used by a Viennese writer, Arthur Schnitzler, who early in his career as a young physician, had become acquainted

---

[5] For trends in the literature of the seventeenth and eighteenth centuries which prepared the way for the later interest in psychopathology, see Praz (1933).

with Freud's work. Hoffman discusses the spread of the stream of consciousness novel in English and American writings, and throws some light on the problem of reverie in general; he might have supported his argumentation by drawing on the material and the suggestions contained in Varendonck's book on the daydream (1921).

Hoffman's presentation is most successful where the analysis of individual writers is concerned. Particularly the essays devoted to Sherwood Anderson and James Joyce are illuminating and inspiring. So are those on Thomas Mann and Kafka; however, one does not quite understand why they should have been included. Had the attempt been made to represent Freudian influence on German writers as thoroughly as his influence on writers in the English language, others would have had to be mentioned: Hermann Hesse, Robert Musil, Hermann Broch, Albrecht Schaeffer, to name only a few.[6] Had Hoffman's thesis included the Freudian influence on the German literature of his age, one would find it hardly understandable why the reaction of French and Italian writers and poets to the same challenge should have been overlooked. Briefly, it seems that Hoffman would have been better advised to limit his presentation to those fields where his original research laid a firm foundation: the American scene.[7]

The greatest merit in Hoffman's approach lies in the attempt sharply to distinguish between the scientific function of Freud's hypotheses and the use which the writers make of them. The autonomy of the writer's creation, his social function, has been stressed by many who tried to approach the study of literature with psychoanalytic concepts. Hoffman follows a path on which Herbert Read, Edmund Wilson and Kenneth Burke have preceded him. He has elaborated in great detail and with supreme skill their views. He has neglected to explore the host of contributions to his subject that are contained in psychoanalytic journals that frequently deal with writers whose work he discusses. It is even more regrettable that such classical contributions as those of Hanns Sachs and Ernest Jones escaped his attention.

Within the confines of literary criticism itself at least the work of two men might have offered Hoffman additional stimulation. These are the essays of the Swiss literary historian, Walter Muschgg, who discussed the relationship of psychoanalysis to literary criticism in broad historical perspectives, and the brilliant books of the Englishman, William Emp-

6 Particularly Hesse's contribution to the subject (1926, 1931) deserve to be considered and reconsidered.

7 For a more comprehensive discussion of the influence of psychoanalysis on contemporary literature, see, for instance, Selander (1931).

son, who has embodied Freud's findings on overdetermination in his concept of poetic ambiguity. In their work, and in Hoffman's valuable book, psychoanalysis has become a tool of the critic. No attempt is made to transform criticism into psychological analysis, but rather to use the new scientific psychology, in the setting of the critic's assignment. There is some reason to believe that whatever integration has been achieved will be enlarged and improved in years to come. The more clearly established and the better presented psychoanalytic hypotheses become, the more are they likely to be useful to those who attempt to apply them.

Chapter 12

PRINCE HAL'S CONFLICT

For well over a century some of Shakespeare's critics have pointed to inconsistencies in the character of Henry, Prince of Wales (later King Henry V), occasionally explained by the poet's lack of interest, whose attention, it is said, was concentrated mainly on the alternate but "true" hero, Falstaff. This seemed the more plausible since most of the puzzling passages or incidents occur in King Henry IV, Parts I and II of the trilogy; however, closer examination of three inconsistencies, to which critics are wont to refer as typical of others, seems to throw new light on the psychological conflict with which Shakespeare has invested the hero of the trilogy.[1]

Prince Hal's first appearance on the stage as Falstaff's friend and Poins's companion is concluded by the soliloquy in which he reveals his secret intentions. While he has just made plans to riot with the gang and to rob the robbers, his mind turns to the future.

> I know you all, and will awhile uphold
> The unyok'd humour of your idleness:
> Yet herein will I imitate the sun,
> Who doth permit the base contagious clouds
> To smother up his beauty from the world,
> That, when he please again to be himself,
> Being wanted, he may be more wonder'd at,
> By breaking through the foul and ugly mists
> Of vapours that did seem to strangle him.
> If all the year were playing holidays,
> To sport would be as tedious as to work;
> But when they seldom come, they wish'd-for come,
> And nothing pleaseth but rare accidents.
> So, when this loose behaviour I throw off,
> And pay the debt I never promised,
> By how much better than my word I am,

[1] It is generally assumed that Part I of King Henry IV was written in 1596 or 1597, immediately or soon after the completion of King Richard II, and Part II in 1597 or 1598. King Henry V must have been completed shortly before or some time during 1599. See H. Spencer (1940).

> By so much shall I falsify men's hopes,
> And, like bright metal on a sullen ground,
> My reformation, glittering o'er my fault,
> Shall show more goodly and attract more eyes
> Than that which hath no foil to set it off.
> I'll so offend, to make offence a skill;
> Redeeming time when men think least I will.[2]

Some critics feel that this announcement deprives the play of part of its dramatic effect: the change in the Prince's behavior should surprise the audience as it does the personages on the stage. The anticipation, we are told, was forced on the poet as a concession to the public. Henry V appeared to the Elizabethans as the incarnation of royal dignity and knightly valor. His early debauches had therefore to be made part of a morally oriented plan; but some critics find the price of justification too high, since it leaves a suspicion of hypocrisy on the Prince's character.

The second inconsistency is seen in the course of the Prince's reformation which proceeds in two stages. In Part I, Prince Hal returns to his duties when the realm is endangered by rebels; at Shrewsbury, he saves the King's life and defeats Percy Hotspur in combat; but while the war against other rebels continues, we find him back in Eastcheap feasting with his companions. His final reformation takes place at the King's deathbed. Critics usually account for this protracted and repeated reformation by assuming that the success of the Falstaff episodes in Part I suggested their continuation in Part II, an argument supported by the widely accepted tradition that Falstaff's revival in *The Merry Wives of Windsor*, after the completion of the trilogy, was at the special request of Queen Elizabeth. It has nevertheless been emphasized that the concluding scenes of Part II follow in all essential details existing tradition.

The third and most frequently discussed inconsistency is King Henry V's treatment of his former companions with merciless severity. Falstaff, who waits to cheer the new King, is temporarily arrested and, while he hopes that Henry will revoke in private his public pronouncement, we later hear that he has hoped in vain. The King's harshness has broken his heart. In the "rejection of Falstaff,"[3] who has won the audience's heart, the dramatist has "overshot his mark"; the King's reformation could have been illustrated by gentler means, and some critics suggest how this could have been achieved without offending the Old Knight. The formula of banishment, however, is only partly Shakespeare's invention since it paraphrases traditional accounts.

2 *King Henry IV*, Part I, Act 1, Sc. 2.
3 See Bradley (1934) whose censure of Shakespeare is moderate compared to that of Hazlitt (1848).

This tradition originated soon after Henry V suddenly died in Paris, at the age of thirty-five, crowned King of England and France (1421). The tradition grew in chronicles and popular accounts, hesitantly at first, more rapidly later, when Henry's striving for European leadership and hegemony in the Channel appeared as an anticipation of the political goals of Tudor England. In Shakespeare's time, fact and legend had become firmly interwoven.[4]

Prince Henry (of Monmouth, born 1387) was early introduced to affairs of state. He was twelve years old when, in 1399, his father succeeded Richard II. At fifteen he took personal control of the administration of Wales and of the war against the Welsh. He had shared in this task since 1400, initially guided by Henry Percy, Hotspur, who at that time was thirty-nine, three years older than the Prince's father. In 1405 Hotspur led the rebellion of the Percies and attacked the Prince's forces at Shrewsbury. Supported by the King and his army, Henry of Monmouth carried the day. The rebellion and the pacification of Wales kept the Prince busy until 1408 or 1409. He then entered politics as leader of the parliamentary opposition against the King's council. Repeated illnesses complicated Henry IV's negotiations with Parliament that at the time of his uprising against Richard II had vested royal power in him. Since 1406 rumors concerning his abdication had been spreading. In 1408 he was thought to have died in an attack of seizures "but after some hours the vital spirits returned to him." From January, 1410 to November, 1411 the Prince governed England through the council, supported by the King's half brothers, Henry and Thomas Beaufort. In November, 1411 Henry IV took over again and dismissed the Prince from the council. One of the reasons for the Prince's dismissal was his desire for an active policy in France. It seems that, initially without the King's consent, he had arranged for a small expeditionary force to be sent to the continent in support of Burgundy against the Royal House of France; later the King agreed to the expedition but the Prince had to renounce his intention to lead the forces.

The circumstances that led to Henry of Monmouth's removal from the council are not entirely clear. It seems that Henry IV was motivated by the suspicion that the Prince intended to depose him. The Prince issued public statements denying such intention, and demanded the punishment of those who had slandered him. He finally forced an interview on the King, during which a reconciliation took place. The struggle between father and son was terminated by Henry IV's death in 1413.

[4] For the legend of Prince Hal see especially Kabel (1936, pp. 363-416).

According to the chronicle of the fifteenth and sixteenth centuries, Henry of Monmouth's character changed after his accession to the throne. The early chronicles do not state in detail wherein the conversion consisted. They familiarize us, however, with two areas in which the Prince's attitude was different from that of the later King. The first of these areas is less well defined than the second: during the conflict with his father, the Prince appeared twice at court "with much peoples of lords and gentles." This show of strength was meant to exercise pressure on King and council. During his reign Henry V never used similar methods; no appeal to forces outside "government" is attributed to him, neither in his dealings with Parliament nor with the baronage. Within the framework of his age he was a rigorously constitutional monarch. Somewhat better defined is the change of the Prince's attitude to the Church. The noble leader of the Lollards, Sir John Oldcastle, was the Prince's personal friend, and at least by tolerance, the Prince seems vaguely to have favored the cause for which he stood. Shortly after Henry V's accession to the throne the persecution of the Lollards was intensified. Sir John was arrested and asked to abandon his error. He refused any compromise, succeeded twice in escaping, but he was finally, in 1417, executed after Parliament had determined on the extirpation of Lollardy as heresy.

The legendary versions of the Prince's reformation elaborated these incidents later on; in their earliest formulation they simply stated: "that the Prince was an assiduous center of lasciviousness and addicted exceedingly to instruments of music. Passing the bounds of modesty he was the fervent soldier of Venus as well as of Mars; youthlike, he was tired with her torches and in the midst of the worthy works of war found leisure for excess common to ungoverned age" (Kingsford, 1901, p. 12). Later sources place the Prince's reformation in relation to the conflict with his father: the baronage that had adopted the Prince as leader becomes a group of irresponsible delinquents. Among this group the name of Sir John Oldcastle appears. The fanatic leader of a religious sect thus underwent the transformation into Sir John Falstaff, whose name was substituted by Shakespeare only after Oldcastle's descendants had complained of what seemed a vilification of their ancestor; but various traces of the original name are extant in Shakespeare's text. The banishment of Falstaff then may be considered as an elaboration of Henry V's persecution of the Lollards whom he once had favored. Other elements of the legendary tradition are inserted with clearly moralistic intentions: the Prince's reformation is used to exemplify the nature of royal responsibility. Thus Sir Thomas Elliott in his treatise, *The Book*

Called the Governor (1536), introduced the tale of Prince and Chief-justice according to which the King confirms that Chiefjustice in office who, in the royal name, had once arrested the riotous Prince. The image of Henry V was thus idealized into that of the perfect Renaissance ruler (T. Spencer, 1942).

Shakespeare borrowed these and similar incidents of his trilogy from a variety of sources, but mainly from the second edition of Raphael Holinshed's *Chronicles of England, Scotland and Ireland* (1587).[5] In addition to historical sources he relied upon a popular play produced a few years earlier. So closely does he follow *The Famous Victories of Henry V* that it seems as if he had set himself the task to retain as many as possible of the incidents familiar to his audience in spite of the total transformation of the context. Without commenting in detail upon this transformation—though such a comparison would permit one to support the hypothesis here to be proposed—it suffices to point to its general direction. The historical facts concerning the conflict between Henry IV and his son and "heir apparent," Henry of Monmouth, had been blurred by legend. The conversion of the Prince became the dominant theme, a conversion modeled after that of the life of the saints. Shakespeare returns to the core of this tradition, or rather rediscovers that core, in the sources accessible to him. He centers his attention on the conflict between father and son which is made to account for both the Prince's debauchery and his reformation.

The conflict between father and son appears in Part I of Henry IV in three versions, each time enacted by one central and two related characters.[6] The theme is manifestly stated by the King in the introductory scene of the trilogy, when he compares Henry of Monmouth to Henry Percy.

> Yea, there thou makest me sad and makest me sin
> In envy that my Lord Northumberland
> Should be the father to so blest a son,
> A son who is the theme of honour's tongue;
> Amongst a grove, the very straightest plant;
> Who is sweet fortune's minion and her pride:
> Whilst I, by looking on the praise of him,
> See riot and dishonour stain the brow
> Of my young Harry. O! that it could be prov'd
> That some night-tripping fairy had exchang'd
> In cradle-clothes our children where they lay,

[5] See Ax (1912).

[6] That the repetition of one theme in various configurations indicates its central position was pointed out by Jekels (1933).

And called mine Percy, his Plantagenet!
Then would I have his Harry, and he mine.[7]

The position of the Prince between Falstaff and the King is almost as explicitly stated; he has two fathers, as the King has two sons. When he enacts with Falstaff his forthcoming interview with his father, the theme is brought into the open.[8] It is not limited to court and tavern, the centers of the "double plot," as W. Empson (1935) calls it, but extends to the rebel camp. Henry Percy stands between a weak father, Northumberland, who is prevented by illness from participating in the decisive battle, and a scheming uncle, Worcester, who plans the rebellion, conceals from Percy that the King offers reconciliation and drives him thus to battle and to death.

The three versions of the father-son conflict compelled Shakespeare to deviate from his sources and thereby to enrich the stage: he sharpened the report of the chronicles on the rebellion of the Percies in order to create the contrast of Worcester and Northumberland; he reduced Henry Percy's age from a slightly older contemporary of Henry IV to a somewhat older contemporary of the Prince—and he invented Falstaff.

The triangular relationships are not only similar to each other, since they all contain variations of the theme of good and bad fathers and sons, but within each triangle the parallel figures are closely interconnected; thus the two Harrys, whom Henry IV compares, form a unit; Hotspur's rebellion represents also Prince Hal's unconscious parricidal impulses.[9] Hotspur is the Prince's double. Impulses pertaining to one situation have thus been divided between two personages;[10] but though in the triangles the characters are paired and contrasted, each of the play's personages transcends the bondage to his function in this thematic configuration. They have all outgrown the symmetry which they serve, into the fullness of life.

To appraise Falstaff as a depreciated father figure is to grasp the superficial aspect of a character who, more than any other of Shakespeare, has enchanted readers and audiences since his creation. Franz Alexander (1933) finds two principal psychoanalytic explanations for this universal enchantment: Falstaff's hedonism, he says, represents the uninhibited gratification of an infantile and narcissistic quest for pleas-

---

[7] *King Henry IV*, Part I, Act 1, Sc. 1.

[8] The idea of the travestied interview itself is borrowed from *The Famous Victories of Henry the Fifth*. There the Prince and his companion enact the Prince's subsequent interview with the Chiefjustice.

[9] This point was made by Alexander (1933), and by Empson (1935, p. 43).

[10] Ernest Jones (1911, 1949) speaks in a similar connection of decomposition.

ure, a craving alive to some extent in every one of us; this hedonism, moreover, is made acceptable by contrast: one turns with relief from the court or the rebel camp to the tavern. In accordance with the last is the traditional antithesis of "tragic King and comic people" (Empson) used by Shakespeare to emphasize a moral antithesis. From Prince Hal's point of view, Falstaff is a contrast to the King, who represents another version of the unsatisfactory paternal image. Henry IV succeeded his cousin Richard II by rebellion and regicide. The feeling of guilt that over-shadowed his life becomes manifest when on his deathbed, in addressing the Prince, he reviews the sorrows that the unlawfully acquired crown inflicted on him.

> How I came by the crown, O God forgive;
> And grant it may with thee in true peace live![11]

In this great scene Prince Henry's mood accords with his father's; he too is burdened with guilt. In the preceding scene he finds his father sleeping, and believes him to be dead. Shakespeare, adapting this scene from the chronicle play, has added a prop device: the crown which lies next to the King's bed.[12] The crown inspires the Prince with awe and apprehension. He longs to possess it, but "the best of gold" is "the worst of gold"; it endangers the bearer. He wages "the quarrel of a true in-heritor," controls his desire and, in a mood of contemplation, concludes that royal responsibility is a heavy burden. He has overcome the hostile impulse against the dying King and can now reply to his father:

> You won it, wore it, kept it, gave it me;
> Then plain and right must my possession be;[13]

It is an attempt to reassure: "Since I have come guiltless into the possession of the crown, since I refrained from regicide and parricide, I shall rightfully be King"; yet in the greatest crisis of his life, the Prince, now King Henry V, reveals that his apprehension has not been van-quished. The night before the battle of Agincourt, when his outnum-bered army is weakened by disease, and confidence is more than ever required, he turns to prayer to avert divine retaliation for his father's crime that, with the crown, seems to have moved to his shoulders.

[11] *King Henry IV*, Part II, Act IV, Sc. 5.

[12] The very crown that literally he had taken from Richard II. See *Richard II*, Act IV, Sc. 1.

[13] *King Henry IV*, Part II, Act IV, Sc. 5.

O God of battles! steel my soldiers' hearts;
Possess them not with fear; take from them now
The sense of reckoning, if the opposed numbers
Pluck their hearts from them! Not to-day, O Lord!
O, not to-day, think not upon the fault
My father made in compassing the crown!
I Richard's body have interred anew;
And on it have bestow'd more contrite tears
Than from it issu'd forced drops of blood:
Five hundred poor I have in yearly pay,
Who twice a day their wither'd hands hold up
Toward heaven, to pardon blood; and I have built
Two chantries, where the sad and solemn priests
Sing still for Richard's soul. More will I do;
Though all that I can do is nothing worth,
Since that my penitence comes after all,
Imploring pardon.[14]

The essential passages of this prayer follow Holinshed's *Chronicles* wherein it is reported that after his succession to the throne Henry V had King Richard's body ceremoniously interred in Westminster Abbey and made specified donations in commemoration. Reference to this incident and the place in which it is made invite comment. By reintroducing the theme of the tragic guilt attached to the House of Lancaster, Shakespeare establishes a link between Henry V and his older plays that dramatize the downfall of the Lancastrian Kings (Henry VI, Richard III). The victory of Agincourt and the life of Henry V are thus made to appear as a glorious interlude in a tragic tale of crime and doom; however, the King's prayer before the battle reveals the structure of the conflict which Shakespeare embodied in his character: the desire to avoid guilt and to keep himself pure of crime is paramount in Henry V. In one passage of the prayer the King recalls the tears he shed on Richard's coffin, a detail not recorded by Holinshed, and yet obviously suggested by other passages of the *Chronicle*. It may well be considered a hint— the only one we find in the trilogy—that there ever existed a personal relationship between Richard II and the son of his banished cousin Henry of Lancaster—Henry of Monmouth. During the last months of his rule King Richard II sailed for Ireland to quell a local rebellion and he took Henry of Monmouth with him. The young Prince seems to have attracted the King's attention. The Prince was knighted by King Richard, Holinshed records, "for some valiant act that he did or some other favourable respect." Shakespeare was undoubtedly familiar with this account and very probably familiar with reports of the Prince's reaction

---

[14] *King Henry V*, Act IV, Sc. 1.

to the news of his father's rebellion. Young Henry of Monmouth is said to have replied to a question of Richard's that he could not be held responsible for his father's deed.

In Shakespeare's *King Richard II* no direct reference is made to the relationship between Prince Hal and Richard,[15] but the theme to which we refer is present and clearly emphasized: one entire scene is devoted to it, the first in which the Prince is mentioned. Henry IV, newly enthroned, meets with his Lords—but his son is absent.

> Can no man tell of my unthrifty son?
> 'Tis full three months since I did see him last:
> If any plague hang over us, 'tis he.
> I would to God, my lords, he might be found:
> Inquire at London, 'mongst the taverns there,
> For there, they say, he daily doth frequent,
> With unrestrained loose companions,
> Even such, they say, as stand in narrow lanes,
> And beat our watch, and rob our passengers;[16]

The Prince has dissociated himself from the court that his father won by treason. In silent protest he has turned to the tavern rather than to participate in regicide.[17] Regicide dominates the scene that starts with Henry IV's quest for his absent son. The last of Richard's followers and the new King's cousin, the Duke of Aumerle, confesses to Henry IV that he has plotted against his life. Before Aumerle can complete his confession, the Duke of York, his father and the uncle of Henry IV, forces his way into their presence. He doubts whether the purpose of Aumerle's audience be murder or repentance and is prepared to surrender his son.[18] This is the environment from which the Prince withdraws, to which he prefers the vices of Eastcheap and the freedom of Falstaff's company.

In *King Henry IV*, Part II, the contrast between court and tavern is

[15] One might conjecture that Shakespeare preferred not to refer to the personal relationship between Prince Hal and King Richard since he needed a more mature Prince, not a boy of twelve.

[16] *King Richard II*, Act V, Sc. 3.

[17] Only once Henry V states openly his disapproval of his father's actions, and then in a highly restrained fashion. When wooing, somewhat abruptly, Katherine of France he says

> . . . I dare not swear thou lovest me; yet my blood begins to flatter me that thou dost, notwithstanding the poor and untempering effect of my visage. *Now beshrew my father's ambition! He was thinking of civil wars when he got me.* . . . (Italics added.)

[18] York himself had plotted against Richard II and seeks his son's punishment out of a displaced feeling of guilt. Some of the complexities of this relationship were elucidated by Taylor (1927).

reëmphasized in a scene in which Falstaff's carefree vice is justaposed with John of Lancaster's virtuous villainy. This younger brother of Prince Hal is in command of the campaign against the still surviving rebels. Falstaff serves in his inglorious army. Lancaster promises the rebels pardon; they accept his offer and he breaks his word to send them to the gallows. We have just witnessed this monstrous performance— taken directly from Holinshed's *Chronicles*—when Lancaster and Falstaff meet. The "sober blooded youth" provokes Falstaff's soliloquy in praise of Sherristack and of Prince Hal, whose valor has not made him addicted to "thin potations."

Falstaff's loving praise of the Prince, and what others say when they refer to the Prince in the latter part of Part II of Henry IV remind us once more of how well he has succeeded in deceiving the world. His conversion upon his accession to the throne comes as a surprise to the court and to the tavern. Only the audience, having been in his confidence from his first soliloquy, are enabled to understand the contradictions in his behavior as being a part of his paramount conflict.

When Shakespeare familiarized himself with the youth of Henry V this conflict must have imposed itself upon his mind as one that would unify the various traits and incidents reported. The tendentious accounts in the *Chronicles* had not fully obliterated the traces of antagonism in the relationship between the Prince and the King. This antagonism, the legends of the Prince's debauchery and conversion, and other elements that the dramatist found in his sources, he wove into a plausible character. The Prince tries to dissociate himself from the crime his father had committed; he avoids contamination with regicide because the impulse to regicide (parricide) is alive in his unconscious. When the King's life is threatened he saves the King and kills the adversary, who is his alter ego. In shunning the court for the tavern he expresses his hostility to his father and escapes the temptation to parricide. He can permit himself to share Falstaff's vices because he does not condone the King's crime; but hostility to the father is only temporarily repressed. When finally he is in possession of the crown, he turns against the father substitute; hence the pointed cruelty of Falstaff's rejection. Both paternal figures between which the Prince oscillates have less meaning to him than appears at first. What he opposes to them is different and of an exalted nature: his ideals of kingship, royal duty and chivalry. These ideals are with him when he first appears on the stage; they grow in and with him throughout the tragedy, and they dominate throughout the five acts of *King Henry V*.

These ideals, one might speculate, may have been modeled on an idealization of Richard II, the murdered King, whom Prince Hal as a boy had accompanied to Ireland and whose favor he had won. Richard, however, was hardly fit to serve as model of a great king. Shakespeare has drawn him as a weak and irresponsible man, who depended presumptuously on the trappings of royalty for his kingship, on that ceremony that meant so little to Henry V and for which he substituted royal duty. One may conjecture this to have been a further reason why Shakespeare did not explicitly refer to the existence of a personal relationship between Prince Henry and King Richard. But all this is speculative. Opposed to it is solid evidence of the importance of moral conflicts in the personality of Henry V; it would be easy to demonstrate from metaphors and puns alone, with which the poet speaks through the hero, his proclivity to such conflicts. His major actions and interests all indicate too the Prince's search for moral justification.

While living the roistering life of the tavern, his thirst for glory won in battle—but only battle with a moral purpose—and chivalry was great; hence the Prince's bitter caricature of Hotspur.

> . . . I am not yet of Percy's mind, the Hotspur of the North; he that kills me some six or seven dozen of Scots at a breakfast, washes his hands, and says to his wife, 'Fie upon this quiet life! I want work.' 'O my sweet Harry,' says she; 'how many hast thou killed to-day?' 'Give my roan horse a drench,' says he; and answers, Some fourteen' an hour after; 'a trifle, a trifle.'[19]

There is jubilant relief when Percy turns to rebellion and the Prince can finally fight an envied rival, and in the service of a just cause liberate and use his own aggressive impulses; hence also, before the invasion of France, the preoccupation with legal points; and finally, on the night before Agincourt, the protracted debate with Williams, the soldier. Assuming that his partner in discussion is "Harry le Roy" an English commoner, the soldier argues

> . . . There are few die well that die in a battle; for how can they charitably dispose of anything, when blood is the argument? Now, if those men do not die well, it will be a black matter for the king that led them to it. . . .[20]

Henry goes to great lengths to refute this thesis. He contends that the King is answerable only for the justice of his cause and cannot be answerable for "the particular endings of his soldiers," since "every subject

19 *King Henry IV*, Part I, Act II, Sc. 4.
20 *King Henry V*, Act IV, Sc. 1.

is the King's, but every subject's soul is his own." The moving subtleties of this theological discourse[21] lead to the King's soliloquy on ceremony and royal destiny:

> Upon the king! let us our lives, our souls,
> Our debts, our careful wives,
> Our children, and our sins lay on the king!
> We must bear all. O hard condition,
> Twin-born with greatness, subject to the breath
> Of every fool, whose sense no more can feel
> But his own wringing! What infinite heart's-ease
> Must kings neglect that private men enjoy!
> And what have kings that privates have not too,
> Save ceremony,—save general ceremony?
> And what art thou, thou idol ceremony?[22]

Summoned to battle, the King kneels in prayer in which he disclaims any complicity in his father's crime; thus prepared, the hero can conquer.

Henry V's preoccupation with morals is not glorified by Shakespeare nor presented as the dominant virtue of "a Christian soldier"; it is shown in its dynamic interplay with opposite tendencies, and occasionally—with a slightly ironical smile—exposed as a pretense. While the King is urging the clergy to establish his claim to the throne of France, the audience knows that he has forced the support of the Church by political pressure. The bishops, who have accepted the deal and supplied the garbled justification, are well aware of the King's burning desire for conquest. We are left in doubt as to whether it is political shrewdness or self-deception which prompts the King to pose the question:[23]

> May I with right and conscience make this claim?[24]

Ambiguities and schisms of motivation are characteristic of the King. He flees to the tavern to escape from the evils of the court—but he becomes a past master of licentious living. He strives for humane warfare, and protects the citizens of conquered Harfleur;[25] but when the French

21 Canterbury says of the newly enthroned Henry V (Act I, Sc. 1.):
  Hear him but reason in divinity
  And, all admiring, with an inward wish
  You would desire the King were made a prelate.

22 *King Henry V*, Act IV, Sc. 1.

23 A somewhat similar analysis of this passage has been given by Traversi (1941), who in a remarkable essay stresses the importance of "cool reasoning" and "self-domination" in the King's character.

24 *King Henry V*, Act I, Sc. 2.

25 Traversi (1941) notes that when the King presents his ultimatum to Harfleur his passion rises, and that in accepting the surrender he regains self-control.

break the laws of warfare in attacking the English encampment and killing the boys, Henry has every French prisoner's throat cut. The "friction between flesh and spirit" (Traversi), between impulse and inhibition, is fully resolved only when from moral scrutiny Henry proceeds to heroic venture, when as leader of men who are determined to fight with a clear conscience against overwhelming odds, he feels himself one among peers:

We few, we happy few, we band of brothers.[26]

The inconsistencies in Prince Hal's character that some of Shakespeare's critics thought to have detected are not inconsistencies but attempts to resolve a conflict which is in some of its elements similar to Hamlet's. In Hamlet the oedipus is fully developed, centering around the queen. In Shakespeare's historical dramas women are absent or insignificant. Prince Hal's struggle against his father appears therefore in isolation, enacted in male society. Hamlet stands between a murdered father and a murderous uncle. Prince Hal's father murdered his second cousin—and predecessor—to whom the Prince had an attachment. Thus the crime is in both cases carried out by the father or by his substitute—the King in Hamlet—while both heroes are battling against the murderous impulse in their own hearts.

The psychological plausibility of Prince Hal as a dramatic character is not inferior to that of Hamlet, whatever the difference in depth and dramatic significance of the two plays may be. While only one part of the oedipal conflict is presented, the defenses which Prince Hal mobilizes in order to escape from his internal predicament are well known from the clinical study of male youths. In our analysis of the Prince's character we have implicitly referred mainly to two mechanisms: first, to the formation of the superego; second, the displacement of filial attachment onto a father substitute.

The Prince, in his thoughts, compares the King, his father, with an ideal of royal dignity far superior to the father himself. This ideal, derived from paternal figures but exalted and heightened, is his protection in the struggle against his parricidal impulses and against submission to the King. This mechanism operates in some form or other in every boy's development at the time of the resolution of the oedipal conflict. During this process the superego acquires part of its severity and some of its autonomy. It is a process subject to many vicissitudes, as illustrated by a clinical example.

26 *King Henry V*, Act IV, Sc. 3.

A boy of eight approached his father, a distinguished judge, with a request for advice. He held two one dollar bills and wanted to know whether he might keep them. They had been acquired by the sale to neighbors of pencils which a mail order house had sent him on his request. Upon the receipt of the two dollars he was to be sent a premium to which he now preferred the money. The judge asked to see the advertisement to which the boy had responded and the letter of the mail order house. After reading both he ruled: "You may keep the money; they have no right to make such contracts with minors."

When thirty-five years later the incident was recalled in analysis it appeared that he had not only lost confidence in all authority since that time, but also that when he had asked his father's advice he was testing him. He had grown suspicious that the father did not live up to the principles—sexual and moral—he advocated, and when in his own conflict he sought the father's advice, he had hoped that the father would support his own hesitant moral views. When this expectation was disappointed, he acquired a cynical independence. The compulsion to live up to his ideal became part of a complex neurotic symptomatology.

In one detail only did this patient resemble Prince Hal: his own moral standards assured his independence from all paternal figures and were used as aggressive reproach in every contact with them. Prince Hal uses not only his ideal of moral integrity as reproachful contrast against his father, but also his own playful depravity. The second mechanism of defense the Prince mobilizes is no less common than the first. He adopts an extrafamilial substitute who, true to a pattern frequently observed, is the antithesis of the father. Falstaff is closer to the Prince's heart than the King; he satisfies the libidinal demands in the father-son relation through his warmth and freedom. Yet the Prince proves superior to Falstaff in wit and royal reveling: he triumphs over both father and father substitute.[27] He is paramount in license as he will be paramount in royal dignity.

Literary critics seem of late weary of the intrusion of psychoanalysis. However politely, they assert—and rightly so—their independence.[28] This essay is a psychological analysis which attempts only to underline a few universal, unconscious mechanisms, and is not intended as literary criticism. It suggests that Shakespeare had puzzled about the nature of

[27] The son's superiority over the father occurs also in other connections in the trilogy. Hotspur is superior to both Worcester and Northumberland and Aumerle is superior to his father, York, who first betrays King Richard before he betrays his own son.

[28] See Trilling's excellent essay, *Freud and Literature* (1947), or Knights' essay, *Prince Hamlet* (1946).

Henry V's personality, and that already, while writing the last act of *Richard II,* was aware of the conflict on which he intended to center the character development of the King. Shakespeare's plan, suggested in this case by the nature of the tradition about the subject, must have been one of the trends of thought that, on various levels of awareness, directed him in writing the trilogy. It is not suggested that the plan was complete from the beginning; it might have manifested itself to the poet during his work, i.e., it might have been preconscious before. Moreover, some elements we here consider part of this plan probably never reached consciousness. What answer Shakespeare might have given if asked why Henry V kills Falstaff by his harshness is comparatively irrelevant. What counts is that he had the King do so, and he surely must have known that this could hardly be popular with his audience. Such internal consistency, the final parricide, can only have been conceived by one who in creating had access to his own unconscious impulses.

If investigations similar to the one here attempted, but more complete and authoritative, were carried out systematically; if they were to comprehend all of Shakespeare's work and, at least for purposes of comparison, the works of other Elizabethans; if conflicts and their varied or preferred solutions, and those omitted by one author, one group of authors, one period, or one cultural area were collated—such an application of psychoanalysis might be integrated with the work of the literary historian or critic.

Plot and character are clearly not the only, and not always the most important, tools of the dramatic poet. Psychoanalysis suggests other approaches for the study of poetic language, its metaphors and hidden meanings.[29] Systematic investigation in this area may lead to other types of integration than the study of plot or character. The combination of various sequences of such systematic studies might finally lead to a topic in which critics and psychoanalysts are equally interested and about which they are both, each in his own field, almost equally ignorant: the nature of the artist's personality, a question that must be studied in its cultural variations before generalizations can be made.

Psychoanalysis has frequently attempted short cuts, mostly by correlating one of the artist's works with an occurrence noted by his biographers,[30] assumptions that can rarely be verified.

29 See Sharpe (1946). See here also Chapter 10.

30 This procedure was initiated in 1900 by a remark of Freud who envisaged the possibility that Shakespeare's choice of Hamlet as a topic and the treatment of the conflict might have to do with the death of Shakespeare's father and his son Hamnet.

Clinical analysis of creative artists suggests that the life experience of the artist is sometimes only in a limited sense the source of his vision; that his power to imagine conflicts may by far transcend the range of his own experience; or, to put it more accurately, that at least some artists possess the particular gift to generalize from whatever their own experience has been. One is always tempted to look for a cue that would link this or that character to its creator's personality. Falstaff, it has been said, is clearly Shakespeare himself. Why not Percy or Richard II? Are they not equally alive, equally consistent? Could not for each of these characters that very same psychological plausibility be claimed, that we here claim for Prince Hal? Such a quest seems futile and contrary to what clinical experience with artists as psychoanalytic subjects seems to indicate. Some great artists seem to be equally close to several of their characters, and may feel many of them as parts of themselves. The artist has created a world and not indulged in a daydream.

This writer is not exempt from the temptation to detect a neat connection between the artist and one of his characters. I therefore record my own venture in this direction, with appropriate reservations. At the time Shakespeare was working on Richard II, and studying the life of Prince Hal, he reëstablished the prestige of the Shakespeare family (which had been lost through his father's bankruptcy) by purchasing a coat of arms. The motto chosen is one that might well have been used to characterize Prince Hal's striving for the crown: "Non sanz droict."

Part Five

Psychology of Creative Processes

Chapter 13

ON INSPIRATION

Let us take the spirit of language as a guide for our first steps. The various meanings of the word "inspiration" show a single conception developing along a progressive scale.[1] The *literal* meaning is best illustrated by the narrative in Gen. ii, 7: "And the Lord God formed man of the dust of the ground and breathed into his nostrils the breath of life; and man became a living soul." The usage of the word "inspiration" in modern times is, however, twofold. It comprehends the action of inhaling as well as the action of blowing on, or into, the passive as well as the active part of the process.

The *metaphorical* usage to which I shall mainly refer transposes the bodily action on to the mental plane. The action of inspiring and the condition of being inspired refer to the mind. "A special immediate action or influence of the spirit of God or some divine and supernatural being" (*Shorter Oxford Dictionary*, 1936) takes hold of a person. He becomes an instrument of the Divine, and his works are "inspired" in the same way as those books of the Bible which are thought to have been written under divine influence and have retained a special place in the religious belief of man. From this conception—which, for the purpose of this paper, I shall call the "full metaphorical meaning of inspiration" and which is based upon the immediate substitution of spiritual influence for breath—all other figurative meanings of the word derive.[2] Two of them, however, are further differentiated. We sometimes

[1] See for a general discussion Lafora (1927), Bradley (1929), and since the publication of the present paper (1939) also Bowra (1949). In the present context, "inspiration" and "creation" are considered as psychological phenomena only. No connotation of value is implied in these words.

[2] If, for instance, one describes as inspiration "the utterance or publication of particular views or information on some public matter, if prompted from some influential quarter" (*Oxford Dictionary*), the relation even to the literal meaning is still apparent. The scene, when a Government official gives information to a reporter, is still a distant relation of the biblical one.

call spontaneous ideas, visions, or conceptions "inspiration" (*Encyclopaedia Britannica,* 11th edition) , and we speak of the "inspiring" influence of a person upon others. I shall refer to these meanings as the second and third stages of metaphorical usage. Divergent as they undoubtedly are, they still have a common basis. They both describe changes in the attitude of man, the first a change in his mind which arises suddenly, the second a change in his emotional life, mostly due to the influence of another person. Both these changes, however, are characteristic of states of inspiration in the full metaphorical sense. But in the latter the alteration of the normal attitude is not limited to the mental and emotional condition of the person; it also embraces his physical state. This alteration generally arises suddenly and is ascribed to the influence of some spirit. The concept of inspiration is intended to account for these states: it is an explanation on the animistic level. In order to replace it by a scientific explanation we shall have to enumerate some of the characteristics of such states.

In their purest form they are found in primitive society. They appear mainly in the religious sphere, which includes almost all productive mental activities. The inspired persons are mainly priests, medicine men, or prophets. At a later stage—if we can speak of evolution where such uncertainty still prevails—the poet and, in exceptional cases, men of action join them. These men of action, however, are not the mythical heroes, not the great revolutionaries; they are rather of the type of "the prophet as leader."[3] The states of inspiration are not permanent. They take hold of the individual for a certain time. They are mostly connected with a partial loss of consciousness and are almost habitually accompanied by various sorts of more or less uncoördinated motor activities.

The clinical classification of these states is not always easy. They sometimes show characteristics of epileptic or—perhaps more frequently —hystero-epileptic states (*morbus sacer*) or else a more or less complicated hysterical symptom formation. But while there seems to be a certain variety of clinical syndromes which may predispose to these states, the psychological conception of the belief in inspiration and of the processes occurring in it aims at a solution that will not be limited to any one of these clinical conditions. These highly complex processes may be described as phenomena of regression. In clinical cases this regression is likely to lead to a withdrawal of ego control from many of

3 For illustrative material see now Arlow's suggestive study of the consecration of the prophet (1951) , which has a bearing on several of the topics discussed in the present study.

the higher mental activities. As an example we have mentioned that the coördination of motor activities is frequently affected. To add another most characteristic feature, in states of inspiration speech becomes automatic. It is not the subject who speaks but a voice from out of him. The pronouncements of this voice from him are unknown before the state of inspiration has arisen. It is the voice of his unconscious, he communicates it to others, and he himself becomes part of the public.

In such communications the unconscious is supreme. They are always prophecy or poetry of some kind. The vision of the future is, of course, largely based upon the interaction of wish and fantasy (the main contents of the unconscious) with the preconscious understanding of the needs and desires of the community. The essence of vaticination has in fact always been the unconscious connection between the prophet and the client, the forecast of the future being based upon the experience of the past. The poets of old were hardly distinguished from priests and prophets. Their main province was myth, that is to say the past of the tribe or the common fantasy about that past, in which terrible deeds occurred, incest and murder, similar to those which mold the fantasy life of early childhood. The story of this past is not entrusted to consciousness. In a state similar to that of intoxication, elated, in a trance, not conscious of what he does—thus Plato, to whom we owe this first description of the state of inspiration—the poet sings his song. The voice of God speaks through him to men. Obviously all similar states, when the prophet acts as leader, when he codifies the law or writes down what has been revealed to him, are based upon analogous mental experiences. We are perhaps thus justified in saying that the inspired leadership of primitive society consists of individuals who are distinguished among other qualities which do not enter into the framework of our present deliberation by a certain disposition to communicate with the repressed wishes and fantasies in themselves by the use of special mechanisms. These mechanisms are in the nature of projection and introjection. What comes from inside is believed to come from without. The "voice of the unconscious" is externalized and becomes the voice of God, who speaks through the mouth of the chosen. This process of externalization constitutes one decisive element of the phenomenon of inspiration, but not the whole of it.[4] The knowledge which the voice communicates is not only derived from God, but literally given by him. The awareness itself

---

[4] For the purpose of this paper a further differentiation may be valuable. If the externalized thought is projected on to some special supernatural being, it may, when communicated to the tribe, bear some features of this being as he is known by tradition. This is the case of prophecy.

is a result of inspiration as well as a part of it, and thus the driving of the unconscious toward consciousness, the process of becoming conscious, is attributed to the influence of the Divine. In other words, an alteration of cathexis inside the person, the bursting of the frontiers between the unconscious and the conscious, is experienced as an intrusion from without. We may therefore say that the conception of inspiration is connected with two emotional experiences. Though they are intimately interwoven with each other and may, therefore, not always be distinguished by the individual himself, they may be separated here for the sake of our presentation: in the concept of inspiration impulses, wishes and fantasies derived from the unconscious[5] are attributed to a supernatural being and the process of their becoming conscious is experienced as an action of this being upon the subject, and thus *activity* is turned into *passivity*.[6]

Before we attempt to carry this trend of thought any further we shall have to consider some of the conditions which may account for the universality and the tenacity of the belief in inspiration. Two main purposes seem to be served by that belief: one concerns its social and the other its individual aspect. Through the idea of inspiration the communication gains in authority, and the person who communicates it is relieved of the burden of responsibility. The increase in authority is best exemplified if we think of the concept of revelation. The revealed truth is of a quality other than that of truth acquired through human effort. It is beyond criticism as well as beyond doubt. The problem of responsibility, however, is more complicated; it is intimately linked up with anxiety and guilt. In speaking of archaic social conditions we may say that the tale the poet tells derives from or touches upon the forbidden sphere of wishes, desires, and impulses. Under the assumption of inspiration not he but the Divine is acting; he is not responsible, his feelings of guilt are relieved, and no anxiety need arise.

The full metaphorical meaning of inspiration, however, underwent an alteration even in the ancient world, and thus it became a term des-

[5] In a more detailed study distinctions would have to be made concerning the structural character of what has been projected, whether it is derived from the id—the only case mentioned above—from the ego or the superego; for such distinctions in visionary states see Money-Kyrle (1933).

[6] One is once more reminded of the twofold meaning of the word "inspiration." See lately also Bergler (1950, p. 118) who comments on one part of Houseman's self-observation: "All this shows that oral elements are predominant, although frequently cloaked in more superficial forms of 'conception.' In other words, the narcissistic mechanism of reversal ('I produce') is frequently in contradiction with the feeling 'Something is forced upon me.'"

ignating special conditions of creation, though without losing the whole of its original meaning. Just as the prerogatives conceded to the man of genius are still derived from the days in which *ingenium* had its full mythological meaning, so the consideration granted to those who are in this special state of creativeness still reflects the older conception. This relation does not exist for the public only, it is not only a sociological one, but it remains true of the creators themselves, it has a full psychological sense.

In many autobiographical descriptions, especially by poets or artists, we hear that the creative states are states of special excitement.[7] This excitement may be favored by certain conditions and may be evokable by certain stimuli, but as a rule it cannot be controlled altogether. In these conditions the individual may feel more or less elated or depressed, extremely vital or ill. The act of creation becomes extremely easy, sometimes progressing at great speed, and a feeling arises that "the real work is done by some unseen collaborator" (R. L. Stevenson).

Out of a great variety of autobiographical descriptions I want to choose one which impresses me by its moderation and prudence. In his Leslie Stephen Lecture at Cambridge on *The Name and Nature of Poetry* (1933) A. E. Housman describes what one might fittingly call his individual experience of poetic inspiration. "I think that a production of poetry is less an active than a passive and involuntary process." He compares it with human or animal secretion and stresses the fact that it is painful and accomplished in a state near to illness.

> Having drunk a pint of beer at luncheon—beer is a sedative to the brain and my afternoons are the least intellectual portions of my life —I would go out for a walk. As I went along, thinking of nothing in particular, there would flow into my mind with sudden and unaccountable emotion, sometimes a line or two of verse, sometimes a whole stanza at once, accompanied, not preceded, by a vague notion of the poem as a whole. Then there would usually be a lull and perhaps the spring would bubble up again. I say bubble up, because the source of the suggestion thus proffered to the brain was an abyss.

This abyss Housman is inclined to locate in "the pit of the stomach."

While here the veil of understatement disguises the emotional upheaval of the creative state under a cover of self-irony, we may imagine that other, less critical minds would be inclined to describe analogous

[7] For an anthology of quotations see now particularly Harding (1940). It is hardly necessary to stress that Nietzsche's (1945, I, p. 497) description of the experience of inspiration of "what poets of a stronger age understood by the word" has a place of its own in the literary tradition.

though less fruitful experiences in terms of the full metaphorical meaning of inspiration. In Housman's words, however, another meaning of that word is implied: that which I suggested should be called the "second stage of metaphorical usage." In this sense inspiration designates, as we said, the sudden arising of visions or thoughts, and in this sense inspiration may be called almost the everyday version of the creative process which we all know as a flash of thought.

I should like to discuss this phenomenon in connection with scientific thinking, where the sudden experience concerns some step in the attempt to solve a problem.[8] Summarizing some of the results of recent psychological research, we may emphasize the following points. The work of the mind in research and discovery does not consist only in a continuous application to the quest for a solution. A part of the work is done in preconscious elaboration, the result of which comes into consciousness in sudden advances. It is almost always possible to find traces of an interrelation between some external stimuli and this preconscious process.[9]

Some of the greatest scientific discoveries are attributed to chance by the discoverers themselves, just as Newton's observation of a falling apple is alleged to have been the source of his discovery of the law of gravitation. A closer analysis of such cases, which play a considerable part in typical biographies of scientists, has, as Paulhan (1901) has shown, proved beyond all doubt that what appears to be chance is in fact an observation impregnated with previous preconscious experiences. The making of the observation is in itself a part of the preconscious process. In the words of Louis Pasteur: "Le hasard ne favorise que les esprits préparés" (Delacroix, 1931). The idea, however, that the discovery originated from the observation which chance offered and that the whole of the mental process involved was indeed started by chance,

---

[8] For further literature and some new data see Partridge (1938). What is said here can be applied in a similar but not in a totally identical sense to other kinds of creative activities. Normally in scientific thinking ego control is strongest, and emotional conditions least noticeable. (See for an elaboration Chapter 14.) For an opposite view which attributes at least poetic inspiration exclusively to "the delighted perception" see now, e.g., a charming but not too-well-advised essay by Donaghy (1944).

[9] Psychoanalytic experience leads us to confirm this point of view and to stress one part of this relation. We have in our daily work ample opportunity to watch how observations are directed by the mind, that is to say, how human beings notice what they are prepared to see. As Anna Freud once put it, one can almost predict, in the course of an analysis with a woman patient, when she is going to read in a newspaper that an operation has been performed on a hermaphrodite. On another plane, self-observation confirms that even our research work can be hampered or promoted by our dependence on these factors.

through an inspiration, deserves some further comment. Chance is always tinged by the conception of fate. It stands for what in religious terms may be called the will of God, in the last analysis for God himself.[10] And thus our path seems to have led us back to the problem of inspiration. The belief in the part played by chance in scientific discoveries repeats on another plane the idea of the voice of the unconscious which is externalized and attributed to God. In order to account for this similarity several arguments may be adduced. Scientific thinking is in itself never sharply separated from the realm of the unconscious, and the psychoanalysis of inventors and research workers shows that there is an intimate connection between these higher mental functions and unconscious wishes and desires and their infantile roots (Lorand, 1950). This argument concerning the id aspect of scientific thought may be supplemented by another which might be called the superego aspect. Any research or discovery may, in some sense, be an attempt to trespass across established boundaries and thus be related to infantile situations in which such attributes were forbidden and dangerous. But a third argument may still be added; it concerns the aspect of ego psychology. The working of our mind in productive thinking is, as we have said, not based on steady application only. It is most probably connected with changes of cathexis which may take the character of sudden, as it were eruptive, processes. The part attributed to chance would then properly be described as rationalization. But this description is true only in a somewhat superficial sense. It does not take into account one further element: that of the excitement sometimes connected with productive thinking, even if that excitement is less noticeable than with any other sort of creative activity. Such excitement is of a libidinal nature. Evidence is easily accessible in so far as "normal" conditions of creative activity are concerned.[11] The evidence, however, which I should like to mention here, as shortly as possible, concerns its pathological aspect, i.e., states of excitement connected with unsuccessful creative activity in thinking and in scientific research. I have chosen the two following cases for the sake of contrast. In the first the symptom of intellectual inhibition

10 It is hardly necessary to justify this substitution here. One argument only may be quoted. In mythology, where all inventions and discoveries are either inspired or considered as products of a Promethean impulse, a number of typical legends occur in which the acquisition of new insight or a new conquest in the fight against nature is either ascribed to some father imago (to some great teacher), or else to Chance as a *locum tenens*.

11 A closer investigation of the circumstances favoring creative activities seems, for instance, to prove that certain habits—they might be called the "working" or "creative" habits of an individual—are no less full of meaning than his sleeping or any other habits.

is of a comparatively simple structure—the structure only is to be considered—in the second the process used is akin to inspiration.

The first patient, a man in his early forties, has had a fairly successful professional career. He is a learner, an examination type, and has endeavored to add to his name a variety of letters—many more than his father, who had worked successfully in the same field. The rivalry with this beloved father dominates all the spheres of the patient's activity. His whole life is a somewhat exaggerated repetition of his father's life, and his obedience to his father's principles and moral conceptions has taken a turn toward caricature. He distorts any father figure he meets in his life by means of the mechanism of projection and he then fights the dummy he has set up. This fight is clearest in the intellectual field. While his faculty for learning is extreme and his records in cramming have won him admiration—his memory is extraordinary and literally every other word he speaks is a quotation—he feels entirely unable to think for himself and is actually shaken by anxiety when faced with a new problem. His first impulse is to seek help, some authority to quote: in terms of instinctual life, some formula to take in and then to apply. But sometimes, under special conditions, he tries to fight that authority. Any success in this fight—his outlook is in many ways a modern one, almost that of a revolutionary—has the greatest emotional value. It is an achievement more desirable than any other. "And I have at last found that out for myself," he will exclaim in deep excitement. It is a victory in a conflict, a victory of activity over passivity, and as such an almost exact repetition of certain of his attempts to overcome the shock of circumcision, experienced in his fifth year, though traces of this attitude were discernible in some much older material, in aggressive impulses connected with anal experiences.

The second case concerns a man in his thirties who, among many other difficulties, shows an almost complete inhibition in working, which forms a severe impediment to his career as a scientific worker.[12] While any kind of routine work is easily achieved, any form of creative activity is associated with extreme difficulties and accompanied by a number of severe physical and mental symptoms. These difficulties are partly determined by an unconscious identification with his father, which follows the line of aggressiveness and guilt. Whereas his grandfather, whose tradition he wishes to continue, had been a famous academic teacher, his father has, owing to an inhibition in his powers of scientific research, failed to reach high academic honors. More interesting, however, than

---

[12] For a fuller account of this case, see now Kris (1951 a).

this part of the problem are the patient's attempts to overcome the inhibition. I should like to mention two of them. He can attempt productive work if, by means of alcohol or drugs, he has worked himself up into a state of excitement, in which work is done in a rapture. The second method is more complicated. He manages to find some authority in his own or in a neighboring field of research whom he induces to give him some advice about his work. His reaction to this advice is twofold. He endeavors to prove its futility, or he is afraid of committing a plagiarism. Closer analysis, however, shows that his wish to take away another person's ideas is no stronger than his fear that his own ideas may be used by this same person or by someone else. And furthermore the advice he gets is exactly the sort of advice he wants to get, the sort of advice which he had, in fact, himself suggested. Here the mechanisms of projection and introjection are at work and the process is akin to inspiration, one of the differences being that instead of "an unseen collaborator" —to use Stevenson's words—the collaborator is a person in the outside world. No less than the first method, that of oral gratification, the second method, the "taking advice" and dealing with it, produces states of marked general excitement. In these states the whole pace of his life seems to be accelerated. His attitude is changed. Indeed, one is almost tempted in this connection to use the word "inspired." As regards the historical background it may be briefly added that analogous tendencies expressed themselves in his latency period when he stole books from his father in order to buy sweets; they were rooted in childhood in a passive oral fantasy of incorporating his father's penis.[13]

In both of these cases a homosexual fantasy forms the background of experiences in the intellectual field, the sexualization being obviously responsible for the failures. The climax in the old fantasy is replaced in the first case by the intellectual fight and the deep satisfaction which eventually ensues, in the second case by the states of excitement. In this second case, however, the aggressive meaning of creative activity leads to the quest for an authority, whose advice frequently represents the pa-

[13] The phase of analysis which deals with these problems was *initiated* by a dream in which the conflict with his father was represented as a fight in which books were used as weapons. The oral-aggressive impulse persisted almost undisturbed in the patient's predilection for eating brains.—Since the publication of this paper (1939) Bergler has stressed the importance of the defense against oral impulses ("oral masochism") in numerous clinical contributions dealing in part with the psychology of "writers." I am inclined to view these findings and earlier ones by Brill (1931) in relation to Freud's suggestions on structural characteristics in the "artist," which might in varying degrees of intensity apply to creative individuals in many fields. See pp. 25f.

tient's own ideas. Here, *si parva licet componere magnis,* lies the analogy with the state of inspiration in the full metaphorical sense.[14]

The sexual character of the concept of fertilization through respiratory functions, which is the nucleus of inspiration in its literal sense, has been discussed by Ernest Jones (1914).[15] He has stressed the fact "that respiratory processes tend to be interpreted in the unconscious in terms of alimentary ones" and "that breath receives much of its importance . . . through the conception of internal pneuma." He has described how the conception of the soul derives from that of anal procreation "which has gradually been purged from all material grossness" until the "purest and least sexual form of procreation, the one most befitting the creator himself," has been established. While this purification, as described by Jones, was mostly concerned with the pregenital implication connected with the fertilizing power of breath, the various meanings of inspiration with which we began show how the purification is concerned here with the elimination of the sexual implication. In the full metaphorical sense inspiration implies a state of a sometimes scarcely veiled sexual character which is best exemplified by reports of the changes in sex actually occurring with the shahmans of certain Mongolian tribes.[16] The sexual connotation, however, has disappeared in the second stage of the metaphorical usage. Here inspiration designates a process of ego activity only, the sudden appearance of ideas. In the third stage, when we speak, for instance, of the inspiring effect of leadership, emphasis is laid once again on a libidinal relationship. But this libidinal relationship concerns the superego. Thus we may say that the various meanings of the word inspiration seem to be differentiated by a varying degree of desexualization.

This point of view, however, does not concern the various meanings of the word inspiration only. The states of inspiration themselves may be more or less sexual in character and where inspiration is an element in creative activities of any kind a certain degree of desexualization seems to be a precondition of success. The spirit of language, however, the connotations attached to respiratory functions, direct our attention to another point: to the importance of pregenital elements in fantasies connected with inspiration. It is my impression that this is a never absent feature of these fantasies. Instead of discussing the clinical evidence here, I should like to recall Housman's words: the "natural secretion like

---

14 We may here recall that one of the main effects of inspiration in primitive society is that of relieving the feeling of anxiety and thus of appeasing the guilty feelings connected with creation.

15 For further clinical evidence see Fenichel (1931), and now Greenacre (1951).

16 Some details have been given by Maenchen-Helffen (San Francisco) in a lecture delivered in 1937 before the Academic Association for Medical Psychology in Vienna.

turpentine in the fire" or the "morbid secretion like the pearl in the oyster," the bubbling up from an abyss, "the pit of the stomach," and "the pint of beer" which initiates the process, speak for themselves. The process of inspiration is here clearly expressed in oral, intestinal and anal terms. This is not astonishing if we think that on the level of pregenital meaning creation itself signifies anal production. But the pregenital elements in the fantasies connected with inspiration stand in a special framework. The fantasies—I can speak only of men—are centered around the father and around the conflict between active and passive tendencies.[17] While in autobiographical descriptions of creative states pregenital connotations are frequently implied or even expressed, as in Housman's words, the relation to the father figure is better hidden. In Housman's skeptical self-analysis this part of the fantasy seems to have found an expression in the following words: "I have rarely written poetry unless I was rather out of health, and the experience, though pleasurable, was generally agitating and exhausting." This is the description of a process in which passivity is indeed supreme. In terms of our theory we might say: the path leads from anal activity to homosexual passivity and thus another well-known meaning of creation is evoked—that of giving birth to a child.

At this point a number of problems arise which I shall not be able to approach in this connection.[18] I think, however, that at least two of them should be mentioned. How far are pregenital experiences themselves responsible for such fantasies as the one which found its expression in Housman's words and how far is the pregenital element due to regression? That is to say, how far have they kept their older meaning and how far are they influenced by the fact that the individual has reverted from the genital to an earlier stage? This question is connected with a second one. The process of inspiration being based upon the reintrojection of what was formerly projected, it may be asked how far this process is in itself influenced by earlier experiences of using the same mechanisms, especially as "the voice of the unconscious," which is externalized, contains results of former introjections.

The answer to these questions is obviously linked up with the discussion of the theories presented in the last decade mainly by Melanie Klein, Ernest Jones—especially in his paper on the phallic phase (1933)—Joan Riviere and other British psychoanalysts. Though

[17] I would now be inclined to stress that the passive attitude to the father revives the older passive attitude to the mother. See Kris (1951 b), where the discussion concerning the use of the words passive and active is carried one step further. See also here, p. 317.

[18] One of these problems concerns the process of inspiration in women, another is the problem of adolescence, during which states of inspiration are of great frequency.

it is obvious that no attempt can be made here to approach the questions raised in these researches, it is my impression that in the fantasies connected with inspiration the genital elaboration of pregenital experiences is evident, and that the pregenital layers constitute nothing specific.[19] It is clearly impossible here to discuss this specificity in a strict sense, which would enable us to predict what kind of people are likely to experience inspiration. It is meant for the framework of fantasies and mechanisms connected with inspiration as compared with similar elements in several other somewhat comparable emotional conditions. Such conditions include the various kinds of visionary states, various states of grace and possession, and especially the state of ecstasy. I am inclined to believe that in all these states the fantasies are of the same general nature, especially in so far as the use of projection and introjection is concerned; in all of them they are desexualized and raised to the plane of a mental process. The state nearest to inspiration is ecstasy. "What had been projected as a vision of God is now in ecstasy taken back into the ego, but not as an antithesis between ego and super-ego or between ego and God: ego and God are one." This description, given by Helene Deutsch (1927), could be applied as such to the first of the steps constituting inspiration in its full metaphorical meaning.[20] We have tried to show that there is another, a second step connected with it: that the driving of the unconscious toward consciousness is experienced as an intrusion from without—an attitude of a passive nature *par excellence*. The decisive difference, however, can be formulated more clearly. In ecstasy the process results in an emotional climax only; in states of inspiration it leads to active elaboration in creation.[21] The process is dominated by the ego and put to its own purposes—for sublimation in creative activity.[22] Thus inspired creation solves an inner contest, sometimes as a compromise between conflicting forces, sometimes as a defense against one particularly dangerous instinct. Where man seems to be at the peak of his activity, in creation, he is still sometimes inclined to bend his head to the Almighty and to be carried back to the period when dependence on objects in the outside world dominated his life.

19 See Chapter 14, particularly pp. 314ff.

20 See now also H. B. Lee (1949 b, p. 241), who stresses "that it is the reconciliation with conscience and with its projections as God or Muse, which permits the creating ego to view its work as revealed from an outside source and which results in the pleasure of the quality which we call spiritual." "The Muse is, of course, none other than the projection to the supernatural of the idealized mother" (1948, p. 515). H. B. Lee's views are in this respect similar to those of Bergler (1950).

21 Ecstasy seems more frequent among women, inspiration among men.

22 For an identical formulation see now Mosse (1951).

Chapter 14

ON PRECONSCIOUS MENTAL PROCESSES

I. INTRODUCTION

In recent psychoanalytic writings preconscious mental processes are rarely mentioned, even when fundamentals are discussed (Alexander, 1948). In publications further removed from psychoanalytic experience, the psychoanalytic connotations of the term "preconscious" are entirely lost.[1] This would not be remarkable or invite comment were it not that, in the area of ego psychology, certain aspects of preconscious mental activity have been studied with greater care and by a larger number of investigators than ever before in the history of psychoanalysis: to quote Freud's last formulation on the subject, ". . . the inside of the ego which comprises above all the intellectual processes has the quality of being preconscious" (1939, p. 42).

The reciprocal relationship between the development of ego psychology and therapeutic technique has not only led to an increased concern with the "psychic surface" and many details of behavior, but also to specific advice as to the handling of the relationship of preconscious to unconscious material in therapy, advice that is sometimes too rigidly formulated, and yet eminently important. Briefly stated, this advice is to wait until what you wish to interpret is close to consciousness, until it is preconscious (Freud, 1939). One may object that this example from psychoanalytic technique proves that our interest in preconscious processes is not "genuine" or independent, but that these processes seem important only as far as they facilitate access to an understanding of unconscious processes, the "real" subject matter of psychoanalysis. This objection is reminiscent of a period in psychoanalysis when interest was centered on the id, when only the repressed was considered as "real" psychic material, when defense was seen as a screen, resistance was considered a force of evil, and when what was a phase in

[1] Murray (1938) distinguishes between preconscious and unconscious processes, without using the term preconscious; Murphy (1947) speaks of unconscious and preconscious processes without distinction.

the development of psychoanalysis was declared to be the only legitimate and relevant field of psychoanalytic investigation. Anna Freud's felicitous formulation (1936) of the equal distribution of interest between the id, the ego, the superego and reality stimulated and enhanced the attitude of clinical psychoanalysis. This equal distribution of interest most definitely embraces rational thought and fantasy in their interrelations with conflict and—at least recently—in their significance as manifestations of the individual's capacity to act in a sphere free from conflict (Hartmann, 1939 a). I therefore conclude that not preconscious mental processes generally, but only certain aspects of these processes have recently been less explicitly discussed. The term, rather than the phenomena, and certain of the theoretical connotations of the term have become unpopular.

It seems to me that in reëxamining some of the theoretical problems connected with preconscious mental processes in the context of current knowledge, we may gain access to implications of psychoanalytic theory that deserve increased attention. Before us lies the project which Freud started when in the eighteen-nineties he planned a treatise of which a draft has recently come to light (Freud, 1950) : a psychoanalytic psychology, normal and abnormal.

II. Problems and Main Assumptions

One of the immediate reasons for the relative neglect of preconscious mental processes may well lie in the history of psychoanalytic theory. Freud's ideas were constantly developing, his writings represent a sequence of reformulations, and one might therefore well take the view that the systematic cohesion of psychoanalytic propositions is only, or at least best, accessible through their history. The clearest instance of such a reformulation was the gradual introduction of structural concepts. The introduction of these new concepts has never fully been integrated with the broad set of propositions developed earlier. Many of Freud's views on preconscious mental processes are contained in writings (1915-1917) in which he discusses functions of the system Pcs, later attributed to the ego. In sharp contrast to these early formulations stands Freud's later consideration of "preconscious" merely as a "mental quality" (1932 a, 1939) .

In defining the quality of the preconscious, Freud follows Breuer: preconscious is what is "capable of becoming conscious," and he adds, "capable of becoming conscious easily and under conditions which frequently arise." It is different from unconscious processes "in the case of which such a transformation is difficult, can only come about with considerable expenditure of energy or may never occur" (1932 a, p. 96). However, this general differentiation is a somewhat simplified rendering of complex problems which Freud discussed in other of his writings. Three of these problems have here been selected for brief discussion.

First, not all preconscious processes reach consciousness with equal ease. Some can only be recaptured with considerable effort. What differences exist between the former and the latter?

Second, preconscious mental processes are extremely different from each other both in content and in the kind of thought processes used; they cover continua reaching from purposeful reflection to fantasy, and from logical formulation to dream-like imagery. How can these differences be accounted for?

Third, when preconscious material emerges into consciousness the reaction varies greatly. The process may not be noticed—the usual reaction if the preconscious process is readily available to consciousness. But emergence into consciousness can be accompanied by strong emotional reactions. How may we account for these reactions?

The theoretical assumptions made to differentiate preconscious from unconscious mental processes have varied considerably. At a time when Freud still characterized the preconscious as a functional system, he considered verbalization as one of its functions.[2] Unconscious thoughts, he believed, had to pass through the stage of verbalization on their way to consciousness; feelings could reach consciousness "directly" (1915 a, b). Freud later avoided the obvious pitfalls of this assumption: "The presence of speech gives a safe clue to the preconscious nature of the process . . ." but ". . . the connection with a verbal memory trace cannot be considered as a prerequisite" (1939, p. 43). The difference between preconscious and unconscious mental processes, however, is explained by assumptions concerning the nature of the prevalent psychic energy: unconscious processes use mobile psychic energy; preconscious processes bound energy. The two degrees of mobility correspond to two types of discharge characterized as the primary and secondary processes. We are thus faced with the delimitation between the id and the ego. Note that two sets of assumptions are here suggested by Freud (the types of energy, free and bound, and the types of discharge, the primary and secondary processes) to account for the same events; the formulation in terms of energy permits differentiations in degree, in shading; the formulation in terms of process states extremes. Hypotheses of transi-

---

2 See Nunberg (1932), who treats the system Pcs and the ego as parallel concepts.

tions between extremes seem to me, to Hartmann (1950) and, possibly for other reasons, to Rapaport (1950), preferable.[3]

The assumption that the ego directs countercathexes against the id is essential to any study of preconscious mental processes; also essential is the assumption that a preconscious process from which the ego withdraws cathexis becomes subject to cathexis with id (mobile) energy and will be drawn into the primary process (the basic assumption of the psychoanalytic theory of dream formation). The reverse (unconscious material becomes preconscious) occurs when id derivatives are cathected with ego energy and become part of preconscious mental processes at a considerable distance from the original impulse. They may do so if changes in the distribution of countercathexis have taken place, e.g., if the level of conflict has been reduced and the id impulse has become more acceptable; also, they may sometimes enter preconscious mental processes at a considerable price in terms of symptoms. Id contents may also reach consciousness without ever becoming preconscious. Metaphorically speaking, they may become accessible to the ego not from within but from without. They then appear as percepts, acquiring at once, as it were, the hypercathexis required for consciousness. This is an abnormal (or rare) pathway to consciousness, the pathway of hallucination. We consider it by contrast as normal when preconscious material reaches consciousness by a further increase in cathexis, the hypercathexis mediated by attention. In some cases, however, this hypercathexis cannot become effective without considerable effort. This is the reason why we assume the working—at the passage into consciousness—of countercathectic energies that would prevent what is, to some extent, ego-dystonic from entering full awareness.

III. RECOGNITION, RECALL, AND INTEGRATION

The conditions under which ego-dystonic preconscious material may reach consciousness have in psychoanalysis been studied in many contexts, mainly in relation to lapses of memory, and in psychoanalytic therapy when a dream, a thought, or a fantasy is about to elude recall or has done so. It is well known that in these instances voluntary effort or concentration of attention does not always succeed in recapturing elusory thought. But when such an attempt fails, self-observation may be successful in pitting one ego function against another and achieve its end by reëstablishing links that have been lost: the various stages of the pre-

---

[3] Freud was naturally aware of this problem. He explicitly stated (1917) that the primary process is unknown to preconscious thinking, or rarely admissible.

conscious thought process are repeated, until, so to speak, the chain again hangs firmly together. This process can best be studied in situations in which the thought process and the self-observation occur in distinct phases; for instance, when subjects, preferably analyzed, interpret their own "doodling."[4] The report of such an instance permitted insight into the stages of recapture.

A woman of forty, successfully psychoanalyzed, reported at the end of treatment that though she had never had any training in drawing, she was in the habit of "doodling," particularly when concentrating on some external stimulus. During a concert she was "doodling" on the program —one of her preferred patterns—a flower with three leaves. This time, however, she drew only two; then the "drawing hand became independent" and when later she looked at the product, she found a variety of ornaments all varying the theme of two or three leaves. The external circumference of the leaves formed a semicircle, but their tips never touched each other. The patient was able to interpret its meaning. After an interrruption of many months she had had a menstrual period. She had been worried, and treatment with hormones had had no effect. The "doodling" revealed the reaction to the reappearance of menstruation. The absence of the third leaf represented lack of intercourse during menstruation. The leaves that almost touched each other represented "the egg cell that is about to burst open." The patient now recalled that the thought whether or not to have a third child disturbed her during the initial phases of the concert. She reported that soon after having started to "doodle" she was able to listen with great ease and pleasure. This seemed to indicate a frequent if not a regular circumstance: the ideas hidden in "doodles" are often ideas of which the ego wants to liberate itself.

While in this case the attempt at recapturing a trend of thought by recapitulation of its stages proceeded consciously, this process frequently remains preconscious and only its results reach awareness. Without any further instances, many analysts are likely to share the impression that what we describe as concatenation of free associations leading to a missing link in the patient's thoughts frequently—though perhaps not regularly—indicates that the patient's ego has preconsciously already established a unity of context, or reëstablished its control over an ego-dystonic impulse or area of thought.[5] Frequently this control can be

4 See pp. 90ff.
5 For the general theory of free associations in psychoanalysis see Hartmann (1927), Bernfeld (1934).

established only by analytic interpretation that indicates the context which, in other structurally simpler cases, was established by self-observation. The psychic concatenation, or the establishing of the unity of context, is due to the synthetic function of the ego;[6] we are thus faced with a general principle that may well deserve to be reëmphasized. It is valid for the analytic process as a whole, not only for its parts. Cases in which during analysis material recurs which requires interpretation at repeated intervals are attributed to a lack of assimilation of the interpretation, or of the material, and indicate that the synthetic function of the ego is insufficiently established. Conversely, progress in analysis can frequently be described as successful assimilation preventing renewed repression.[7]

The preconscious process that is under the control of the synthetic function of the ego is safe against withdrawal of preconscious cathexis and hence against repression; as a rule it has effortless access to consciousness.

This hypothesis is not limited to the dynamics prevailing in psychological lapses of memory or tongue; it applies to the dynamics of the wider field of analytic observation. One aspect of psychoanalytic therapy is best described by focusing on the patient's ability to recall the past: "[If] the interpretation has removed obstacles to recall, the forgotten memory can take its place within awareness. It is naturally not assumed that in such cases the interpretation produced recall; rather the situation existing previous to the interpretation, the one which suggested the interpretation, must be described as incomplete recall (and therefore, as in some measure similar to the situation in which the memory trace was laid down). Interpretation therefore acts here as a help in the completion of recall. Incomplete recall had announced itself by a variety of signs in the individual's behavior . . ." (Kris, 1947) —which the interpretation uses to reconstruct the original event from which the behavioral pattern was derived. The aim of similar steps in interpretation can be accurately described by the term "recognition," frequently used in the study of memory. When recall is not yet possible, recognition may already be accomplished. The vicissitudes of the relationship between recognition and recall are particularly familiar in reconstructions of infantile experiences. While few, if any, case histories go to the length to which Freud went when, in the case of the Wolf-man, he studied

---

6 Nunberg (1931). For a distinction between synthetic and organizing (integrative) function see Hartmann (1939 a, 1947).

7 See Nunberg (1937); French (1936, 1945). The later repression of phases of a successful analysis, while little investigated, does not contradict this view.

the reactions of the patient to various alternative reconstructions (1918), it seems to be the general experience that in many instances reconstructions must be varied and modified until they are correct. These various steps may all be described in terms of stages in the interaction of recognition and recall.

The suggestion that historical interpretations in analysis stimulate memory to recognition leading to recall is in accord with experimental findings. These experiments show how recognition improves recall or guarantees retention.[8] The theoretical, psychoanalytic explanation of the relationship between recognition and recall is that the synthetic function of the ego, establishing a context, is in the case of recognition facilitated by the help of perception (in our example, the analyst's interpretation). Recall then fills a gap, fits into a pattern.

If we examine the function of recognition in relation to mental qualities, an initial formulation suggests itself: what can be mobilized in recognition must have been preconscious. I should like to stress this formulation and to consider it as well established; and yet, it might be advantageous not to apply it too rigidly. We are familiar with cases in which a historical interpretation gradually—sometimes over extended periods of treatment—opens the way to the recall of repressed material. The complexity of the interdependent factors during the psychoanalytic process is such that we can surely not assume that any one single operation is responsible for major dynamic changes; thus any release from repression depends on the strength of defenses used for the purposes of countercathexis which, in turn, depends on the ego's capacity to cope with the prevailing intensity of conflict. It seems therefore reasonable to assume that facilitation of the ego's integrative or synthetic function by recognition is one of the dynamic factors leading to recall.[9]

The relation of recognition to recall of the repressed can be tentatively described in these terms: since the "original" situation has been recognized, previously not sufficiently invested id derivatives can be integrated into the pattern indicated by the reconstruction; this in turn strengthens the ego's position, permits a reduction of countercathexes and the gradual infiltration of further material—a result in the end not

[8] The unfortunate limitation of these investigations to nonsense syllables makes it difficult to establish closer links between the laboratory findings and psychoanalytic observations (Postman et al., 1948).

[9] When Alexander and French, in recent publications, claim that recall of the repressed is not the reason for an increase in the integrative function of the ego but a consequence of it (1946, pp. 287 ff.), they have not improved the view they contradict; the two factors are better described as dependent variables. They constitute what modern theory of logic terms circular causality.

dissimilar to sudden recall, in cases in which the interpretation has led to the spectacular revival of repressed traumata. In both types of cases the full investment by the ego, the syntonicity of the event with superego and id strivings may then lead to the feeling of certainty, to the change from "I know of" to "I believe." With such expressions Lewin (1939) contrasts two levels of analytic experience. He links the second, that of certitude, to the reëstablishment of infantile omniscience. From the point of view of the present deliberation we attribute the triumph of believing to the complete investment by the ego, to what in Freud's terms might well be described as essential progress in the individual's mental organization.

IV. DISCHARGE AND REGRESSION

It is a strange fact that, in spite of all varieties of clinical experience which throw light on preconscious mental processes, the main source of reference for many of these processes should have remained for almost thirty years a book of the Belgian psychologist Varendonck, entitled *The Psychology of Daydreams* (1921), which reports a great variety of self-observed thought processes.[10] There are obvious and admitted gaps in Varendonck's reports. Upon closer inspection we discover a number of contradictions and suspect the influence of his character traits, a fact to which Rapaport has recently drawn my attention. What few theoretical views Varendonck develops are centered on two thoughts: the relation of all preconscious activity to wish fulfillment—mostly to the fulfillment of conscious wishes—and the assumption that preconscious mental processes follow laws of their own, sharply separated from the laws of conscious thinking.

The value of Varendonck's material consists in the fact that his reports cover a wide range of phenomena. We read of deliberations on the question of whom to choose as faculty reporter for his doctoral dissertation; of self-punitive fantasies in which he loses both legs in the attempt to escape from military service; of castles in Spain of a more conventional type. Many of Varendonck's fantasies are verbal only; others are full of imagery, and some replete with condensations and symbols that are to some degree reminiscent of dreams.

This variety cannot be ascribed to the personal qualities of one observer. Material from certain patients in psychoanalysis confirms such a variety in preconscious thinking. Unpublished experimental investiga-

10 For a systematic survey of the literature see recently Seeman (1951). Among the older writings a most stimulating paper by G. H. Mead (1925/1926) should be mentioned which opened new and wide perspectives.

tions (Rudel, 1949) show that, when asked to report their daydreams, college students record a variety of phenomena that represent what might be called the "stream of preconsciousness" in highly varied expressions of highly varied contents. These are the impressions that justify my introductory remarks on the existence of two continua, one reaching from solving problems to dreamlike fantasy, and one reaching from logical cohesive verbal statements to dreamlike imagery. Both continua, I believe, occur with some frequency in preconscious mental processes.

The first and up to now only relevant critical evaluation of Varendonck's book, from the psychoanalytic point of view, is Freud's introduction to it (1921). It has rarely, if ever, been quoted, and in the German translation of Varendonck's book it was not fully reproduced. In studying ". . . the mode of thought activity to which one abandons oneself during the state of distraction and into which we readily pass before sleep and upon incomplete awakening . . ." Varendonck has rendered a valuable service. While Freud appreciates confirmation found for his views on the psychology of dreams and "defective acts," he sharply opposes Varendonck's central thesis. Freud asserts that there is no difference between preconscious and conscious mental processes. What Varendonck calls daydreaming does not owe its peculiarities to ". . . the circumstance that it proceeds mostly preconsciously. . . . For that reason I think it is advisable, when establishing a distinction between the different modes of thought activity not to utilize the relation to consciousness in the first instance." Freud suggests that one should distinguish in daydreams, as well as in the chain of thoughts studied by Varendonck, freely wandering fantastic thinking as opposed to intentionally directed reflection, since it is known "that even strictly directed reflection may be achieved without the coöperation of consciousness."

If we take this distinction as our starting point and remember that the economic and structural approach, the study of cathexes and ego function, has proved its value in discussing problems in the psychology of preconscious mental processes, we are easily led to one area of deliberation. The ego, we assume, has two kinds of bound energy at its disposal: neutralized energy, and libido and aggression in their non-neutralized form (Hartmann, Kris, and Loewenstein, 1949). Fantastic, freely wandering thought processes tend to discharge more libido and aggression and less neutralized energy; purposeful reflection and solving problems, more neutralized energy. In fantasy, the processes of the ego are largely in the service of the id. Not only the id, however, is involved. Naturally, the superego and "narcissistic" strivings play their part. The content of freely wandering fantasies is extended over the pleasure-unpleasure continuum; hence the probability that in this kind of process, the discharge of nonneutralized libido and aggression will be maximized. In reflective thinking the contrary is likely. Reflective thinking, according to Freud (problem solving, as we would prefer to say), serves to a higher degree the autonomous ego interests. Discharge of libido and aggression is therefore likely to be minimized, and that of neutralized ego energy to be of greater relevance.[11]

We now turn to a brief discussion of the second continuum of preconscious thought processes, that which extends between logical verbalization and fantastic imagery; the hypnagogic fantasies to which Freud refers in the passage quoted above, some of Varendonck's wandering fantasies, and fantasies of the more fanciful patients in psychoanalysis designate the area of the phenomena in question. We are clearly dealing with problems of ego regression.

The very fact that such phenomena of ego regression are infinitely more frequent in fantasy than in deliberative preconscious processes suggests that in fantasy the discharge of libido and aggression may have in general a greater proximity to the id—to mobile energy discharges. The id, as it were, intrudes upon ego functions.

Topographically, ego regression (primitivization of ego functions) occurs not only when the ego is weak—in sleep, in falling asleep, in fantasy, in intoxication, and in the psychoses—but also during many types of creative processes. This suggested to me years ago that the ego may use the primary process and not be only overwhelmed by it.[12] This idea was rooted in Freud's explanation of wit (1905 a) according to which a preconscious thought "is entrusted for a moment to unconscious elaboration," and seemed to account for a variety of creative or other inventive processes. However, the problem of ego regression during creative processes represents only a special problem in a more general area. The general assumption is that under certain conditions the ego regulates regression, and that the integrative functions of the ego include voluntary and temporary withdrawal of cathexis from one area or another to regain improved control (Hartmann, 1939 a, b, 1947). Our theory of sleep is based upon the assumption of such a withdrawal of cathexis. Sexual functions presuppose similar regressive patterns, and the inability to such suspension of ego control constitutes one of the well-known symptoms of obsessional, compulsive characters.

The clinical observation of creators and the study of introspective

11 Alternatively one might speak here of "degrees of neutralization" of the energy discharged; see Hartmann (1950).

12 See here pp. 26ff.

reports of experiences during creative activity tend to show that we are faced with a shift in the cathexis of certain ego functions. Thus a frequent distinction is made between an inspirational and an "elaborational" phase in creation.[13] The inspirational phase is characterized by the facility with which id impulses, or their closer derivatives, are received. One might say that countercathectic energies to some extent are withdrawn, and added to the speed, force, or intensity with which the preconscious thoughts are formed. During the "elaborational" phase, the countercathectic barrier may be reinforced, work proceeds slowly, cathexis is directed to other ego functions such as reality testing, formulation, or general purposes of communication. Alternations between the two phases may be rapid, oscillating, or distributed over long stretches of time.

In ascribing to the ego the control of regression in terms of shifts in the cathexis of ego functions, which can be related to or pitted against each other in various ways, we gain a frame of reference that might in the present tentative state of our knowledge prove useful in various ways. Consider, for example, the shift of cathexis between the ego function of perception (the system Pcpt) and preconscious thought. The individual, immersed in preconscious thought, takes less notice of his environment. Idle fantasies are given such a pejorative description as decrease of attention or, with Freud, of being distracted by fantasy. At this point we seem to gain a further and improved understanding of one problem. It is generally assumed that preconscious thought processes become conscious by hypercathexis. We now realize that there are various degrees of hypercathexis. If energy is diverted from the perceiving function of the ego to fantasy, this in itself may not lead to consciousness but simply to an intensification of the preconscious process. Emergence into consciousness would still be dependent on other conditions.

The automatic functions of the ego are commonly considered to include a special kind of preconscious processes which become conscious only in the case of danger or under other special requirements (Hartmann, 1939 a). Consciousness in these instances is no guarantee of improved function; on the contrary, automatic (habit) responses in driving automobiles or the use of tools, for instance, seem to have undoubted advantages. Similarly, the shift from consciousness to preconsciousness may account for the experience of clarification that occurs when after intense concentration the solution to an insoluble problem suddenly presents itself following a period of rest. Briefly, we suggest that the hypercathexis of preconscious mental activity with some quantity of

---

[13] See Chapter 13.

energy withdrawn from the object world to the ego—from the system Pcpt to preconscious thinking—accounts for some of the extraordinary achievements of mentation.[14]

V. Reactions to Reaching Consciousness

The appropriateness of describing thought processes in terms of cathexis and discharge is further supported if we turn to some reactions of individuals upon becoming conscious of their preconscious fantasies or of the result of their preconscious productive deliberation.[15]

The privileges of fantasy are manifold. When fantasy has taken us far afield we do not as a rule experience shame or guilt—shame, for instance, for having arrogated some of the properties of infantile omnipotence, guilt because the fantasy may have been ruthless and antisocial. Patients may feel ashamed or guilty in reporting such fantasies, although they did not feel so while they were engaged in them or when they recalled them. There is a feeling of not being responsible for one's fantasies.

Tentatively, we assume that in preoccupation with fantasy the ego withdraws cathexis from some functions of the superego. Our knowledge does not permit us to be more specific. One gains the impression that while the ego ideal loses its importance for the individual, the punitive tendencies of the superego are enforced[16] in some for whom self-punitive measures are part of the fantasy. In others the hypercathexis of the ego ideal is predominant, while the function of critical self-observation seems reduced.

The absolution from guilt for fantasy is complete if the fantasy one follows is not one's own. This accounts for the role of the bard in primitive society and, in part, for the function of fiction, drama, etc., in our society. Opportunity for discharge or catharsis is guiltlessly borrowed. A close study of the phenomenology of the subjective experiences connected with fantasy, autogenous or borrowed, tends to confirm the opinion that feelings of relief (temporary or protracted), or of saturation (and final disgust), can all easily be explained by well-known psychodynamics.

---

[14] For a good descriptive summary of these achievements see Delacroix (1939). Recent literature has added particularly striking observations in the field of mathematical inventions; see Hadamard (1949) and McCulloch (1949).

[15] Not all reactions to "becoming conscious" are here considered; "negation" and the "feeling of uncanniness," for instance, are purposely omitted.

[16] Alternatively, one might say neutralized energy is withdrawn from the superego; aggressive energy remains vested in it and leads to unpleasure in fantasy.

A feeling of relief and discharge, similar to that provided by fantasy, can also be gained when the successful solution of a problem has been achieved—when a piece of preconscious deliberation has come to a satisfactory conscious conclusion. The indisputable satisfaction which attends the solution of a problem is usually described in terms of the gratification of a sense of mastery, feelings of triumph from achievements related to ego interests (Hartmann, 1950), feelings of self-esteem which reduce intrapsychic tension as between superego and ego, etc. It seems useful to consider in addition the possibility that the solution of problems—including all areas of creativity—affords pleasure through the discharge of neutral energy used in the pursuit of creative thinking.[17] This consideration is new neither in psychoanalysis nor elsewhere in psychology. It is frequently referred to as functional pleasure.[18] When Freud's interest was still close to the investigation of the psychology of thinking, he stated in *Wit and Its Relation to the Unconscious*: "When our psychic apparatus does not actually act in search of some urgently needed gratifications we let this apparatus itself work for pleasure gain. *We attempt to gain pleasure from its very activity.*" There can be little doubt that the activity to which Freud refers is chiefly the discharge of quantities of neutralized energy. An elaboration of this theory seemed to lead to improved understanding of aesthetic experience.[19]

The gradual steps in the slow . maturation of solving a problem sometimes extend over years. There is a considerable similarity or analogy between some aspects of this problem of thought formation and the problem of preconscious lapses. A solution once found may be forgotten, return after some time and be fitted into its frame of reference, or it may never again be recaptured. Undoubtedly combinations of all psychodynamic factors may interact to produce such results; and yet such forgetting, such selectivity of memory may be due also to a lack of integration necessary for the solution of the problem.

The appropriate material for the study of these phenomena is the history of science, and what Gestalt psychology can contribute has recently been tested in describing the development of Einstein's theory (Wertheimer, 1945).

Freud's recently published *Aus den Anfängen der Psychoanalyse* pro-

[17] In speaking of the pleasurable discharge of neutral energy we assume that this energy need not be ideally—i.e., fully—bound and that the degree of immobility and neutralization of energy may be to some extent independent variables (Hartmann, 1950).

[18] For other aspects of functional pleasure, see p. 210.

[19] See here, p. 63.

vides an opportunity to study some of these problems in relation to psychoanalysis itself. This book consists of a series of intimate letters, notes, essays, and drafts written by Freud between 1887 and 1902. During these years Freud reports to a correspondent the emergence of new ideas and their subsequent slipping away, also, about premonitions of hypotheses to come, and a large set of related phenomena. In 1895 Freud became aware of the main psychological mechanism of dream formation and established a link between the dream mechanism and symptom formation. But his theory of symptom formation was then incomplete and in large part unusable, and the link between the two was dropped. For two years Freud forgot that he had once seen this connection, and he treated dream and neurosis as disconnected and alternative fields of his interest until in 1897 he temporarily reëstablished the connection, forgot it again, and only one year later fully established it, experiencing what in fact was a rediscovery, as a great and triumphant revelation. It took three years to safeguard this finding against lapses of memory, as it was only at the end of this period that the theory was integrated, infantile sexuality was discovered, and the problem of regression made accessible to closer investigation.

Examples of this kind indicate that only when the ego has completed its synthetic function by eliminating contradiction within the theory are the parts of the theory protected against slipping from conscious awareness. We may now revise and amplify the conditions required to eliminate the countercathexis between preconsciousness and consciousness. To the two conditions stated—ego syntonicity and full cathexis with neutral energy as prerequisites and consequences of integration[20]—we now add that ego syntonicity consists not only of freedom from conflict in the intersystemic sense (id and superego), but also in the intrasystemic sense (Hartmann, 1950) in relation to the various ego functions. In solving problems, the feeling of fitting propositions together satisfies the requirement of the synthetic function; critical examination of the context satisfies the requirements of reality testing in an extended sense.[21]

To return from this detour to the central question of reactions to the reaching of awareness of preconscious thought processes, let me repeat that normally there is an absence of reactions. In many instances of both fantasy and creativity, discharge and satisfaction can be experienced.

[20] The degree of cathexis with libido or aggression is clearly variable and related to ego syntonicity.

[21] In this direction lies the further psychoanalytic exploration of reactions to completed tasks and incompleted ones, i.e., to a topic which has been treated with great insistence by experimental psychologists.

The mere feeling of relief is more manifest in fantasy, a mixture of relief and satisfaction more evident in creativity and solving problems. But there are instances in which these same experiences appear in a special form, in which the feeling exists that awareness comes from the outside world. This is obviously true of hallucinations, but it is also true of revelation or inspiration.[22] In revelation or inspiration a preconscious thought is attributed to an outside agent from which it has been passively received. The literal and the attenuated meanings of the term form a continuum; we speak of inspiration also when a percept stimulates thought. Newton, who attributed the discovery of the law of gravity to the observation of a falling apple, is an instance. The perception there acted as a factor precipitating previously organized preconscious ideas waiting for the stimulus.[23]

Why do creators of all kinds so often prefer to attribute their achievements to the influence of such external agents as chance, fate, or a divine providence? One motivation is avoidance of the wrath and envy of the gods; but there are other more significant and deeper motivations. The feeling of full control and discharge of tension in the state of becoming aware of significant ideas or achievements mobilizes deep layers of the personality. In the case of ecstatic revelation the hallucinatory character of the experience is manifest.

We believe that in the process of becoming conscious the preconsciously prepared thought is sexualized, which accounts for the experiences accompanying revelation. Id energies suddenly combine with ego energies, mobile with bound and neutralized cathexes, to produce the unique experience of inspiration which is felt to reach consciousness from the outside. Unconscious fantasies at work in some specific instances of these experiences can be reconstructed, and in Chapter 13 I tried to demonstrate the variety of experiences that are derived from the repressed fantasy of being impregnated and particularly of incorporating the paternal phallus. It has since become plausible that additional fantasies are involved. The feeling of triumph and release from tension remind the individual of a phase in his development in which passivity was a precondition of total gratification, and in which the hallucinated wish fulfillment became reality: the period of nursing. We find here another approach to the full intensity of believing and its relation to infantile omniscience as described by Lewin: the analytic process and the insight it produces can be experienced in terms of an archaic wish ful-

22 See Chapter 13.

23 In a delightful chapter of his autobiography, Walter B. Cannon (1945) has described phenomena of this order under the heading: Gains From Serendipity.

fillment. Changes in cathexis during the working of the psychic apparatus tend, I suggest, to be generally experienced in terms of such an archetype. The maturing of thought, the entry into awareness from preconsciousness to consciousness tend to be experienced as derived from outside, as passively received, not as actively produced. The tendency toward passive reception takes various shapes and forms, appears under the guise of various modalities, but the subjective experience remains one of reception. When, after the completion of his theory of dreams, Freud was urged to publish his theories of sexuality, he answered to his urging friend: "If the theory of sexuality comes, I will listen to it."

This relationship between creativity and passivity exemplifies once more one of the leading theses of this presentation: the integrative functions of the ego include self-regulated regression and permit a combination of the most daring intellectual activity with the experience of passive receptiveness.

Bibliography and Index

BIBLIOGRAPHY

Abercrombie, L. 1926, *Theory of Poetry*. New York: Harcourt, Brace & Co.

Abraham, K. 1913, *Dreams and Myths*. New York: Nervous and Mental Disease Publication.

—— 1921, Contributions to the Theory of the Anal Character. *Selected Papers on Psycho-Analysis*. London: Hogarth Press. (New edition 1942.)

Adolf, H. 1951, The Essence and Origin of Tragedy. *The Journal of Aesthetics and Art Criticism*, X.

Alexander, F. 1933, A Note on Falstaff. *Psychoanalytic Quarterly*, II.

—— 1948, *Fundamentals of Psychoanalysis*. New York: W. W. Norton & Co.

—— and French, T. M. 1946, *Psychoanalytic Therapy*. New York: The Ronald Press.

Allport, G. W. 1942, *The Use of Personal Documents in Psychological Science*. Social Science Research Council Bulletin, 49.

Anastasi, A. and Foley, J. P., Jr. 1940-1942, A Survey of the Literature on Artistic Behavior in the Abnormal (in 4 parts):

    1941 (I), Historical and Theoretical Background, *Journal of General Psychology*, XXV.

    1941 (II), Approaches and Interrelationships. *Annals of the New York Academy of Sciences*, XLII.

    1940 (III), Spontaneous Productions. *Psychological Monographs*, LII, No. 6.

    1941 (IV), Experimental Investigations. *Journal of General Psychology*, XXV.

—— 1940, The Study of "Populist Paulers" As an Approach to the Psychology of Art. *Journal of Social Psychology*, XI.

—— 1943, An Analysis of Spontaneous Artistic Productions by the Abnormal. *Journal of General Psychology*, XXVIII.

—— 1944, An Experimental Study of the Drawing Behavior of Adult Psychotics in Comparison with That of a Normal Control Group. *Journal of Experimental Psychology*, XXXIV.

Anonymous 1898, *The Famous Victories of Henry the Fifth*. London: Thomas Crede.

Anthroposco, O. 1784, *Geschichte der Physiognomik*. Leipzig.

Arieti, S. 1950, New Views on the Psychology and Psychopalliology of Wit and the Comic. *Psychiatry*, XIII.

Aristotle, see Butcher, S. H.

Arlow, J. A. 1951, The Consecration of the Prophet. *Pschoanalytic Quarterly*, XX.

Arnheim, R. 1949, The Gestalt Theory of Expression. *Psychological Review*, LVI.

—— 1951, Perceptual and Aesthetic Aspects of the Movement Response. *Journal of Personality*, XIX.

Arundel, R. M. 1937, *Everybody Pixillated*. Boston: Little Brown.

Aschaffenburg, G. 1915, *Handbuch der Psychiatrie. Allgemeine Symptomatologie der Psychosen*. Allgemeiner Teil 3. Abteilung I. Leipzig und Wien: Franz Deuticke.

Ashbee, C. R. 1928, *Caricature*. London: Chapman & Hall.

Auden, W. H. 1948, My Guilty Vicarage: Notes on the Detective Story by an Addict. *Harpers Magazine*.

Audry, J. 1924, La folie dans l'art. Lyon: *Medical*.

Auerbach, J. G. 1950, Psychological Observations on Doodling in Neurotics. *Journal of Nervous and Mental Disease*, CVII.

Ax, H. 1912, *The Relation of Shakespeare's Henry IV to Holinshed's Chronicle*. Freiburg im Breisgau: D. Lauber.

Axelrad, S. and Maury, L. 1951, Identification as a Mechanism of Adaptation. In *Psychoanalysis and Culture*. Edited by G. B. Wilbur and W. Muensterberger. New York: International Universities Press.

Axelrad, S., see Ginzberg, E.

Baldinucci, G. 1681, *Vocabulario Toscano dell' arte del disegno*. Firenze.

—— 1682, *Vita del Cavalier G. L. Bernini*. Firenze.

Bartlett, E. M. 1937, *Types of Aesthetic Judgment*. London: George Allen and Unwin.

Bartlett, P. 1951, *Poems in Process*. New York: Oxford University Press.

Baudouin, C. 1929, *Psychanalyse de l'art*. Paris: Felix Alçan.

Baynes, H. G. 1940, *The Mythology of the Soul: A Research into the Unconscious from Schizophrenic Dreams and Drawings*. Baltimore: Williams and Wilkins. (Reissued, London: Methuen & Co., Ltd., 1949.)

Becker, P. E. 1934, Das Zeichnen Schizophrener. *Zeitschrift für die gesamte Neurologie und Psychiatrie*, CXLIV.

Bellak, L. 1945, On the Psychology of Detective Stories and Related Problems. *Psychoanalytic Review*, XXXII.

Bellori, G. 1672, *Le vite de pittori, scultori, et architetti moderni*. Roma.

Bender, L. 1937, Art and Therapy in the Mental Disturbance of Children. *Journal of Nervous and Mental Disease*, LXXXVI.

—— 1947, Childhood Schizophrenia. *American Journal of Orthopsychiatry*, XVII.

Benjamin, J. D. 1950, Methodological Considerations in the Validation and Elaboration of Psychoanalytical Personality Theory. *American Journal of Orthopsychiatry*. XX.

Beres, D. 1951, A Dream, a Vision, and a Poem: A Psychoanalytic Study of the Origins of the Rime of "The Ancient Mariner." *International Journal of Psycho-Analysis*, XXXII.

Berger, A. 1895 (1932), Seelenchirurgie (Review of Breuer and Freud, *Studies in Hysteria*). Wien: *Neue Freie Presse*, December 2; partly republished in *Psychoanalytische Bewegung*, IV, 1932.

Bergler, E. 1937, A Clinical Contribution to the Psychogenesis of Humor. *Psychoanalytic Review*, XXIV.

—— 1944, A Clinical Approach to the Psychoanalysis of Writers. *Ibid.*, XXXI.

—— 1945 (a), Mystery Fans and the Problem of Potential Murders. *American Journal of Orthopsychiatry*, XV.

—— 1945 (b), On a Five-Layer Structure in Sublimation. *Psychoanalytic Quarterly*, XIV.

—— 1947, Psychoanalysis of Writers and of Literary Production. In *Psychoanalysis and the Social Sciences*, I. Edited by G. Róheim. New York: International Universities Press.

—— 1950, *The Writer and Psychoanalysis*. New York: Doubleday & Co.

——, see Jekels, L.

Bergmann, G. 1935, Zur analytischen Theorie literarischer Wertmassstäbe (mit einer Bemerkung zur Grundlagendiskussion). *Imago*. XXI.

Bernfeld, S. 1922, Bemerkungen über Sublimierung. *Imago*, VIII.

—— 1929, *The Psychology of Infants*. London: Kegan Paul.

—— 1931, Zur Sublimierungstheorie. *Imago*, XVII.

—— 1932, Der Begriff der Deutung in der Psychoanalyse. *Zeitschrift für angewandte Psychologie*, XLII

—— 1934, Die Gestalttheorie. *Imago*, X.

Bernfeld, S. C. 1951, Freud and Archaeology. *American Imago*, VIII.

Bertschinger, H. 1911, Illustrierte Halluzinationen. *Jahrb. f. psa. Forsch.*, III.

Binyon, L. 1937, A Note on Richard Dudd. *Magazine of Art,* XXX.
Birnbaum, K. 1933, Methodologische Prinzipien der Pathographie. *Zeitschrift für die gesamte Neurologie und Psychiatrie,* CXLIII.
— 1935, *Die Welt der Geisteskranken.* Berlin: Springer.
Blum, A. 1916 (a), *L'estampe satirique en France pendant les guerres de religion.* Paris: Giard et Briet.
— 1916 (b), *La Caricature révolutionnaire.* Paris: Jouve & Cie.
Bonaparte, M. 1939, A Defense of Biography. *International Journal of Psycho-Analysis,* XX.
Born, W. 1945, Unconscious Processes in Artistic Creation. *Journal of Clinical Psychopathology and Psychotherapy,* VII.
— 1946, The Art of the Insane. *Ciba Symposia,* VII.
Bowling, W. G. 1925/1926, The Wild Prince Hal in Legend and Literature. *Washington Studies, Humanist Series,* XIII.
Bowra, C. M. 1949, *The Creative Experiment.* London: Macmillan.
Bradley, A. C. 1929, Inspiration. In *A Miscellany.* London: Macmillan.
— 1934, The Rejection of Falstaff. In *Oxford Lectures on Poetry.* London: Macmillan.
Bradley, B. and Meyerson, W. S. 1937, *Picture Puzzles and How to Solve Them.* New York: Harper & Brothers.
Brauer, H. and Wittkower, R. 1931, *Die Zeichnungen des Gianlorenzo Bernini.* Berlin: Heinrich Keller.
Breuer, J. and Freud, S. 1895, *Studien über Hysterie.* Wien: Deuticke.
Brierley, M. 1950, *Trends in Psycho-Analysis.* London: Hogarth Press.
Brill A. A. 1916, see Freud, S., 1905 a.
— 1931, Poetry as an Oral Outlet. *Psychoanalytic Review,* XVIII.
— 1941, The Mechanisms of Wit and Humor in Normal and Abnormal Psychopathic States. *Psychiatric Quarterly,* XIV.
British Museum Catalogue of Prints and Drawings in the British Museum, Division I. Political and Personal Satires, 1870. 6 Vols.
Brugsch, T. and Levy, F. H. 1926, *Die Biologie der Person. Ein Handbuch der allgemeinen und speziellen Konstitutionslehre.* Wien: Urban & Schwarzenberg.
Brunswick, R. M. 1940, The Preoedipal Phase of Libido Development. *Psychoanalytic Quarterly,* IX.
Bühler, K. 1927, *Die Krise der Psychologie.* Jena: Fisher.
— 1930, *The Mental Development of the Child.* New York: Harcourt, Brace & Co.
— 1933, *Ausdruckstheorie.* Jena: Fischer.
— 1934, *Sprachtheorie. Die Darstellungsfunktion der Sprache.* Jena: Fischer.
Bullough, E. 1912, Psychical Distance. *British Journal of Psychology,* V.
— 1919 (a), The Relation of Aesthetics to Psychology. *Ibid.,* X.
— 1919 (b), Mind and Medium in Art. *Ibid.,* XI.
— 1921, Recent Work in Experimental Aesthetics. *Ibid.,* XII.
Bürger-Prinz, H. 1932, Ueber die künstlerischen Arbeiten Schizophrener. In Bumke's *Handbuch der Geisteskrankheiten,* IX.
Burke, K. 1941, *The Philosophy of Literary Form.* Baton Rouge: Louisiana State University Press.
— 1945, *A Grammar of Motives.* New York: Prentice-Hall.
Burlingham, D. T. 1934, Mitteilungsdrang und Geständniszwang. *Imago,* XX.
Burt, C. and others, 1933, *How the Mind Works.* London: George Allen and Unwin.
Butcher, S. H. 1951, *Aristotle's Theory of Poetry and Fine Art.* With a critical text and translation of "The Poetics," with a prefatory essay by John Gassner. 4th Edition. New York: Dover Publications, Inc.
Buxbaum, E. 1941, The Role of Detective Stories in Child Analysis. *Psychoanalytic Quarterly,* X.

Buytendijk, J. J. and Plessner, H. 1925/1926, Die Deutung des mimischen Ausdrucks: Ein Beitrag zur Lehre vom Bewusstsein des anderen Ich. *Philosophischer Anzeiger*, I.
Bychowski, G. 1947, The Rebirth of a Woman. *Psychoanalytic Review*, XXXIV.

Cameron, N. 1938 (a), Individual and Social Factors in the Development of Graphic Symbolization. *Journal of Psychology*, V.
—— 1938 (b), Functional Immaturity in the Symbolization of Scientifically Trained Adults. *Ibid.*, VI.
Cannon, W. B. 1945, *The Way of an Investigator*. New York: W. W. Norton & Co.
Capgras, E. 1911, Ecrits et poésies d'une démente précoce. *L'Encèphale*, VI.
Cattell, R. B. and Luborsky, L. B. 1947, Personality Factors in Response to Humor. *Journal of Abnormal and Social Psychology*, XLII.
——, see Luborsky, L. B.
Chatterji, N. N. 1951, Schizophrenic Drawing. *Samiksa*, V.
Christensen, E. O. 1944, Freud on Leonardo da Vinci. *Psychoanalytic Review*, XXXI
Clark, Sir K. 1939, *Leonardo da Vinci. An Account of His Life and Development*. Cambridge: University Press.
Cowell, J. G., see Schube, P. G.
Croce, B. 1922, *Aesthetics*. London: Macmillan.
—— 1923, L'Umorismo. In *Problemi di estetica e contributi alla storia dell' estetica Italiana*. Second Edition. Bari: Laterza.

Darwin, C. 1904, *Expression of the Emotions*. London: Murray.
Davis, R. 1928, Caricature of To-day. Special Autumn Number of *The Studio*.
Davison, C. and Kelman, H. 1939, Pathological Laughing and Crying. *Archives of Neurology and Psychiatry*, XLII.
Delacroix, H. 1939, L'Invention et le génie. In *Nouveau Traité de Psychologie*. Edited by G. Dumas. Paris: Felix Alçan.
del Solar, C., see Gellert, E.
Deri, F. 1939, On Sublimation. *Psychoanalytic Quarterly*, VIII.
Deri, M. 1931, Naturobjekt und Menschenwerk. Ueber einen Unterschied in der Betrachtung natürlicher und künstlerischer Sachverhalte. *Imago*, XVII.
Deutsch, H. 1927, Ueber Zufriedenheit, Glück und Ekstase. *Internationale Zeitschrift für Psychoanalyse*, XIII.
—— 1934, Don Quijote und Donquijotismus. *Imago*, XX.
—— 1944-1945, *The Psychology of Women*. 2 Vols. New York: Grune & Stratton.
Dietrich, A. 1897, *Pulcinella, pompejanische Wandbilder und römische Satyrspiele*. Leipzig.
Dilthey, A. 1897, Die Einbildungskraft des Dichters. Bausteine für eine Poetik. In *Gesammelte Schriften*, VI. Leipzig-Berlin: B. G. Teubner.
Donaghy, J. L. 1944, On the Nature of Inspiration and the Genesis of Poetry. *The Dublin Magazine*.
Dooley, L. 1934, A Note on Humor. *Psychoanalytic Review*, XXI.
Drommard, G. 1909, *La Mimique chez les alienés*. Paris: Felix Alçan.
Dumas, G. 1933, L'Expression des émotions. In *Nouveau Traité de Psychologie*, III. Paris: Felix Alçan.

Ehrenzweig, A. 1948/1949, Unconscious Formation in Art. *British Journal of Medical Psychology*, XXI and XXII.
Eidelberg, L. 1945, A Contribution to the Study of Wit. *Psychoanalytic Review*, XXXII.
Eisenstein, V. 1948, Obsessive Hobbies. *Psychoanalytic Review*, XXXV.
Eisler, R. 1910, *Weltenmantel und Himmelszelt*. München: O. Beck.

Eliot, T. S. 1942, *The Music of Poetry. The Third W. P. Ker Memorial Lecture.* Glasgow: Jackson, Son & Company.

Empson, W. 1931, *The Seven Types of Ambiguity.* New York: Harcourt, Brace & Co.

—— 1935, *Some Versions of the Pastoral.* London: Chatto & Windus.

—— 1951, *The Structure of Complex Words.* London: Chatto & Windus.

Engerth, G. 1933, Zeichenstörung bei Patienten mit Autotopagnosien. *Zeitschrift für die gesamte Neurologie und Psychiatrie,* CXLIII.

Erickson, M. H. and Kubie, L. S. 1938, The Use of Automatic Drawing in the Interpretation and Relief of a State of Acute Obsessional Depression. *Psychoanalytic Quarterly,* VII.

Erikson, E. H. 1942, Hitler's Imagery and German Youth. *Psychiatry,* V.

Evenson, H. 1926, Die Geisteskrankheit des Vincent Van Gogh. *Allgemeine Zeitschrift für Psychiatrie,* LXXXIV.

—— 1936, Psychiatrie und schaffende Kunst. *Acta Psychiatrica,* XI.

Eysenck, H. J. 1942, The Appreciation of Humour: An Experimental and Theoretical Study. *British Journal of Psychology,* XXXII.

—— 1943, An Experimental Analysis of Five Tests of "Appreciation of Humour." *Educational and Psychological Measurements,* III.

—— 1944, National Differences in the Sense of Humor: Three Experimental and Additional Studies. *Character and Personality,* XIII.

Fairbairn, W. R. D. 1938 (a), Prolegomena to a Psychology of Art. *British Journal of Psychology,* XXVIII.

—— 1938 (b), The Ultimate Basis of Aesthetic Experience. *Ibid.,* XXIX.

Fay, H. M. 1912, Réflection sur l'art et les aliénés. *Aesculape,* II.

Federn, P. 1931, Der neurotische Stil. *Abhandlungen aus der Neurologie, Psychiatrie, Psychologie und ihren Grenzgebieten.* Berlin: Karger.

Fehrle, E. 1930/1931, Das Lachen im Glauben der Völker. *Zeitschrift für Volkskunde,* Neue Folge II.

Félibien, A. 1676, *Des Principes de l'architecture, de la sculpture, de la peinture, etc., avec un dictionnaire des termes propres à chaque de ces arts.* Paris.

Fenichel, O. 1928, Ueber organlibidinöse Begleiterscheinungen der Triebabwehr. *Internationale Zeitschrift für Psychoanalyse,* XIV.

—— 1931, Ueber respiratorische Introjektion. *Ibid.,* XVII.

—— 1939 (a), The Counter-Phobic Attitude. *International Journal of Psycho-Analysis,* XX.

—— 1939 (b), *Problems of Psychoanalytic Technique.* Albany: The Psychoanalytic Quarterly, Inc.

—— 1943, The Misapprehended Oracle. *American Imago,* III.

—— 1945, *The Psychoanalytic Theory of Neurosis.* New York: W. W. Norton & Co.

—— 1946, On Acting. *Psychoanalytic Quarterly,* XV.

Ferdière, G. 1947, Introduction à la recherche d'un style dans le dessin des schizophrènes. *Annales Medico-Psychologiques,* 105, II.

—— 1951, Le dessinateur schizophrène. *L'évolution psychiatrique.*

Ferenczi, S. 1913, Lachen. In *Bausteine zur Psychoanalyse,* IV. Bern: Hans Huber.

—— 1919, Thinking and Muscle Innervation. In *Further Contributions to the Theory and Technique of Psycho-Analysis.* London: Hogarth Press, 1926.

—— 1922, The Psyche as an Inhibitory Organ. *Ibid.*

Flach, A. 1928, Die Psychologie der Ausdrucksbewegung. *Archiv für die gesamte Psychologie,* LXV.

—— 1934, Psychomotorische Gestaltbildung im normalen und pathologischen Seelenleben. *Ibid.,* LXXI.

Flournoy, H. 1933, Le Problème des hallucinations au point de vue psychanalytique. *Archives Suisses de Neurologie et de Psychiatrie,* XXXII.

Flugel, J. C. 1942, Sublimation: Its Nature and Conditions. *British Journal of Educational Psychology*, XII.

Foerster, H. v. (ed.) 1949, *Cybernetics. Circular, Causal and Feedback Mechanisms in Biological and Social Problems.* New York: Josiah Macy, Jr. Foundation.

Foley, J. P., see Anastasi, A.

Foulkes (Fuchs), S. H. 1936, Zum Stande der heutigen Biologie. *Imago*, XXII.

Fraenger, W. 1922, *Die trollatischen Träume des Pantagruel: Ein Holzschnittfratzenbuch.* Zürich-Erlenbach: Eugen Reutsch Verlag.

French, T. M. 1936, A Clinical Study of Learning in the Course of a Psychoanalytic Treatment. *Psychoanalytic Quarterly*, V.

—— 1945, Integration of Social Behavior. *Ibid.*, XIV.

——, see Alexander, F.

Fretet, J. 1946, *L'Aliénation poétique, Rimbaud, Mallarmé, Proust.* Paris: J. B. Janin.

Freud, A. 1923, The Relation of a Beating Fantasy to a Daydream. *International Journal of Psycho-Analysis*, I.

—— 1936 (1946), *The Ego and the Mechanisms of Defence.* New York: International Universities Press.

—— 1951, Observations on Child Development. In *The Psychoanalytic Study of the Child*, VI. New York: International Universities Press.

Freud, S. 1895, *Studies in Hysteria.* (With Breuer.) Translation A. A. Brill. New York: Nervous and Mental Disease Monographs, 1936.

—— 1900, *The Interpretation of Dreams.* Translation A. A. Brill. Revised edition (in accordance with 8th German edition). London: Allen & Unwin, 1932; New York: Macmillan, 1937. Included in *The Basic Writings of Sigmund Freud.* New York: Modern Library, 1938.

—— 1904 (a), *The Psychopathology of Everyday Life.* Translation A. A. Brill. New York: Macmillan, 1914; London: Fisher Unwin, 1914; London and New York: Penguin Books, 1938. Included in *The Basic Writings of Sigmund Freud.* New York: Modern Library, 1938.

—— 1904 (b), Psychopathic Characters on the Stage. *Psychoanalytic Quarterly*, XI.

—— 1905 (a) *Wit and Its Relation to the Unconscious.* Translation A. A. Brill. New York: Moffat, Yard, 1917; London: Kegan Paul, 1922. Included in *The Basic Writings of Sigmund Freud.* New York: Modern Library, 1938.

—— 1905 (b), *Three Contributions to the Theory of Sex.* Translation A. A. Brill. Revised edition (in accordance with 4th German edition). New York: Nervous and Mental Disease Monographs, 1930. Included in *The Basic Writings of Sigmund Freud.* New York: Modern Library, 1938. New authorized translation James Strachey, *Three Essays of the Theory of Sexuality.* London: Imago Publ. Co., 1949.

—— 1905 (c), Fragment of an Analysis of a Case of Hysteria. *Collected Papers*, III. London: Hogarth Press.

—— 1907, *Delusion and Dream.* Translation Helen M. Downey. New York: Moffard, Yard, 1917; London: Allen & Unwin, 1921.

—— 1908, The Relation of the Poet to Daydreaming. *Collected Papers*, IV. London: Hogarth Press.

—— 1909 (a), Notes Upon a Case of Obsessional Neurosis. *Ibid.*, III.

—— 1909 (b), The Family Romance of Neurotics. *Ibid.*, V.

—— 1910 (a), *Leonardo da Vinci.* Translation A. A. Brill. New York: Dodd, Mead, 1932; London: Kegan Paul, 1922.

—— 1910 (b), The Antithetical Sense of Primal Words. *Collected Papers*, IV. London: Hogarth Press.

—— 1911 (a), Formulations Regarding the Two Principles in Mental Functioning. *Ibid.*, IV.

—— 1911 (b), Psychoanalytic Notes upon an Autobiographical Account of a Case of Paranoia (Dementia Paranoides). *Ibid.*, III.

—— 1912/1913, *Totem and Taboo.* Translation A. A. Brill. New York: New Republic, 1931; London: Routledge, 1919; London and New York: Penguin Books, 1938; included in *The Basic Writings of Sigmund Freud.* New York: Modern Library, 1938. New authorized translation James Strachey. New York: W. W. Norton & Co.

—— 1913, The Occurrence in Dreams of Material From Fairy-Tales. *Collected Papers,* IV. London: Hogarth Press.

—— 1915 (a), Repression. *Ibid.*

—— 1915, (b), The Unconscious. *Ibid.*

—— 1917, *Introductory Lectures on Psycho-Analysis.* Translation Joan Riviere. Revised Edition. London: Allen & Unwin, 1929; New York (but under the title *A General Introduction to Psychoanalysis*): Liveright, 1935 and Garden City Publishing Co., 1943.

—— 1919, The Uncanny. *Collected Papers,* IV. London: Hogarth Press.

—— 1920, *Beyond the Pleasure Principle.* Translation C. J. M. Hubback. London: Hogarth Press, 1922. New York: Boni and Liveright, 1922.

—— 1921 (a), *Group Psychology and the Analysis of the Ego.* Translation James Strachey. London: Hogarth Press, 1922; New York: Liveright, 1940.

—— 1921 (b), Introduction to J. Varendonck (1921).

—— 1923 (a), A Neurosis of Demoniacal Possession in the Seventeenth Century. *Collected Papers,* IV. London: Hogarth Press.

—— 1923 (b), *The Ego and the Id.* Translation Joan Riviere. London: Hogarth Press, 1927.

—— 1924 (a), The Economic Problem of Masochism. *Collected Papers,* V. London: Hogarth Press.

—— 1924 (b), Neurosis and Psychosis. *Ibid.*, II.

—— 1926 (a), *The Problem of Anxiety.* Translation H. A. Bunker. New York: W. W. Norton & Co., 1936.

—— 1926 (b), *Inhibitions, Symptoms and Anxiety.* Translation Alix Strachey. London: Hogarth Press, 1936.

—— 1928 (a), Humour. *Collected Papers,* V. London. Hogarth Press.

—— 1928 (b), Dostoevsky and Parricide. *Ibid.*

—— 1930 (a), *Civilization and Its Discontents.* Translation Joan Riviere. London: Hogarth Press, 1930; New York: Cape & Smith, 1930.

—— 1930 (b), Ansprache im Frankfurter Goethe Haus. *Gesammelte Werke,* XIV. London: Imago Publ. Co., 1948.

—— 1931 (a), Female Sexuality. *Collected Papers,* V. London: Hogarth Press.

—— 1931 (b), Libidinal Types. *Ibid.*

—— 1932 (a), *New Introductory Lectures on Psychoanalysis.* New York: W. W. Norton & Co., 1933.

—— 1932 (b) The Acquisition of Power over Fire. *Collected Papers,* V. London: Hogarth Press.

—— 1935, Postscript, 1935. Included in revised edition of *An Autobiographical Study.* London: Hogarth Press.

—— 1937, Analysis Terminable and Interminable. *Collected Papers,* V. London: Hogarth Press.

—— 1939, *An Outline of Psychoanalysis.* New York: W. W. Norton, 1949.

—— 1950, *Aus den Anfängen der Psychoanalyse. Briefe an Wilhelm Fliess, Abhandlungen und Notizen aus den Jahren 1887-1902.* London: Imago Publishing Co.

Friedlander, K. 1942, Children's Books and Their Function in Latency and Prepuberty. *American Imago,* III.

Friedman, J. and Gassel, S. 1950, The Chorus in Sophocles' Oedipus Tyrannus. *Psychoanalytic Quarterly,* XIX.

Frois-Wittman, J. 1929, Considérations psychanalytiques sur l'art moderne. *Revue Française de Psychanalyse*, III.
—— 1937, *Art, Inconscient et Réalité*. Deuxième Congrès Internationale d'Esthétique et de la Science de l'Art. I. Paris: Felix Alçan.
Fry, R. 1920, *Vision and Design*. London: Chatto & Windus.
Fuchs, E. 1901, *Die Karikatur der europäischen Völker vom Altertum zur Neuzeit*. Berlin: Hoffman.
—— 1906, *Die Frau in der Karikatur*. München: A. Lange.
—— 1916, *Der Weltkrieg in der Karikatur*. München: A. Lange.
—— 1921, *Die Juden in der Karikatur*. München: A. Lange.

Gadelius, B. 1922, *Det mänskliga Själslivet*. Stockholm: Geber.
Garfinkel, L., see Zimmerman, J.
Gassel, S., see Friedman, J.
Gassner, J., see Butcher, S. H.
Gaunt, W. 1945, *The Aesthetic Adventure*. New York: Harcourt, Brace & Co.
Gellert, E. 1950-1951, An Etiological Analysis of Laughter as Observed in the Preschool Child. Term Paper (unpublished) with the assistance of P. Keefer, supervised by C. del Solar. New Haven: Yale University.
Gero, G. 1933, Review of S. Bernfeld (1932). *Imago*, XIX.
—— 1939, Zum Problem der oralen Fixierung. *Internationale Zeitschrift für Pyschoanalyse*, XXIV.
Ginsburg, S., see Ginzberg, E.
Ginzberg, E., Ginsburg, S. W., Axelrad, S. and Herma, J. L. 1951, *Occupational Choice: General Theory*. New York: Columbia University Press.
Glover, E. 1924, The Significance of the Mouth in Psycho-Analysis. *British Journal of Medical Psychology*, IV.
—— 1931, Sublimation, Substitution and Social Anxiety. *International Journal of Psycho-Analysis*, XII.
—— 1934, Medical Psychology or Academic (Normal) Psychology. Problems in Orientation. *British Journal of Medical Psychology*, XIV.
—— 1947, Basic Mental Concepts, Their Clinical and Theoretical Value. *Psychoanalytic Quarterly*, XVI.
—— 1950, *Freud or Jung*. New York: W. W. Norton & Co.
Gombrich, E. H. 1934/1935, Zum Werke Giulio Romanos. *Jahrbuch der kunsthistorischen Sammlungen in Wien*.
—— 1947, *Cartoons and Progress*. London: Contact Publications, Ltd.
—— 1951, Meditations on a Hobby Horse or the Roots of Artistic Form. In *Aspects of Form*. Ed. by L. L. Whyte. London: Lund Humphries.
—— and Kris, E. 1940. *Caricature*. London: The King Penguin Books.
Gomperz, H. 1905, *Weltanschauungslehre*. Jena: Diederichs.
—— 1906, Ueber einige Voraussetzungen naturalistischer Kunst. *Beilage zur Münchner Allgemeinen Zeitung*.
—— 1929, *Ueber Sinn und Sinngebilde, Verstehen und Erklären*. Tübingen: J. B. C. Mohr.
Götz, B. 1933, Review of Kris, E. (1932). *Deutsche Literatur Zeitung*.
Graber, G. H. 1931, Zwei "Witzbilder." *Zeitschrift für psychoanalytische Pädagogik*, V.
Graewe, H. 1936, Geschichtlicher Ueberblick über die Psychologie des kindlichen Zeichnens. *Archiv für die gesamte Psychologie*, XCVI.
Grand-Carteret, J. 1885, *Les Moeurs et la caricature en Allemagne*. Paris.
—— no date, *Les Moeurs et la caricature en France*. Paris.
Greenacre, P. 1945, Conscience in the Psychopath. *American Journal of Orthopsychiatry*, XV.

—— 1951, Respiratory Inspiration and the Phallic Phase. In *The Psychoanalytic Study of the Child*, VI. New York: International Universities Press.

Grisar, H. and Heege, F. 1922, *Luthers Kampfbilder, Luther-Studien*. Freiburg: Herder.

Grose, F. 1791, *Rules for Drawing Caricatures*. London.

Grotjahn, M. 1940, Ferdinand the Bull: Psychoanalytical Remarks about a Modern Totem Animal. *American Imago*, I.

—— 1947, Symbolism in the Drawing of a Transvestite. *Samiksa*, I.

—— 1948, Transvestite Fantasy Expressed in Drawing. *Psychoanalytic Quarterly*, XVII.

—— 1949, Laughter in Psychoanalysis. *Samiksa*, III; reprinted in *The Yearbook of Psychoanalysis*, VI. New York: International Universities Press.

Gutheil, E. 1935, Musical Daydreams. *Psychoanalytic Review*, XXII.

Guttmann, E. and Maclay, W. S. 1937, Clinical Observations on Schizophrenic Drawings. *British Journal of Medical Psychology*, XVI.

—— See Maclay, W. S.

Hadamard, J. 1949, *The Psychology of Invention in the Mathematical Field*. Princeton: Princeton University Press.

Haecker, V. and Ziehen, T. 1931, Beitrag zur Lehre von der Vererbung und Analyse der zeichnerischen und mathematischen Begabung, insbesondere mit Bezug auf die Korrelation zur musikalischen Begabung (Schluss). *Zeitschrift für Psychologie*, CXXI.

Haigh, S. S. 1935, Review of Symons (1934). *Psychoanalytic Quarterly*, IV.

Harding, R. E. M. 1940, *An Anatomy of Inspiration and an Essay on the Creative Mood*. Third edition, 1948. Cambridge: W. Heffer & Sons.

Hart, H. H. 1950, The Integrative Function in Creativity. *Psychiatric Quarterly*, XXIV.

Hartlaub, G. F. 1920, Der Zeichner Josephson. *Genius, Zeitschrift für wertende und alte Kunst*, I.

Hartmann, H. 1927, *Die Grundlagen der Psychoanalyse*. Leipzig: Georg Thieme.

—— 1930, Gedächtnis und Lustprinzip: Untersuchungen an Korsakow Kranken. *Zeitschrift für Neurologie und Psychiatrie*, CXXVI.

—— 1939 (a) Ich-Psychologie und Anpassungsproblem. *Internationale Zeitschrift für Psychoanalyse und Imago*, XXIV. Translated in part in Rapaport (1951).

—— 1939 (b), Psychoanalysis and the Concept of Health. *International Journal of Psycho-Analysis*, XX.

—— 1944, Psychoanalysis and Sociology. In *Psychoanalysis Today*. Edited by S. Lorand. New York: International Universities Press.

—— 1947, On Rational and Irrational Action. In *Psychoanalysis and the Social Sciences*, I. Edited by G. Róheim. New York: International Universities Press.

—— 1948, Comments on the Psychoanalytic Theory of Instinctual Drives. *Psychoanalytic Quarterly* XVII.

—— 1950, Comments on the Psychoanalytic Theory of the Ego. In *The Psychoanalytic Study of the Child*, V. New York: International Universities Press.

—— 1952, The Mutual Relationship in the Development of the Ego and Id. *Ibid.*, VII (in press).

—— and Kris, E. 1945, The Genetic Approach in Psychoanalysis. *Ibid.*, I.

———— and Loewenstein, R. M. 1946, Comments on the Formation of Psychic Structure. *Ibid.*, II.

———— 1949, Notes on the Theory of Aggression. *Ibid.*, III/IV.

———— 1951, Some Psychoanalytic Comments on Culture and Personality. In *Psychoanalysis and Culture*. Edited by G. B. Wilbur and W. Muensterberger. New York: International Universities Press.

Hassmann, O. and Zingerle, H. 1913, Untersuchungen bildlicher Darstellungen und sprachlicher Aeusserungen bei der Dementia Praecox. *Journal für Psychologie und Neurologie*, XX.

Hazlitt, W. 1848, *Characters of Shakespeare's Plays.* 4th Edition. London: C. Templeman.

Hecker, E. 1873, *Die Physiologie und Psychologie des Lachens und des Komischen.* Berlin: Ferd. Dümmlers.

Heege, F., see Grisar, H.

Heimann, A., see Salomon, R.

Heller, P. 1951, The Writer's Image of the Writer. A Study in the Ideologies of Six German Authors. 1918-1933. Doctoral Dissertation, Columbia University (unpublished).

Hendrick, I. 1942, Instincts and the Ego During Infancy. *Psychoanalytic Quarterly,* XI.

—— 1943 (a), Work and the Pleasure Principle. *Ibid.,* XII.

—— 1943 (b), The Discussion of the "Instinct to Master." *Ibid.,* XII.

Herland, L. 1938, *Gesicht und Charakter.* Wien: Saturn Verlag.

Herma, J., see Ginzberg, E.

Herzfeld, E. and Prager, L. 1929, Verständnis für Scherz und Komik beim Kinde. *Zeitschrift für angewandte Psychologie,* XXIV.

Herzfeld, M. 1925, *Leonardo da Vinci, der Denker, Forscher und Poet.* Jena: Diederich.

Hesse, H. 1926, Künstler und Psychoanalyse. In *Almanach der Psychoanalyse.* Wien: Psychoanalytischer Verlag.

—— 1931, Notizen zum Thema Dichtung und Kritik. *Neue Rundschau.*

Hitschmann, E. 1913, Swedenborg's Paranoia. *Zentralblatt für Psychoanalyse,* III. English Translation: *American Imago,* V. 1949; reprinted in *The Yearbook of Psychoanalysis,* VI. New York: International Universities Press, 1950.

—— 1930 (a), Zur Psychologie des jüdischen Witzes. *Psychoanalytische Bewegung,* II.

—— 1930 (b), Die Bedeutung der Psychoanalyse für die Biographik. *Ibid.*

Hodin, J. P. 1949, Two Swedish Masters. *The Norseman,* VII.

Hoffman, F. J. 1945, *Freudianism and the Literary Mind.* Baton Rouge: Louisiana State University Press.

Hogarth, W. 1758, *The Bench.* London.

Homburger, A. 1922, Ueber die Entwicklung der menschlichen Motorik und ihre Beziehungen zu den Bewegungsstörungen der Schizophrenie. *Zeitschrift für die gesamte Neurologie und Psychiatrie,* LXXXVIII.

Hoops, R. 1934, Der Einfluss der Psychoanalyse auf die englische Literatur. *Anglistische Forschungen* (herausgegeben von Dr. J. Hoops), LXXVII.

Housman, A. E. 1933, *The Name and Nature of Poetry. Leslie Stephen Lecture.* Cambridge: University Press.

Hupp, C. 1930, *Ehrenschelte und Schandbild.* München-Regensburg.

Huschke, A. 1821, *Mimische und physiognomische Studien.* New Edition: *Der Körper als Ausdruck.* Edited by W. Rink. Dresden: Dr. Madaus & Co.

Hyman, S. E. 1948, *The Armed Vision. A Study in the Methods of Modern Literary Criticism.* New York: Alfred Knopf.

Isaacs, S. 1933 (1940), *Social Development in Young Children. A Study of Beginnings.* London: George Routledge & Sons.

Jacobson, E. 1946, The Child's Laughter, Theoretical and Clinical Notes on the Function of the Comic. In *The Psychoanalytic Study of the Child,* II. New York: International Universities Press.

Jacobsson, J. 1946, Nöeken motwet hos Ernst Josephson, ett tema med variationer. Göteborg: Kungl Vetenskaps—och Vitterhets—Samhölles Handlingar. Sgätte Följden Ser A, III.

Jaspers, K. 1923, *Allgemeine Psychopathologie.* (Third Edition 1923, Fifth Edition 1948.) Berlin: Springer.

—— 1926, *Strindberg und Van Gogh.* Bern: Hans Huber.

Jekels, L. 1926, Zur Psychologie der Komödie. *Imago,* XII.

—— 1933, Das Problem der doppelten Motivgestaltung. *Ibid.*, XIX.
—— and Bergler, E. 1934, Uebertragung und Liebe. *Ibid.*, XX.
Jenkins, W., see Postman, L.
Jensen, W. 1903, *Gravida*. Dresden und Leipzig: Carl Reissner.
—— 1907, Drei unveröffentlichte Briefe. *Psychoanalytische Bewegung*, I. 1929.
Jones, E. 1911, A Psychoanalytic Study of Hamlet. In *Essays in Applied Psycho-Analysis*, 1st edition. London: Hogarth Press, 1923.
—— 1912, Analytic Study of a Case of Obsessional Neurosis. In *Papers on Psycho-Analysis*. Fourth Edition. London: Ballière Tindall & Cox, 1938.
—— 1914, The Madonna's Conception Through the Ear. In *Essays in Applied Psycho-Analysis*, II. London: Hogarth Press, 1951.
—— 1933, The Phallic Phase. *International Journal of Psycho-Analysis*, XIV.
—— 1949, *Hamlet and Oedipus*. London: S. Gollancz.
—— 1950, The Death of Hamlet's Father. *International Journal of Psycho-Analysis*, XXXI.
Jung, C. G. 1911-1912, Wandlungen und Symbole der Libido. *Jahrbuch für psycho-analytische und psychopathologische Forschungen*, II and III.
Juynboll, W. R. 1934, *Het komische genre in de italiaansche Schilderkunst gedurende de 17 en de 18 eeuw*. Leiden: N. V. Leidsche Uitgevers—Maatschappij.

Kabel, P. 1908, Die Sage von Heinrich V. bis zur Zeit Shakespeares. *Palaestra*, LXIX.
Kaila, E. 1932, Die Reaktion des Säuglings auf das menschliche Gesicht. *Annales Universitatis Aboenis*, XVII.
Kane, E. K. 1928, *Gongorism and the Golden Age: A Study of Exuberance and Un-restraint in Arts*. Chapel Hill: University of North Carolina Press.
Kanner, L. 1931, Judging Emotions From Facial Expressions. *Psychological Monographs*, XLI.
Kanzer, M. 1948, The Passing of the Oedipus Complex in Greek Drama. *International Journal of Psycho-Analysis*, XXIX. Reprinted in *The Yearbook of Psychoanalysis*, V. New York: International Universities Press.
—— 1950, The Oedipus Trilogy. *Psychoanalytic Quarterly*, XIX.
Kaplan, A. 1946, Definition and Specification of Meaning. *Journal of Philosophy*, XLIII.
Kasanin, J. S. 1944, *Language and Thought in Schizophrenia*. Berkeley: University of California Press.
Katan, M. 1940, Die Rolle des Wortes in der Schizophrenie und Manie. *Internationale Zeitschrift für Psychoanalyse und Imago*, XXV.
Katz, D. and R. 1928, *Gespräche mit Kindern*. Berlin: Springer.
Kauders, O. 1931, Zur Kenntnis und Analyse der psychomotorischen Störungen. (Abhandlungen aus der Neurologie und Psychiatrie, Heft LXIV.) Berlin: S. Karger.
Kelman, H., see Davison, C.
Kenderdine, M. 1931, Laughter in the Pre-School Child. *Child Development*, II.
Kingsford, C. L. 1901, *Henry V, The Typical Medieval Hero*. New York: G. P. Putnam & Sons.
Kirschbaumer, L. 1940, Poetry in Schizophrenia and Other Psychoses. *Journal of Nervous and Mental Disease*, XCI.
Klein, M. 1929, Personification in the Play of Children. *International Journal of Psycho-Analysis*, X. Reprinted in *Contributions to Psycho-Analysis*. London: Hogarth Press. 1948.
Kluckhohn, C. 1945, Personal Documents in Anthropological Science. In *The Use of Personal Documents in History, Anthropology and Sociology*, by Louis Gott-schalk, Clyde Kluckhohn and Robert Angell. Social Science Research Council Bulletin, LIII.

Knight, L. C. 1946, *Explorations*. London: Chatto & Windus.
Kraepelin, E. 1909-1913, *Psychiatrie*. Leipzig: Barth.
Krapf, E. E. 1948, Georg Christoph Lichtenberg psicoanalista clandestino del siglo XVIII. *Rivista de Psicoanalisis*, VI.
Kraus, G. 1941, Vincent van Gogh en de Psychiatrie. *Psychiatrische en Neurologische Bladen*. (With extensive bibliography.)
Krautheimer, R., see Salomon, R.
Kretschmer, E. 1930, *Medizinische Psychologie*. Fourth Edition. Leipzig: Georg Thieme.
Kries, J. von. 1925, Vom Komischen und vom Lachen. *Archiv für Psychiatrie und Nervenheilkunde*, LXXIV.
Kris, E. 1926, Der Stil rustique. In *Jahrbuch der Kunsthistorischen Sammlungen in Wien*.
—— 1932, Die Charakterköpfe des Franz Xaver Messerschmidt. Versuch einer historischen und psychologischen Deutung. In *Jahrbuch der Kunsthistorischen Sammlungen in Wien*.
—— 1943, Some Problems of War-Propaganda. *Psychoanalytic Quarterly*, XII.
—— 1944, Art and Regression. *Transactions of the New York Academy of Sciences*, VI, Series II, No. 7.
—— 1947, The Nature of Psychoanalytic Propositions and Their Validation. In *Freedom and Experience. Essays Presented to Horace Kallen*. Edited by S. Hook and M. R. Konvits. Ithaca, New York: Cornell University Press. Reprinted in *Psychological Theory, Contemporary Readings*. Edited by M. Marx. New York: Macmillan, 1951.
—— 1949, Roots of Hostility and Prejudice. In *The Family in a Democratic Society*. Anniversary Papers of the Community Service Society of New York. New York: Columbia University Press.
—— 1950, Notes on the Development and on Some Current Problems of Psychoanalytic Child Psychology. In *The Psychoanalytic Study of the Child*, V. New York: International Universities Press.
—— 1951 (a), Ego Psychology and Interpretation in Psychoanalytic Therapy. *Psychoanalytic Quarterly*, XX.
—— 1951 (b), Some Comments and Observations on Early Autoerotic Activities. In *The Psychoanalytic Study of the Child*, VI. New York: International Universities Press.
——, see Freud, S. (1950). Introduction and Notes.
——, see Gombrich, E. H.
——, see Hartmann, H.
——, see Hartmann, H., and Loewenstein, R. M.
—— and Kurz, O. 1934, *Die Legende vom Künstler*. Wien: Krystallverlag.
—— and Speier, H., and associates, 1944, *German Radio Propaganda. Report on German Home Broadcasts During the War*. Oxford: University Press.
Kubie, L. S. 1934, Body Symbolization and the Development of Language. *Psychoanalytic Quarterly*, III.
—— see Erickson, M. H.
Kurz, O., see Kris, E.

Lafora, G. H. 1930, Don Juan and Other Psychological Studies. In *A Psychological Study of Cubism and Expressionism*. London: Butterworth.
Laforgue, R. 1928, Ueberlegungen zum Begriff der Verdrängung. *Internationale Zeitschrift für Psychoanalyse*, XIV.
Lagerloef, S. 1908, *Christ Legends*. New York: Henry Holt.
Landauer, K. 1926, Die kindliche Bewegungsunruhe, das Schicksal der den Stammganglien unterstehenden triebhaften Bewegungen, *Internationale Zeitschrift für Psychoanalyse*, XII.

—— 1927, Automatismus, Zwangsneurose und Paranoia. *Ibid.*, XIII.

Landis, C., see Roman, R.

Lange, F. 1937, *Die Sprache des menschlichen Antlitzes*. München: J. F. Lehmann.

Lange-Eichbaum, W. 1928 (1932), *The Problem of Genius*. New York: Macmillan.

Langfeld, H. S. 1920, *The Aesthetic Attitude*. New York: Harcourt, Brace & Co.

—— 1937, The Role of Response in Aesthetic Experience. In *Deuxième Congrès International d'esthétique et de la science de l'art*, I. Paris: Felix Alçan.

Lasswell, H. 1948, *Power and Personality*. New York: W. W. Norton & Co.

Le Brun, C. 1667, *Traité sur les passions*. Méthode pour apprendre à dessiner les passions proposée dans une conférence générale et particulière. Paris.

Lee, H. B., 1947 (a), On the Aesthetic State of Mind. *Psychiatry*, X.

—— 1947 (b), The Cultural Lag in Aesthetics. *Journal of Aesthetics and Art Criticism*, VI.

—— 1948, Spirituality and Beauty in Artistic Experience. *Psychoanalytic Quarterly*, XVII.

—— 1949 (a), Projective Features of Contemplative Artistic Experience. *American Journal of Orthopsychiatry*, XIX.

—— 1949 (b), The Values of Order and Vitality in Art. In *Psychoanalysis and the Social Sciences*, II. Edited by G. Róheim. New York: International Universities Press.

—— 1949 (c), The Creative Imagination. *Psychoanalytic Quarterly*, XVIII.

——, see also Levey, H. B.

Lee, V. (Paget, V.) 1913, *The Beautiful*. Cambridge: Cambridge University Press.

Leites, N., see Wolfenstein, M.

Leonardo, see Vinci, L.

Lersch, P. 1932, *Gesicht und Seele. Grundlagen einer mimischen Diagnostik*. München: Reinhardt.

Levey, H. B. 1938, Poetry Production as a Supplemental Emergency Defense Against Anxiety. *Psychoanalytic Quarterly*, VII.

—— 1939, A Critique of the Theory of Sublimation. *Psychiatry*, II.

—— 1940, A Theory Concerning Free Creation in the Inventive Arts. *Ibid.*, III.

——, see also Lee, H. B.

Levine, E. L., see Schilder, P.

Levine, J., see Redlich, F. C.

Levy, F. H., see Brugsch, T.

Lewin, B. D. 1939, Some Observations on Knowledge, Belief and the Impulse to Know. *International Journal of Psycho-Analysis*, XX.

—— 1950, *The Psychoanalysis of Elation*. New York: W. W. Norton Co.

Lewis, N. D. C. 1925, The Practical Value of Graphic Art in Personality Studies. (1. An Introductory Presentation of the Possibilities.) *Psychoanalytic Review*, XII.

—— 1928, Graphic Art Productions in Schizophrenia. *Proceedings of the Association for Research in Nervous and Mental Disease for 1925*, V.

Linton, R. 1945, *The Cultural Background of Personality*. New York: D. Appleton-Century Co.

Lipps, J., see Meyer-Gross, W.

Lips, E. 1937, *The Savage Hits Back*. New Haven: Yale University Press.

Liss, E. 1938, The Graphic Arts. *American Journal of Orthopsychiatry*, VIII.

Listowell, Earl of 1933, *A Critical History of Modern Aesthetics*. London: George Allen and Unwin.

Loewenstein, R. M., see Hartmann, H.

Loewy, E. 1930, Ursprünge der bildenden Kunst. *Almanach der Akademie der Wissenschaften in Wien*.

334 BIBLIOGRAPHY

Lorand, S. 1950, A Note on the Psychology of the Inventor. In *Clinical Studies in Psychoanalysis*. New York: International Universities Press.

Low, D. 1935, *Ye Madde Designer*. London: The Studio, Ltd.

Lowenfeld, H. 1941, Psychic Trauma and Productive Experience in the Artist. *Psychoanalytic Quarterly*, X.

Lowenfeld, V., see Münz, L.

Lowes, J. L. 1927, *The Road to Xanadu*. Boston: Houghton Mifflin.

Luborsky, L. B. and Cattell, R. B., 1947, The Validation of Personality Factors in Humor. *Journal of Personality*, XV.

—— see Cattell, R. B.

Ludwig, H. 1910, *Ich Will. Die Himmelsleiter*. Leipzig: Max Spohr.

Ludwig, K., see Vinci, L.

Luquet, G. H. 1930, Le Rire dans les légendes océaniennes. *Journal de Psychologie Normale et Pathologique*, XXVII.

Lynch, B. 1936, *A History of Caricature*. London: Faber and Gwyer.

Machover, K. 1949, *Personality Projection in the Drawing of the Human Figure*. Springfield, Ill.: Charles C. Thomas.

Maclay, W. S., see Guttmann, E.

—— Guttmann, E., and Meyer-Gross, W. 1938, Spontaneous Drawings as an Approach to Some Problems in Psychopathology. *Proceedings Royal Society of Medicine*, XXXI.

Mahler, M. S. 1949, Psychoanalytic Evaluation of Tics: A Sign and Symptom in Psychopathology. In *The Psychoanalytic Study of the Child*, III/IV. New York: International Universities Press.

Mahon, D. 1947, *Studies in Seicento Art and Theory*. London: Studies of the Warburg Institute, XVI.

Maloney, J. M. and Rockelein, L. 1948. An Insight into Richard Wagner and His Work. A Psychoanalytical Fragment. *American Imago*, V.

—— 1949, A New Interpretation of Hamlet. *International Journal of Psycho-Analysis*, XXX.

Malvasia, G. 1678, *Felsina pittrice*. Bologna.

Mann, T. 1936, *Freud und die Zukunft*. Jena: S. Fischer. Reprinted in *Almanach der Psychoanalyse*, 1937.

—— 1948, The Infant Prodigy. *Stories of Three Decades*. New York: Alfred A. Knopf.

Mannheim, K. 1940, *Man and Society in an Age of Reconstruction. Studies in Modern Social Structure*. London: Kegan Paul, Trench, Trubner & Co., Ltd.

Maschmeyer, E. 1926, Ein Beitrag zur Kunst der Schizophrenen. *Archiv für Psychiatrie*, LXXVIII.

Maslow, A. H. 1949, The Expressive Component of Behavior. *Psychological Review*, LVI.

Maury, L., see Axelrad, S.

McCulloch, W. S., see H. Foerster (1949, p. 170).

McFarlane, K. B. 1936, The Lancastrian Kings. In *The Cambridge Medieval History*, VIII. Cambridge: Cambridge University Press.

Mead, G. H. 1925/1926, The Nature of Aesthetic Experience. *International Journal of Ethics*, XXXVI.

Menninger, K. A. 1938, *Man Against Himself*. New York: Harcourt, Brace and Co.

—— 1942, *Love Against Hate*. New York: Harcourt, Brace and Co.

Merzbach, A. 1930. Symbolische Selbstzeichnungen aus der Psychose eines Jugendlichen und ihre Verwertbarkeit. *Zeitschrift für die gesamte Neurologie*. CXXVII.

Meyer-Gross, W., see Maclay, W. S.

—— and Lipps, J. 1929/1930, Das Problem des primitiven Denkens. *Philosophischer Anzeiger*, IV.

Meyerson, W. S., see Bradley, B.

Michailov, N. 1935, Zur Begriffsbestimmung der Laienmalerei. *Zeitschrift für Kunstgeschichte*, IV.

Migliorini, G. 1939, Automatismi superiori: il riso. *Revista di Psicologia normale e patologica*, XXXV, Series 3.

Millner, S. L. 1948, *Ernst Josephson*. New York: Machmadim Art Editions.

Minkowska, M. 1937, Van Gogh. Les relation entre sa vie, sa maladie et son oeuvre. *Deuxième Congrès Internationale d'esthétique et de la science de l'art*, I. Paris. Felix Alçan.

Moellenhoff, F. 1940, Remarks on the Popularity of Mickey Mouse. *American Imago*, I.

Mohr, F. 1906-1907, Ueber Zeichnungen von Geisteskranken und ihre diagnostische Verwertbarkeit. *Journal für Psychologie und Neurologie*, VIII.

Money-Kyrle, R. 1933, A Psychoanalytic Study of the Voices of Joan of Arc. *British Journal of Medical Psychology*, XIII.

Morgenthaler, W. 1918, Uebergang zwischen Zeichnen und Schreiben bei Geisteskranken. *Schweizer Archiv für Neurologie und Psychiatrie*, II.

—— 1921, Ein Geisteskranker als Künstler. *Arbeiten für angewandte Psychiatrie*, I.

Morris, C. 1946, *Signs, Language and Behavior*. New York: Prentice-Hall.

Mosini, A. 1646, *Diverse Figure*. Bologna.

Mosse, E. P. 1940, Painting-analysis in the Treatment of Neuroses. *Psychoanalytic Review*, XXVII.

—— 1942, Color Therapy. *Occupational Therapy and Rehabilitation*, XXI.

—— 1951, Psychological Mechanisms in Art Production. *The Psychoanalytic Review*, XXXVIII.

Münz, L. and Loewenfeld, V. 1934, *Plastische Arbeiten Blinder*. Brünn: Rudolf M. Rohrer.

Murphy, G. 1947, *Personality*. New York: Harper & Bros.

Murray, H. A. 1934/1935, The Psychology of Humor. *Journal of Social and Abnormal Psychology*, XXIX.

—— 1938, *Explorations in Personality*. New York: Oxford University Press.

—— 1949, Introduction to *Pierre and the Ambiguities*, by H. Melville. New York: Hendricks House.

Muschgg, W. 1930, *Psychoanalyse und Literaturwissenschaft*. Berlin: Dunker und Dürmhaupt.

—— 1933, Dichtung als archaisches Erbe. *Imago*, XIX.

Naecke, P. 1913, Einige Bemerkungen bezüglich der Zeichnungen und anderer künstlerischer Aeusserungen von Geisteskranken. *Zeitschrift für die gesamte Neurologie*, XVII.

Napoli, P. J. 1946, Finger Painting and Personality Diagnosis. *Genetic Psychology Monographs*, XXXIV.

Naumburg, M. 1947, *Studies of the "Free" Art Expression of Behavior Problem Children and Adolescents as a Means of Diagnosis and Therapy*. New York: Nervous and Mental Disease Monographs, LXXI.

—— 1950. *Schizophrenic Art: Its Meaning in Psychotherapy*. New York: Grune & Stratton.

Nicholes, E. L. 1950, The Shadowed Mind: A Study of the Change in Style of Poetry of John Clare Resulting from the Effects of the Schizophrenic Process. Doctoral Thesis, New York University, unpublished.

Nicolai, F. 1781, Reisebeschreibung durch Deutschland und die Schweiz. Nebst Bemerkungen über Gelehrsamkeit, Industrie, Religion und Sitten, VI. Leipzig.

Nietzsche, F. (1945), *Ecce Homo. Collected Writings*, I. New York: Citadel Press.

Nunberg, H. 1920 (1948), On the Catatonic Attack. In *Practice and Theory of Psychoanalysis*. New York: Nervous and Mental Disease Monographs, LXXIV.

—— 1931 (1948), The Synthetic Function of the Ego. *Ibid.*

—— 1932, *Allgemeine Neurosenlehre auf psychoanalytischer Grundlage.* Bern-Berlin: Hans Huber.

——1937, Theory of the Therapeutic Results of Psychoanalysis. *International Journal of Psycho-Analysis,* XVIII.

Orloff, C. 1937, Le Modèle et l'artiste. In *Deuxième Congrès International d'esthétique et de science de l'art, II.* Paris: Felix Alçan.

Paden, W. D. 1942, *Tennyson in Egypt: A Study of Imagery in His Earlier Work.* Lawrence, Kansas: University of Kansas Publications, Humanistic Studies, No. 27.

Paget, V., see Lee, V.

Panofsky, E. 1924, Idea. *Studien der Bibliothek Warburg.*

Parsons, J. P. 1747, Human Physiognomy Explained in the Crounian Lectures on Muscular Motion, for the year 1746 read before the Royal Society, being a supplement to the Philosophical Transactions for that year.

Partridge, C. 1938, Scientific Thought. *Journal of Psychology,* V.

Paulhan, F. 1901 (1930), *Psychologie de l'invention.* 4th Edition. Paris: Felix Alçan.

Pfeifer, R. A. 1923, *Der Geisteskranke und sein Werk: Eine Studie über schizophrene Kunst.* Leipzig: Kroener.

Pfister, O. 1913 (a), Kryptolalie, Kryptographie und unbewussstes Vexierbild bei Normalen. *Jahrbuch für psychoanalytische und psychopathologische Forschungen,* V.

—— 1913 (b), Die Entstehung der künstlerischen Inspiration. *Imago,* II.

—— 1917, *The Psychoanalytic Method.* New York: Moffat, Yard. (Contains a condensation of the paper of 1913.)

—— 1923, *Expressionism in Art: Its Psychological and Biological Basis.* Translated by B. Low and M. A. Muegge. New York: Dutton.

Plessner, H., see Buytendijk, J. J.

Pollnow, H. 1928, Historisch-Kritische Beiträge zur Physiognomik. *Jahrbuch für Characterologie,* V.

—— 1937, L'Analyse pathographique. Histoire du problème. In *Deuxième Congrès International d'Esthétique et de la Science de l'Art,* I. Paris: Felix Alçan.

Porta, G. B. 1601, *De humana physiognomia,* IV. Napoli.

Postman, D. L., see Postman, L.

Postman, L., Jenkins, W. O., Postman, D. L. 1948, An Experimental Comparison of Active Recall and Recognition. *American Journal of Psychology,* LXI.

Pottier, H. E. 1916, Les Origines der la caricature dans l'antiquité. *Annales du Musée Guimet.* Paris.

Prager, L., see Herzfeld, E.

Praz, M. 1933, *The Romantic Agony.* London: Oxford University Press.

Prinzhorn, H. 1919, Das bildnerische Schaffen der Geisteskranken. *Zeitschrift für die gesamte Neurologie und Psychiatrie,* LII.

—— 1922 (a), *Bildnerei der Geisteskranken.* Berlin: Springer.

—— 1922 (b), Gibt es schizophrene Gestaltungsmerkmale in der Bildnerei der Geisteskranken? *Zeitschrift für die gesamte Neurologie und Psychiatrie,* LXXVIII.

—— 1926, *Die Bildnerei der Gefangenen.* Berlin: Axel Juncker.

Radar, M. M. 1935, *A Modern Book of Esthetics.* New York: Henry Holt & Co.

Rank, O. 1907 (4th Edition, 1925), *Der Künstler. Ansätze zu einer Sexualpsychologie.* Wien: H. Heller.

—— 1909 (1913), *Myth of the Birth of the Hero.* New York: Nervous and Mental Disease Monographs, XVIII.

—— 1911, Die Lohengrinsage. Ein Beitrag zur Motivgestaltung und Deutung. *Schriften zur angewandten Seelenkunde,* XIII.

—— 1912 (2nd Edition, 1927), *Das Inzestmotiv in Dichtung und Sage. Grundzüge einer Psychologie des dichterischen Schaffens*. Leipzig-Wien: F. Deuticke.
—— 1919, *Psychoanalytische Beiträge zur Mythenforschung. Gesammelte Studien aus den Jahren 1912/1914*. Wien: Internationale Psychoanalytische Bibliothek, IV.
—— 1932, *Art and Artist, Creative Urge and Personality Development*. New York: Alfred A. Knopf.

Ransom, J. C. 1941, The New Criticism. *New Directions*.

Rapaport, D. 1950, On the Psychoanalytic Theory of Thinking. *International Journal of Psycho-Analysis*, XXXI.
—— 1951, *Organization and Pathology of Thought. Selected Sources*. (Translation and commentary by D. R.) New York: Columbia University Press.

Rapp, A. 1949, A Phylogenetic Theory of Wit and Humor. *Journal of Social Psychology*, XXX.

Read, H. 1936, *In Defense of Shelley and Other Essays*. London: William Heineman.
—— 1937. *Art and Society*. London: William Heineman.
—— 1938, *Collected Essays in Literary Criticism*. London: Faber & Faber.
—— 1951 (a), Psycho-Analysis and the Problem of Aesthetic Value. *International Journal of Psycho-Analysis*, XXXII.
—— 1951 (b), *Art and the Evolution of Man*. London: Freedom Press.

Redlich, F. C., Levine, J., and Sohler, T. P., 1951, A Mirth Response Test. Preliminary Report on a Psychodiagnostic Technique Utilizing Dynamics of Humor. *American Journal of Orthopsychiatry*, XXI.

Rees, H. E. 1942, *A Psychology of Artistic Creation, as Evidenced in Autobiographical Statements of Artists*. New York: Bureau of Publications, Teachers College, Columbia University.

Regis, E. 1882, Les aliénés peints par eux-mêmes. *L'Encéphale*, II.

Reich, A. 1949, The Structure of the Grotesque-Comic Sublimation. *Bulletin of the Menninger Clinic*, XIII. Reprinted in *The Yearbook of Psychoanalysis*, VI. New York: International Universities Press.

Reik, T. 1929 (a), Lust und Leid im Witz. *Imago*, XV.
—— 1929 (b) *Lust und Leid im Witz. Sechs psychoanalytische Studien*. Wien: Internationaler Psychoanalytischer Verlag.
—— 1933, *Nachdenkliche Heiterkeit*. Wien: Internationaler Psychoanalytischer Verlag.

Reinach, S. 1911, Le Rire rituel, *Revue de l'Université de Bruxelles*. Also in *Cultes religions et mythes*. IV, 1912.

Reitman, F. 1939, Facial Expression in Schizophrenic Drawings. *Journal of Mental Science*, LXXXV.
—— 1947, The "Creative Spell" of Schizophrenics after Leucotomy. *Ibid.*, XCIII.
—— 1950, *Psychotic Art*. New York: International Universities Press.

Réja, H. 1901, L'art malade: dessins de fous. *Revue universelle*, I.
—— 1907, *L'art chez les fous*. Paris.

Rickman, J. 1940, On the Nature of Ugliness and the Creative Impulse (Marginalia Psychoanalytica II). *International Journal of Psycho-Analysis*, XXI.
—— 1948, The Nature of Ugliness and the Creative Impulse. *Ibid.*, XXIX.

Rockelein, L. A., see Maloney, J. M.

Roe, A. 1947, Personality and Vocation. *Transactions of the New York Academy of Science*, Series 2, IX.

Róheim, G. 1943, On Sublimation. *Psychoanalytic Quarterly*, XII.

Roman, R. and Landis, C. 1945, Hallucination and Mental Imagery. *Journal of Nervous and Mental Disease*, CII.

Rorschach, H. 1913, Analytische Bemerkungen über das Gemälde eines Schizophrenen. *Zentralblatt für Psychoanalyse und Psychotherapie*, III.
—— 1914, Analyse einer schizophrenen Zeichnung. *Ibid.*, IV.

Roos, A. 1935, New Light on the Grylli. *Journal of Hellenic Studies*.

Rudel, R. 1949, The Function of Daydreams. Master's Thesis (directed by M. Scherer) at the Graduate Faculty of Political and Social Sciences, New School for Social Research, New York.

Sachs, H. 1924, *Gemeinsame Tagträume*. Wien: Internationaler Psychoanalytischer Verlag.

—— 1942, *The Creative Unconscious*. Cambridge: Sci.-Art Publishers.

Salomon, R. 1936, *Opicinus de Canistris*. *Weltbild und Bekenntnisse eines avignonensischen Klerikers des vierzehnten Jahrhunderts*. Mit Beiträgen von A. Heimann und R. Krautheimer. London: The Warburg Institute.

Sapas, E. 1918, Zeichnerische Reproduktion einfacher Formen durch Geisteskranke. *Schweizer Archiv für Psychiatrie*, IV.

Saussure, R. de 1934, Ueber genetische Psychologie und Psychoanalyse. *Imago*, XX.

Schäfer, T. 1934, Ueber gebärdliche Verhaltensweise bei Kindern. *Archiv für die gesamte Psychologie*, XCI.

Scherer, M., see Rudel, R.

Schilder, P. 1918, *Wahn und Erkenntnis*. Berlin: Springer.

—— 1923, *Seele und Leben*. Wiesbaden: Bergmann.

—— 1931, Studies Concerning the Psychology and Symptomatology of General Paresis. Translated in Rapaport (1951).

—— 1935 (1950), *The Image and Appearance of the Human Body*. New York: International Universities Press.

—— 1942, *Goals and Desires of Man*. New York: Columbia University Press.

—— and Levine, E. L. 1942, Abstract Art as an Expression of Human Problems. *Journal of Nervous and Mental Disease*, XCV.

Schlenther, P. No date, *Henrik Ibsens sämtliche Werke in deutscher Sprache*. Durchgesehen und eingeleitet von G. Brandes, J. Elias und P. Schlenther. Introduction to Volume VI. Berlin: S. Fischer Verlag.

Schlosser, J. V. 1924, *Die Kunstliteratur*. Wien: Anton Schroll & Co.

Schneider, D. E. 1950, *The Psychoanalyst and the Artist*. New York: Farrar, Straus & Co.

Schube, P. G. and Cowell, J. G. 1939, Art of Psychotic Persons. *Archives of Neurology and Psychiatry*, XLI.

Searl, M. N. 1933, Play, Reality and Aggression. *International Journal of Psycho-Analysis*, XIV.

Sears, R. N. 1934, Dynamic Factors in the Psychology of Humor. Doctoral Thesis, Harvard University Library (unpublished).

Sedlmayr, H. 1930, *Die Architektur Borrominis*. Berlin: Frankfurther Verlagsanstalt.

Seeman, W. 1951, The Freudian Theory of Daydreams: An Operational Analysis. *Psychological Bulletin*, XLVIII.

Selander, S. 1931, The Influence of Psychoanalysis in Modern Literature. *Dagens Nyheter*, December 5 and 6. (Abstracted in *Psychoanalytische Bewegung*, III.)

Sharpe, E. 1930, Certain Aspects of Sublimation and Delusion. *International Journal of Psycho-Analysis*, XI.

—— 1935, Similar and Divergent Unconscious Determinants Underlying the Sublimations of Pure Art and Pure Science. *Ibid.*, XVI.

—— 1946, From King Lear to the Tempest. *Ibid.*, XXVII. Reprinted in *Collected Papers on Psycho-Analysis*. London: Hogarth Press, 1950.

—— 1950, An Unfinished Paper on Hamlet. *Ibid.*

Silberer, H. 1909, Report on a Method of Eliciting and Observing Certain Symbolic Hallucinations. In Rapaport (1951).

—— 1910, Phantasie und Mythos. *Jahrbuch für Psychoanalyse und psychopathologische Forschungen*, I.

Slochower. H. 1941, Freud and Marx in Contemporary Literature. *The Sewanee Review*.

Snijder, G. A. 1934, Das Wesen der kretischen Kunst. Versuch einer Deutung. *Jahrbuch des Deutschen Archäologischen Institut, Archäologischer Anzeiger,* IL.

Sohler, T. P., see Redlich, F. C.

Sonnenfels, 1768, *Vom Verdienst des Portraitmalers.* Wien.

Speier, H., see Kris, E.

Spencer, H. 1940, *The Art and Life of William Shakespeare.* New York: Harcourt, Brace & Co.

Spencer, T. 1942, *Shakespeare and the Nature of Man.* New York: Macmillan.

Sperling, O. E. 1951, Illusions, Naive and Controlled. *Psychoanalytic Quarterly,* XX.

Spielrein, S. 1931, Kinderzeichnungen bei offenen und geschlossenen Augen. Untersuchungen über die unterschwelligen kinästhetischen Vorstellungen. *Imago,* XVII.

Spitz, R. A. with the assistance of Wolf, K. M. 1946, The Smiling Response: A Contribution to the Ontogenesis of Social Relations. *Genetic Psychology Monographs,* XXXIV.

Sterba, R. 1928, Bemerkungen zum dichterischen Ausdruck des modernen Naturgefühls. *Imago,* XIV.

—— 1930, Zur Problematik der Sublimierungslehre. *Internationale Zeitschrift für Psychoanalyse,* XVI.

—— 1939, The Significance of Theatrical Performance. *Psychoanalytic Quarterly,* VIII.

—— 1940 (a), The Problem of Art in Freud's Writings. *Psychoanalytic Quarterly,* IX.

—— 1940 (b), Aggression in the Rescue Fantasy. *Ibid.*

Strauss, L. 1941, Persecution and the Art of Writing. *Social Research,* III.

Sully, J. 1904, *Essai sur le rire.* Paris: Felix Alçan.

Suter, J. 1912, Die Beziehung zwischen Aufmerksamkeit und Atemvorgang. *Archiv für die gesamte Psychologie,* XXV.

Symons, A. J. A. 1934, *The Quest for Corvo. An Experiment in Biography.* London: Cassel & Co.

Tarachow, S. 1948, Remarks Concerning Certain Examples of Late Medieval Ecclesiastical Art. *Journal of Clinical Psychopathology,* IX.

—— 1949, Remarks on the Comic Process and Beauty. *Psychoanalytic Quarterly,* XVIII.

—— 1951, Circuses and Clowns. In *Psychoanalysis and the Social Sciences,* III. Edited by G. Róheim. New York: International Universities Press.

Tate, A. 1941, *Reason in Madness.* New York: Putnam.

Tatlock, I. S. P. 1943, Geoffrey of Monmouth's Vita Morlini. *Speculum: A Journal of Medieval Studies,* XVIII.

Taylor, M. P. 1927, A Father Pleads for the Death of His Son. *International Journal of Psycho-Analysis,* VIII.

Toulzac, M. 1901, *Rire et pleurer spasmodique.* Paris: E. Witski & Cie.

Traversi, D. A. 1941, Henry V. *Scrutiny,* IX.

Trilling, L., 1945, Art and Neurosis. *Partisan Review.*

—— 1947. Freud and Literature. *Horizon.*

—— 1950, *The Liberal Imagination* (Reprints of the two papers listed above). New York: Viking Press.

Utitz, E. 1911, *Die Funktionslust im aesthetischen Verhalten.* Leipzig.

Vanlar, C. 1903, La Psychologie du rire. *Bulletin Académie Royale de Bruxelles.* Clane de Science, Série IV.

Varendonck, J. 1921, *The Psychology of Daydreams.* London: Allen and Unwin.

Villamil, J. P. L., 1933, Matiz intenso e religiosidad en el contenido inconsciente del psiquismo humano. *Los progressos de la Clinica,* No. 254, Madrid.

Vinchon, J. 1926, *L'Art et la folie.* Paris: Stock.

—— 1927, L'Art dément. *Aesculape*, XVII.
Vinci, Leonardo da. 1882, *Das Buch von der Malerei* (1270). Editor K. Ludwig. *Quellenschriften für Kunstgeschichte*, XVIII.
Voigt, G. 1880, *Die Wiederbelebung des klassischen Alterthums*. Berlin: G. Reimer.
Vossler, K. 1932, *Spirit of Language in Civilization*. New York: Harcourt, Brace & Co.

Waelder, R. 1933, The Psychoanalytic Theory of Play. *Psychoanalytic Quarterly*, II.
—— 1934 (1936) Das Freiheitsproblem in der Psychoanalyse und das Problem der Realitätsprüfung. *Imago*, XX.
—— 1936, The Principle of Multiple Function. *Psychoanalytic Quarterly*, V.
Wahlin, K. 1911, Ernst Josephson, 1851-1906. *En Minnestekning Sveriges Allmanna Kunstforenings Publication*, XIX.
Wangh, M. 1950, Othello: The Tragedy of Iago. *The Psychoanalytic Quarterly*, XIX. Reprinted in *The Yearbook of Psychoanalysis*, VII. New York: International Universities Press.
Weiss, J. 1947, A Psychologic Theory of Formal Beauty. *Psychoanalytic Quarterly*, XVI.
Weitz, M. 1951, *Philosophy of the Arts*. Cambridge, Mass.: Harvard University Press.
Werner, H. 1933 (1948), *Comparative Psychology of Mental Development*. New York: Harper & Bros.
Wertham, F. 1941, *Dark Legend, A Study in Murder*. New York: Duell, Sloan & Pearce.
Wertheimer, M. 1945, *Productive Thinking*. New York: Harper & Bros.
Westerman-Holstijn, A. J. 1924, Die psychologische Entwicklung Vincent van Goghs. *Imago*, X.
Weygandt, W. 1925, Zur Frage der pathologischen Kunst. *Zeitschrift für die gesamte Neurologie und Psychiatrie*, XCIV.
White, W. A. 1930, The Language of Psychoses. *American Journal of Psychiatry*, IV.
Wilson, E. 1945, *Axel's Castle*. New York: Scribner's.
—— 1941, *The Wound and the Bow*. Boston: Houghton, Mifflin & Co.
Winterstein, A. von (A. v. W.) 1913, G. Ch. Lichtenberg und die Psychoanalyse. *Zentralblatt für Psychoanalyse und Psychotherapie*, III.
—— 1929, Motorisches Erleben im schöpferischen Vorgang. *Psychoanalytische Bewegung*, I.
—— 1934, Contributions to the Problem of Humor. *Psychoanalytic Quarterly*, III.
Witte, O. 1930, Untersuchung über die Gebärdensprache. *Zeitschrift für Psychologie*, CXVI.
Wittkower, R., see Brauer, H.
Wolf, K. M., see Spitz, R. A.
Wolfenstein, M. 1947, The Impact of a Children's Story on Mothers and Children. *Monographs of the Society for Research in Child Development*, No. 42 (1946).
—— 1951, A Phase in the Development of Children's Sense of Humor. In *The Psychoanalytic Study of the Child*, VI. New York: International Universities Press.
—— and Leites, N. 1947, The Analysis of Themes and Plots. *Annals of the American Academy of Political and Social Science*.
—— 1950, *Movies: A Psychological Study*. Glencoe, Ill.: The Free Press.
Wright, T. 1865, *A History of Caricature*. London.
Wulff, M. 1936, Zur Arbeit von E. Kris "Bemerkungen zur Bildnerei der Geisteskranken." *Imago*, XXII.
Wundt, W. 1900, *Völkerpsychologie, I. Die Sprache*. Vierte Auflage, 1921. Stuttgart: A. Koerner.

Ziehen, T., see Haecker, V.
Zilboorg, G. 1941, *A History of Medical Psychology*. New York: W. W. Norton & Co.
Zilsel, E. 1918. *Die Geniereligion. Ein kritischer Versuch über das Moderne Persönlichkeitsideal*. Wien: Braumüller.

—— 1926, *Die Entstehung des Geniebegriffes. Ein Beitrag zur Ideengeschichte der Antike und des Frühkapitalismus.* Tübingen: J. C. B. Mohr.

Zimmermann, J. and Garfinkel, L. 1942, Preliminary Study of the Art Productions of the Adult Psychotic. *Psychiatric Quarterly,* XVI.

Zingerle, H., see Hassmann, O.

BIBLIOGRAPHICAL NOTE

Chapter 1 has been rewritten and enlarged for the present publication. It combines material previously used on two occasions. In the fall of 1938 a series of three lectures was given at the London Institute of Psycho-Analysis. A shorter version, in German, of these lectures was published under the title "Probleme der Aesthetik" in *Internationale Zeitschrift für Psychoanalyse und Imago,* XXVI, 1941. The title and certain parts of Chapter 1 were taken from a paper written for *Psychoanalysis Today,* edited by S. Lorand, New York, International Universities Press, 1946.

Chapter 2 is based on a paper read to the Vienna Psychoanalytic Society in October, 1934. It was published in *Imago,* XXI, 1935, under the title "Zur Psychologie der älteren Biographik dargestellt an der des bildenden Künstlers" and reprinted in the *Almanach der Psychoanalyse,* 1937.

Chapter 3 is based on a paper read to the Academic Association for Medical Psychology in Vienna in May, 1936, and published in *Imago,* XXII, 1936. A Japanese translation was published in *Tokio Zeitschrift für Psychoanalyse,* VII, 1933.

Chapter 4 is based on a paper read to the Vienna Psychoanalytic Society in November, 1932, and was published in *Imago,* XIX, 1933. A Spanish translation appeared in *Revista de Psicoanalisis,* III, 1945/46.

Chapter 5 is based on a paper read to the New York Psychoanalytic Society in March, 1945 and was published in *The Psychoanalytic Quarterly,* XV, 1946.

Chapter 6 is based on a paper read to the XIII International Congress of Psychoanalysis in Lucerne, 1934. It was published in *Imago,* XX, 1934, and in the *International Journal of Psycho-Analysis,* XVII, 1936.

Chapter 7 is based on a paper read to the Warburg Institute of London University in May, 1937; it was published in the *British Journal of Medical Psychology,* XVII, 1938.

Chapter 8 is based on a paper read to the British Psycho-Analytical Society in May, 1937, and was published in the *International Journal of Psycho-Analysis,* XIX, 1938.

Chapter 9 is based on a paper read to the XIV International Congress of Psychoanalysis in Marienbad, 1936, and was published in *Internationale Zeitschrift für Psychoanalyse und Imago,* XXIV, 1939, and in the *International Journal of Psycho-Analysis,* XXI, 1940.

Chapter 10 was originally published in *Philosophy and Phenomenological Research*, VIII, 1948.

Chapter 11 was originally published in *The Psychoanalytic Quarterly*, XV, 1946.

Chapter 12 was originally published in *The Psychoanalytic Quarterly*, XVII, 1948.

Chapter 13 was originally published in the *International Journal of Psycho-Analysis*, XX, 1939.

Chapter 14 is based on a paper presented at the Annual Meeting of the American Psychoanalytic Association in Montreal, 1949, and was published in *The Psychoanalytic Quarterly*, XIX, 1950. It has been reprinted in *The Yearbook of Psychoanalysis*, VII, edited by S. Lorand, New York, International Universities Press, 1951. A slightly different version has been reprinted in part with extensive annotations by D. Rapaport in his *Organization and Pathology of Thought. Selected Sources*. New York, Columbia University Press.

INDEX

Abercrombie, L., 259, 321
Abraham, K., 78, 218, 219, 232, 321
Active repetition of passive experiences, 41-42, 59, 182, 207, 210
Actor, psychology of, 28, 40, 42-43
Adolescence, psychology of, 83-84, 94, 234
Adolf, H., 40, 321
Aeschylus, 47
Aesthetic barrier, 147
Aesthetic experience
  characteristics of, 31, 59
  pleasure in, 22, 59, 63
  theory of, 243, 315
  types of, 63
Aesthetic illusion, 39-47
  and actor, 43
  and ego control, 45-46, 61-63
  and energy discharge, 46, 63
  and magic, 49
  and participation, 40-41, 44, 46
  and reality testing, 41
  and sequence of responses, 56
  function of, 44-45, 63
  roots of, 42
Aesthetics, 59-60, 79, 188, 202, 210
Agathon, 188
Agglutination, 106
Aggression (see also Destruction and Psychic Energy), 175, 180, 192-193, 214-216, 220, 231-234
Agucchi, 189
Aiken, C., 270
Alexander, F., 173, 278, 309, 321
Allegory, 257
Allport, G. W., 58, 321
Ambiguity
  aesthetic, 243-264
  and primary process, 104
  of expression, 108
  types of, 245-251
Amphiboly, 245
Anastasi, A., 87, 89, 91, 102, 106, 112, 151-153, 321, 326
Andersen, H. C., 69
Anderson, S., 271
Animal phobias, 31-32, 39
Anlage, 71
Anthropology, 18, 73, 121, 224

Anthroposco, O., 239, 321
Apocryphal gospel, 70
Archimedes, 65
Architect, 80-82, 126, 151-169
Aretino, 195
Arieti, S., 185, 321
Aristophanes, 188, 195
Aristotle, 45, 62-63, 227, 239, 321, 323
Arlow, J. A., 292, 321
Arnheim, R., 21, 55, 321
Arnold, M., 254
Art
  and ritual, 57, 67, 159-160, 253, 256
  antinaturalistic, 77-78
  as communication, 16, 31, 37, 47-56, 60-62, 243, 254
  as social control, 39, 57
  as sorcery, 61, 80, 159-160, 203
  as therapy, 95-96
  cathartic effect of, 45-46, 62
  comparative approach to, 88, 91, 105-106
  critic's response to, 57
  function of, 31, 37, 39, 45-46, 61, 79, 128, 167, 203
  gestalt approach to, 21-22
  history and development of, 15, 21, 30, 40, 47-50, 67, 73-74, 108, 142, 189-203, 262-263
  in social and historical setting, 21, 29, 57, 66-67, 108, 189-203, 262-263
  interdisciplinary approach to, 18
  limitations of psychoanalytic approach to, 19-22, 31
  magic function of, 47-51, 61, 80, 168, 203
  media of, 28-29, 54, 62
  neoplatonic theory of, 115, 196-203
  of cave dwellers, 50-51, 106
  of eidetics, 106
  primitive, 49, 57, 88, 91, 105-106
  psychoanalytic approach to, 13-31, 128-129
  relation between function, form and content, 49, 105, 142-143, 168
  stringencies in, 19, 21, 62, 252-264
  survival value of, 62, 263

theory of, 46, 73, 79, 88, 189, 243
use of psychoanalysis in, 30, 267-272
Artist (*see also* Painter, Poet *and* Sculptor)
accounts of process of creation by, 53, 59, 90, 293, 295-296
and mythology, 47-48, 73-74, 293
and philosopher, 21, 48
and scientist, 21, 47
anonymity of, 66-67
as aesthetic person, 58, 133, 261
as empirical person, 58, 133, 261
as magician, 47-48, 78, 164
as rebel, 47-48, 80, 150, 166
compared to priest, 39, 79, 293
compared to teacher, 39
competing with gods, 48, 81, 150, 166
"divine," 79, 81
freedom of, 79-80, 115, 166, 197-203
identification with audience, 61, 167
image of, 64-84, 129, 150
in historical setting, 21, 29, 67, 73-74, 79
in search of model, 53-54
legends of, 64-84, 149-150
living up to biographical model, 69, 82-83, 150
measure of greatness, 19-20
narcissism of, 35, 80
oral tendencies of, 20, 299
passivity of, 139-143, 166, 294-302
pathographic approach to, 19, 21, 31, 58, 128-129, 287-288
precocity of, 71-72
psychology of, 25-26, 80, 115-117, 287-288, 299-300
psychotic, *see* Psychotic Artist
recognition of, 47-48, 66-68, 198-199
relation to audience, 38-39
relation to his work, 60-61, 80, 131-132
relation of life history to work, 17, 31, 71, 287-288
relation to model, 51-53, 74, 113, 135-150
roots of admiration for, 47-49
-s, competition among, 74-76
social position of, 47-48, 66-68, 78, 198-199
suicide of, 80-82
typical delusions of, 81, 138, 149-150, 164-169
voyeurism of, 20
Artistic productions (*see also* Art)
and body image, 56, 114
as copy of nature, 75, 115, 190
as document of process of creation, 30

deceiving effect of, 75
distance from instinctual conflict, 39
hierarchy of, 28
in course of analysis, 24
multiplicity of meanings, 25, 243-264
of blind child, 56
of insane, *see* Psychotic Productions
structure of, 62
surpassing nature, 74, 115
Arundel, R. M., 90, 321
Aschaffenburg, G., 153, 321
Ashbee, C. R., 321
Attention, 208
Auden, W. H., 44, 321
Audience (*see also* Re-creation)
artist's identification with, 61, 167
degree of participation by, 40-41
distance from art work, 46-47, 56, 256-257
identification with artist, 61-63, 167
identification with artist's model, 55
identification with play characters, 43
kinesthetic reaction of, 55-56
role of, 38-39, 60-63
stratification of, 57
structure of response of, 54-55, 61-63, 255-257
turning from passivity to activity, 58-59, 62
Audry, J., 153, 321
Auerbach, J. G., 90, 321
Ax, H., 277, 321
Axelrad, S., 20, 27, 321, 328, 334

Baldinucci, G., 189, 196, 322
Bartlett, E. M., 55, 322
Bartlett, P., 61, 322
Bateson, G., 83
Baudouin, C., 78, 87, 322
Baynes, H. G., 87, 322, 326
Bechterew, 219
Becker, P. E., 152, 322
Bell, C., 217
Bellak, L., 44, 322
Bellori, G., 189, 322
Bender, L., 55, 114, 322
Benjamin, J. D., 14, 322
Beres, D., 24, 322
Beresford, J. D., 268
Berger, A., 265, 322
Bergler, E., 20, 25-26, 35, 44, 187, 288, 294, 299, 302, 322
Bergmann, G., 141, 322
Bergson, H., 174, 179, 221, 263
Bernfeld, S., 26, 64, 218, 307, 322, 328

Bernfeld, S. C., 64, 322
Bernini, G. L., 175, 191, 192, 194, 322
Bertschinger, H., 87, 98, 152, 322
Bibring, E., 179, 232
Binyon, L., 95, 323
Biographer, attitude to hero, 64-67
Biographical formulae
  and actual life experiences, 81
  and myths, 69-70
  of architects, 81-82
  of painter and sculptors, 64-74
  roots of, 64-74
Biographical interest, psychology of, 58
Biography
  as a literary category, 64, 66
  enacted, 83
  function of, 64-66
  hero's youth in, 67-74
  of artists, 57-58, 66-83, 287-288
  role of tradition in, 64-83
  psychology of, 64-80
Birnbaum, K., 58, 142, 323
Bisexuality, in creation, 25, 150, 161-162, 167
Blake, W., 95
Bleuler, E., 144
Blum, A., 193, 323
Boccaccio, 68
Body image, 55-56, 114
Bonaparte, M., 58, 323
Born, W., 26, 87, 95, 323
Bosch, H., 199
Bouman, 106
Bowling, W. G., 323
Bowra, C. M., 291, 323
Bradley, A. C., 274, 291, 323
Bradley, B., 103, 323, 335
Brauer, H., 189, 190, 194, 323, 340
Breuer, J., 23, 219, 265-266, 304, 322, 323, 326
Brierley, M., 26, 117, 323
Brill, A. A., 196, 206, 269, 299, 323, 326-327
Brissaud, 219
Broadside, 180, 189-203
Broch, H., 271
Brugsch, T., 236, 323, 333
Brunswick, R. M., 42, 323
Bühler, K., 50, 77, 92, 105, 210, 217-218, 239, 323
Bullough, E., 46, 256, 323
Bunker, H. A., 327
Bürger-Prinz, H., 153, 323
Burke, K., 249, 271, 323
Burlingham, D. T., 181-182, 323
Burt, C., 31, 56, 323

Butcher, S. H., 63, 321, 323, 328
Butler, S., 270
Buxbaum, E., 44, 323
Buytendijk, J. J., 218, 236-237, 324, 336
Bychowski, G., 87, 324

Cameron, N., 92, 178, 324
Cannon, W. B., 317, 324
Capgras, E., 324
Caricature, 103-105, 114, 136, 173-203
Carracci, A. and L., 189-190, 195, 199-200, 202
Cartoonist, typical conflict of, 28
Cassirer, E., 224
Cattell, R. B., 215, 324, 334
Chain drawings, 102
Chatterji, N. N., 125, 324
Childhood schizophrenia, 114
Child (ren)
  art of, 88, 91, 105-106
  as artist, 68-74
  attitude to, 72-73
  development of, 21, 41, 53, 55, 178, 206-210, 223-224, 229
  drawings of, 178, 192, 197
  fun of, 182-183, 211
  laughter of, 205
  luxury of movement, 222
  play of, 41-42, 77, 182-183, 205, 209-211, 214
  smiling of, 227-229
  speech of, 178, 206-207, 223-226
  urge to communicate of, 181
Christ, syncretistic account of childhood of, 70, 72
Christensen, E. O., 19, 324
Cicero, 222, 227
Cimabue, 68-69, 74
Circus, 214
Clang associations, 100, 124
Clare, J., 93, 335
Clark, K., 19, 324
Clown, 213, 215-216, 233
Coleridge, S. T., 23, 24, 47
Comedy, 188, 213
Comic (see also Jokes, Humor and Wit), 63, 173-216, 233
  and cultural differentiation, 183
  and sublime, 63, 187, 202
  as defense against anxiety, 146, 214-216
  definition of, 174, 217
  distinguished from wit and humor, 204-205
  double-edged character of, 181-183, 199, 214-216

experimental investigations of, 212
infantile character of, 205-207
perception of, 204
social character of, 180-181, 185, 204
subjective aspects of, 185
time-bound, 176
unknown to children, 212
Communication
aesthetic, 254-256
and art, see Art, As Communication
and gesture, 50, 112, 218
and representational art, 49-50
intended, 136, 218
media of, 49-50, 92, 218
mimic, see Expressive Movements
representational compared to verbal, 50
standards of interpretation, 245, 255-257
tactile root of, 55
unconscious, 116, 218
Comparative psychology, 105
Confession compulsion, 181
Conflicts
and personality development, 20-21
and recurrent themes, 19, 23, 69
typical, 28-29
ubiquity of, 17
Connoisseur, 57-58, 62, 260
Consciousness
hypercathexis of, 306, 313-314
motor theory of, 55-56
pathways to, 38, 167, 306
reactions to reaching, 314-318
Corvo, Baron, 35-39
Cowell, J. G., 152, 324, 338
Creation
and re-creation, 31, 51-53, 56-63
as divine prerogative, 78-79
Creative activity
and free association, 30
and inspiration, 30, 59-61, 167-168, 291-302, 316-317
and passivity, 139-143, 166, 294-302, 314-318
and structure of personality, 26
and the unconscious, 25-28, 53, 59-60, 115-116, 148, 291-302, 316-317
and typical conflicts, 26
defensive, 29, 35
function of, 115-116, 128, 168
influence of bisexuality on, 25
influence of life history, 19, 58
influence of oral-masochistic tendencies, 20, 25-26
influence of psychoanalysis on, 20, 29

influence of trauma on, 25
influence of voyeurism, 20
perception in, 53, 115-116
phases of, 59, 61
psychotic, see Psychotic Artist and Psychotic Productions
success and failure of, 29
Creative spell, 88-90, 93-94, 106, 126, 151-169
Critic, see Connoisseur
Croce, B., 58, 132, 187, 261, 324
Counterphobic attitude, 210
Ctesicles, 184

Daedalus, 48, 75, 78, 166
Dancer, typical conflict of, 28
Dante, 68, 118
Darwin, C., 217-218, 224, 234, 237
Daumier, 191
Davis, R., 196, 324
Davison, C., 219, 324, 331
Daydream (see also Preconscious), 32-39, 77
and narrative art, 31-39, 44, 147
and masturbation fantasy, 33-35
experimental investigation of, 310-311
of hero's discovery, 71
Decomposition, 278
Defense
and neutralization, 53
by substitution, 285
comic as, 215
specificity of, in artist, 20
unification of, 20
Delacroix, H., 296, 314, 324
Del Solar, C., 212, 324, 328
Delusion, 81, 87, 93, 95, 97, 129, 136-150, 164-169
Denial, 42, 139
Depersonalization, 142
Deri, F., 26, 324
Deri, M., 15, 19, 324
Descartes, 208
Destruction (see also Aggression), 52, 76, 117, 125, 127, 159-160, 168, 185
Deus artifex, 79, 81, 161
Deutsch, H., 186, 187, 232, 266, 302, 324
Dewey, J., 251, 254, 256
Dietrich, A., 324
Dilthey, A., 129, 324
Don Quixote, 186, 194
Donaghy, J. L., 296, 324
Donne, 258, 260
Doodling, 90-91, 102, 307
Dooley, L., 173, 216, 324

Dostoyevski, 270
Dramatic art, 39-40
Drawing, as construction and destruction of image, 51-52
Dream
  and art work, 24-25, 177, 199, 253-254
  and caricature, 175-176
  and childhood fantasies, 42, 253
  and daydreams, 38
  and life history, 19
  and wit, 176
  depicting of, 30
  Dürer on, 199
  interpretation, 116, 178, 246
Drommard, G., 222, 324
Dudd, R., 95, 322
Dujardin, E., 270
Dumas, G., 219, 222, 239, 324
Dürer, 198-199
Duris of Samos, 76

Eastman, M., 260
Ecstasy, 302
Ego
  and affect, 177, 225
  and comic, 204-216
  and conflict, 21, 45-46
  and development of style, 92
  and energy discharge, 25-28, 46, 53, 62-63, 185, 225, 305-306, 310-311
  and expression of aggression, 136, 175, 231-234
  and fantasy, 311-312
  and humor, 204
  and laughter, 220-229
  and primary process, 60, 99, 103, 177, 206-207, 305-306, 312
  and regression, 28, 41, 77, 129, 177, 205, 293-297, 301, 312, 318
  and smiling, 229
  autonomy of functions of, 20-21, 27, 29, 53, 63, 114, 206, 208, 219, 222, 226, 312-313
  complete investment of, 310, 316
  conflict-free sphere of (see also Ego, autonomy of functions), 304
  control of aggression, 180, 215-216
  control of motility, 112, 219-220, 226-239
  delay of discharge, 37-38
  development of, 21, 38, 41, 53, 204-216
  in art and psychosis, 60, 93, 312
  in ecstasy, 302
  loss of control of, 77, 116, 177, 201, 206, 225

pleasure and control, 45, 63, 207
primary autonomy, 20
psychology, 18, 19, 84, 87-88, 105-106, 167, 219, 297, 303-304
relation to id, 25, 46, 60-62, 115-116, 129, 185, 305-306
relation to reality in psychosis, 93, 100, 234-235
secondary autonomy, 20, 27
self-regulation of, 28
strength, 103
synthetic function of, 308-309, 316
syntonicity, 316
weakness, 105, 221, 312
Ehrenzweig, A., 22, 324
Eidelberg, L., 181, 324
Eidetic, 106
Einstein, A., 315-316
Eisenstein, V., 89, 324
Eisler, R., 78, 324
Eitingon, M., 94
Elaboration, 59-62, 116
  preconscious, 180, 185, 313
Elation, 293
Eliot, T. S., 58, 59, 248-249, 255, 260, 325
Elliott, Sir T., 276-277
Embellishments, 63, 95
Empathy, kinaesthetic, 55
Empson, W., 25, 243, 248-250, 258-259, 271-272, 278-279, 325
Endowment (see also Talent)
  special, and magic, 47-56
  special, relationship to divine, 40
Engerth, G., 113, 325
Erasmus, 195
Erickson, M. H., 91, 325, 332
Erikson, E. H., 65, 325
Evenson, H., 95, 153, 325
Expressionism, 88, 108, 199
Expression
  and language, 218, 223-226
  cultural variations of, 218, 224
  development of, 222-226
  disturbances of, 111-113, 128-150, 218, 224, 229-239
  experimental investigations of, 235-239
  interpretation of, 218, 231, 235-237
  melody of movements, 236
  privatization of, 126
  search for, 111, 144-150, 235
  social character of, 218, 228
  toto corpore, 224-225, 227
Expressive behavior (see also Mimic and Gesture), 217-239
Eysenck, H. J., 185, 215, 325

Fairbairn, W. R. D., 16, 325
Fairy tales, 42
Falstaff, 194, 204, 273-288
Family romance, 69-72
Fantasies
  anal, 145-146
  and creative imagination, 17, 293-302
  and fairy tales, 42
  and masturbation, 33-35, 37
  and play, 32-33
  depicting of, 30
  dynamics of, 310-318
  hidden in doodles, 91, 307
  of being discovered as genius, 71-72
  of inside of female body, 125
  oral, 140-141, 317
  rescue, 71
Fay, H. M., 153, 325
Federn, P., 325
Fehrle, E., 233, 325
Félibien, A., 191, 325
Fenichel, O., 43, 93, 116, 139, 210, 214, 219, 226, 229, 232, 245, 300, 325
Ferdière, G., 87, 325
Ferenczi, S., 219, 222, 226, 232, 325
Feuillet, O., 69
Fiction, *see* Narrative Art
Filefo, 195
Films, psychological study of, 18
Flach, A., 236, 325
Fliess, W., 23, 327
Flournoy, H., 115, 325
Flugel, J. C., 26, 326
Foerster, H. v., 326, 334
Foley, J. P., 87, 89, 91, 102, 106, 112, 151-153, 321, 326
Folk art, 91
Folklore, 72-73
Forgetting, 315-316
Form, 22, 49, 92, 105, 142-143, 147, 161, 168, 266
Form niveau, 92
Foulkes, S. H., 99, 326
Fraenger, W., 326
Free association
  and preconscious, 307
  as artistic expression, 30
French, T. M., 308-309, 321, 326
Fretet, J., 30, 326
Freud, A., 33-34, 38, 39, 41, 93-94, 234, 296, 304, 326
Freud, S., 13-29, 34, 38, 41-42, 45, 55, 58, 63-64, 69, 72, 78, 83, 93, 100, 104-106, 116, 126, 139, 147, 164, 167, 173-174, 176-178, 180, 182-184, 186-187, 196-197,

204-210, 212, 216, 219-220, 222-223, 227-229, 231, 235, 237, 246-247, 263, 265-272, 287, 299, 303-306, 309, 313-318, 322-324, 326-328, 332
  influence on literature, 267-272
  Inhibition, Symptom and Anxiety, 87-88, 106
  on activity-passivity, 41-42
  on ambiguous words, 246, 247
  on believing, 310
  on biographers, 64
  on children's play, 41-42, 183, 211
  on comparative psychology, 105
  on daydreams, 34, 311-312
  on distinction of dream and daydream, 147, 167, 311
  on dreams, 22, 246, 311
  on ego control of primary process, 116, 305, 311-312
  on fairy tales, 42
  on family romance, 69
  on fusion of energy, 28
  on *Gravida*, 23-24
  on humor, wit, jokes, and the comic, 25, 104, 173-174, 176, 178, 180, 182, 186-187, 196-197, 204-209, 211-212, 216, 220, 222
  on kinaesthetic experiences, 55
  on Leonardo da Vinci, 19-22
  on libidinal types, 216
  on motility, 219, 223, 229, 237
  on object and word representation, 100
  on origin of smiling, 227-228, 231
  on poets, 22-23, 266
  on pleasure gain from psychic apparatus, 63, 315
  on preconscious, 206, 303-306, 311-318
  on primary and secondary process, 27, 177, 206, 305
  on psychoanalysis and archeology, 64
  on psychotic's relationship to reality, 93, 100
  on repression, 25, 29
  on resemblance of case histories and novels, 266
  on restitution, 93, 235
  on Schreber, 93, 108, 139, 164
  on Shakespeare, 287
  on sublimation, 26
  on tragedy, 42, 45
  on Wolf-man, 309
  review of *Studies in Hysteria*, 265
Friedlander, K., 42, 327
Friedman, J., 18, 328
Frois-Wittman, J., 62, 328

Fry, R., 56, 328
Fuchs, E., 328
Fuchs, S. H., *see* Foulkes, S. H.
Functional pleasure, 32, 210-211, 315

Gadelius, B., 97, 328
Galileo, 202
Garfinkel, L., 328, 341
Garrick, 43
Gassel, S., 18, 328
Gassner, J., 63, 323, 328
Gaunt, W., 36, 328
Geibel, E., 165
Gellert, E., 212, 324, 328
Genius, 47, 64, 79-80
  and insanity, 151, 169
  as target of ambivalence, 80
  divine origin of, 74
  misunderstood, 81
  religion of, 73-74
Gero, G., 64, 218, 328
Gestalt psychology, 21-22, 239, 248
Gestures, 112, 178-179, 207
  and words, 50, 223-226
Ginsburg, S., 20, 328
Ginzberg, E., 20, 321, 328, 330
Giotto, 68, 118
Glover, E., 15, 26, 225, 266, 328
Goethe, 23, 132, 213
Goldsen, J., 45
Gombrich, E. H., 8, 49, 54, 75, 173, 189-203, 328, 332
Gomperz, H., 17, 77, 328
Götz, B., 136, 141-142, 328
Goya, 30
Graber, G. H., 212, 328
Graewe, H., 55, 328
Grand-Carteret, J., 328
Greenacre, P., 267, 300, 328-329
Grimace, 136-147, 179, 225, 233
Grisar, H., 193, 329
Groos, K., 210
Grose, F., 329
Grotesque, psychology of, 179, 213-214
Grotjahn, M., 87, 212, 233, 329
Gruhle, H. W., 235
Grylli, 102
Gutheil, E., 58, 329
Guttmann, E., 90, 102, 153, 329, 334

Hadamard, J., 314, 329
Hadrian VIIth, A Romance, 36-37
Haecker, V., 71, 329, 340
Haigh, S. S., 36-37, 329
Hallucination, 53, 101, 306, 317

Hals, F., 194
Hamlet, 18, 47, 58, 260, 285-287
Happy ending, demand for, 42-43
Harding, R. E. M., 59, 253, 295, 329
Hart, H. H., 26, 329
Hartlaub, G. F., 108, 329
Hartmann, H., 8, 15, 16, 17, 20, 21, 26, 27, 28, 29, 38, 64, 126, 177, 206, 219, 304, 306, 307-308, 311-313, 315-316, 329, 332, 333
Hassmann, O., 89, 329, 341
Hawthorne, N., 23
Hazlitt, W., 274, 330
Hecker, E., 232, 330
Heege, F., 193, 329, 330
Heimann, A., 124, 330, 338
Heller, P., 65, 330
Hendrick, I., 211, 330
Henry IV, 273-288
Henry V, 273-288
Hephaestus, 48, 75, 78, 166
Heracles, 69
Herland, L., 217, 233, 330
Herma, J. L., 20, 328, 330
Herzfeld, E., 183, 212, 330, 336
Herzfeld, M., 113, 330
Hesse, H., 271, 330
Hill, F., 95
Histiography, 73-74
Hitschmann, E., 58, 96, 186, 330
Hobbes, 23, 207-209
Hodin, J. P., 95, 108, 330
Hoelderlin, 93
Hoffman, F. J., 265-272, 330
Hogarth, W., 192, 197, 330
Holinshed, R., 277, 280, 282
Homburger, A., 222, 223, 234, 330
Homer, 75
Hoops, R., 268, 330
Horror vacui, 107, 126
Housman, A. E., 256, 294-296, 300-301, 330
Humor *(see also* Comic, Jokes *and* Wit), 173, 187-188, 204-205, 215-216, 238, 247
Humorist, melancholic disposition of, 186, 216
Hupp, C., 193, 330
Huschke, A., 239, 330
Huxley, A., 268
Hyman, S. E., 25, 330
Hysteria, 98
Hystero-epileptic states, 292

Iatmul, 83

Ibsen, H., 43, 82
Identification
    and aesthetic reaction, 55-58, 61-63
    and imitation, 56
    and kinesthesia, 55-56
    and orality, 55-56, 299
    and over- and under-distance, 47
    and professional ethics, 83
    and reality testing, 42
    and succession of generations, 83
    of artist with God, 48, 81, 150, 166
    of audience with characters of play, 43
    of author with hero, 36
    role of body image in, 55-56
    shifts in, 28, 62
    with artist, 56-59, 61-63
    with biographical models, 83
    with leader, 57
    with the ridiculed, 208-209
Idealization, 53, 64, 282-283
Idols, 49
Illmarinen, 75
Illustrations, functions of, 50
Image
    devotional, see Idols
    function of, 49
    identity of, with model, 49, 76-77
    magic power of, 48, 76-78, 160, 200-203
    of the body, see Body image
Imitation, as aggression, 178-180
Incorporation, 163, 167, 299
Infant prodigy, 70-74
Inspiration
    admiration of, 30, 47, 67, 190
    and elaboration, 61
    and pregenital fantasies, 299-302
    and regression, 59, 167
    and skill, 30, 253
    in process of creating, 54, 59-61, 166,
        254, 291-302, 317
    in scientific thinking, 296-297
    secularization of, 79
Instinct to master, 211
Instinctual energy (see also Psychic En-
    ergy)
    break-throughs of, 38, 46
    fusion of, 28, 47, 52
    strength of, 72
Introjection, 166, 293, 299, 301-302
Introspection, 24, 59-60
Intuitive psychology, 22-23, 88, 265-266
Isaacs, S., 210, 330

Jacobson, E., 209, 330
Jacobsson, J., 97, 330

James, H., 23
Jaspers, K., 93, 95, 115, 153, 330
Jekels, L., 187, 188, 213, 277, 322, 330-331
Jenkins, W., 309, 331, 336
Jensen, W., 23-24, 331
Jerusalem, W., 210
Jevreinoff, N. N., 113
Joke, 103-105, 176, 180, 202, 206, 207, 211,
        214-216, 220-221, 247
    experimental investigation of, 215
    Jewish, 186
    understanding of, 104, 181
Jones, E., 18, 167, 215, 221, 260, 269, 271,
        278, 300, 301, 331
Josephson, E., 95-98, 107-110, 329, 330, 335
Joyce, J., 268, 271
Jung, C. G., 15, 78, 82, 87, 152, 268, 270,
        328, 331
Juynboll, W. R., 174, 190, 331

Kabel, P., 275, 331
Kafka, F., 271
Kaila, E., 227, 331
Kane, E. K., 257, 331
Kanner, L., 237, 331
Kant, 46, 256
Kanzer, M., 18, 331
Kaplan, A., 8, 243-264, 331
Kasanin, J. S., 331
Katan, M., 93, 331
Katz, D. and R., 182, 331
Kauders, O., 236, 331
Kelman, H., 219, 324, 331
Kenderdine, M., 206, 331
Kingsford, C. L., 276, 331
Kirschbaumer, L., 331
Klages, L., 88, 237
Klein, M., 210, 232, 301, 331
Kluckhohn, C., 121, 331
Knight, L. C., 286, 332
Kovacs, S., 232
Kraepelin, E., 139, 332
Krapf, E. E., 332
Kraus, G., 95, 332
Krautheimer, R., 332, 338
Kretschmer, E., 106, 332
Kries, J. von, 238, 332
Kris, E., 13, 14, 15, 16, 26, 28, 29, 38, 41,
        42, 57, 65, 66, 114, 115, 126, 129, 136,
        138, 141, 143, 146, 167, 173, 198, 207,
        222, 238, 253, 265, 298, 301, 308, 311,
        328, 329, 332, 339
Kubie, L. S., 91, 178, 325, 332
Kurz, O., 66, 115, 332

Lafora, G. H., 291, 332
Laforgue, R., 76, 332
Lagerloef, S., 70, 332
Landauer, K., 219, 222, 332-333
Landis, C., 115, 333, 337
Lange, F., 218, 333
Lange-Eichbaum, W., 58, 151, 333
Langfeld, H. S., 43, 55, 333
Language, acquisition of, 206-207, 224
  ambiguity of, 245-264
  and expressive behavior, 218, 223-224
  compared to representational art, 92
  in schizophrenia, 100-101, 103
  in science, 250-251
  of the body, 218-220, 224, 238-239
  poetic, 243-264, 287
  prehistoric, 251
Lasswell, H., 41, 57, 333
Lattimore, R., 75
Laughter, 204-239
  and smiling, 227-229
  as defense against anxiety, 232-233
  as social act, 220-226
  control of, 226-229
  in brain-injured, 219
  in group formation, 221
  variety of meanings of, 231-234
Lavater, 134, 217
Lawrence, D. H., 36, 268
Leadership
  and traumatic experiences, 32-33
  and psychological intuition, 31
  artistic, 29-30
  in primitive society, 293
Le Brun, C., 134-135, 138, 333
Lee, H. B., 16, 31, 59, 60, 79, 117, 302, 333
Lee, V., 55, 333
Legend
  of birth of hero, 68, 74
  of deceptive power of art work, 75-77
  of discovery of talent, 68-74, 82-83
  of Pygmalion, 76
Leites, N., 18, 333, 340
Leonardo da Vinci, see Vinci, L.
LeRoy, O., 76
Lersch, P., 217, 333
Levey, H. B., 26, 333
Levine, E. L., 55, 333
Levine, J., 215, 333, 337
Levy, F. H., 236, 323, 333
Lewin, B. D., 105, 187, 310, 333
Lewis, N. D. C., 87, 152, 333
Lewisohn, L., 270
Libidinal types, 216
Libido, see Psychic energy

Lichtenberg, G. C., 23, 134, 217, 332
Liebermann, M., 191-192
Life experiences, detachment from, 35
Life history
  influence of, 19, 21, 31, 71
  influence of endowment on, 21
Linton, R., 65-66, 333
Lippmann, W., 269
Lipps, J., 105, 333, 334
Lipps, T., 55
Lips, E., 105, 333
Liss, E., 333
Listowell, Earl of, 46, 55, 333
Literature, see Narrative Art and Poetry
Literary criticism, 24, 243-288
Loewenstein, R. M., 8, 15, 16, 26, 28, 38,
  126, 311, 329, 332, 333
Loewy E., 50, 333
Lombroso, 151
Longinus, 263
Lorand, S., 9, 297, 329, 334, 342, 344
Low, D., 192, 334
Lowenfeld, H., 25, 334
Lowenfeld, V., 56, 114, 334, 335
Lowes, J. L., 24, 254, 334
Luborsky, L. B., 215, 324, 334
Lucian, 195
Ludwig, H., 112, 334
Ludwig, K., 334, 340
Luquet, G. H., 233, 334
Lynch, B., 334

Macaulay, R., 268
Macbeth, 265
Machover, K., 114, 334
Maclay, W. S., 90, 102, 153, 329, 334
Maenchen-Helffen, A., 300
Magic, 47-50, 77, 256
  and drama, 40
  and effigy, 180, 183, 193, 201-203
  and value, 184-185
  apotropaic, 138, 213
  in caricature, 179
  in ritual, 138
  sympathetic, 51
Mahler, M. S., 232, 334
Mahon, D., 189, 334
Mallarmé, 259
Maloney, J. M., 18, 43, 334
Malvasia, 190, 334
Mania, 89-90, 187, 216
Mann, T., 73, 83, 270, 271, 334
Mannheim, K., 17, 334
Marx, K., 268
Maschmeyer, E., 153, 334

Maslow, A. H., 219, 334
Masturbation, 33-34, 37
Maugham, W. S., 268
Maury, L., 8, 27, 321, 334
McCulloch, W. S., 314, 334
McFarlane, K. B., 334
Mead, G. H., 310, 334
Melville, H., 23, 24, 335
Memory, 306-308
Menninger, K. A., 26, 334
Meryon, C., 95
Merzbach, A., 152, 334
Messerschmidt, F. X., 81, 83, 95, 111-112, 128-150, 235
Mestrovic, 69
Metaphor, 258, 263, 270, 287
Meyer, C. F., 23
Meyer-Gross, W., 90, 102, 105, 333, 334
Meyerson, W. S., 103, 323, 335
Michailov, N., 91, 335
Michelangelo, 74, 114-115, 198
Migliorini, G., 219, 335
Millner, S. L., 97, 108, 335
Mimic (see also Expressive Behavior)
  and diagnosis, 112, 144, 235-236
  disturbances of in schizophrenia, 112, 136-149, 234-236
  function of, 112
  magic function of, 136-147
  ontogenesis of, 145
Minkowska, M., 95, 335
Model
  for structural inquiries, 106
  of artist, see Artist, Relation to Model
  ontogenetic, 77, 184
Modigliani, 108
Moellenhoff, F., 213, 335
Mohr, F., 87, 107, 335
Monakow, C. von, 236
Money-Kyrle, R., 294, 335
Morgenthaler, W., 153, 165, 335
Morris, C., 250, 335
Mosini, A., 335
Mosse, E. P., 87, 302, 335
Motility, 112-114, 219-239
Motor discharge, in artistic activity, 54
Muensterberger, W., 322, 329
Münz, L., 56, 114, 334, 335
Murphy, G., 303, 335
Murray, H. A., 24, 186, 215, 303, 335
Muschgg, W., 79, 166, 263, 271, 335
Music, 22
Musil, R., 271
Mystery fan, psychology of, 44-45
Mythology, 17, 31, 48, 297

Naecke, P., 152, 335
Napoli, P. J., 335
Narrative art, 265, 272
  and daydream, 33-35
  as defense, 35
  as wish fulfillment, 35, 42
  autobiographical elements in, 35
Naumburg, M., 87, 96, 335
Negation, 314
New Testament, 70
Nicholes, E. L., 8, 93, 335
Nicolai, F., 132, 138, 140-143, 145-147, 149, 335
Nietzsche, F., 23, 155, 270, 295, 335
Nonsense talk, 200, 205-207
Nunberg, H., 52-53, 144, 166, 224, 305, 308, 335-336

Occupational therapy, 90
Omnipotence of thought, 49, 53, 77, 82, 161, 206, 213
Ontogeny, see Model, ontogenetic
Opicinus de Canastris, 118-127, 338
Oppenheim, 219
Oracle, 245
Oral incorporation, see Inspiration
Orality, and memory, 55-56, 299
Orloff, C., 53, 336
Othello, 23

Paden, W. D., 24, 336
Paget, V., see Lee, V.
Painter
  and medicine man, 51
  compared to poets, 47-48
  genesis of vocational choice, 52-53
  in literary tradition, 51
  social position of, 47-49
Painting
  and component drives, 53
  and motor discharge, 54
  as construction and destruction of image, 51-52
Panofsky, E., 115, 190, 198, 336
Pappenheim, E., 8, 151-169
Parody, 175
Parrhasios, 75
Parsons, J. P., 135, 336
Partridge, C., 296, 336
Pascal, 23
Pasteur, L., 296
Pathognomy, see Physiognomy
Pathography, 58, 149
Paul, J., 213
Paulhan, F., 296, 336

Perception
 and hallucination, 115
 and inner vision, 53, 115
 and need, 41
 and motility, 55-56
 and recall, 309
 in process of creation, 53-54
Petrarch, 118
Pfeifer, R., 90, 95, 107, 110, 336
Pfister, O., 22, 87, 91, 336
Phidias, 47
Philippon, 196
Philology, 64, 93, 206, 233
Physiognomy, 133-147, 195, 217-239
Piaget, J., 178
Picasso, 53
Picture puzzles, see Rebus
Pirandello, 43
Plato, 23, 60, 74, 151, 169, 187, 190, 227, 254, 293
Play
 function of, 32-33, 182
 of child, see Children, play of
 on shapes, 101-106, 152, 196-203
 on words, 101, 103-104, 152, 206, 247, 257
Plessner, H., 218, 236-237, 324, 336
Plot, and instinct gratification, 38-39
 double, 278
Poet, communicating unconscious wishes, 293-294
 compared to painters and sculptors, 47-48
Poetry, 243-264
 standards of interpretation, 243-244, 249, 258-264
Pollnow, H., 58, 217, 336
Porta, G. B., 138, 195, 336
Portraiture, 194-195
Postman, D. L., 309, 336
Postman, L., 309, 331, 336
Pottier, H. E., 233, 336
Poussin, N., 190
Praegnanz, 22
Prager, L., 183, 212, 330, 336
Praxiteles, 76
Praz, M., 30, 270, 336
Preconscious fantasy thinking, 91
Preconscious, thought processes, 24, 28, 91, 174, 180, 183, 206, 208, 259, 303-318
 and unconscious, 104, 206, 303-306
 and wish fulfillment, 310
 during creation, 101, 103
 variety of, 305, 310

Predisposition, see Talent
Primary process, 25, 27, 98-106, 116, 221, 254, 263, 305-306, 312
 ego control of, 28, 60, 103, 105, 116, 176, 196-198, 206-207
 in psychosis, 152, 206
 overwhelming ego, 60, 103, 125, 206
Prinzhorn, H., 88, 90-92, 94, 99-103, 106-107, 109, 114, 151-153, 165, 336
Projection, 109, 115-116, 150, 203, 293, 298, 301-302
Projective tests, 20, 115
Prometheus, 48, 78, 166
Proportion, 81, 137-138, 149-150
Proust, 17, 23
Psychic apparatus, pleasure from, 63, 182, 315
Psychic energy (see also Instinctual Energy)
 and laughter, 221-222, 225-226
 and perception, 22, 53, 55, 62, 306-310
 and thought processes, 27, 305-306, 311-318
 bound, 27, 305-306, 311, 315
 economy of, 22, 188, 204-205
 incomplete neutralization, 46, 312
 modes of discharge, 38-39, 53, 59, 63, 126, 305-306, 310-318
 neutralization of, 26, 27, 28, 31, 38-39, 46, 53, 61-63, 232, 311, 315-316
 saving of, 175-176, 178, 186, 204-205, 221
 shifts in cathexis of, 63, 312-314
 transformation of, 26-27, 63
Psychic systems
 shifts in cathexis of, 61-62
 shifts in levels of, 25, 28, 61-63, 259
Psychoanalysis
 an "open system," 16
 and archeology, 64
 and history, 64
 and literature, 265-272, 286
 and social sciences, 16
 applied to art, 13-31, 287-288
 contributions to psychology of art, 13-31, 265-272, 286-288
 development of, 13-14, 17-19, 23, 128-129, 173-174, 267, 304
 hypothesis of, 13-31
 influence on art, 30-31, 265-272
 reactions to, 265, 269
 schools of thought in, 14-15, 287
 technique of, see Psychoanalytic Technique
 validation of, 14, 17, 18

Psychoanalytic technique, 19-20, 29, 106, 303-304, 306-310, 317-318
Psychotic art
and delusional system, 87, 93, 95, 97, 156-169
and differential diagnosis, 87, 152-153
function of, 158-159
primary process in, 98-106
role of symbols in, 87, 107-108
Psychotic artist
identification with God, 150, 156-169
origin of delusions of, 82
Psychotic productions, 61, 87-169
admiration for, 108, 151, 260
and diagnostic categories, 87, 89, 92, 95, 109
and disturbances of motility, 112-114
and factor of training, 89-94, 107, 110
change of style in, 92, 94-98
characteristics of, 99-144
compared to productions of normals, 89-94, 101-102, 169
rendering of human face in, 106-114, 142-146
unintelligibility of, 95, 99, 110
Psychotics
incidence of "creative spell," 88-89, 152
spontaneous artistic creations by, 87-117
Puns, 100, 196, 200, 206, 257

Quintilian, 207

Rabelais, 199
Radar, M. M., 46, 55, 336
Rank, O., 15, 17, 69, 336-337
Ransom, J. C., 337
Rapaport, D., 16, 28, 91, 219, 306, 310, 337, 338, 344
Raphael, 108, 194
Rapp, A., 176, 337
Read, H., 8, 31, 91, 105, 263, 271, 337
Reality
definition of, 15
transformation of, 141
Reality testing
and secondary elaboration, 103, 313
in children, 41, 53
Rebus, 103, 176
Recall, 306-310
Recognition
and abstract art, 54
and preconscious, 24, 306-310
of subject matter, 54-56
Recovery (see also Restitution), 93
Re-creation, 56-63, 202, 243-244, 249, 251-260, 263

Redlich, F. C., 215, 333, 337, 339
Rees, H. E., 59, 337
Regis, E., 337
Regression, 105, 129, 138, 203, 205, 207, 215, 220-221, 253-254, 263
and ego control, 28, 60-63, 167, 169, 177, 180, 197-198, 202, 220-221, 253, 263, 293, 312, 318
and inspiration, 59
and newly acquired functions, 41
and progression, 61, 184
Reich, A., 179, 214, 337
Reik, T., 104, 173, 179, 180, 181, 182, 186, 238, 337
Reinach, S., 233, 337
Reitman, F., 111, 152, 153, 337
Réja, H., 152, 337
Religion, 73, 79, 292
Rembrandt, 194
Remission, 97
Representational art
ambiguity of, 49
and body response, 56
and language, 92
and magic, see Magic
responses to, 55-59
Repression
and introspection, 24
definitions of, 269-270
flexibility of, 25, 29, 291-302, 317-318
of phases of analysis, 308
Restitution (see also Recovery), 93-94, 100, 106, 112, 114, 116, 144, 168, 235
Richard II, 273, 279, 281, 283, 286-288
Richards, I. A., 250
Richter, see Paul, Jean
Rickman, J., 25, 117, 337
Riddle, 176
Ritual, 57, 67, 159-160, 253, 256
Rivière, J., 301, 327
Rjepin, I., 113
Rockelein, L., 18, 43, 334, 337
Roe, A., 20, 337
Róheim, G., 26, 224, 329, 333, 337, 339
Rolfe, F. W., see Corvo, Baron
Roman, R., 115, 333, 337
Ronsard, 201
Rorschach, H., 87, 337
Roos, A., 102, 337
Rousseau, J. J., 30
Rudel, R., 311, 338

Sachs, H., 21, 33, 38, 60, 79, 167, 271, 338
Salomon, R., 117, 121, 122, 123, 124, 330, 332, 338
Sapas, E., 152, 338

Saussure, R. de, 178, 338
Schaeffer, A., 271
Schäfer, T., 224, 338
Scherer, M., 338
Schilder, P., 55-56, 114, 152, 153, 219, 226, 333, 338
Schiller, 46, 132
Schizophrenia
    concepts in, 160
    concepts of, 93
    intact part of personality, 126, 161, 169
    motility disturbances in, 106-114, 136-149, 234-236
    restitution in, *see* Restitution
Schlenther, P., 43, 338
Schlosser, J. v., 198, 338
Schneider, D. E., 25, 26, 59, 338
Schnitzler, A., 270
Schopenhauer, 270
Schreber, 93, 108, 139, 164
Schube, P. G., 152, 324, 338
Sculptor
    compared to poets, 47-48
    descendants of cultural heroes, 48
    in literary tradition, 51
    motor discharge in work of, 54
    social position of, 47-49
Searl, M. N., 210, 338
Sears, R. N., 215, 338
Secondary process, 25, 27, 305
Sedlmayr, H., 21, 338
Seeman, W., 310, 338
Segantini, 69
Selander, S., 271, 338
Seneca, 227
Shakespeare, 23, 58, 248, 265, 273-288
Sharpe, E., 20, 26, 58, 116, 287, 338
Silberer, H., 91, 338
Sinclair, M., 268
Skill (*see also* Talent) , 30, 61, 253
Slochower, H., 338
Smiling, 205, 227-230
Snijder, G. A., 106, 339
Social psychology, 57
Social sciences, 18, 66, 184
Socrates, 188
Sohler, T. P., 215, 337, 339
Sonnenfels, 230, 339
Sophocles, 17, 23
Source material, evaluation of, 64-66, 128-129, 149-150
Speier, H., 65, 332, 339
Spencer, H., 210, 238, 273, 339
Spencer, T., 277, 339
Sperling, O., 40, 339
Spielrein, S., 55, 113, 339

Spitz, R. A., 227-228, 238, 339, 340
Ssorin, A., 113
Status personality, 65-66
Stein, G., 260
Sterba, R., 14, 26, 41, 55, 71, 339
Stereotypy, 106-114, 140-146, 235
Stevenson, R. L., 295
Stimulus word, 244, 249
Strachey, J., 326-327
Strauss, L., 245, 339
Stream of consciousness, 271
Stream of preconsciousness, 311
Style
    and energy discharge, 22, 38-39, 62, 142, 159
    and imagery, 38
    and response, 62
    changes of, 30, 77, 92, 94-98, 133, 137-148, 153, 159, 161, 168-169, 192-194, 262
    decorative, 257
    development of, 92, 133, 143
    psychology of, 21-22
Stylization, 142
Sublimation, 31, 39, 80
    and fusion of energy, 28
    and vocational choice, 52-53
    conditions favoring it, 26-28
    definition of, 26-27
    in creative activity, 27-28, 302
Sublime, 63, 187-188
Sully, J., 224, 339
Superego
    and artistic leadership, 57
    and audience, 38
    and fantasy, 314
    and the comic, 183, 185-187
    and wit, 207
    formation of, 285-286
    in aesthetic response, 62
    in ecstasy, 302
    in humor, 207
    in joke, 215
    in understanding of comic, 181
Surrealism, 30, 151, 199
Suter, J., 226, 339
Swedenborg, 96, 330
Switch words, 246
Symbol formation, 168, 177
Symbolism
    in children's play, 209-210
    in fairy tales, 42
Symbols, 87, 244-245, 251
    private, 95-97, 254
Symons, A. J. A., 37, 329, 339

Talent
  and conflict, 29
  and structure of activity, 29
  hereditary factors in, 71
  inhibition of, 91
  legend of discovery of, 68-74
  nature of, 20
Tarachow, S., 117, 213-214, 216, 339
Tate, A., 257, 339
Tatlock, I. S. P., 127, 339
Taylor, M. P., 281, 339
Tennyson, A., 24
Thinking (see also Thought Processes)
  in images, 106
  psychology of, 303-318
Thomas, D., 270
Thought processes (see also Primary and
    Secondary Process)
  and motor discharge, 223
  archaic, 91, 99
  preconscious, see Preconscious
Tic, significance of, 146, 232
Titian, 194
Toulzac, M., 230, 339
Traditional themes
  ubiquity of, 17, 31
  variations of, 18
Tragedy, 62, 188, 213
Traversi, D. A., 284-285, 339
Travesty, 175, 213
Traumatic experiences, 25, 31-33, 39
Trilling, L., 23, 29, 286, 339

Uexküll, J. von, 236
Uncanny, 199, 213, 314
Unconscious
  archaic, 152
  collective, 82
  onto- and phylogenetic nexus, 105
  "voice of," 293, 301
Underdistance, 56, 256-258
Unification, tendency to, 187, 302
Utitz, E., 210, 339

Van Gogh, 30, 94-95, 325, 330, 332, 335
Vangaard, T., 97
Vanlar, C., 225, 339
Varendonck, J., 91, 271, 310-312, 327, 339
Vasari, G., 73-74, 198
Verbigerations, 100, 103, 124
Verse (see also Poetry), formal qualities
  of, 62-63
Villamil, J. P. L., 89, 153, 339
Vinchon, J., 339-340
Vinci, Leonardo da, 19, 21, 22, 53, 79, 113,

229, 324, 330, 333, 334, 340
Virgil, 255
Visual imagery
  in daydreams, 38
  archaic nature of, 38, 50, 91
Vocational choice, 20, 28-29, 51-52
Voigt, G., 195, 340
Vossler, K., 251, 340

Waelder, R., 177, 182, 340
Wahlin, K., 96, 340
Walpole, H., 268
Wangh, M., 23, 340
Weiss, J., 22, 340
Weiss, R., 237
Weitz, M., 14, 340
Weltuntergang, 123, 127, 164
Werner, H., 105, 340
Wertham, F., 18, 340
Wertheimer, M., 315, 340
Wesensschau, 88
West, R., 268
Westerman-Holstijn, A. J., 95, 340
Weygandt, W., 94, 95, 153, 340
White, W. A., 340
Wieland, 78
Wilbur, G. B., 322, 329
Wilson, E., 250-251, 271, 340
Winterstein, A. von, 55, 134, 173, 340
Wit (see also Comic, Humor, and Jokes),
  204, 207, 213, 247
Witte, O., 224, 340
Wittkower, R., 189, 190, 194, 323, 340
Wolf, K. M., 227-228, 237, 238, 339, 340
Wolfenstein, M., 18, 42, 206, 333, 340
Woolf, L. and V., 268
Work
  capacity for, 20
  inhibition of, 297-299
Works of art, see Artistic productions
Wright, T., 340
Writer (see also Artist and Poet), reac-
  tion of to psychoanalytic interpreta-
  tions, 23-24
Wulff, M., 113, 114, 340
Wundt, W., 106, 238-239, 340

Zeuxis, 74-75
Ziehen, T., 71, 329, 340
Zilboorg, G., 127, 340
Zilsel, E., 73, 340-341
Zimmerman, J., 328, 341
Zingerle, H., 89, 329, 341
Zweig, S., 24

Illustrations

FIG. 1
Psychotic Artist. *(Fairy Tale)*

FIG. 2
Psychotic Artist. *(Portrait)*

FIG. 3
Ernst Josephson.
(Pan)

FIG. 4
Ernst Josephson.
(David and Goliath)

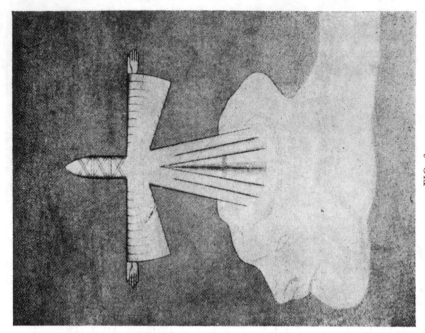

FIG. 6
Psychotic Patient. (*Anti-Christ*)

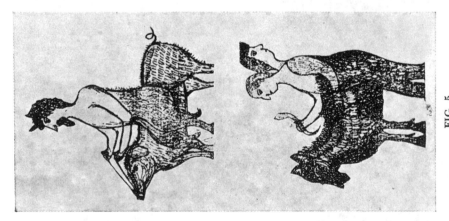

FIG. 5
Hysterical Patient. (*Drawings*)

FIG. 7
Psychotic Patient. *(The Shepherd)*

FIG. 8
Psychotic Patient. *(Six Heads)*

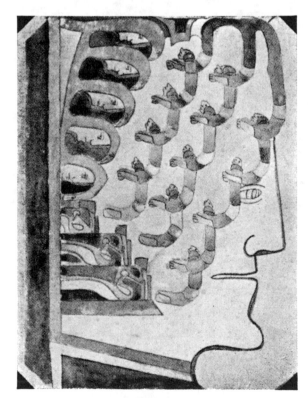

FIG. 9
Psychotic Patient. *(Profile)*

FIG. 10
Cameo.
(Combination of Heads)

FIG. 11
German 19th Century.
(Caricature of Napoleon)

FIG. 12
Psychotic Patient.
(Hindenburg)

FIG. 13
Psychotic Patient.
(Emperors)

FIG. 14
Ernst Josephson. *(Adam)*

FIG. 15
Ernst Josephson. *(Drawing)*

FIG. 16
Ernst Josephson. (*Drawing*)

FIG. 17
Ernst Josephson. *(Portrait)*

FIG. 18
Psychotic Patient. *(Drawing)*

FIG. 19a and b

Psychotic Patient. (*A Photograph and Its Copy*)

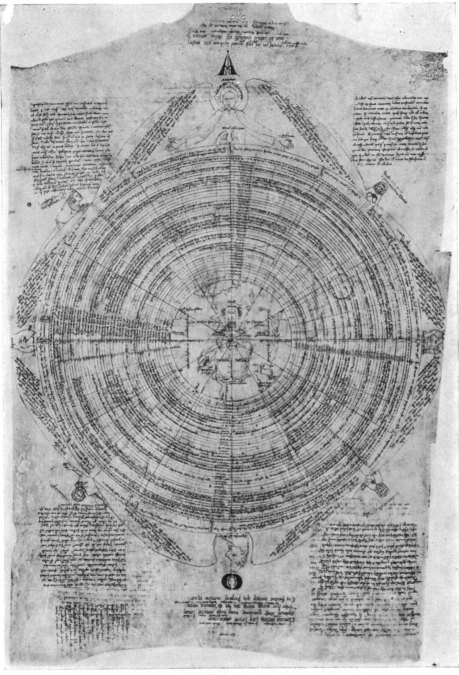

FIG. 20
Opicinus de Canistris. (*Autobiography*)

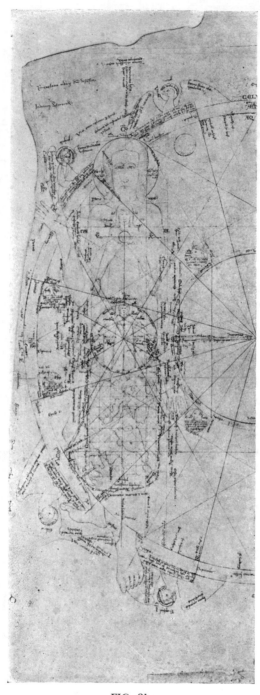

FIG. 21
Opicinus de Canistris.
(*Christ and the Universe*)

FIG. 23
F. X. Messerschmidt.
(*The Artist How He Imagined
Himself Laughing*)

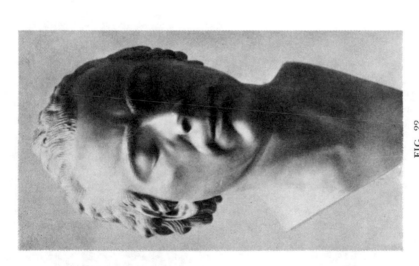

FIG. 22
F. X. Messerschmidt.
(*Quiet Peaceful Sleep*)

FIG. 24
F. X. Messerschmidt.
(*The Courageous General*)

FIG. 25
F. X. Messerschmidt.
(*The Melancholic One*)

FIG. 26
F. X. Messerschmidt.
(*A Surly Old Soldier*)

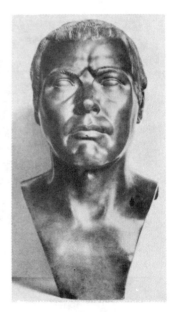

FIG. 27
F. X. Messerschmidt.
(*The Reliable One*)

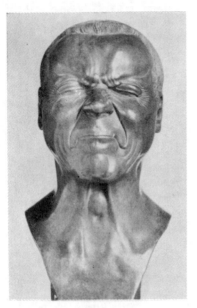

FIG. 28
F. X. Messerschmidt.
(The Ill-Humored One)

FIG. 29
F. X. Messerschmidt.
(The Satirizing One)

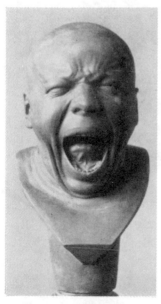

FIG. 30
F. X. Messerschmidt.
(The Yawning One)

FIG. 31
F. X. Messerschmidt.
(The Obstinate One)

FIG. 32
F. X. Messerschmidt.
(*A Haggard Old Man With
Aching Eyes*)

FIG. 33
F. X. Messerschmidt.
(*Just Rescued From Drowning*)

FIG. 34
F. X. Messerschmidt.
(*A Hanged One*)

FIG. 35
F. X. Messerschmidt.
(*The Vexed One*)

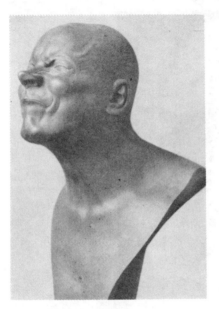

FIG. 36
F. X. Messerschmidt.
(Strong Odor)

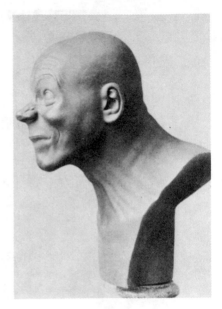

FIG. 37
F. X. Messerschmidt.
(A Simpleton)

FIG. 38
F. X. Messerschmidt.
(An Old Cheerful Smiler)

FIG. 39
F. X. Messerschmidt.
(A Hypocrite and Slanderer)

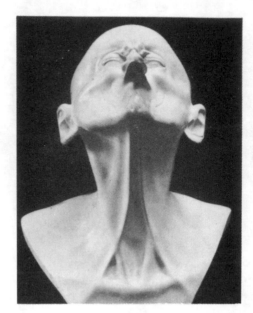

FIG. 40
F. X. Messerschmidt.
(First Beak Head)

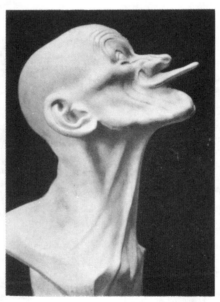

FIG. 41
F. X. Messerschmidt.
(Second Beak Head)

FIG. 42
F. X. Messerschmidt.
(The Sinister Man)

FIG. 43
F. X. Messerschmidt.
(The Incapable Bassoonist)

FIG. 44
F. X. Messerschmidt.
(Afflicted with Constipation)

FIG. 45
F. X. Messerschmidt.
(Grief Locked Up Inside)

FIG. 48
F. X. Messerschmidt.
(*The Troubled One*)

FIG. 47
F. X. Messerschmidt.
(*The Enraged and Vengeful
Gypsy*)

FIG. 46
F. X. Messerschmidt.
(*Childish Weeping*)

FIG. 50

F. X. Messerschmidt. (*The Capuchin Monk Fessler*)

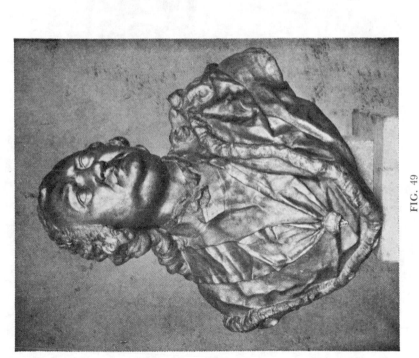

FIG. 49

F. X. Messerschmidt. (*Jan van Swieten*)

FIG. 51

Psychotic Architect. (*Victory*)

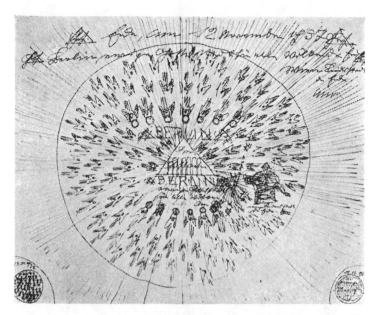

FIG. 52
Psychotic Architect. *(Sphera)*

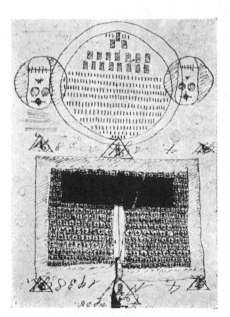

FIG. 53
Psychotic Architect.
(Eternal Hell)

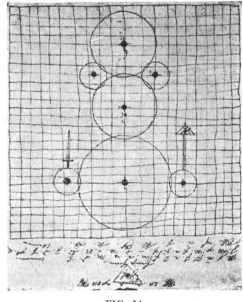

FIG. 54
Psychotic Architect.
(The Dies Are Cast)

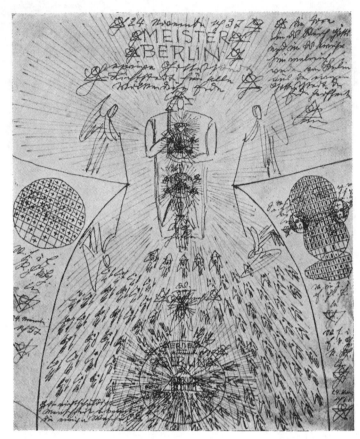

FIG. 55

Psychotic Architect. *(Sphera and Damnation)*

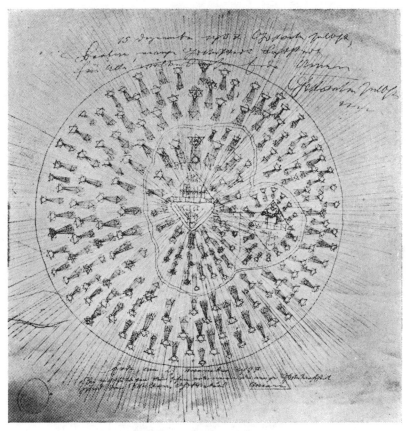

FIG. 56
Psychotic Architect. *(Sphera and the Stars of David)*

FIG. 57
Psychotic Architect. *(The Universe)*

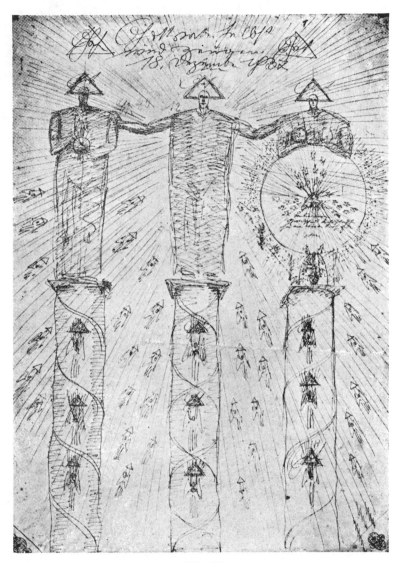

FIG. 58
Psychotic Architect. (*God Father Himself*)

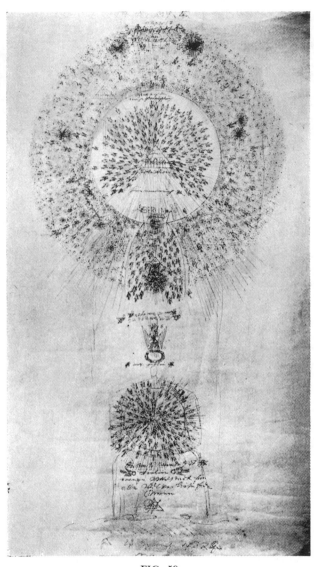

FIG. 59
Psychotic Architect. *(Ostensory)*

FIG. 61
Psychotic Architect. (*The Process of Sculpturing*)

FIG. 60
Psychotic Architect. (*God, the Sculptor*)

FIG. 63
Italian 17th Century. (*Caricature*)

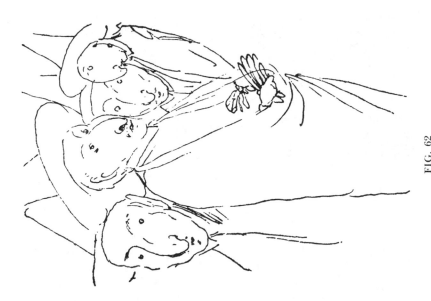

FIG. 62
Italian 17th Century. (*Caricature*)

FIG. 64
Italian 17th Century. *(Dwarfs)*

FIG. 65
Honoré Daumier. *(Napoleon III)*

FIG. 66
Greek Art. *(Dwarf)*

FIG. 67
Lorenzo Bernini. *(Captain of the Fire Brigade)*

FIG. 68
Lorenzo Bernini. *(Cardinal Scipione Borghese)*

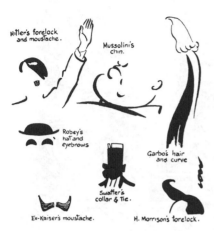

FIG. 69
David Low. (*Tabs of Identity*)

FIG. 70
Early Christian Period.
Wall Engraving.
(*Mock Crucifix*)

FIG. 71
German 15th Century.
(*Man on the Gallows*)

FIG. 72
Dutch 17th Century.
(*The Preacher and the Devil*)

FIG. 73
Italian 17th Century. *(Sketches and Caricatures)*

FIG. 74
Giovanni Battista Porta. *(The Man and the Ram)*

FIG. 76
Corneliss Floris. (*Ornament*)

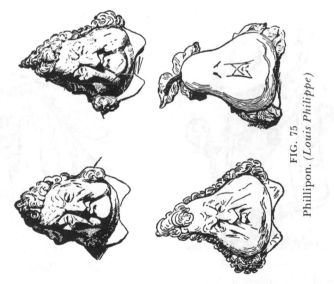

FIG. 75
Phillipon. (*Louis Philippe*)

FIG. 77
"Rabelais." *(Grotesque Figure)*

FIG. 78
"Rabelais." *(Grotesque Figure)*

FIG. 79
Hieronimus Bosch.
(Grotesque Figure)